SONGS
America Voted By

IRWIN SILBER

SONGS
America Voted By

IRWIN SILBER

A thoroughly factual
and entertaining history
of the candidates, the
parties, the issues,
the songmakers, and the
words and music that
won – and lost – American
presidential elections

**Stackpole
Books**

For Nina

SONGS AMERICA VOTED BY

Copyright © 1971 by Irwin Silber

First paperback edition, 1988
Published by
STACKPOLE BOOKS
Cameron and Kelker Streets
Harrisburg, Pa. 17105

Cover illustration by Pat Topper

ISBN 0-8117-2275-9
Library of Congress Catalog Card Number 79-162451

Printed in U.S.A.

Library of Congress Cataloging-in-Publication Data

Songs America voted by.

   Bibliography: p.
   1. Campaign songs. I. Silber, Irwin, 1925–
M1659.7.S66 1988   88-750704
ISBN 0-8117-2275-9

Contents

Union and Washington. Songs of ratification and national unity in the young republic.
    The New Roof (A New Song for Federal Mechanics)
    God Save Great Washington

Adams and Jefferson and Liberty. Songs of the first great political quarrel from the campaigns of 1796, 1800, and 1804.
    American Spirit
    Adams and Liberty
    The Son of Liberty
    Jefferson and Liberty

Madison Appears and Monroe Is the Man. Campaign songs of a united people, 1808, 1812, 1816, 1820.
    Madison, Union and Liberty
    Monroe Is the Man

Old Hickory: Half Horse and Half Alligator. The emergence of Andrew Jackson and the beginnings of the party system. Songs of the Adams vs. Jackson years from the campaigns of 1824, 1828, and 1832.
    The Hunters of Kentucky
    Little Wat Ye Wha's A-Comin'
    Adams and Clay
    The Hickory Tree
    Jackson Toast

6

Where to Find Often Used Melodies

The following melodies are used for more than one song in this book. A title appearing in italics indicates that the melodic line is printed with that song. All others have the lyrics only.

Acknowledgments

One way to realize the interdependency of contemporary life is to undertake a book of this kind. It quickly becomes apparent that not only is "no man an island," but that long-cherished concepts of "originality" and "individualism" may have much less to do with life in the future than we presently suspect.

In any event, it is quite clear that the present work is the fruit of many labors. One does not thank those propagandists of other times for their efforts, but merely acknowledges their efforts as the raw material of history. Similarly, it is impossible to thank those historians and philosophers—Benjamin Franklin, Thomas Jefferson, John Stuart Mill, Karl Marx, Charles and Mary Beard, John D. Hicks, Matthew Josephson, William Appleman Williams, Eugene H. Roseboom—whose work provided both guidance and information in the preparation of this study. Their work, after all, has now become a part of the common cultural heritage.

In a more particular way, however, I should like to acknowledge the assistance and active concern of a number of institutions and individuals whose resources have been utilized for this work. I am especially indebted to William Lichtenwanger, Head of the Music Division of the Library of Congress, for his unfailing cooperation and interest. Without his help and the resources of the mammoth collection he directs, this work would not have been realized. Equally crucial was the superb private collection of election campaign songs of Mr. Lester Levy of Pikesville, Maryland. Mr. Levy was both generous and thoughtful in making his material available to me. I hope that readers of this work who are interested in the general subject of American popular music will look into Mr. Levy's fine survey study of period music (1820-1900), *Grace Notes in American History,* published by the University of Oklahoma Press.

Other important sources of campaign song material were the Music Division of the New York Public Library, the Political History Division of the Smithsonian Institution, the New York Historical Society, the Tennessee State Library and Archives, the Harry S. Truman Library in Independence, Missouri, the American Antiquarian Society, the New Hampshire Historical Society, the Calvin Coolidge Memorial Room of the Forbes Library in Northampton, Massachusetts, and the Music Library of Baylor University in Texas. A special word of thanks to Joseph Hickerson of the Folksong Archive at the Library of Congress, Gus Miller of the Republican National Committee, Edmund Soule, the Music Librarian at the University of Oregon, and Brooke Whiting, Assistant Head of the Special Collections Department at the University of California in Los Angeles. All provided much useful material.

Several publications were extremely helpful by publishing inquiries of mine which resulted in correspondence from people all over the country who either remembered campaign songs or happened to have material in their possession. These were the *New York Times Book Review, Library Journal, Variety, Billboard,* and *Notes Magazine.* There is no practical way to mention the names of all those who responded to these inquiries, but their suggestions were almost universally helpful.

The cooperation of those music publishers whose copyrighted songs are included in this book was, naturally, indispensable. Without their enlightened interest, most of the songs from the campaign of 1908 until today would not have been available for publication. I especially want to thank Irwin Snyder of Warner Brothers Music, Mr. V. Matarainen of the Jerry Vogel Music Co., Herbert E. Marks of the E. B. Marks Co., Mr. Theodore Jackson and Irving Berlin Music, Inc., Mr. Sammy Cahn, and Lenore Terry of the Index Department of ASCAP for very specific help in tracking down and documenting a number of important songs.

The disappointments in this area were surprisingly few. The main one is the absence of a campaign song for the 1968 Democratic nominee, Hubert Humphrey. A campaign song on Mr. Humphrey's behalf was written and sung extensively, but it was an unauthorized parody to a popular show tune and the copyright owner refused to give permission to reprint it. Similarly, it would have been logical to include the songs "Happy Days Are Here Again" and "Row, Row, Row With Roosevelt" for the 1932 and 1936 campaigns, but in both cases the copyright owners refused permission. A good song on behalf of Thomas Dewey's 1944 campaign, "Dewey—We Do!", was eliminated because it was not possible to track down either the present copyright proprietor or the composer.

Every effort has been made to ascertain the copyright status of the songs in this book. In no case have I knowingly printed a copyrighted composition without first obtaining permission of the owner. In the event that an inadvertent error has been made in this connection, I would appreciate hearing from the appropriate party so that the proper credit may be given in future editions.

Two people who made invaluable contributions to this work are Oscar Brand and Jerry Silverman. I worked with Oscar many years ago to produce an LP record of presidential campaign songs for Folkways Records, and his continuing interest in the subject and my efforts have been extremely helpful. Jerry Silverman supervised the final music preparation for the songs and, as always, was perceptive and creative, as well as conscientious.

Along at the end of a page of this kind, the author (almost always male) expresses a note of gratitude (almost always patronizing) for his life's mate who managed to type the manuscript, proofread the galleys, change the diapers, and keep dinner warm while the work was in progress. My partner in life, Barbara Dane, and I do not have that kind of relationship and her contribution to this book cannot be measured in terms of either secretarial or domestic chores. But her incisive intelligence, her vast musical experience, her deep-seated commitment to mutual principles, as well as her comradely love have enriched my life beyond measure and are, of course, reflected in these pages.

Introduction

This book is an anthology of one particular set of political paraphernalia—the songs with which American political parties and movements have attempted to sing their presidential candidates into office. As such, one may view the collection as a journey into nostalgia, re-creating for a moment the excitement and slogans and color of bygone years.

But these songs are more than remembrances. They are also melodic footnotes to our history, lyrical insights into the issues and personalities of that quadrennial national ritual by which Americans have acted out the form, if not always the substance, of democracy for almost 200 years.

We are not concerned here with the, at best, dubious literary worth of such creatures of the moment as "Clear the Way for Hayes and Wheeler" or "Hooray for Bill McKinley and that Brave Rough Rider Ted." These songs make no pretense at being great or lasting literature. But it is precisely in their topicality that they concern us, for with historical perspective we see how the appeals to prejudice and morality, compassion and jingoism, class interest and self-interest, reveal the social values of other times.

Their worth to us stems from the fact that they were designed not so much to reflect an age as to influence the course of events. But because their intent is so overwhelmingly immediate to their own time, they are able to speak to us across the decades of other men and other agonies. These songs, these musical antiques, are but the casual artifacts of history, occasionally capturing the essential quality of a moment of the past, sometimes transfixing us with an emotional reality which goes beyond the recitation of facts or the analysis of social forces.

Antiques they are; and the trouble with antiques, especially the historical kind, is the antiquarian attitude they all too often induce. For the most part, the collection, codification and study of historical ephemera—whether military uniforms, almanacs, period furniture or campaign songs—has been left to latter-day pseudo-innocents who seem determined to invent a past which never existed.

This tendency to retreat into the past, into some era in which life was presumably simpler and less discordant, has been a perennial characteristic of America's attitudes towards its own history. In earlier times, the romanticization of the past was the dominant theme of almost all historical writing, so that successive generations came to maturity imbued with the contrived myths of George Washington's inability to lie about the cherry tree affair and Abraham Lincoln trudging through the snow for ten miles in order to give a customer the correct change. Perhaps the schoolteachers of those earlier days who so gleefully helped propagate these outrages believed that they were helping to inculcate necessary ideas of virtue and honesty in their young charges. If so, the process does not seem to have had any notable effect on the conduct of those children when they grew up and were forced to confront life as it really is. The one notable achievement of this romanticization of history has been not the cultivation of a righteous moral code in the body politic, but the development of a profoundly healthy skepticism towards institutions which attempt to pass off such nonsense as fact.

Historical writing in general has come a long way in the past fifty years. The "revelations" of the Beards that economic self-interest had somewhat more to do with the policies of the Founding Fathers than did the abstract principles of Justice, Freedom and Equality shocked the national naiveté at first, but now we take such analysis in stride, understanding that truth is not only stranger than fiction, it is ultimately more fascinating, more complex and more satisfying.

But is it really necessary to discuss principles of historical analysis when the subject matter is such ephemera as the political campaign songs of American presidential elections? There might seem to be a lack of proportion here. Some may feel it takes all the fun out of the matter. A song, after all, is only a song. Why worry it to death? Others may find the whole process vaguely unpatriotic, preferring to regard such materials somehow as among the lesser shrines of the American experience, if not to be worshipped, at least to be cherished as semisacrosanct relics of less divisive times. And there are undoubtedly still some who prefer to keep the process of assembling these kinds of political artifacts relatively uncomplicated and separate from the other, more demanding disciplines of historical analysis.

Unfortunately, these attitudes have tended to dominate this aspect of historical study heretofore. As a result, such subjects enjoy little standing in scholarly circles, offering to the "serious" researcher perhaps an occasional footnote or a momentary diversion. But in treating here with political campaign songs, we have an opportunity to do much more than evoke nostalgia.

Much may be learned by examining the content of these ballads. True, we will not add particularly to our understanding of the underlying economic significance of the tariff controversies of the nineteenth century from the free trade versus protection songs of the Cleveland-Harrison and Bryan-McKinley campaigns. But we will learn something about how the popular mood perceived this question, and we will also learn something about the whole political mechanism of attempting to win popular support for policies which are in the specific interest of one group in society.

As with all literature, and most especially consciously contrived propaganda, it would be a mistake to take these campaign ballads at face value. One can only understand them in the total social-political context of their time and function. But surely, some fascinating additional dimension is added to our comprehension of American attitudes towards the Spanish-American War when we come across the following, to the tune of "On the Banks of the Wabash," in a 1900 McKinley re-election campaign song:

From the thralldom of Spain's cruel rule in Cuba,
Brave McKinley set the suffering people free.
He unfurled the Stars and Stripes in Porto Rico,
Liberation and expansion—Don't you see? . . .

A better day has dawned upon the islands
Since the Stars and Stripes, proud emblem of the free,
Floats o'er them, not for conquest, but for freedom,
Not for thralldom, but for priceless liberty.

Come shake your dull noddles, ye pumpkins, and bawl,
And own that you're mad at fair Liberty's call;
No scandalous conduct can add to your shame,
Condemn'd to dishonor, inherit the fame.

Campaign singing, while clearly an adjunct to the electoral process, actually predates the Republic. We don't know whether or not there were any campaign songs in the New York City elections of 1734 when some popular candidates successfully challenged supporters of Governor Cosby. But when the election was over and the governor's men had been defeated, some enthusiastic partisans of the people's cause wrote "A Song Made Upon the Election of New Magistrates for This City," which hailed "you good lads that dare oppose all lawless power and might," who "shew you boldly dare/Stand up to save your country dear."

Enraged, the governor summoned a hand-picked grand jury which promptly condemned the song (and a companion piece) to "be burnt before the City Hall . . . by the hands of the Common Hangman." Political songs have been in trouble in this country ever since.

In both England and the Colonies, the political song became a fairly common literary device. To what extent these "songs" were actually sung is hard to determine. One imagines a group of young men in the back room of a local tavern gleefully harmonizing the lyrics from a broadside sheet, but it is probable that, with few exceptions, the "songs" were circulated primarily as poetic polemics.

In the hectic pre-Revolutionary days, a "battle of the ballads" erupted in the pages of Colonial newspapers between rebellious Whigs and loyalist Tories. John Dickinson's "Liberty Song," written in 1768, was a musical and political omen of what was to shortly follow. Written to the melody of "Hearts of Oak," it was one of the first songs to incorporate the increasingly popular concept of "American":

Come join hand in hand, brave Americans all,
And rouse your bold hearts at fair Liberty's call;
No tyrannous acts shall suppress your just claim,
Or stain with dishonor America's name.

Dickinson's song evoked scores of "replies" to the same tune, penned by outraged Loyalists, such as this one from a Boston Tory:

Songs such as these flourished in the period of pre-Revolutionary agitation, appearing mostly as penny broadsides or in the columns of Colonial newspapers. Again, whether they were actually sung to any appreciable extent is difficult to ascertain.

In the postwar period several judiciously anonymous bards maintained the practice with occasional comments on one or another of a variety of local issues. A number of such songs were tributes to Washington and were a small part of the process which eventually resulted in the selection of Washington as the first president. A small burst of political odes helped to whip up enthusiasm for the Constitution during the ratification campaign of 1788; and later, during the 1790s, songs partisan to the respective ideologies of Adams and Jefferson began to appear, reflecting the accelerating political divisiveness of the period.

For the most part, however, campaign singing was a minor device for influencing voters and winning elections up until 1840. Few political songs of that era have survived the ruthlessness of time; and of these, only one or two were even conceived of as actual campaign songs.

There was little to suggest in all of the political campaigns before it that the year 1840 would erupt in an explosion of campaign music which was not only unprecedented in history but which has rarely been matched since. The famous "Tippecanoe and Tyler Too" campaign marked the beginning of a new era in American politics. For the first time, a "modern" political campaign took shape. Parades, banners, slogans, marching clubs, party newspapers, songbooks, sheet music and all of the other accouterments of electioneering suddenly descended on the citizenry with all of the fervor of an evangelical revival and all the productivity of a new industry. The reasons for this new type of campaign are not hard to find. The political process in the United States had reached a new level of development. Andrew Jackson had revolutionized American politics by constructing an on-going, vital party machine which functioned all year round and was built on the basis of rewarding supporters in massive numbers with the "spoils" of federal office. So effective was this machine that organized opposition to it did not develop for some time. But by 1840, the smell of office and the incentive of reward were strong enough to bring a semblance of unity to the Whig opposition. The Harrison-Van Buren campaign which ensued left its mark on the elective process for some three-quarters of a century afterwards.

From 1840 to 1916, campaign music was an indispensable part of every presidential election. Professional songwriters vied with enthusiastic amateurs for the endorsement of party professionals. Major music publishers prepared elaborately decorated sheet music—songs, waltzes, grand marches, polkas and *galops* in honor of Henry Clay, Ulysses Grant, Samuel Tilden, Rutherford Hayes, James Garfield and almost all the rest of that exclusive fraternity of successful and unsuccessful presidential candidates. For this was the age of pianoforte music with popular pieces of the day selling as many as 1,000,000 copies. The rewards for success were enormous while the investment was low; and so publishers gave a receptive ear to anyone offering a song for his campaign favorite. But like all good entrepreneurs, the music publishers did not leave to chance that which could be stimulated. Composers and lyricists were hired to write campaign music every four years and, especially towards the end of the nineteenth century, it was common practice for writers to compose pieces for both candidates. In 1896, an enterprising composer by the name of W. L. Needham published a piece of sheet music called "The Political Quartet." Using one tune and a common refrain, it combined four songs in one—with verses on behalf of the Republican, Democratic, Prohibition and Populist parties. The chorus for all seasons went:

> Onward freemen, hail to the cause we defend,
> We'll sweep the country from ocean to ocean you
>   may depend,
> Doubt not, comrades, every one do a good share,
> Stand by the flag and be true to our leader,
>   and we'll get there.

During this same period, the campaign songster (a collection of lyrics without music) became standard equipment along with the official campaign biography. Consisting of collections of song lyrics, parodies

to popular tunes of the day and standard patriotic airs, campaign songsters were sold and circulated by bookstores, newsstands and local party organizations.

The decline of campaign singing began with the end of World War I. Neither Warren Harding nor James Cox were able to inspire the musical muses beyond a handful of puerile efforts in 1920, and Calvin Coolidge and John Davis did little better four years later, although a few people may still recall "Keep Cool and Keep Coolidge" with a fondness which speaks more for nostalgia than musical quality. Herbert Hoover and Al Smith did a little better in 1928, although Smith would seem to have had the better of the ballads—probably because New York's governor had earned a certain popularity among the song-writing clan of Democratic New York City, many of whom answered the call of the campaign. The general popular support of Roosevelt's first two campaigns brought forth a goodly batch of songs while, largely on the strength of a *Chicago Tribune*-sponsored song-writing contest, Alf Landon was inundated with parodies to "Oh! Susannah" in the 1936 election.

After that, however, it was all downhill. The only significant exception to the pattern was the ill-fated campaign of Henry Wallace on a third party ticket in 1948, a campaign which would seem to have inspired as many songs as it did votes. This was largely the result of the coincidence of the burgeoning left-oriented folk song revival of the period with Wallace's candidacy, but after Wallace's disastrous defeat, campaign songs have played only the most perfunctory of roles in presidential elections.

In today's electronic age, the old-fashioned election campaign is dead. The torchlight parades, the candidate's barbecue, the stump speech and the campaign song have all passed into history. In their time, they served a purpose. If these devices were used, as they always have been, to obfuscate issues and manipulate minds, they were also reflections of a certain since-vanished primitive democracy in a time when a candidate had to face his peers as a man and a human being.

Taken as a total body of expression, these songs have something to tell us about who we are and what we have been. If we read their message right, they may even tell us something of what lies ahead.

The Early Years (1788-1836)

From Washington to Jackson

There was a time—hopefully it is past—when the suggestion that the American Revolution was fought for anything except those lofty principles stated in the Declaration of Independence was viewed as a nefarious attempt to somehow diminish the stature of America's "founding fathers." There probably are still some who view any form of historical analysis which takes into account personal and class self-interest as a suspect enterprise—especially when applied to the period of the country's formation. The real significance of the American Union and the Constitution on which it is based, however, is not that they rise above such interests, but that they precisely elevate such interests to the level of national policy.

The American Constitution represents the historically necessary triumph of the developing business forces over the other constituent parts of the revolutionary struggle. For no other class—farmers, artisans, shopkeepers—were capable of unleashing the powerful social energy which a rising American bourgeoisie could. The Constitutional document makes a number of crucially important concessions to other sectors of the population—necessary because their support was required to enact it—but remains basically the charter by which the American free enterprise system was given the political superstructure for its fullest development. For the needs of a developing capitalist class cut across state lines and required a uniformity of laws, currency and local custom, and a centralized government capable of enforcing a national will which might come into conflict with local usage.

Union and Washington

But even a document was not enough. A unifying personality, a leader in whom all could have confidence, was also required. That leader was provided in the personage of George Washington, whose undisputed prestige and dedication to the new nation *as a whole* were as indispensable to the successful launching of the United States as was the Constitution itself. And so in 1788 while the question of ratification of the Constitution racked the land, the propagandists penned verses like:

> No more shall Anarchy bear sway,
> Nor petty states pursue their way,
> But all united firm as one,
> Shall seek the general good alone.
> > Great Washington shall rule the land,
> > While Franklin's council aids his hand.

From "A New Federal Song," words by Eli Lewis, music by Edward Tyler, as printed in *The Pennsylvania Packet and Daily Advertiser,* August 5, 1788.

The most popular song created on behalf of ratification was the work of Francis Hopkinson, a signer of the Declaration of Independence, and a well-known author and composer.

THE NEW ROOF
(A New Song for Federal Mechanics)

Words: Francis Hopkinson
Tune: "To Anacreon in Heaven" ("Star-spangled Banner")

Come muster, my lads, your mechanical tools,
Your saws and your axes, your hammers and rules;
Bring your mallets and planes, your level and line,
And plenty of pins of American pine;
> For our roof we will raise, and our song still shall be,
> A government firm and our citizens free.

Come, up with the plates, lay them firm on the wall,
Like the people at large, they're the ground-work of all.
Examine them well and see that they're sound,
Let no rotten parts in our building be found;
> For our roof we will raise, and our song still shall be,
> Our government firm, and our citizens free.

Now hand up the girders, lay each in his place,
Between them the joists must divide all the space.
Like assembly-men, these should lie level along,
Like girders, our Senate prove loyal and strong.
> For our roof we will raise, and our song still shall be,
> A government firm, over citizens free.

The rafters now frame—your King-Posts and braces,
And drive your pins home, to keep all in their places;
Let wisdom and strength in the fabric combine,
And your pins be all made of American pine.
> For our roof we will raise, and our song still shall be,
> A government firm, over citizens free.

Our King-Posts are Judges—How upright they stand,
Supporting the Braces, the Laws of the Land—
The laws of the land, which divide right from wrong,
And strengthen the weak by weak'ning the strong.
> For our roof we will raise, and our song still shall be,
> Laws equal and just for a people that's free.

Up! up with the rafters—each frame is a State!
How nobly they rise! their span, too, how great!
From the north to the south, o'er the whole they extend,
And rest on the walls, while the walls they defend.
> For our roof we will raise, and our song still shall be,
> Combined in strength, yet as citizens free.

Now enter the purlins, and drive your pins through,
And see that your joints are drawn home, and all true;
The purlins will bind all the rafters together,
The strength of the whole shall defy wind and weather;
> For our roof we will raise, and our song still shall be,
> United as States, but as citizens free.

Come, raise up the turret—our glory and pride—
In the centre it stands—o'er the whole to preside;
The sons of Columbia shall view with delight
Its pillars and arches and towering height.
> Our roof is now raised, and our song still shall be,
> A Federal head, o'er a people still free.

Huzza! my brave boys, our work is complete,
The world shall admire Columbia's fair seat;
Its strength against tempests and time shall be proof,
And thousands shall come to dwell under our roof.
> Whilst we drain the deep bowl, our toast still shall be,
> Our government firm, and our citizens free.

Written 1787-1788; first appearance in print Feb. 6, 1788, in the *Pennsylvania Gazette.*

While nothing resembling a partisan election campaign was waged on behalf of George Washington, both popular and practical political sentiment combined in tribute to the former commander of the Continental Army. In a certain sense, the growing partisanship of the times between urban mercantile interests and the small, independent landholders was obscured by the general unanimity in support of Washington. It was only Washington, in fact, who was able to forestall the burgeoning conflict which would erupt a decade later and climax in the historic election of 1800.

In the general period 1786-1788, many lyrical tributes to Washington were composed. They could hardly be considered "campaign" songs, as such, but they did reflect not only the wide respect and unifying force of Washington; they were also a part of the general expression which moved the country towards conferring the presidency on the man from Mount Vernon.

GOD SAVE GREAT WASHINGTON

Words: Anonymous

Tune: "God Save the King" ("America")
(From the *Philadelphia Continental Journal,*
    April 7, 1786)

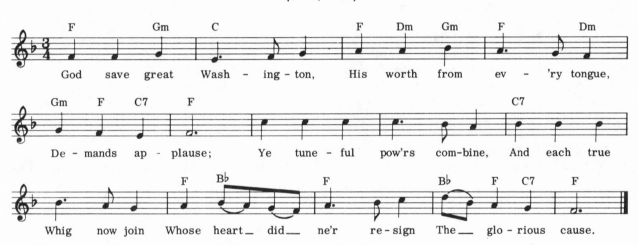

God save great Washington, His worth from ev'ry tongue, Demands applause; Ye tuneful pow'rs combine, And each true Whig now join Whose heart did ne'r resign The glorious cause.

Adams and Jefferson and Liberty

The American Union was barely four years old and Washington's admonition against "the daemon of party spirit," delivered in 1790, was still a stated aspiration of the new nation, when the very real divisions of American society found their political form in the emergence of political parties in 1792. The Federalists, led largely by Alexander Hamilton and John Adams, represented the essentially conservative interests of the rising new mercantile class of the Middle Atlantic and New England states. For a period of time, the wealthier southern planters made common cause with the Federalists, until specific sectional concerns drove a wedge between them. Thomas Jefferson and James Madison were the dominant spokesmen for the Republicans, who found themselves increasingly opposing the Federalists on a wide range of specific issues.

Although Washington himself was leaning more and more to the Federalist Party, the unifying influence of his prestige managed to keep both factions together in a rather uneasy coalition within the government. Both Adams and Jefferson urged Washington to run for re-election in 1792, probably since neither wanted to take responsibility for the inevitable party split which was bound to follow his presidency.

By 1796, however, the lines had been so sharply

drawn that the struggle was on in earnest. It was a struggle which would be fought out over the next two decades and while the Federalists won the first round, it was the only one in which they triumphed.

The campaigning in the election of 1796 was intense, but much of it took place behind the closed doors of state legislatures and in the halls of Congress. We have no evidence, therefore, of any surviving campaign song or poetry from that contest. But Adams' victory, a narrow one, was barely achieved before the partisanship which would culminate in the election of 1800 was well under way.

The Federalists, out of a combination of economic ties with the British and fear of the "anarchistic" spirit of the French Revolution, enacted the Alien and Sedition Laws of 1798, designed to curb criticism of the President. The Republicans, whose agrarian constituency viewed the British with great suspicion, identified with the populist ideals of the French Revolution. Struggling against an overstrong central power in their own country, the Republicans found ideological nourishment in the spirit of French liberty.

It is against this background that the musical overtures to the 1800 election were composed. Federalist lyricists utilized the war spirit of 1798 to identify their cause with that of national patriotism. A particularly martial version of "Yankee Doodle" invoked a rather ungenteel image to stir up American valor:

AMERICAN SPIRIT

Sing Yankee Doodle, that fine tune,
Americans delight in;
It suits for peace, it suits for fun,
It suits as well as fighting.

Chorus:
Yankee Doodle, mind the tune,
Yankee Doodle dandy,
If Frenchmen come with naked bum,
We'll spank 'em hard and handy.

Bold Adams did in Seventy-Six,
Our Independence sign, sir,
And he will not give up a jot,
Tho' all the world combine, sir. *(Cho.)*

From *The Federal Songster.*

On a somewhat more exalted level, another poet celebrated:

Adams, the man of our choice, guides the helm,
No tempest can harm us, no storm overwhelm....
The Federal Constitution, boys,
  and the President forever.

From "The Federal Constitution and Liberty Forever,"
words by Mr. Milns (not otherwise identified), and
music by J. Hewitt (1798).

Among the most ardent of the Federalist songwriters was Robert Treat Paine, Jr., a sort of ne'er-do-well son of a signer of the Declaration of Independence. Paine was originally named Thomas, but he subsequently appealed to the Massachusetts Legislature to change that for his father's name on the grounds that since the notorious "infidel" Thomas Paine had borne it, he "had no Christian name." Under his new name, Paine wrote several pro-Adams songs, including "The Green Mountain Farmer" and "Adams and Liberty." The latter was composed in 1798 "at the request of the Massachusetts Charitable Fire Society" and is reported to have netted its author the then fabulous sum of $750.

ADAMS AND LIBERTY

Words: Robert Treat Paine, Jr.

Tune: "To Anacreon in Heaven" ("The Star-spangled Banner")

Ye___ sons of Co-lum-bia who brave-ly have fought For those rights which un-
long taste the bless-ings your val-or has bought, And your sons reap the

stained from your sires have de-scend-ed, May you
soil which your fath-ers de-

fend-ed; Mid the reign of mild
peace, May your na-tion in-crease, With the glo-ry of Rome, and the

wis-dom of Greece; And ne'er shall the___ sons of Co-lum-bi-a be___

slaves,___ While the earth___ bears a plant, or the sea rolls a wave.

In a clime whose rich vales feed the marts of the world,
　Whose shores are unshaken by Europe's commotion,
The trident of commerce should never be hurled
　To increase the legitimate powers of the ocean;
　　But should pirates invade,
　　Tho' in thunder arrayed,
Let your cannon declare the free charter of trade;
　For ne'er shall the sons, etc.

The fame of our arms, of our laws the mild sway,
　Had justly ennobled our nation in story,
Till the dark clouds of faction obscured our young day,
　And enveloped the sun of American glory;
　　But let traitors be told,
　　Who their country have sold,
And bartered their God for his image in gold,
　That ne'er shall the sons, etc.

While France her huge limbs bathes, recumbent in blood,
　And society's base threats with wide dissolution,
May peace, like the dove who returned from the flood,
　Find an ark of abode in our mild constitution.
　　But though peace is our aim,
　　Yet the boon we disclaim,
If bought by our sovereignty, justice, or fame;
　For ne'er shall the sons, etc.

'Tis the fire of the flint each American warms;
    Let Rome's haughty victors beware of collision;
Let them bring all the vassals of Europe in arms,
    We're a world by ourselves, and disdain a provision.
        While with patriot pride
        To our laws we're allied,
No foe can subdue us, no faction divide;
    For ne'er shall the sons, etc.

Our mountains are crowned with imperial oak,
    Whose roots, like our liberties, ages have nourished;
But long ere our nation submits to the yoke,
    'Not a tree shall be left on the field where it flourished.
        Should invasion impend,
        Every grove would descend
From the hill-tops they shaded, our shores to defend;
    For ne'er shall the sons, etc.

Let our Patriots destroy Anarch's pestilent worm,
    Lest our liberty's growth should be checked by corrosion;
Then let clouds thicken round us—we heed not the storm;
    Our realm fears no shock but the earth's own explosion;
        Foes assail us in vain
        Though their fleets bridge the main,
For our altars and laws, with our lives we'll maintain;
    For ne'er shall the sons, etc.

Should the tempest of war overshadow our land,
    Its bolts could ne'er rend Freedom's temple asunder;
For unmoved at its portals would Washington stand,
    And repulse with his breast the assaults of the thunder;
        Of its scabbard would leap,
        His sword from the sleep,
And conduct, with its point, every flash to the deep!
For ne'er shall the sons, etc.

Let fame to the world sound America's voice:
    No intrigue can her sons from the government sever;
Her pride is her Adams—his laws are her choice,
    And shall flourish till Liberty slumbers forever.
        Then unite heart and hand,
        Like Leonidas' band,
And swear to the God of the ocean and land
    That ne'er shall the sons, etc.

Whatever discretion had kept campaign songs from making their appearance before then, the critical election of 1800 was ushered in by what may have been the first actual presidential election campaign songs in American history. Supporters of John Adams were singing "Adams and Liberty," but Jeffersonians, organized into Democratic-Republican societies and appealing to the popular sentiment, created new ballads which explicitly asked citizens to vote for their man.

After attacking "men in pow'r [who] cry 'Sedition,'" one such song said:

If you peace and freedom love,
Act with circumspection,
Ev'ry foe to these remove,
At your next election,
Chuse for chief Columbia's son,
The immortal Jefferson.
He will ever-ever-ever-ever stand,
    Watching o'er your freedom.

From *"Watching O'er Your Freedom"* (1800).

Another, "The Son of Liberty," was a singing biography of the man from Monticello, referring to such highlights of Jefferson's career as his drafting of the Declaration of Independence and his service as American Minister to France from 1785 to 1790. The words of the song were set to the tune of "Variety," unfortunately not available.

THE SON OF LIBERTY

Words: Anonymous

Tune: "Variety" by Charles Dibdin

Music lend thy pleasing aid,
Freedom's will must be obeyed,
Sing, she cries with life and glee,
To the son of liberty.
    Sing, she cries with life and glee,
    To the son of liberty.

He the Declaration framed,
Independence, that proclaimed,
Columbia owes that great decree,
To the son of liberty.
    Columbia owes that great decree,
    To the son of liberty.

Acting in a noble cause,
He abolished cruel laws,
Set the mind and body free,
He's the son of liberty.

Sent unto a foreign court,
There he firmly did support,
His country's rights and dignity,
Like a son of liberty.

And at home his actions tell,
That he filled his station well,
Bold intriguers foiled we see,
By the son of liberty.

Reason, knowledge, truth combined,
Deep research with learning joined,
Virtue, mild philosophy,
Form the son of liberty.

Public virtue, private worth,
In his character shine forth,
Jefferson the great is he,
And the son of liberty.

Few like Jefferson we find
'mong the sons of human kind,
Friend of peace and honesty
Is the son of liberty.

Hark! what voices rend the sky!
Lo, the sovereign people cry,
Jefferson shall leader be,
Honored son of liberty.

Some songs did not bother to hide behind euphemisms or generalities. To the tune of "Yankee Doodle," Jeffersonians sang:

See Johnny at the helm of State,
Head itching for a crowny,
He longs to be, like Georgy, great,
And pull Tom Jeffer downy.

Jefferson's campaign songs were echoed in a number of celebratory pieces after his election. One anonymously created broadside, "composed for the 4th of March, 1801," the day of Jefferson's inauguration, concerned the Federalist attempt to set up a standing army. (Hamilton actually was the force behind the proposal; he viewed himself as its commander and may even have dreamed of the possibility of utilizing that position to take over the reins of government, since he was barred from election to the presidency by reason of his birth in the West Indies. Adams, somewhat more wisely, as it turns out, favored building up a navy.)

Some swore Johnny Adams the nation should steer,
With an Army and Navy we'd nothing to fear,
But this useless parade will I hope disappear,
    A useless expense to Columbia,
    Nor feed on Columbian roast beef.

The most popular of these post-election songs was the work of Robert Treat Paine, the same writer who had composed "Adams and Liberty." It was not

25

the last time that a songwriter would switch sides so precipitously. Paine, naturally enough, called his song "Jefferson and Liberty" and wrote it to the tune of an old Irish reel. The "reign of terror" mentioned in the first stanza of the song referred to the period of political inquisition, arrests of newspaper editors, etc., highlighted by the Alien and Sedition Acts, by which the Adams Administration made serious inroads on the Bill of Rights. The phrase also served to hurl back at the Federalists the charge that the Republicans were overly sympathetic to the French Revolution and its "reign of terror."

JEFFERSON AND LIBERTY

Words: Robert Treat Paine, Jr.   Tune: "Gobby-O"

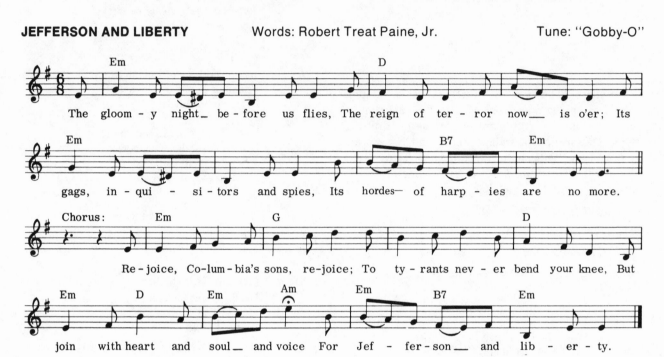

The gloom-y night_ be-fore us flies, The reign of ter-ror now__ is o'er; Its gags, in-qui-si-tors and spies, Its hordes— of harp-ies are no more.

Chorus: Re-joice, Co-lum-bia's sons, re-joice; To ty-rants nev-er bend your knee, But join with heart and soul_ and voice For Jef-fer-son__ and lib-er-ty.

O'er vast Columbia's varied clime,
Her cities, forests, shores and dales,
In rising majesty sublime,
Immortal Liberty prevails.

Hail, long expected, glorious day!
Illustrious, memorable morn,
That Freedom's fabric from decay
Rebuilds, for millions yet unborn.

His country's surest hope and stay,
In virtue and in talents tried,
Now rises to assume the sway,
O'er Freedom's Temple to preside.

Within its hallowed walls immense,
No hireling Bands shall e'er arise,
Arrayed in Tyranny's defense,
To crush an injured people's cries.

No Lordling here, with gorging jaws,
Shall wring from Industry its food;
Nor fiery bigots' Holy Laws
Lay waste our fields and streets in blood.

Here Strangers from a thousand shores,
Compelled by Tyranny to roam,
Shall find, amidst abundant stores,
A nobler and a happier home.

Here Art shall lift her laureled head,
Wealth, Industry and Peace divine,
And where dark pathless Forests spread,
Rich fields and lofty cities shine.

From Europe's wants and woes remote,
A dreary waste of waves between,
Here plenty cheers the humblest cot,
And smiles on every Village Green.

Here, free as air's expanded space,
To every soul and sect shall be
The sacred priv'lege of our race,
The Worship of the Deity.

These gifts, great Liberty, are thine;
Ten thousand more we owe to thee—
Immortal may their mem'ries shine
Who fought and died for Liberty.

What heart but hails a scene so bright,
What soul but inspiration draws,
Who would not guard so dear a right,
Or die in such a glorious cause?

Let Foes to Freedom dread the name,
But should they touch the sacred Tree,
Twice fifty thousand swords shall flame
For Jefferson and Liberty.

From Georgia to Lake Champlain,
From seas to Mississippi's shore,
The Sons of Freedom loud proclaim,
The Reign of Terror now is o'er.

Reportedly first performed in public March 11, 1801, at a festival in Wallingford, Connecticut, in commemoration of Jefferson's election.

Paine's own "Adams and Liberty" was parodied by a Jeffersonian who used the Anacreon tune to call for Jefferson's re-election in 1804:

Calumny and falsehood in vain raise their voice,
To blast our great President's fair reputation;
Yet Jefferson still is America's choice,
And he will her liberties guard from invasion.
  'Tis the wretches who wait
  To unite Church and State
The name of our Jefferson ever to hate.
But ne'er shall the sons of Columbia be slaves,
While the earth bears a plant or the sea rolls its waves.
. . . .

At freedom's fair temple see Jefferson stand,
Firm and unmoved by the thunder of faction.
Let all true Americans join heart in hand
To aid, to promote, and support his election.

Also titled "Jefferson and Liberty" and appearing in a broadsheet of "Patriotic Songs" which were "selected for the fourth of July, 1803, and sung at Portsmouth, N.H."

Madison Appears and Monroe Is the Man

The election of 1800 effectively ended Federalist power, and Jefferson's two eventful terms reduced the party of Hamilton and Adams to little more than a sectional faction. While James Madison clearly had significant qualifications for the presidency in his own right—as the "father of the Constitution," author of the influential Federalist Papers and secretary of state—his election in 1808 was more an endorsement and reassertion of Jeffersonian rule than anything else. The only Madison campaign song the author has been able to find is more a tribute to Jefferson and a renewal of old issues than a paean to Madison.

MADISON, UNION AND LIBERTY

Words: Anonymous (from an 1808 broadside)   Music: No tune indicated

As yon effulgent orb of light
With beaming glory sinks to rest,
Veiled in a gloomy cloud of night
His splendors vanish from the West,
So *Jefferson* to shade retires,
But *Madison*, like morn, appears,
Fresh confidence and hope inspires,
And light again the nation cheers.
    Huzza for Madison! Huzza!
    For Union and America!

Late have the foes to freedom sought
Our happy Union to divide;
For which our heroes bravely fought,
For which our patriots bravely died.
But vain their efforts yet have proved,
The temple, still unshaken, stands,
Nor by the power of faction moved,
Nor levelled by rebellion's hands.
    Huzza for Liberty! Huzza!
    For Union and America!

For should the Tories all unite,
And join again with British foes,
Hell would rejoice at such a sight,
But heav'n in justice interpose;
Millions of freemen, firm and brave,
Would grasp the keen avenging steel,
Lightning would storm o'er every wave
And thunders from our Navy peal.
   To blast the wretch who dare betray
   The PEOPLE OF AMERICA.

Then join, ye friends of Freedom, join!
For lo! Sedition marches forth;
With whom infernal fiends combine,
The South to sever from the North;
To crush the traitors of our land,
Be ready at a moment's call,

United—safely shall we stand—
Divided—we are sure to fall:
   Long may Columbians live to see
   Pow'r, Union, Peace and Liberty.

The "Virginia Succession" brought James Monroe to the presidency in 1816. The Federalists, gasping for breath, barely mounted some token opposition, and by the time of Monroe's second candidacy he had the field completely to himself. The election of 1820, in which Monroe received every electoral college vote but one (that one cast solely to maintain Washington as the only unanimous choice of the nation), was both the high-water point of Democratic-Republican rule and the end of the Virginia dynasty which had seen four of our first five chief executives come from that state.

MONROE IS THE MAN   Words: Anonymous   Tune: "Young Lochinvar" by Joseph Mazzinghi (1811)

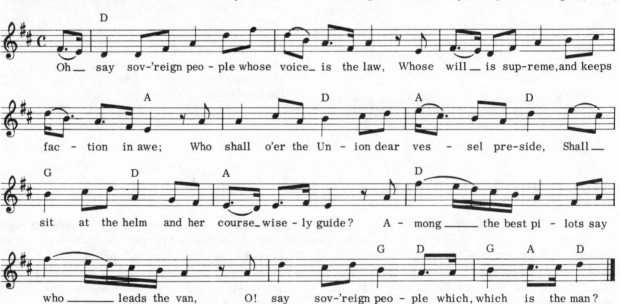

Oh— say sov'reign peo - ple whose voice— is the law, Whose will— is sup-reme, and keeps fac - tion in awe; Who shall o'er the Un - ion dear ves - sel pre-side, Shall— sit at the helm and her course—wise - ly guide? A - mong—— the best pi - lots say who —— leads the van, O! say sov'reign peo - ple which, which is the man?

Is it him whose whole life has so constantly shewn,
That the cause of the people was ever his own?
The firm friend of freedom in every sphere,
Whose conscience 'mong kings and 'mong courts still was clear.
Whose actions grow brighter the nearer we scan,
O! say sov'reign people—which—which is the man?

Who cares not for office for pow'r or for place,
But whose merits and virtues the highest would grace,
Whose country's his Idol, her good all his care,
And in the worst times who did never despair;
In Peace and in War—who can act and can plan,
O! say sov'reign people—which—which is the man?

O! 'tis easy to tell without speaking his name,
So well is he known in the records of fame,
To him much we owe, and on him we depend,
We can ne'er be deceived in so faithful a friend;
He's the Man that we love—for to hate him who can,
MONROE—yes MONROE—he indeed is the Man.

Old Hickory: Half Horse and Half Alligator

The relative equanimity characteristic of the election campaigns from 1804 to 1820 came to a rude and permanent ending with the election of 1824 and the first of the Adams-Jackson contests. The unity of interest which had produced the strong wave of nationalism of the preceding twenty years was shattered by the emergence of strong sectional pulls reflecting the diverse needs of a New England merchant and manufacturing establishment, a growing southern plantation aristocracy based on slavery, and a burgeoning western frontier.

Despite Henry Clay's lien on the mantle of the West, it was Andrew Jackson, the hero of New Orleans, who emerged as the main popular figure of the 1824 election. Frontier egalitarianism likewise appealed to workingmen of the North, and Jackson began to make serious inroads in both New York and Pennsylvania. The rise of Old Hickory frightened the conservative seaboard interests who supported John Quincy Adams, while Henry Clay, enraged and overwhelmed by the Jacksonian tide, cast his lot with Adams.

The result was an electoral stalemate in which Jackson, Adams and Clay split the vote. Eventually, as the result of a deal between Clay and Adams, the House of Representatives elected the New Englander, despite the fact that Jackson had beaten him in both the electoral and popular vote.

The only song which one can attribute to the 1824 campaign with any degree of certainty is "The Hunters of Kentucky," a popular ballad recounting Jackson's victory over the British at New Orleans in 1815. The song itself was actually written some years earlier by Samuel Woodworth, best known, perhaps, as the author of "The Old Oaken Bucket." Its first appearance in print was in 1822, and it was subsequently used in all the Jackson campaigns as a theme song.

THE HUNTERS OF KENTUCKY   Words: Samuel Woodworth   Tune: "Unfortunate Miss Bailey"

1. Ye gen-tle-men and la-dies fair, Who grace this fa-mous cit-y, Just lis-ten if you've time to spare, While I re-hearse this dit-ty, And for the op-por-tu-ni-ty con-ceive your-selves quite luck-y, For 'tis not of-ten that you see A hunt-er of Ken-tuck-y. Oh, Ken-tuck-y, the hunt-ers of Ken-tuck-y! Oh, Ken-tuck-y, the hunt-ers of Ken-tuck-y!

We are a hardy, free-born race,
Each man to fear a stranger;
Whate'er the game we join in chase,
Despoiling time and danger;
And if a daring foe annoys,
Whate'er his strength and forces,
We'll show him that Kentucky boys
Are alligator horses. *(Cho.)*

I s'pose you've read it in the prints,
How Packenham attempted
To make Old Hickory Jackson wince,
But soon his scheme repented;
For we, with rifles ready cock'd,
Thought such occasion lucky,
And soon around the gen'ral flocked
The hunters of Kentucky. *(Cho.)*

You've heard, I s'pose how New Orleans
Is fam'd for wealth and beauty,
There's girls of ev'ry hue it seems,
From snowy white to sooty.
So Packenham he made his brags,
If he in fight was lucky,
He'd have their girls and cotton bags,
In spite of old Kentucky. *(Cho.)*

But Jackson he was wide awake,
And was not scared at trifles,
For well he knew what aim we take
With our Kentucky rifles.
So he led us down to Cypress swamp,
The ground was low and mucky,
There stood John Bull in martial pomp,
And here was old Kentucky. *(Cho.)*

A bank was raised to hide our breasts,
Not that we thought of dying,
But that we always like to rest,
Unless the game is flying.
Behind it stood our little force,
None wished it to be greater,
For ev'ry man was half a horse,
And half an alligator. *(Cho.)*

They did not let our patience tire,
Before they showed their faces;
We did not choose to waste our fire,
So snugly kept our places.
But when so near we saw them wink,
We thought it time to stop 'em,
And 'twould have done you good I think,
To see Kentuckians drop 'em. *(Cho.)*

They found, at last, 'twas vain to fight,
Where lead was all the booty,
And so they wisely took to flight,
And left us all our beauty.
And now, if danger e'er annoys,
Remember what our trade is,
Just send for us Kentucky boys,
And we'll protect ye, ladies. *(Cho.)*

While the campaign of 1824 was relatively free of musical invective, the 1828 contest, which was clearly destined to be a renewal of the fray between the same contenders, produced at least a handful of singing rousers and several tons of insult. The Adams supporters, on the defensive ever since 1824, unleashed an attack on Jackson whose scurrilousness has rarely been matched in history. One pro-Adams newspaper wrote:

General Jackson's mother was a Common Prostitute brought to this country by the British soldiers! She afterwards married a MULATTO MAN with whom she had several children, of which number GENERAL JACKSON is one!

Other papers circulated a story which cast doubt on the legality of Jackson's marriage, while still another made the following comment on the use of the Hickory Tree as a campaign symbol:

Among the debasing irrationalities of which the friends of General Jackson have been guilty is that of planting hickory poles or trees in their vicinities, as significant of their attachment to this candidate to whom that distinctive nick-name has been given. . . . Such of these trees as may survive, could they tell to posterity of the drunken orgies they had witnessed, of the scenes of intemperance which had been exhibited around, would make the next generation blush for that which had preceded it.

And when Democrats charged that under the continuation of "Johnny" Adams' rule, "War, Pestilence and Famine's Coming," Adams' supporters responded with the following reply:

LITTLE WAT YE WHA'S A-COMIN'

Words: From the *Cincinnati Gazette* (July 30, 1828)
Music: Traditional Scottish tune, "Highland Muster Roll"

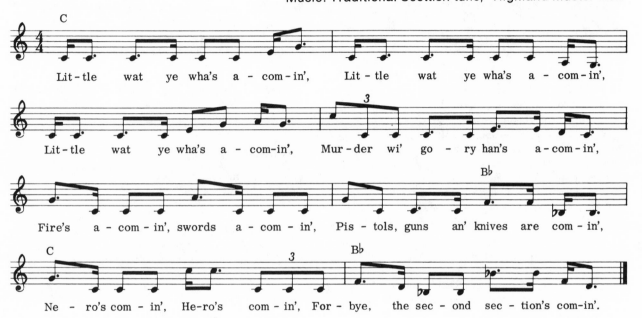

Little wat ye wha's a-comin',
Little wat ye wha's a-comin',
Little wat ye wha's a-comin',
Martial an' Lynch's Law are comin',
Slavery's comin', knavery's comin',
Plunder's comin', Blunder's comin',
Robbing's comin', Jobbing's comin',
    An' a' the plague o' War's a-comin'.

Little wat ye wha's a-comin',
Little wat ye wha's a-comin',
Little wat ye wha's a-comin',
JUGGERNAUT himsel' is comin',
He'll fret and fume, he'll shoot and stab,
He'll stamp an' swear "like any drab,"
He'll play Jack Cade—hang honest men,
    An' after that Calhoun's a-comin'.

Not all the Adams songs were quite so vituperative, although it did seem that the president's partisans hated Jackson much more heartily than they supported their chief. In a bid to boost Henry Clay for the vice-presidency on Adams' ticket, Ohio Republicans sang of "Adams and Clay," reviving the tune, if not the spirit, of earlier days and another Adams. But even here they could not completely resist the temptation to take some swipes at the Opposition.

ADAMS AND CLAY

Words: From the *Cincinnati Gazette* (Aug. 15, 1828)
Tune: "The Star-spangled Banner"

Here's a pledge to the Star Spangled Banner so fair!
Fill! Fill to the brim with a patriot's devotion,
But temp'ring its radiance, let mercy be there,
The beacon, the bound of our fiercest emotion,
   Ere the nights which we hold
   To a Tyrant are sold,
While peace is still resting on cottage and fold.
With hearts turned to rapture, let's hail this bright day,
Beneath the bland influence of Adams and Clay.

Of the peal of the shot—of the flash of the steel,
Which purchased this moment, let gratitude tell.
The flash was terrifick—and dreadful the peal
When invaders, not countrymen, felt it and fell.
   And wailed the acclaim
   Of the Hero's fierce name,
In rattling to fragments the trumpet of fame.
Let's remember the blessings which dawned on this day,
And hail their continuance in Adams and Clay.

But if blessings so valued are fleeting and brief,
If affliction must visit our best and our rarest,
Let famine blow mildew on each golden sheaf,
Let pestilence strike midst our best and our fairest;
   But, oh, from our land,
   Avert the fell hand,
That would sink us beneath a stern tyrant's command,
Lest darkling and joyous [*sic*] clouds rise on the day
That is dawning so brightly on Adams and Clay.

But the name-calling wasn't all on the Adams side by any measure. Jackson supporters accused the president of having arranged, while minister to Russia, for the seduction of an American girl by the Czar. Old Hickory was hailed as the "man of the people" while Adams was castigated as a snob and an aristocrat.

THE HICKORY TREE

Tune: None indicated

While Jonny was lounging on crimson and down,
And stuffing both pockets with pelf,
Brave Andrew was pulling John Bull's colors down,
And paying his army himself.

While Jonny was gorging the fat of the land
And bartering for Cod, d'ye see—
Brave Jackson was feeding his patriot band,
On nuts of the Hickory tree.

While Jonny made journeys, yet never stirred out,
At twenty-five dollars per day,
Bold Jackson o'er mountains and swamps took his rout,
And mortgaged his lands for the pay.

When Jonny had bought his commission of Clay,
And mounted the throne, d'ye see,
Brave Jackson disgusted at rogues turn'd away
And again sought his Hickory Tree.

Another Jackson song reflected the depth of the feelings aroused by the "deal" of 1824 which had denied Old Hickory the presidency:

JACKSON TOAST

Words: From the *Lancaster Journal*
Tune: "Auld Lang Syne"

Though Adams now misrules the land,
And strives t'oppress the free,
He soon must yield his high command
Unto "Old Hickory."

Chorus:
Then toast our Jackson, good and great,
The man whom we admire,
He soon will mount the chair of state,
Which patriots all desire.

And though Corruption's baleful voice
Did formerly prevail—
Once more he'll be the people's choice,
Though demagogues assail.

Now Johnny Q. and Henry Clay,
With all the people's foes,
Are giving, as they pass away,
Their last convulsive throes.

And Liberty will reign once more,
O'er all the brave and free—
When Jackson shall her rights restore,
To their first purity.

Let Freemen, then, their goblets fill,
And drink to him whose name
Stands sanctioned by the People's Will,
First on the roll of fame.

Tippecanoe and Tyler Too

The First Great Singing Campaign, the Historic Election of 1840

In the history of campaign music in America, the year 1840 represents the Great Divide. Previously campaign singing was, at best, a sometime thing, confined more to a certain satiric versifying in the political journals than to any phenomenon resembling music.

Upon first examination, one is tempted to suggest that songs—as well as the rest of the paraphernalia of the traditional nineteenth-century election campaign—emerged from the Harrison-Van Buren contest as the result of an effort to rouse public interest in what might otherwise have been a most unmemorable race. For neither the personalities of the candidates nor the "burning issues" which supposedly divided them had any particularly distinguishing characteristics.

But 1840 is a tidewater mark in American politics for a variety of reasons, and the development of mass campaign techniques, of which singing may have been the most flamboyant, reflected more deep-going changes in the American electoral pattern—namely, the institutionalization of the party system and the popular selection of presidential electors.

In such a context, a new kind of campaign developed—one which based itself on popular appeal and the glorification of a "standard-bearer" chosen primarily for his ability to win votes.

From the beginning, the campaign waged on behalf of William Henry Harrison was a phenomenon of fury, fervor and frenzy. As has happened many times since in American politics, an overenthusiastic spokesman for the opposition opened the Harrison flood-gates. The Democratic editor of the *Baltimore Republican* suggested, in an editorial written shortly after Harrison's nomination, that the way to treat the ex-general was to "give him a barrel of hard cider and settle a pension of two thousand a year on him, and my word for it, he will sit the remainder of his days in his log cabin...."

As campaign rhetoric of the age went, it was fairly mild stuff. But the astute Whigs, sensing the makings of a popular image, escalated the phrases "log cabin" and "hard cider" to the heights of moral and national virtue, a process whose irony rested in the fact that the image bore little resemblance to the reality. Harrison—a descendant of the Virginia aristocracy, a perennial office-seeker in Ohio, owner of a substantial country home, the nominee of various propertied interests in both the North and South, and the commanding officer in a dubious military victory against Indians almost thirty years earlier—was transformed into the "people's candidate," the hero of Tippecanoe, the incarnation of all the rugged values of candor and independence one associated with the American frontier; and the "log cabin and hard cider" campaign was under way.

The slogans fabricated by the Whig image-makers on behalf of their candidate rested on flimsy foundations indeed. The much-heralded Battle of Tippecanoe (November 7, 1811) was not nearly the military triumph or masterful strategic blow which Whig propagandists proclaimed it some thirty years later. The "victory" by 1,000 crack American troops under Harrison's command over a band of poorly armed Indians fighting with great courage under the inspiration of Tecumseh but without much strategy was far from decisive. Harrison lost about one-fourth of his men. Much of the triumph seems to have consisted in razing the Indian village on Tippecanoe Creek. As the crowning irony of the campaign of 1840, there is little evidence that the aging general had any great taste for hard cider, although it seems he was not averse to the choicer brands of whiskey of the day.

Harrison vs. Van Buren

The Harrison-Van Buren campaign was without precedent in American history. Parades, processions, floats, banners, mass meetings and concerts were just a few of the devices used to attract popular attention and arouse mass excitement. Log cabin newspapers were published while Tippecanoe handkerchiefs, miniatures, medals, almanacs and flags flooded the country. A Van Buren newspaper reports that "city cockneys sport log cabin breast pins, in gold; their sisters and sweethearts anoint themselves with 'log cabin perfumes' and indite their love letters and invitations upon beautifully embossed paper of foreign manufacture, ornamented with the British picture of a log cabin." (It was a favorite charge of the Democrats that British gold was behind the Harrison campaign.)

Where the Whigs outdid themselves, however, was in the realm of song. Log Cabin songbooks and songsters proliferated, marking the first appearance of the campaign songbook in American history. Sheet music—both songs and instrumentals—was published by the carload by enterprising music publishers who enthusiastically hopped on the Harrison bandwagon.

For the most part, the songs were either celebrations of Harrison's "virtues," or blistering mockeries on the political and moral defects of "Little Van." There is no evidence to suggest that Harrison ever had much to do with the north end of a plough, but this did not prevent the Whig rhymesters from singing about the "honest old farmer of North Bend" or the "plain-spoken yeoman" in his fields.

> What though the hero's hard "huge paws"
> Were wont to plough and sow?
> Does that disgrace our sacred cause?
> Does that degrade him? No!
>
> No ruffled shirt, no silken hose,
> No airs does TIP display;
> But like the "pith of worth" he goes
> In homespun "hoddin-grey."

Upon his board there ne'er appeared
The costly "sparkling wine,"
But plain "hard cider" such as cheered
In days of old lang syne.

From "Should Brave Old Soldiers Be Forgot?" arr. by T. Carr, pub. Blake's Log Cabin Music, Phila. 1840.

In a nation still largely agricultural, still enamored of a frontier which always offered another chance, a vast coterie of slick propagandists and party enthusiasts carefully cultivated Harrison's homespun image.

Hurrah! for the farmer of Tippecanoe,
The honest old farmer of Tippecanoe,
With an arm that is strong and a heart that is true,
The man of the People is Tippecanoe.

From "The Farmer of Tippecanoe," to the tune of "The Campbells are Coming" *(Log Cabin and Hard Cider Melodies)*.

With an honest Old Farmer, a merry old song,
And a mug of "hard cider," we'll sit the night long.
Freedom despises all those who deride her,
She trusts in the Whigs, and their mugs of hard cider.

From "With an Honest Old Farmer," no melody indicated *(Harrison Melodies)*.

Far out in the west, where there lives the squatter,
Who hunt with the rifle, and trap for mink and otter;
Old Harrison dashed, when the fuss was just a-brewin',
And he made things fly like a streak of blue ruin.

Then the war being over, he squat him down here,
Raised his log cabin first, then began for to clear;
And as long as old Tipp has a scothold there,
The hungry and thirsty are welcome to share.

From "The Buckeye Song," written by a member of the Fifth Ward Club, New York Tippecanoe Assn. (sheet music pub. by Thomas Birch, 1840).

If Harrison was horny-handed honesty incarnate, Van Buren, quite naturally, was a scheming, manipulative, cowardly aristocrat of dubious parentage whose prime associates were thieves, murderers and scoundrels. (One assumes that the proprieties of the time forbade charging Van Buren with child

molesting and miscegenation.) When he wasn't "Van, Van, the used-up man," he was "King Matty" and worse. Overseer of a "corrupt" administration, Van Buren was held responsible for every mishap of the past forty years. In addition to defeatism and nepotism, the favorite charge against Van Buren was an alleged penchant for "stylish" living and aristocratic tastes, supposedly a contrast to the rough-hewn values of Tippecanoe. The songs said it all:

LITTLE VANNY

Words: Anonymous

Tune: "Rosin the Beau"

You can't make a song to Van Buren,
Because his long name will not do;
There's nothin' about him allurin',
As there is about Tippecanoe!

He never was seen in a battle,
Where bullet and cannon shot flew;
His nerves would be shocked with the rattle
Of a contest like Tippecanoe!

While Harrison marched to the border,
Sly Van stayed at home as you know,
Afraid of the smell of gun-powder—
Then hurrah for Old Tippecanoe!

Little Mat was too tender a dandy,
To shoulder a musket and go
Where Harrison battled so handy
As he did when at Tippecanoe!

But snug in his pretty silk stockings,
And dressed in his broadcloth all new,
He roasted his shins in a parlor—
Not fighting like Tippecanoe.

And now with his gold spoons and dishes,
He lives like a king with his crew;
He'll feast on the loaves and the fishes,
Till we put in Old Tippecanoe.

From *The Tippecanoe Song Book*.

Unabashed and unashamed, the Whigs ascribed every crime and malfeasance imaginable to Van Buren. Given impetus by the Panic of 1837 and the president's own less than ingratiating personality, the charges found a ready response and were sung gleefully throughout the country. The full version of the following devastating portrait of Van Buren covered more than fourteen pages of one songster with a recital of political and personal calumnies rarely matched in the history of campaign song.

There is little evidence to support the numerous charges. In fact, outright lies were joined with half-truths to create the image of a "homespun" Harrison and an "aristocratic" Van Buren. The Whig charge that Van Buren wanted the poor man "to work a week for half a crown" was made out of

whole cloth. The reference to "French Artificial Flowers" was part of an elaborate scheme, largely the work of Charles Ogle, whose book, *The Royal Splendors of the President's Palace,* provided a text for Whig campaign orators who seized on trivialities to lend some substance to their accusations. The reference to England is based on Andrew Jackson's appointment of Van Buren as Minister to Great Britain in 1831, a designation subsequently vetoed by a Calhoun-dominated Senate in an act of personal vengeance.

Some choice verses of this diatribe-laden song follow:

VAN BUREN

Words and music: Anonymous

Who nev-er did a no-ble deed? Who of the peo-ple took no heed? Who is the worst of ty-rant's breed? Van Bu-ren!

Who, while but a little boy,
Was counted crafty, cunning, sly,
Who with the wily fox could vie?
Van Buren!

Who, when an urchin, young at school,
Would of each classmate make a tool,
In cheating, who the roost would rule?
Van Buren!

By scheming who to England went?
By intrigue who is President?
By proxy who has millions spent?
Van Buren!

Who wants to bring the poor man down
To work a week for half a crown?
(Such twenty seven monarchs own)?
Van Buren!

Who when distress and want was ours,
Profusely scattered golden showers?
To buy French Artificial Flowers?
Van Buren!

Who never had an honest thought?
Who to their senses others brought?
And has himself a Tartar caught?
Van Buren!

Who like the wily serpent clings,
Who like the pois'nous adder stings,
Who is more base than basest Kings?
Van Buren!

Who rules us with an iron rod,
Who moves at Satan's beck and nod,
Who heeds not man, who heeds not God?
Van Buren!

Who would his friend, his country sell,
Do other deeds too base to tell,
Deserves the lowest place in Hell?
Van Buren!

From *A Miniature of Martin Van Buren.*

But of all the Whig songs which set the nation to tapping its feet on the way to the polls, none was more popular than "Tip and Ty," the comic glee which gave us the phrase "Tippecanoe and Tyler too" and firmly established the power of singing as a campaign device. With rare exceptions, the authors of campaign ballads are best left in an obscurity from which one rescues them only with a resolute lack of charity. Still, history has no right to exempt the first practitioner of the art from a well-earned notoriety. Alexander Coffman Ross, who wrote the lyrics for "Tip and Ty" (to the tune of a minstrel number, "Little Pigs"), was a jeweler in Zanesville, Ohio in 1840 when the political muse overcame him. A member of his local Tippecanoe Club as well as his church choir, and apparently an amateur clarinetist and singer of modest accomplish-

ment, Ross introduced the song at a Whig meeting in Zanesville, where it was greeted, according to an observer, with "cheers, yells and encores." Later, Ross went on a business trip to New York, where he managed to introduce the song to a Whig rally. The ensuing pandemonium apparently launched the song on the road to nationwide popularity. The *North American Review* called it "in the political canvas of 1840 what the 'Marseillaise' was to the French Revolution. It sang Harrison into the presidency."

Ross's song, oddly enough, does not seem to have been copyrighted (an oversight future campaign songwriters did not make); and a number of different versions of the sheet music appeared, many with a great variety of verses. The version here seems to be Ross's original.

TIP AND TY

Words: Alexander Coffman Ross   Tune: "Little Pigs"

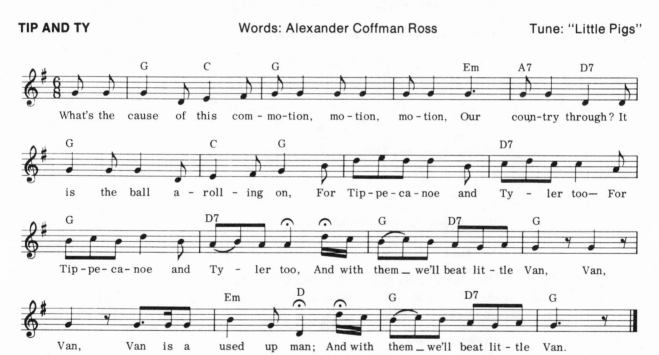

Like the rushing of mighty waters, waters, waters,
On it will go!
And in its course will clear the way
For Tippecanoe and Tyler too. *(Cho.)*

See the Loco standard tottering, tottering, tottering,
Down it must go!
And in its place we'll rear the flag
Of Tippecanoe and Tyler too. *(Cho.)*

The Bay State boys turned out in thousands, thousands, thousands,
Not long ago,
And at Bunker Hill they set their seals
For Tippecanoe and Tyler too. *(Cho.)*

Have you heard from old Vermount, mount, mount,
All honest and true?
The Green Mountain boys are rolling the ball
For Tippecanoe and Tyler too. *(Cho.)*

Don't you hear from every quarter, quarter, quarter,
Good news and true?
That swift the ball is rolling on
For Tippecanoe and Tyler too. *(Cho.)*

Now you hear the Vanjacks talking, talking, talking,
Things look quite blue,
For all the world seems turning round
For Tippecanoe and Tyler too. *(Cho.)*

Let them talk about hard cider, cider, cider,
And Log Cabins too,
It will only help to speed the ball
For Tippecanoe and Tyler too. *(Cho.)*

His latchstring hangs outside the door, door, door,
And is never pulled through,
For it never was the custom of
Old Tippecanoe and Tyler too. *(Cho.)*

He always has his tables set, set, set,
For all honest and true,
To ask you in to take a bite
With Tippecanoe and Tyler too. *(Cho.)*

See the spoilsmen and leg-treasurers, treasurers, treasurers,
All in a stew!
For well they know they stand no chance
With Tippecanoe and Tyler too. *(Cho.)*

Little Matty's days are numbered, numbered, numbered,
Out he must go!
And in his place we'll put the good
Old Tippecanoe and Tyler too. *(Cho.)*

For information concerning Ross and his song, see an article by
Norris F. Schneider in the Zanesville, Ohio *Sunday Times Signal,*
May 17, 1959.

No one will ever know for sure how many Harrison songs were hopefully launched on a bewildered electorate. Hundreds of them found their way into print. For the most part they were parodies to popular tunes of the day, although from time to time a Whig with a bent for composing might assay an original tune as well. But in the great tradition of political singing before and since, it was obviously deemed best to utilize familiar airs. "Yankee Doodle," "Fine Old English Gentleman," " 'Tis My Delight," "Auld Lang Syne," and most especially, that hardy perennial of every election campaign of the nineteenth century, "Rosin the Beau," were freely borrowed, parodied and mangled in the quest for votes.

Songwriters for Harrison pulled no punches in castigating politicians of the opposition. Politicos pilloried in the first song below include Senator Felix Grundy of Tennessee, attorney general for one year in the Van Buren Administration, and a staunch Democrat; Senator Thomas Hart Benton of Missouri, a strong Jackson and Van Buren man; and John C. Calhoun, vice-president for eight years (1825-1833), who had allied himself with the Whigs during Jackson's second term, but who in 1840 supported Van Buren.

The following songs also do their best to magnify Harrison's military accomplishments. The word "Thames," recurring frequently in the songs, refers to a battle during the War of 1812 when Harrison, after displaying considerable ineptitude as a military commander, managed to defeat a British-Indian army on the Thames River in southeast Ontario, October, 1813.

HARRISON

Tune: "Yankee Doodle"

It rather seems that humbug schemes
  Can never more cajole us,
There's such a run for HARRISON
  That nothing can control us.

The Western World the flag's unfurled,
  No faction can divide her;
And all the rest will sign the test,
  "Log Cabin and Hard Cider."

When our frontiers were drenched in tears,
  Their cabins sacked and gory,
He struck the blow, chastised the foe,
  Established peace with glory.

Then join the throng and swell the song,
  Extend the circle wider;
And let us *on* for HARRISON,
  "Log Cabin and Hard Cider."

When British bands and savage clans
  Unitedly assailed us,
Our HARRISON was then the one
  Whose courage never failed us.

Through all the west he stood the test,
  And all his foes confounded,
And held his posts against the hosts,
  By whom he was surrounded.

Though at the Thames some other names
  Come in to grace the story,
He laid the plan and led the van
  To victory and glory.

Then crowd the throng and swell the song,
  And spread his glory wider,
And join the run for HARRISON,
  "Log Cabin and Hard Cider."

Let Grundy sneer and Benton jeer;
  The day of retribution,
We firmly trust 'twill be for us,
  A day of restitution.

And let Calhoun change every moon,
  And every such backslider,
We'll go as one for HARRISON,
  "Log Cabin and Hard Cider."

With HARRISON, our country's one,
  No treachery can divide her,
The thing is done with "HARRISON,
  Log Cabin and Hard Cider."

Come farmers all, attend the call,
  'Tis working like a charmer,
Hitch on the team and start for him,
  For he's a *brother farmer*.

His cabin's fit and snug and neat,
  And full and free his larder,
And though his cider may be hard,
  The times are vastly harder.

With social joys—wives, girls and boys,
  Our cabins and our cider,
We'll shout as one for HARRISON,
  And spread his glories wider.

The South and West will stand the test,
  In spite of every spoiler,
And we'll engage to seal the pledge
  For HARRISON and TYLER.

From *Log Cabin and Hard Cider Melodies.*

THE LOG CABIN
AND HARD CIDER CANDIDATE

Tune: "Auld Lang Syne"

Should good old cider be despised,
And ne'er regarded more?
Should plain log cabins be despised,
Our fathers built of yore?
  For the true old style, my boys!
  For the true old style,
  Let's take a mug of cider now,
  For the true old style.

We've tried experiments enough
Of fashions new and vain,
And now we long to settle down
To good old times again.
  For the good old ways, my boys, etc.

We've tried your purse-proud lords, who love
In palaces to shine,
But we'll have a Ploughman President
Of the Cincinnatus line.
  For old North Bend, my boys, etc.

We've tried "the greatest and the best,"
Of him we've had enough,
And he who in those footsteps treads,
Is yet more sorry stuff.
  For the brave old Thames, my boys, etc.

Then give's a hand, my trusty boys:
And here's a hand for you,
And we'll quaff the good old cider yet
For old Tippecanoe.
  For Old Tippecanoe, my boys, etc.

And surely you will give your votes,
And surely I will too,
And we'll clear the way to the White House
For Old Tippecanoe.
  For Tippecanoe, my boys, etc.

From *The Harrison Medal Minstrel.*

OLD TIPPECANOE   Tune: "Rosin the Beau"

When first near the Thames' gentle waters,
My sword for my country I drew,
I fought for America's daughters,
'Long side of Old Tippecanoe.
    'Long side of Old Tippecanoe, etc.

And now that the good of the nation
Requires that something we do,
We'll hurl little Van from his station,
And elevate Tippecanoe.
    And elevate Tippecanoe, etc.

Again and again fill your glasses,
Bid Martin Van Buren adieu,
We'll please ourselves and the lasses,
And vote for old Tippecanoe.
    And vote for old Tippecanoe, etc.

And who pray is Martin Van Buren,
What wonders did he ever do?
Was he in the Battle of Orleans,
Meigs, Thames or Old Tippecanoe?

Oh! no, he had no taste for fighting,
Such rough work he never could do,
He shirked it off on to brave Jackson,
And the Hero of Tippecanoe.

The Whigs at the coming election,
Will carry their candidates through,
They've made the judicious selection
Of Tyler and Tippecanoe.

The spoilsmen are leaving their party,
Where prospect for office is blue,
Not wishing to stick by poor Matty,
They change for Old Tippecanoe.

They say that he lives in a cabin,
And that he drinks hard cider, too,
Well, what if he did, I am certain,
He's the Hero of Tippecanoe.

The country still loves her old soldiers,
And soon will her gratitude show,
By choosing as chief of her council,
The Hero of Tippecanoe.

For once let the Whigs pull together,
In union their efforts renew,
And this be their watchword in battle,
"The Hero of Tippecanoe."

The times are as hard as they can be,
The Locos acknowledge them so;
What then can be lost by exchanging
Young Van for Old Tippecanoe?

For fear that we should be thirsty,
I'll tell you what we will do,
We'll fill up the gourd with hard cider,
And drink to Old Tippecanoe!

From *The Harrison Medal Minstrel.*

What was the effect of all this? The despairing editor of a Democratic newspaper during the 1840 campaign wrote:

Some of the songs I shall never forget. They rang in my ears wherever I went, morning, noon and night.... Men, women and children did nothing but sing. It worried, annoyed, dumbfounded, crushed the Democrats, but there was no use trying to escape. It was a ceaseless torrent of music, still beginning, never ending. If a Democrat tried to speak, argue, or answer anything that was said or done, he was only saluted with a fresh deluge of music.

Why almost every amateur poet and songwriter in the United States in 1840 should have been won to the Harrison cause remains something of a mystery, although experience teaches us that in such matters a receptive audience may be more important than political ideals. Whatever the reason, the Van Buren campaign was singularly lacking in songs, poetry, slogans, artifacts and—as it turns out—votes. The few examples of Van Buren song-poetry to be found are, like much of the Van Buren campaign, primarily responsive. A few Democratic rhymesters made sport of some of the more obvious Whig pretensions, but no one seems to have drawn any inspiration from Little Van himself.

As befits a party in power, the Democrats attempted to stand on their dignity. One Van Buren partisan wrote in a letter to the editor of the *Manhattan Advertiser:*

Fellow friends—and some that are not friends—the lesson of this epistle is thus: The Whigs have attempted to sing themselves into office. Therefore it remaineth for us to sing their *lullaby,* as hath been our fortune oft aforetime. No doubt they'll squirm a little in the cradle—it's just like them. The idea that the people are to be gulled by *songs,* without the merit of either truth or patriotism, is a chimera of entire Whig origin.

Another Democratic newspaper, the *Albany Argus,* offered its own rejoinder to "Tip and Ty" with the following note:

A Whig paper says Tippecanoe cradles are becoming fashionable among Whig ladies (married or single, the editor sayeth not). We recommend the following nursery ditty as an accompaniment:

> Hush-a-by-baby,
>   Daddy's a Whig,
> Before he comes home
>   Hard cider he'll swig.
> Then he'll be tipsy
>   And over he'll fall,
> Down will come daddy,
>   Tip, Tyler and all.

With hindsight, it is easy to see that the Democrats allowed the Whigs to define the election. By confining themselves to attacks on Harrison and attempting to adopt an imperious stance towards their "upstart" opponents, they only added to the carefully constructed image which the Whig campaign projected. The Democrats, however, did not have the benefit of historical experience. No one had ever encountered a campaign like that of 1840 before and despite themselves, they were swept up in the excitement of the Tippecanoe surge.

Politicians of a later date could have advised them that there is little to be gained in attacking the war record of a popular hero, but the Democrats seemed blissfully unaware of this pitfall and proceeded to belittle the highly acclaimed exploits of Old Tippecanoe, as in this campaign ballad:

BULLET PROOF (or THE HERO WHO NEVER LOST A BATTLE)

Tune: "Auld Lang Syne"

> Oh, no, he never lost a fight!
> He's even bullet proof!
> For why? When e'er the battle raged,
> He always kept aloof!
>   He always kept aloof, my friends,
>   He always kept aloof,
>   And that's the reason why Old Tip
>   Was always bullet proof!
>
> 'Twas very cautious in Old Tip,
> 'Twas very brave and fair—
> The more our British foes came on,
> The more he wasn't there!
>   The more he wasn't there, my friends, etc.
>
> 'Twas very lucky for him, too,
> It was—it was, indeed!
> The more he didn't get a wound,
> The more he didn't bleed!
>
> But while retreating through the wood,
> And through the tangled fern,
> He tore his mustn't-mention-'ems
> And had to put on her'n.
>
> And thus the war path he did tread,
> Through all that fearful fray;
> But always (as old settlers said),
> He ran the other way.
>
> But he had high authority
> To thus preserve his tallow,
> For Falstaff says "discretion is
> The better part of valor."
>
> Then here's a health to *Tip*-Canoe,
> "The hero of defeat,"
> As safe a generalissimo
> As ever beat retreat!
>
> For oft his gallant troops, 'tis said,
> Paternally he'd tell,
> To "stand a little farther off,
> And they could see as well!"
>
> And many a prudent soldier, who,
> To his advice gave heed,
> Went off without a single wound
> To carry home for seed.

And thus the mighty General,
Through all that bloody war,
Escaped with bare a bramble scratch
His sole and only scar!

From the *Albany Argus,* May 18, 1840.

Among the many Democratic charges against Harrison was that the Whig campaign was devoid of principle. Aside from the fact that the spoils of office have always provided principle enough for *all* major political parties, there is a certain element of truth in the accusation, since the Whig coalition brought together a host of forces with contending interests who were united primarily in their opposition to Democratic rule. It was, in fact, the contradictory positions of different elements in the Whig coalition which led to a campaign strategy of personalizing the contest through the image of Old Tippecanoe. So aware were the Whig campaign strategists of the danger inherent in the all too fragile unity in their ranks, that they devised a "front porch" campaign in which Harrison's public appearances were few and far between, confining the candidate's pronouncements to carefully contrived generalities. In fact, a committee of three prominent Whigs—Major David Gwynne, Judge John C. Wright, and Oliver M. Spencer—handled Harrison's political correspondence after the candidate had said a little too much in letters responding to inquiries concerning his political views.

Since Harrison's popularity seemed to grow in almost direct proportion to his studied evasiveness on the issues, the Democrats fumed about "boss control" and candidates who spoke out of both sides of their mouths. One Democratic song lampooned this aspect of the Whig campaign, and Harrison's Committee of Correspondence in particular, but clearly to no avail, since public dissatisfaction with Van Buren only made the General's "above-the-battle" stance that much more appealing:

THE LAST WHIG SONG   Tune: "Old King Cole"

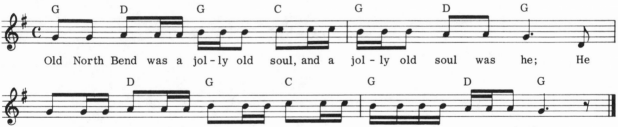

Old North Bend was a jol-ly old soul, and a jol-ly old soul was he; He called for his pipe and he called for his bowl and he called for his Com-mit-tee of Three.

He called for a mug of apple juice,
The best there was in the larder,
And he told his Committee, "Make no excuse,
Every day it is growing harder!"

And the General sat by his own fireside
In the midst of advisers three;
"I'm puzzled," said he, "with my numerous friends;
Why can they not quiet be?

Some ask me one thing, some ask another—
They bother me most to death:
If I say yes and no to this, that and t'other,
'Twill surely take all my breath!

"If I say yes to the North, I'm gone at the South—
I'm glad that the nation's no wider;
I declare I am very much down at the mouth
So give us a swig of that cider!"

The Committee sat—not a word they said,
But they kept up a terrible thinking;
And they watched the nod of the old man's head,
While he the mug of cider was drinking.

At length they spoke—"We've concluded, sir,
That you answer no more of these letters;
'Tis strange how the people, poor ignorant souls,
Will constantly pester their betters.

You can hand them all over to us, North Bend,
We'll be General for you a while—
But we'll give you advice—the advice of a friend—
Drink cider—drink hard, or you'll spile!"

The General nodded, as wont to do,
To this lordly Committee of Three,
And ever since then the old man is mum,
For a still small voice is he!

Go down to North Bend, the old hero you'll find,
As jolly a coon as can be;
But question him not, or he'll send you away
To ask his Committee of Three!

From the *Goshen Democrat* (1840).

Another Democratic charge was that the Whigs were really Federalists in disguise—an accusation with considerable basis in fact. The Whig Party was actually an amalgam of anti-Jackson, antipopulist forces, including the propertied interests who had supported the Federalists twenty years earlier. One Democratic political poet made the case in this song:

WHEN THIS OLD HAT WAS NEW   Words: Anonymous   Tune: "When This Old Hat Was New"

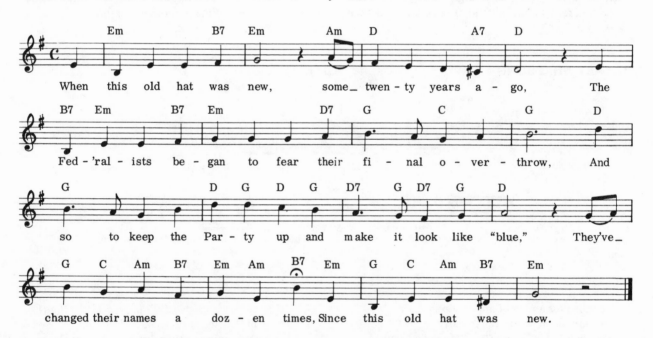

When this old hat was new, they thought the people fools,
And still they hope for Fed'ral ends to find them willing tools,
But though they've often changed their names as knaves are wont to do—
Their doctrines look just as they did—
    When this old hat was new.

When this old hat was new, the Feds despised the poor,
And blushed if ever they were caught within a "cabin" door,
The Democrats alone were found among the toiling crew—
Logs were not rolled in ruffle shirts—
    When this old hat was new.

When this old hat was new, 'tis said, one Henry Clay,
While all the Feds cried out, "Amen!" would thus devoutly pray:
He prayed for "War and pestilence and hungry famine too,
Before a military chief!"—
    When this old hat was new.

When this old hat was new, if I remember well,
Among the heroes of the time, "Old Hickory" bore the bell—
"Dick Johnson" next in honor stood among the noble few—
For Dick was "hero of the Thames"—
    When this old hat was new.

When this old hat was new, the Fed'rals used to boast—
But often found the reckoning to be without their host—
And now they think that Harrison will "run," till all is blue—
Because he used to run so fast—
    When this old hat was new.

When this old hat was new, ere "patent Whigs" were made,
Old Tip was a Federalist and wore the black cockade!
But now he is—the Lord knows what! He's hidden from our view!
Though I suspect he's what he was—
    When this old hat was new.

When this old hat was new, Van Buren was the man
The people loved—altho' abused by all the Federal clan,
A Democrat, unmoved, unchanged—still to his country true,
He's ever been her friend and guard—
    Since this old hat was new!

From the *Albany Argus,* August 29, 1840.

But the Whig image-makers had turned all this upside down, making Van Buren (who was one of the more egalitarian and democratically inclined of our presidents) into an aristocrat and projecting the patrician, Harrison, as the paragon of all the homespun virtues. If the "log cabin and hard cider" campaign was probably the most colorful presidential contest in American history, it may also have been the most ironic.

Locofocos, Whigs and Free-Soilers

War with Mexico and the Great Antislavery Agitation

At no time in the history of the United States has the party system performed worse than in the period from 1840 to 1854. Because American political parties are founded on the principle of winning power—virtually at all costs—the quadrennial presidential election too easily can become an exercise in ideological vagueness and intellectual soporifics.

Clearly the country was headed for a massive explosion over the question of slavery. As has happened to other social systems historically, the slave system had become outmoded. It was a moral as well as material drain on the nation as a whole and, in the age of industrialism which already loomed on the horizon, a totally impractical system for an expanding economy which already had fleeting visions of a world market. But a sizable core of southern planters and slave-owners (and all those in some way dependent on them) had a vast stake in the perpetuation of the slave system. And for those whose direct benefits from slavery were illusory, there were always the psychological benefits which racist ideology helped perpetuate.

The social necessity of the time was the end of slavery. But until the Republican Party was founded in 1854, the American political system had no way of undertaking the task. The Whigs and Democrats, both aiming for popular consensus every four years, devoted their efforts to finding candidates and platforms to please all voters. The result? Men of political mediocrity whose chief characteristics varied from overweening ambition to a remarkable ability for the glittering generality.

Jimmy Polk of Tennessee

"I'd rather be right than President," asserted Henry Clay—and a more ingenuous statement of self-congratulatory politics is difficult to find in the annals of American political history. If there was one principle which goaded Henry Clay throughout his life it was that the cause of the United States would be best served by the election of Henry Clay to the presidency. It was a belief from which he never wavered and it marked his course in American politics for more than two decades. With Harrison's death one month after taking office and John Tyler's running battle with the Whig leadership in Congress, Clay's chance came (for the third and last time) in 1844.

Clay began campaigning for his party's nomination shortly after Tyler had been sworn in. He traveled throughout the country, spoke at party functions, lent his prestige to local candidates, and by the time of the Whig Convention in 1844, he was the nominee by acclamation on the first ballot. Once again, as in 1840, the Whig song-makers set to work. If their verses seemed a little narrower in appeal than those of four years earlier, if their paeans to Old Harry Clay were even more unabashed, if their tone was perhaps more strident than before—this undoubtedly reflected in some subtle way the fact that Clay was popular, first of all, with his party. His voter appeal on a national scale had never really been tested; and as things turned out, this appeal was not nearly as widespread as the Whig faithful had believed.

As early as 1842, Clay partisans were singing: "Do you know a traitor viler, viler, viler/Than Tyler?" "Tippecanoe—but not Tyler too!" wrote one Whig rhymester in the depression following Tyler's ascension, while another expressed a widespread impatience in Whig ranks with:

> Times won't be right, 'tis plain to see,
> Till Tyler runs his race;
> But then we'll have a better man
> To put into his place.
> For now we'll rouse, with might and main,
> And work and work away,
> And work, work, work, work,
> And put in Henry Clay.
>
> From "Workingmen's Song," *The Harry
> Clay Melodist.*

Clay had fully expected to be the power behind Harrison's throne, but Tyler's independence of the Whig Congress and his history as a Democrat created an impossible situation from the beginning. By the time of the '44 campaign, Clay was running more against Tyler than the Democrats.

> Now four years ago the country was stirred,
> By the Whigs who resolved they would be heard;
> They elected their President, Tippecanoe,
> They elected another, a traitor to you.
>
> Now let us try Harry! Now let us try Harry;
> Now let us try Harry who always was true.
>
> From "Great Harry Clay," *The National Clay
> Minstrel.*

When Clay supporters were not berating Tyler, they were reminding one and all of the short-lived glories of Tippecanoe, with the suggestion that only Harry was Old Tip's legitimate political heir.

> Our chosen Chief, alas!—no more
> Shall place his lance in rest—
> But well we know the love he bore
> Our Harry of the West.
>
> From "Harry of the West," *The
> Harry Clay Melodist.*

The songs which sang William Henry Harrison into office were revived for Clay:

> What has caused this agitation, 'tation, tation,
> Our foes betray?
> It is the ball a-rolling on
> To clear the way for Henry Clay,
> To clear the way for Henry Clay.
> For with him we can beat any man, man, man
>   Of the Van Buren clan,
> For with him we can beat any man.
>
> From "Clear the Way for Harry Clay," *Whig
> Songs for 1844.*

In memory of and association with "farmer" Harrison, "farmer" Clay was introduced to the body politic, along with log cabins and hard cider:

FARMER CLAY

Tune: "Yankee Doodle"

Yankee Doodle, Whigs, huzza,
We're done with Captain Tyler,
The man who in his country's flaw,
Shall never more defile her:

Chorus:
For Farmer Clay then boys hurrah,
And proudly here proclaim him,
The great, the good, the valiant Hal
And shout whene'er you name him.

Our noble Harry is the man
The nation most delights in!
To place him first is now the plan,
For this we're all uniting!

Brave Whigs! Where'er the gallant song,
"Log Cabins and Hard Cider"
Was chorused loud and echoed long,
Let this be heard—and wider.

From *The National Clay Minstrel.*

"Who the hell is James K. Polk?" sang the Whigs when the Democratic Convention nominated the first "dark horse" of presidential politics. Some of them thought it was a joke. One of the Whig campaign songs capitalized upon Polk's obscurity by referring to him as "Ex-Speaker Polk of Tennessee." Polk had been speaker of the Tennessee House of Representatives in the period 1835-39, until he was elected governor of the state. He was defeated for re-election as governor in both 1841 and 1843.

JIMMY POLK OF TENNESSEE

Words: J. Greinerl   Tune: "Dandy Jim of Caroline"

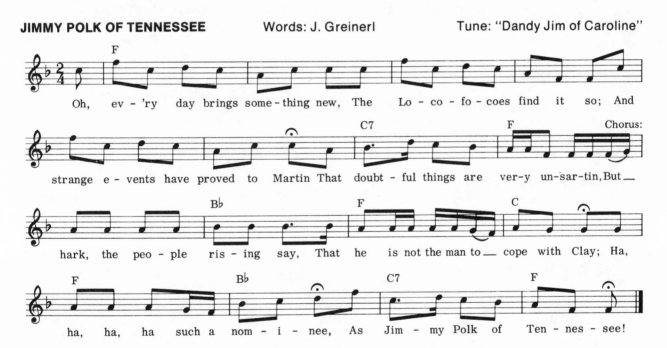

Oh, ev-'ry day brings some-thing new, The Lo-co-fo-coes find it so; And strange e-vents have proved to Martin That doubt-ful things are ver-y un-sar-tin, But hark, the peo-ple ris-ing say, That he is not the man to cope with Clay; Ha, ha, ha, ha such a nom-i-nee, As Jim-my Polk of Ten-nes-see!

Come listen Whigs and Locos all,
Your kind attention here I call,
And mark the burthen of the glee,
Ex-Speaker Polk of Tennessee. *(Cho.)*

Polk's choice occasioned some surprise,
Good Democrats rolled up their eyes,
Our candidate, pray, who is he?
Why James K. Polk of Tennessee. *(Cho.)*

But soon their vast excitement o'er,
They see what ne'er was seen before,
The best selection that could be,
Ex-Speaker Polk of Tennessee. *(Cho.)*

Fall down before a better man,
Than even little Matty Van,
Buchanan too, must bow the knee
To Ex-Speaker Polk of Tennessee. *(Cho.)*

From the original sheet music published by G. E. Blake, Philadelphia, 1844.

It was no accident that campaign singing in America emerged as a not-so-fine art at the same time that a minor revolution in popular culture was taking place. It was in the 1830s and '40s that a truly distinctive and unique American music began to appear. Prior to that time, the country's music was either imported from Europe or consisted of fairly puerile imitations of British and Continental fare. In 1829, Thomas Dartmouth "Daddy" Rice wrote and performed his famous minstrel piece, "Jump Jim Crow." In the decade that followed, Negro minstrelsy became the most popular musical style of the era. And the most prolific of these black-faced song and dance men was Daniel Decatur Emmett, a tunesmith from Ohio who created such staples of musical Americana as "Dixie," "Blue Tail Fly," and "Boatman's Dance." In 1843, Emmett produced a song which took the country by storm and still lives today as an American favorite, "Old Dan Tucker."

Not so surprisingly, the Whigs claimed Emmett as one of their own, though there is no hard evidence that the famous songwriter belonged to their party. They took "Dan Tucker" and created a jingle which enjoyed great popularity during the campaign and which also enjoyed the distinction of being one of the few songs to successfully devise a rhyme for Clay's running mate, Theodore Frelinghuysen.

CLAY AND FRELINGHUYSEN
Tune: "Old Dan Tucker"

A first-rate rhyme was made of late,
By a Whig from the Buckeye State;
It goes to that familiar tune
Which Old Dan Tucker taught the coon.

Chorus:
Hurrah! hurrah! the country's risin',
For Harry Clay and Frelinghuysen!
Hurrah! hurrah! the country's risin',
For Harry Clay and Frelinghuysen.

There's no two names that can be found,
Although you search the country round,
More terror to that clan comprisin',
Than Harry Clay and Frelinghuysen. *(Cho.)*

The Loco's cause is out of season,
For it has neither rhyme nor reason;
The people tried and found it lacking,
Their promises had not good backing. *(Cho.)*

No doubt they'd rather hear us groan,
But that we'll leave to them alone;
For with good Clay and Frelinghuysen,
The way we'll beat them is surprisin'. *(Cho.)*

Clay's a patriot through and through,
And so is Frelinghuysen, too;
They are men of truth and candor,
Who can't be hurt by Loco slander. *(Cho.)*

When Locos see them on our ticket,
'Tis a sight which they grow sick at,
For anything from humbug free
With Locos' systems don't agree. *(Cho.)*

From *The Whig Banner Melodist.*

Four years earlier the Democrats had viewed the Tippecanoe musical histrionics with disdain. This time they had no compunctions about borrowing Harrison's theme song, "Tip and Ty," to celebrate Polk and George M. Dallas, the Democratic vice-presidential candidate:

Oh, what is all this great commotion,
    'motion, 'motion,
Our country through?
It is the ball a-rolling on
For James K. Polk and Dallas too,
For James K. Polk and Dallas too.
With them we shall carry the day, day, day,
Have it all our own way.
With them we shall carry the day.

From "That Same Old Tune," *Western Democratic Melodist.*

Democratic campaign songs did not engage in the kind of panegyrics about Polk which the Whig melodies did for Henry Clay. This may very well have been because the Democratic tunesmiths didn't know much about their dark horse candidate. But more interesting, more fun, and probably a lot more memorable than one more syrupy tribute to the "Farmer of Ashland" or "Young Hickory" (the nickname Democratic campaign strategists pinned on Polk in order to get some of the Jackson magic to rub off) were a series of saucy attacks on Henry Clay, whose checkered career had certainly made him vulnerable enough to such treatment.

"Go home, Harry Clay," the Democrats sang, "your bargain with Adams we've not forgot." They promised they would "send to Kingdom Come H. Clay and Frelinghuysen" and declared that "the ladies" were all such ardent supporters of the Democrats that

> . . . no man will they marry
> Who will vote for old Henry Clay.

> From *The Southern Traveller*, a
> Lafayette, La. weekly newspaper,
> as reported in Moore, *Anti-Clay
> Songs from the Campaign of 1844*.

While both the Whigs and Polk's Democratic rivals equivocated on the issue of Texas, Polk was forthright. He favored annexation and a confrontation with Mexico. And so, quite early in the race, he supported the application of the Texas "independents" for union with the United States, while Clay, fearful of losing the antislavery vote, straddled the issue.

POLK, DALLAS AND TEXAS
Tune: "Old Dan Tucker"

A Psalm we don't object to sing,
But Uncle Sam is now the thing,
He cries, "For Polk and Dallas go,"
And save Texas from Mexico.
   Then Whigs clear the way,
   Whigs give way,
   Whigs give way, 'tis freedom becks us,
   For Polk, for Dallas and young Texas.

Sly Hal and Theodore so grand,
Instead of gaining Sam more land,
They'd sell each acre to the foe,
And sell the people on it too.
   Then Whigs clear the way, etc.

From *The Democratic Songster*.

Democrats sang of "Young Hickory Polk of Tennessee" and once again revived the populist image of Jacksonian democracy with appeals to "workies" and attacks on aristocratic Whiggery.

HARD TIMES
Tune: "The Girl I Left Behind Me"

Hard times, hard times, is all the cry, The country's in confusion; The banks have stopped, but still they try To mystify delusion. They give us trash and keep their cash To send across the waters, To pay for things they've bought of kings To gull our sons and daughters.

Chorus (to the last eight measures of the verse):
Then to the polls, ye noble souls,
The banks now cry for quarters;
But here's their doom, they shall resume,
Or forfeit all their charters.

Shall corporations rule the soil
That Washington defended?
Shall honest people sweat and toil
And have their rights suspended?
Shall we be slaves to pampered knaves,
And banks still be our masters,
Since all they pay from day to day,
Is nothing but shin-plasters? *(Cho.)*

Brave Jackson fought to set us free,
He loves his country dearly;
Then, sons of true democracy,
On, to preserve it fairly.
The name of Clay shall fade away
Before our party's hero;
We'll lay these banks that play such pranks
All just as low as zero. *(Cho.)*

From *The Democratic Songster.*

In a similar vein, another Democratic song reminded voters of the "promises" of 1840:

TWO DOLLARS A DAY AND ROAST BEEF

Tune: "Rosin the Beau"

In the year eighteen hundred and forty,
The song of promised relief,
Which was sung to the poor by the haughty,
Was "two dollars a day and roast beef."

Then the banners were flying and streaming—
To reason the people were deaf;
They went through the universe screaming,
"Two dollars a day and roast beef."

Medals, sashes and badges now flourished,
With portraits betokening grief;
The wearers hoped they'd be nourished
With "Two dollars a day and roast beef."

The wood-chuck, the skunk, and coon, too,
And the fox, that inveterate thief,
Lent their skins to the Whigs with this tune, too,
"Two dollars a day and roast beef."

They swigged and they guzzled hard cider,
In mass beyond all belief;
'Mid the fumes their mouth opened wider—
"Two dollars a day and roast beef."

The star then above the horizon
Was soon overshadowed with grief;
For the people have never set eyes on
"Two dollars a day and roast beef."

The pledges were broken—truth banished,
Where now was the promised relief?
The dream of "two dollars" had vanished,
And also the promised "roast beef."

From *The Western Democratic Melodist.*

As it turned out, the election of 1844 was decided by the narrowest of margins. The vote of New York proved decisive, and Polk's victory by just 5,000 votes was made possible by the presence on the ballot of the abolitionist Liberty Party, whose presidential candidate, James Birney, won 16,000 votes. It may be assumed that Clay, being the less ardent of the annexationists, would have received the major portion of those votes if the Liberty Party had not campaigned. Several critics of "minor" party politics have suggested that the outcome of the election was ironic for the antislavery forces precisely because of this fact. The abolitionists of the era had no such view. They saw Clay as a temporizer who might give the illusion of certain concessions but who would never confront the slave system. The Liberty Party, too, had songs, while poets like John Greenleaf Whittier and James Russell Lowell lent their verses to the antislavery cause. The following song was popularized by the Hutchinson Family Singers, one of the most popular singing groups of the period, and devotedly abolitionist.

WE'RE FOR FREEDOM THROUGH THE LAND   Words: J. E. Robinson   Tune: "The Old Granite State"

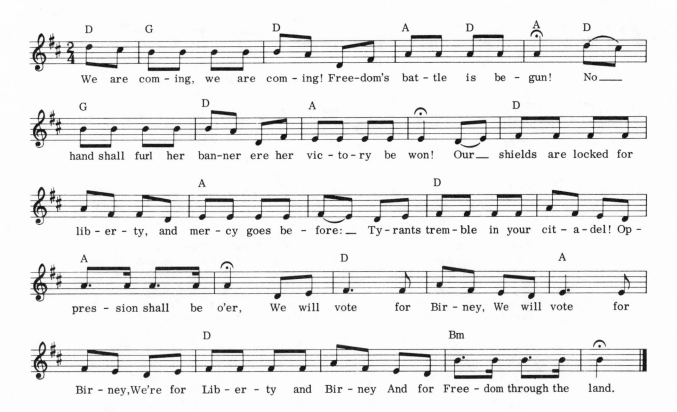

We have hatred, dark and deep, for the fetter and the thong,
We bring light for prisoned spirits, for the captive's wail a song;
We are coming, we are coming! and "No league with tyrant man,"
Is emblazoned on our banner, while Jehovah leads the van!
    We will vote for Birney, etc.

We are coming, we are coming! but we wield no battle brand:
We are armed with truth and justice, with God's charter in our hand,
And our voice which swells for freedom—freedom now and ever more—
Shall be heard as ocean's thunder, when they burst upon the shore!
    We will vote for Birney, etc.

From *The Liberty Minstrel.*

Jesse Hutchinson of the Hutchinson Family Singers wrote the words for the most popular Liberty Party song of the campaign. Like the Democrats and Whigs, the abolitionists, too, used Dan Emmett's tune of "Old Dan Tucker." But the song which Jesse Hutchinson wrote, while it garnered only a relative handful of votes for the antislavery cause, lasted far beyond the immediacy of the 1844 campaign and became a part of the agitational art of the next two decades.

GET OFF THE TRACK   Words: Jesse Hutchinson   Tune: "Old Dan Tucker"

Ho, the car E - man - ci - pa - tion Rides ma - jes - tic thru the na - tion, Bear - ing on its train the sto - ry, Lib - er - ty! A na - tion's glo - ry. Roll it a-long, Roll it a-long, Roll it a-long thru the na - tion, Free-dom's car, E - man - ci - pa - tion.

Men of various predilections,
Frightened run in all directions;
Merchants, editors, physicians,
Lawyers, priests, and politicians.
    Get out of the way! every station!
    Clear the track of 'mancipation!

Let the ministers and churches
Leave behind sectarian lurches;
Jump on board the Car of Freedom,
Ere it be too late to heed 'em.
    Sound the alarm! Pulpits thunder!
    Ere too late you see your blunder!

Politicians gazed, astounded,
When, at first, our bell resounded:
Freight trains are coming, tell these foxes,
With our votes and ballot boxes.
    Jump for your lives! politicians,
    From your dangerous, false positions.

Railroads to Emancipation
Cannot rest on *Clay* foundation.
And the road that *Polk* erects us,
Leads to slavery and to Texas!
    Pull up the rails! Emancipation
    Cannot rest on such foundation.

All true friends of Emancipation,
Haste to Freedom's railroad station;
Quick into the cars get seated,
All is ready and completed.
    Put on the steam! all are crying,
    And the liberty flags are flying.

On, triumphant see them bearing,
Through sectarian rubbish tearing;
The bell and whistle and the steaming,
Startle thousands from their dreaming.
    Look out for the cars while the bell rings!
    Ere the sound your funeral knell rings.

See the people run to meet us;
At the depots thousands greet us;
All take seats with exultation,
In the Car Emancipation.
    Huzza! Huzza! Emancipation
    Soon will bless our happy nation.
    Huzza! Huzza! Huzza!

Rough and Ready Wins the Race

As was the case in 1844, and as it would be again in 1852, the differences between the major party nominees for the presidency in 1848 were minimal. Both Zachary Taylor, the inept but fortune-blessed general who had never even voted in an American election previously, and Lewis Cass, the victim of Polk's dark horse nomination at the Democrats' 1844 convention, planted themselves as firmly as they could in what they conceived to be the middle of the American political spectrum.

A Liberty Party man, summing up the two candidates' views on slavery, struck the aptest note of the campaign: "If one is a Northern man with Southern principles, the other is a Southern Man with Southern principles. Both candidates are utterly unworthy the suffrages of a free people."

The Southern man was General Zachary Taylor, the only Whig besides Harrison to win the presidency. Like Harrison, Taylor was thrust into the role of a popular military hero who, somehow, was supposed to be above the petty strife of partisan politics.

Popular sentiment against the war with Mexico had grown rapidly in the preceding two years, but Polk had been astute enough to get the hostilities over with before the election rolled around. The big question was slavery. Would there be a new Fugitive Slave Law? What about slavery in new states and the District of Columbia? Both parties straddled the issue with the skill of acrobats of long experience.

The Whigs, having garnered considerable experience at this sort of thing, concentrated on image-building. Plain-speaking "Rough and Ready" was their man, supposedly well endowed with the virtues of rugged honesty, sturdy fortitude and homespun

wisdom which the phrase suggested. He was "Old Zack," the essence of reliability, the war hero who had no nose for politics but who was answering the call of a weary people for the same kind of dogged integrity in their political affairs which Taylor had presumably brought to the battlefields of Mexico.

The popular sentiment for Taylor began to mount as early as 1846, even before his political affiliations (if any) were known. The *Rough and Ready Songster,* published that year, contained several score popular ditties celebrating Taylor's military heroics. Taylor was well supplied with credentials, too. He served in the Florida wars against the Indians and was military commander at the Battle of Lake Okeechobee in December of 1837 when the Seminoles were defeated. At the Battle of Monterrey (September 21-23, 1846), American troops under Taylor's command defeated a superior force of Mexicans. The victory was a turning point in the war. Taylor's exploits against Santa Anna, President of Mexico and commander in chief of its armed forces, and the Mexican generals Ampudia and Arista, and his victory at Buena Vista (February 22-23, 1847), the most celebrated of the war, gave added luster to the American commander's laurels.

ROUGH AND READY

Words: Alfred Wheeler   Tune: "Yankee Doodle"

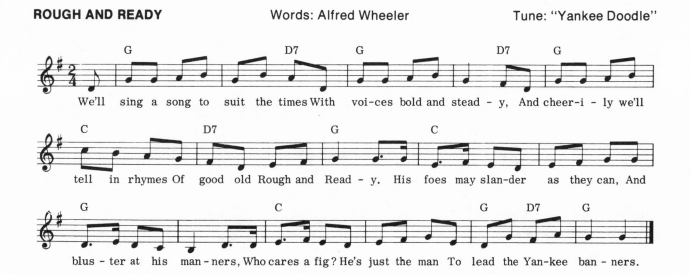

Chorus (to the last eight measures of the verse):
Then Rough and Ready let it ring,
And set the bells a-chiming,
Where'er we go we're bound to sing
His praises in our rhyming.

In Florida he gained a name
That won our admiration,
And loudly has his gallant fame
Been echoed thro' the nation.
  There's not a heart in all the land,
  That beats not firm and steady,
  For the hero of the Rio Grande,
  Old gallant Rough and Ready.

At Monterrey he showed the world
That Yankees ne'er are daunted,
The flag of freedom he unfurled,
And on the towers planted;
  And there it waves in triumph high
  'Mid freemen bold and steady,
  A monument to every eye
  Of gallant Rough and Ready.

Old Zach's the boy for Santa Anna,
Ampudia or Arista,
And long 'twill be ere they forget
The field of Buena Vista.
  Though legions of the foeman swarm,
  Against our brave defenders,
  Old Rough and Ready they will find
  The man who ne'er surrenders.

Success has aye with glory bright
Upon his path attended,
And give him but the chance to fight,
The war will soon be ended.
  And never shall Columbia cease
  To cherish long and steady,
  The man who is in war and peace,
  The same old Rough and Ready.

Now we predict it won't be long,
In spite of Madam Rumor,
Before we sing this very song
In the Halls of Montezuma.
  And then we'll shout in chorus strong,
  With voices firm and steady,
  And this the burden of our song,
  Old gallant Rough and Ready.

From the original sheet music published
by Firth, Hall & Pond, New York,
N.Y., 1847.

A year later, the war hero was the hero-candidate,
and old Rough and Ready, the Bold Soger Boy, was
being serenaded into the White House.

ROUGH AND READY
(or THE BOLD SOGER BOY)   Words: H. P. Gratten   Tune: "The Bold Soger Boy" by Samuel Lover

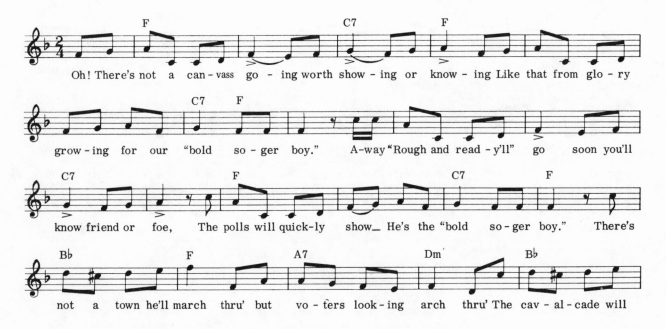

Oh! There's not a can-vass go-ing worth show-ing or know-ing Like that from glo-ry grow-ing for our "bold so-ger boy." A-way "Rough and read-y'll" go soon you'll know friend or foe, The polls will quick-ly show— He's the "bold so-ger boy." There's not a town he'll march thru' but vo-ters look-ing arch thru' The cav-al-cade will

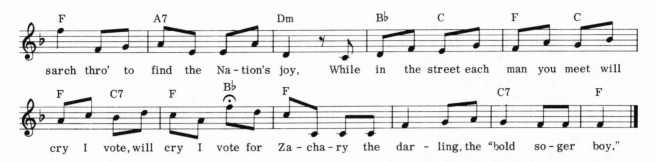

sarch thro' to find the Na-tion's joy, While in the street each man you meet will
cry I vote, will cry I vote for Za-cha-ry the dar-ling, the "bold so-ger boy."

When the rest have got the rout,
Oh! they'll pout, and they'll shout,
Then go the right about
For the "Bold Soger Boy."
When in the White House chair,
Won't that pair tear their hair,
But he'll get there soft and fair,
Will our "Bold Soger Boy."

Sure we see the game before us,
Though with "pledges" they may bore us;
All the people will encore us,
And sing our songs with joy!
What's that we hear?
Repeat that cheer:
It's loud and clear!
Hurrah! we shout,
For Zachary the darling,
The "Bold Soger Boy."

From the original sheet music published by Lee & Walker, Philadelphia, Pa., 1848.

While the songs of '48 were mercifully few, the populist, common-man theme which had been a part of the literature since the partisans of Andrew Jackson had attacked John Quincy Adams as an aristocrat and a snob, surfaced once again. Why the Whig image-manipulators were able to convince the American electorate that their military chieftains were the common man personified is something of a mystery. That they were able to do so on behalf of a southern-born career military man who, during the course of his rise through the ranks, was able to acquire a considerable estate in land and slaves in Louisiana and Mississippi, must stand as a tribute to that penchant for self-delusion which has so frequently been a characteristic of American electoral politics.

If anyone deserved the "common man" sobriquet, it was Lewis Cass. Son of a New Hampshire blacksmith who had fought in the Revolution as an enlisted man, Cass rose to fame as a soldier/frontiersman, riding the law circuit in Ohio, fighting the British at Detroit, exploring the Northwest Territory and making peace with the Indians. Nevertheless, the Taylor men turned Cass's service as ambassador to France during the Jackson Administration against him, insinuating that he was an effete snob who sought to impose foreign manners upon the American people.

OLD ZACK UPON THE TRACK

Tune: "Old Dan Tucker"

Oh, Lewis Cass, he went to France,
King Phillippe showed him how to dance,
He dressed him up in clothes so fine,
Then let him come with him to dine.
   Get out of the way, poor Cass unsteady,
   Thought people were *too* rough and ready.

Cass forthwith set to work to make,
Americans all a court-dress take,
To cost a hundred dollars or more—
And wouldn't introduce the Poor!
   Get out of the way, the toiling masses
   Hate court-dress and courtier Casses!

From *The Rough and Ready Minstrel.*

Scanty though the major party campaign songs were, the Democrats still lagged behind the Whigs in versifying. Did they find such antics beneath their dignity? Perhaps. Whatever the reasons, the Democrats made do with a handful of ditties, none of which became very popular. Characteristically, they tried to make a virtue of their lack of songs:

We need not sing their praise in verse,
While hearts record their fame.
Our history's brightest page will boast
A Cass and Butler name.

From the *Philadelphia Plain-Dealer,*
June 27, 1848.

Actually, Cass had enjoyed a long and distinguished career of service to the American government. As a volunteer during the War of 1812, he won a small degree of fame when he refused to participate in Hull's surrender of the American garrison at Detroit to the British, breaking his sword across his knee in an act of defiance. Governor of Michigan by appointment of Madison, secretary of war to Jackson, ambassador to France and United States senator from Michigan, Cass was as well-known a figure in his own time as he is obscure to history. It was Cass's widely circulated pamphlet, published in 1842, reciting a long history of British infringements on American naval rights, that projected him into the presidential spotlight. A Democratic newspaper in 1848 celebrated his achievements in one of the few Cass songs of that campaign:

THE BRAVE OLD VOLUNTEER

Tune: "The Hunters of Kentucky"

When war's fierce conflict through the land
Sent forth its dread alarms,
The thrilling bugle's sound was heard,
And freemen rushed to arms,
Bold Cass led on our gallant band
To save the vast frontier,
With daring hand our flag sustained,
The brave old Volunteer.

Chorus:
The brave, the brave, the brave old volunteer,
The brave, the brave, the brave old volunteer.

The first to land on hostile shore,
He fought them long and well;
On Canard's bridge and Thames' proud field
Old England's banner fell!
When Hull surrendered to the foe,
And quailed his heart with fear,

Bold Cass refused his sword to yield—
The brave old volunteer!

When England tried, in after years,
To sweep us from the main,
Brave Cass her projects crushed once more—
Defeated her again!
He bore our glorious banner through
The battle and the breeze;
He would not yield to England now
THE FREEDOM OF THE SEAS.

He woke the gallant sons of France,
And roused that slumbering land
To join with him in breaking down
Proud England's tyrant hand.
Their liberated millions rise
With songs of lofty cheer,
And bless the day when first they saw
The brave old volunteer.

Old Europe, rocking to and fro,
And struggling to be free,
In young America beholds
Her glorious destiny.
Let us fulfill our mission here
Their rising hopes to cheer;
He "set the ball in motion" there,
The brave old volunteer.

From Maine to Georgia hear the sound—
'Tis rolling, rushing on,
From Aztec's lofty capital
To distant Oregon.
The ocean-bound republic joins
With voice of mighty cheer,
He'll make a glorious President—
THE BRAVE OLD VOLUNTEER.

From *The Campaign,* June 21, 1848, special newspaper published by the Democratic Party for the campaign, Washington, D.C.

Cass might be a "brave old volunteer," but such euphemisms were a poor substitute for Taylor's military fame. But the Democrats also had a military man on their ticket, General William Orlando Butler, second in command to Taylor at Monterrey, whom they named their vice-presidential candidate. As might be supposed, Butler's presence in the campaign was invoked as frequently as possible, though to no avail.

CASS AND BUTLER   Tune: "Picayune Butler"

They came to town the oth-er day, And told us what the peo-ple say—
Cass and But-ler, 'tis a fact, Oh, they're the ones to clear the track,

1. A-hoo! That
2. A-hoo!

Chorus:
Cass and But-ler's com-ing, com-ing,

Cass and But-ler's come to town.
come to town. A-hoo! A-hoo! A-hoo! A-hoo! A-hoo! A-hoo!

Cass and But-ler's come to town.

Some time ago they met before,
And started the Ball in Baltimore,
  Ahoo!
When Polk and Dallas was the name,
But Cass and Butler's now the game.
  Ahoo!

From a broadside in the Harris
Collection, Brown University.

Perhaps the most significant occurrence of the 1848 election was the appearance of a new party. The Free Soil Party was a loose coalition of "conscience" Whigs (who couldn't stomach Taylor, the slave-holder), "Barnburner" Democrats (radical reformers who were willing to "burn down the barn" if they couldn't change their party and who opposed the "Hunkers," or conservative Democrats), and Liberty Party abolitionists who, unlike some of their fellows, were still attempting electoral politics in the struggle against slavery. After a feverish convention in Buffalo, the newly named Free-Soilers emerged with a curious ticket: ex-President Martin Van Buren at the head and Charles Francis Adams, an antislavery Whig and son of John Quincy Adams, for vice-president.

Following a spirited campaign, the Free-Soilers managed to poll some 10 percent of the total vote. Most likely they took the election away from Cass, since Van Buren's appeal was more to dissident Democrats than unhappy Whigs. The Free Soil platform, while hardly abolitionist, was clearly antislavery. Its slogan, "Free Soil, Free Speech, Free Labor, and Free Men," would reappear eight years later along with the name of the Republicans' first nominee—Frémont!

Like so many third parties which come to birth in a crusading spirit based more on ideological conviction than any practical possibility of victory, the Free-Soilers were able to engender far more songs than their two major party foes.

MARTIN VAN OF KINDERHOOK

Tune: "Dandy Jim of Caroline"

Come, ye hardy sons of toil,
And cast your ballots for Free Soil;
He who'd vote for Zacky Taylor,
Needs a keeper or a jailer.
And he who still for Cass can be,
He is a Cass without the C;
The man on whom we love to look,
Is Martin Van of Kinderhook.
  Martin Van's the one we'll go,
  He is the man for the people, O!
  I look around and find it so,
  Just as they said at Buffalo.

When the Whigs they preach and pray,
For the old man of Monterrey,
I shake my head as up I figures
The price of his two hundred niggers;
When the Hunkers say the man
Is Lewis Cass of Michigan,
Amid the talk of all their lawyers,
I think of sand-banks, snags and sawyers.
  Martin Van's the one, etc.

How the Hunker placemen pale,
As our shouts come on the gale;
How they tremble with dismay,
Looking on our proud array.
Taylor he must take his station,
'Mong the slaves on his plantation,
While the toast around we pass,
"A long good night" to Lewis Cass.
  Martin Van's the one, etc.

From *Free Soil Songs for the People.*

FREE SOIL CHORUS

Tune: "Auld Lang Syne"

All hail, ye friends of liberty,
Ye honest sons of toil,
Come let us raise a shout today
For freedom and free soil.

Chorus:
For freedom and free soil, my boys,
For freedom and free soil,
Ring out the shout to all about,
For freedom and free soil.

We wage no bloody warfare here,
But gladly would we toil,
To show the South the matchless worth,
Of freedom and free soil.

Nor care we aught for party names,
We ask not for the spoils.
But what we'll have is liberty,
For freemen and free soil.

Too long we've dwelt in party strife,
'Tis time to pour in oil,
So here's a dose for Uncle Sam,
Of freedom and free soil.

From *Free Soil Songs for the People.*

Locos All—Great and Small

The chief feature of the desultory campaign of 1852 was that it marked the last significant political gasp of the Whig Party. The unhappy coalition which had grown out of the disastrous Adams-Clay alliance of 1824 had contributed some significant voices to the American political spectrum: Clay himself, Daniel Webster, Horace Greeley, William Seward and a host of others who in later years would form the nucleus of the Republican Party, including the young Illinois congressman who had fiercely opposed the Mexican war, Abraham Lincoln.

But the Whigs had no solution to offer a nation increasingly rent by a single inexorable contradiction—slavery. In 1850, under the guidance of the aging Clay and with the support of the aging Webster, Congress passed the historic Compromise which momentarily forestalled the historical process for another decade. The artful juggling of concessions to various factions while permitting the "peculiar institution" to remain intact and the republic to expand westward was a tribute, perhaps, to the consummate political skill of men not prepared to confront the real historical forces at work. But time was running out for such manipulation of social forces, and the electoral defeat of the Whigs in 1852 which hastened the formation of the Republican Party two years later was merely one more logical step in the historical process.

To be sure, the Whigs who met in Baltimore in June of 1852 could not have been aware that they were about to launch their final campaign. Crassly opportunistic to the end, they came up with still another military hero who, they hoped, would again lead them to victory at the polls and who would also, hopefully, prove somewhat more durable than his two predecessors—Zachary Taylor and William Henry Harrison.

It certainly required no bending of the historical evidence to certify General Winfield "Fuss and Feathers" Scott a genuine military hero. Distinguishing himself at the Battle of Chippewa and seriously wounded at the Battle of Lundy's Lane, Scott emerged from the War of 1812 with a military reputation second only to Jackson's. For the next four decades he served with distinction in the periodic wars against the Indians and then as the chief architect of victory over the Mexicans. Passed by for Harrison in 1840 and again for Taylor in 1848, the Whigs finally turned to him in 1852 in a desperate effort to hold together their rapidly disintegrating party and a rapidly polarizing country. But even the nomination was no simple matter, Scott winning the prize on the fifty-third ballot after it had become clear that Millard Fillmore, who had succeeded Taylor, did not have the votes.

The political realities proved insurmountable. With William Seward as Scott's campaign manager, the southern Whigs were fearful of a Scott administration which would be partial to opponents of the slave system. The Convention then proceeded to adopt a platform which fully endorsed the Compromise of 1850, particularly emphasizing the new Fugitive Slave Law, which had been the major concession to the South. After Scott's somewhat precipitous endorsement of the Whig program (perhaps as a military man rather than a politician Scott was not sophisticated enough to realize that he had no need to concern himself with what the party said), the antislavery, Free Soil elements remained notably cool to his candidacy. The nomination of William A. Graham, former governor of North Carolina and secretary of the navy under Fillmore, as Scott's running mate further alienated the antislavery forces, although they found nothing attractive about the Democratic vice-presidential candidate, Senator William R. King from Alabama.

In all fairness, one cannot say that either Scott or the Whigs were completely lacking in principle. In a fundamental sense, their chief theme had been enunciated two years earlier in 1850 by Daniel Webster, who believed that there was no greater political evil than disunion. With both secession and slavery "abhorrent" to them, the Whigs sought to contain a thunderous eruption with a delicate balancing act. This was the dilemma on whose horns Winfield Scott's presidential candidacy was impaled.

Not surprisingly, therefore, issues were about the last thing the Scott campaign strategists had in mind. The songs for Scott and Graham concentrated, instead, on the General's distinguished career and tried to build up the image of a father figure who would "be the man to guide the Ship of State."

SCOTT, WHO OFT TO VICTORY LED

Tune: "Scots Wha Hae Wi' Wallace Bled"

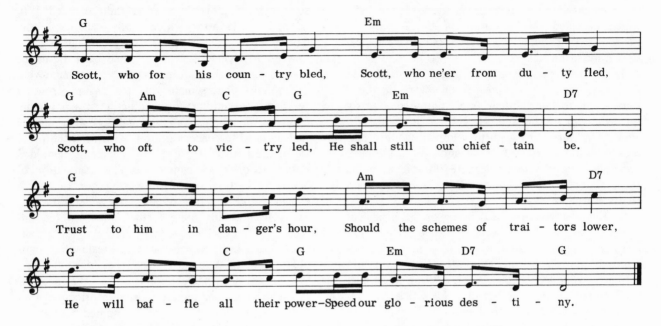

Scott, who for his coun-try bled, Scott, who ne'er from du-ty fled,

Scott, who oft to vic-t'ry led, He shall still our chief-tain be.

Trust to him in dan-ger's hour, Should the schemes of trai-tors lower,

He will baf-fle all their power—Speed our glo-rious des-ti-ny.

Who doth fear a *Pierce* or thrust?
Every *King* shall bite the dust!
Countrymen! a nation's trust
　　Rescue from a bigot's hand.
Who would not reward the brave?
Forth! your country's credit save—
Honor him who honor gave—
　　On with Scott to victory!

From the fame of Chippewa,
Queenston Heights, Niagara,
Old Fort George and Florida,
　　"See the conquering hero comes!"
By the fields of Mexico,
Covered with our country's foe,
He has scattered or laid low;
　　On with Scott, to victory!

From *The Scott Songster.*

Vera Cruz, Cherubusco, Chapultepec—the magic names of military triumph were invoked over and over again by the Whig campaigners. Having proven successful with "Old Tippecanoe" and "Old Rough and Ready," the Whigs created rhymes which made up in political acumen for any poetic shortcomings:

I have voted for Jackson and Taylor,
I have voted for Tippecanoe,
And if I'm spared till November,
I'll vote for old Chippewa, too.

From "I'll Vote for Old Chippewa, Too," *Scott and Graham Melodies.*

But it wasn't all high-minded rhetoric for "Old Chippewa." Franklin Pierce, the Democratic candidate, had served some time in the Mexican War and had been "wounded" during the fight for Mexico City. At least that was the story which first circulated. Closer investigation revealed that Pierce had been injured by a bucking horse, fainted in the saddle, and had to be carried to his tent. If the circumstances surrounding Pierce's involvement in the war were of small concern before the campaign, the Whigs soon remedied that:

Two Generals are in the field,
Frank Pierce and Winfield Scott—
Some think that Frank's a fighting man;
And some think he is not.
'Tis said that when in Mexico,
While leading on his force,
He took a sudden fainting fit
And tumbled off his horse.

From "Scott and Graham," *The Scott Songster.*

Even less subtly, the Whig rhymesters celebrated

Fainting Frank in the rear rank,
When he heard the battle clank,
He tumbled to the ground.

From an 1852 broadside song, "The Fainting General."

As usual, the Whigs had the best of the quadrennial ballad competition. The songs they came up with were generally more professional and easier to sing. And there were more of them. For one thing, the Whigs seemed to have more of a musical ear than the Democrats, generally utilizing the newest and most popular tunes while the Locos were still rehashing the old standards. And so, while Democratic tunesmiths settled for melodies like "The White Cockade" and the perennial "Yankee Doodle" plus some of the older minstrel songs, the Whigs jumped into the fray with the hit melody of the period, "Wait for the Wagon," composed in 1851 by one of the best of the minstrelmen, R. B. Buckley.

WAIT TILL NOVEMBER

Tune: "Wait for the Wagon"

The Democratic Party, boys,
Are crowing mighty fierce,
Since they have nominated
Their "last man"—General Pierce.
They say he'll be elected
In Eighteen Fifty Two,
And march into the White House—
But that he will not do.

Chorus:
Wait till November,
Wait till November,
Wait till November,
And they'll all turn blue!

The Whigs have settled on a choice,
The people will approve—
Old SCOTT and GRAHAM are the boys
To make this nation move.
The Locos say they'll floor them
In Eighteen Fifty Two,
And march into the White House—
But that they'll never do. *(Cho.)*

O, come along, my gallant boys,
We'll shout a loud hurrah,
As we introduce our champion,
The brave old Chippewa.
The Locos think they'll beat him
In Eighteen Fifty-Two,
And march into the White House—
But that they'll never do. *(Cho.)*

Old Scott's the boy, my hearties,
To bring down Loco game,
He's sure to beat both Pierce and King,
For WINfield is his name.
They know they cannot crush him
In Eighteen Fifty-Two,
Then he'll march into the White House,
For that he's bound to do,

Final Chorus:
Wait till November,
Wait till November,
Wait till November,
And the Whigs will put him through.

From *Scott and Graham Melodies.*

As in 1844, the Whigs walked off with the dubious musical honors of the campaign while the Democrats won the election. Or perhaps musical discretion turned out to be the better part of political valor and the voters rewarded the Democrats as the Party which had inflicted the least raucous sounds on them in the guise of campaign song.

What the Democrats lacked in the way of song, however, they made up for with political shrewdness and a combination of sectional and ideological interests which could not be beaten. Again they chose a "dark horse" at their convention, an obscure senator from New Hampshire whose political credentials were impeccable, Franklin Pierce. A New Englander, he had amassed a record of never antagonizing the special interests of the Southern slaveholders. He was for States' Rights and could well afford to express a certain moral repulsion for slavery which he always carefully accompanied with a denunciation of abolitionists as "reckless fanatics." He was, in short, a demagogic nonentity who might appease the New England wing of the party while reassuring the Southerners that they had nothing to fear from a Pierce administration—an assurance which was eminently demonstrated during his four years in office.

There is little evidence to suggest that the songs of the Democratic campaign of 1852 were ever sung. The few to be found are all parodies to popular airs which ran as verse in various Democratic newspapers, a tradition which has always been much more literary than musical. Typical is the following song from the pages of the *Brooklyn Eagle,* a staunchly Democratic journal:

THE LATEST YANKEE DOODLE

Tune: "Yankee Doodle"

"Old Scott," who never took a seat
In halls of legislation—
Is he the man to legislate
For this great Yankee nation?
He's but a soldier—nothing more,
In politics a noodle—
He well may rule brigade or corps
But never Yankee Doodle.

For Yankee Doodle's not the man
To be cajoled so handy,
Catch him sleeping, if you can,
This Yankee Doodle Dandy.

The Democratic song which follows not only castigated the "Coons," as the Whigs were frequently called, but also capitalized upon the conflict between Scott and President Polk during the Mexican-American War. Polk removed Scott from his position as commander of the American Army during the War after Scott had written a letter complaining that the Administration was hamstringing his efforts to win the war. When Scott received the notice of his removal, he immediately sent an apology to Polk, beginning, "Your letter, received as I sat down to take a hasty plate of soup, demands a prompt reply." Subsequently Polk published both of Scott's letters in an effort to justify his actions. General Scott's soup figured prominently in the "Locofoco Song."

LOCOFOCO SONG   Tune: "Nelly Bly"

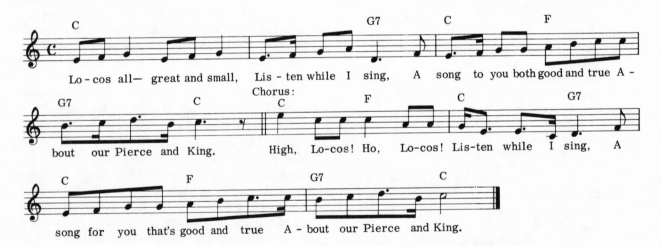

Lo-cos all— great and small, Lis-ten while I sing, A song to you both good and true A-bout our Pierce and King.

Chorus:
High, Lo-cos! Ho, Lo-cos! Lis-ten while I sing, A song for you that's good and true A-bout our Pierce and King.

General Pierce, he is not fierce,
But full of Yankee game,
For he did go to Mexico
The Hottentots to tame.

General Scott, he likes things hot,
Especially his "soup,"
He thinks it good for flesh and blood
Whene'er his spirits droop.

For Pierce and King we'll shout and sing
While on our "winding way,"
So "Coons" look out what you're about
We're bound to win the day.

On next March we'll take the starch
Out of "Fillmore's" collar,
Old Scott we'll beat on the first heat,
And make the "Coons" all holler.

Then Locos all—great and small,
Shout aloud and sing,
A loud huzza! And hip! hurrah!
For our own Pierce and King!

From the *Brooklyn Eagle.*

An interesting "first" of the 1852 campaign was the appearance of the "ethnic" issue. The great waves of Irish immigration of the previous decade were beginning to be felt politically. The Irish vote loomed as decisive, and the Democrats with their big city organizations and popular appeal to the "little man" had gotten there early. Scott attempted to make inroads among the Irish, but the Democrats dug up a letter the general had written ten years earlier reflecting typical nativist prejudices. The Democrats even claimed that Pierce's father, Benjamin Pierce, one-time governor of New Hampshire, came from Ireland although he was actually born in Chelmsford, Massachusetts in 1757.

The following song from the *New York Democratic Free Press* mercilessly hammered away at many of Scott's campaign handicaps. Again the Democratic songwriters played up the general's difficulties with President Polk during the Mexican War. The fire in Scott's rear, mentioned in the song, referred to his allegation that he had "a fire upon my rear, from Washington, and the fire, in front, from the Mexicans." The Democrats also effectively exploited Whig hypocrisy on the issue of the war itself. The Whigs had been highly critical of the War with Mexico, and attacked Polk for initiating it. But in 1852 (as in 1848), they tried to make political capital out of the exploits of a hero of the war.

Pierce's supporters also gleefully called attention to the split in Whig ranks on the question of slavery. The Whig platform endorsed the Compromise of 1850, including the Fugitive Slave Law. The "Higher Law" Whigs professed the principle that there was an even higher law than the U.S. Constitution, God's law against slavery.

In view of Scott's many campaign liabilities, the Democratic songwriters predicted (correctly, as it turned out) that he would "get up Salt River," i.e., be defeated at the polls. The expression "up Salt River" occurred throughout nineteenth-century campaigning. One story has it that an anti-Whig boatman forced Henry Clay to miss a campaign appearance in 1828 by rowing him up Salt River, but the incident is of dubious authenticity.

The "poor Greeley" addressed in the chorus of the song was Horace Greeley, editor of the *New York Tribune,* who had been a prominent figure in Whig ranks for more than a decade. After Scott's nomination, Greeley commented that many of the antislavery Whigs liked Scott but "spit upon the platform." "Billy York" was probably a reference to William Seward of New York, Scott's campaign manager.

DEMOCRATIC SONG
Tune: "Oh! Susannah"

I had a dream the other night
When all around was still,
I dreamed I saw Old 'Pultepec
A-sliding down the hill.
The "hasty" soup was in his hand,
The "fire was in his rear,"
His Free Soil allies wouldn't stand
But scattered far and near.

Chorus:
Oh, poor Greeley,
Don't you spit on me,
I'm getting up Salt River
With the platform on my knee.

He had a pack of letters, too,
He'd wrote since '41,
With principles of every hue,
Weighing about a ton;
The whole was fast upon his back
And really crushed him down,
And not a Whig of all the pack
Could stop to lift a pound.

He called the Irish long and loud
From Patrick up to Harney,
But Paddy only grinned and bowed,
And "jist he twigged the blarney."
"Arrah, I'm not a native coon,
Nor caught with trashy writin',
Your 'indignation fired' too soon
You'd better stick to fightin'."

"But Franklin Pierce's the boy for me,
His father came from Erin,
His father's son is frank and free,
We like his fine appearin'."
But still poor Scott kept slipping past,
A-down that slippery hill,
He called on Billy York at last,
And called both loud and shrill.

But Billy's feet were slipping, too,
His darkies wouldn't draw,
He couldn't make them hold the two,
"Platform" and "Higher Law."
Poor Greeley sweat and Greeley braced
To stop the general slide,
But Greeley's morals double faced,
Slid onward with the tide.

Those mystic epaulettes he grasped,
Scott wore in '48,
"His brains were never here," he gasped,
But all this comes too late,
"That horrid war we used to hate,
We love it dearly now,
We never talked of bloody graves—
Dang it anyhow."

Thus in this vision of the night
When all around was still,
I saw the Whigs in motley flight
Far down that slippery hill.
While Democrats were on the brow
And made the welkin ring,
Old Coon we've fairly caught you now—
Hurrah for Pierce and King!

"Free Speech, Free Soil, Free Men, Frémont!"

The Campaign of 1856 and the Birth of the Republican Party

From time to time, over the course of almost two centuries, the American political system has exploded with the suddenly unleashed energy of emerging social forces which the established political structure could no longer contain. Jefferson's agrarian triumph in 1800, Bryan's populist appeal of 1896 and Roosevelt's antidepression, prolabor thrust of 1932 are all examples of such historical moments.

None of these, however, could match the fervor and impact of those campaigns which were a part of the agony of the Republic's most profound rendering—the destruction of the slave system. The elections of 1856, 1860 and 1864 were themselves such an integral part of this process that the political struggles centering in those campaigns proved to be decisive in the ordering of historical events.

The campaign of '56 provided the first indication of the crusading spirit of that period which would, a few years later, become the emotional motive force of the Civil War. The emergence of the Republican Party as a major political grouping no longer bound by the intersectional coalition politics of its predecessors, provided the format through which a fundamental realignment of social and political forces could take place.

Like all new major parties in history, a common hostility to the prevailing political power provided a necessary unity to many of its diverse elements. Free Soilers, "conscience" Whigs, reform Democrats, antiforeign nativists, westward expansionists, and antislavery men of varied hues made up the core of the new party. In time, the nativist elements split off to form the American Party (more popularly known as the Know-Nothings), which fielded a separate slate in the '56 campaign.

The fulcrum of all this was a forthright opposition to the slave system. It was a stance which came decked out in a litany of moral principles, though it's doubtful that "morality" by itself has ever made much difference to history. To understand that the moral fervor of antislavery itself had roots in the fact that the slave system had become an impediment to the growth of an industrial capitalist society is not to cast aspersions on the convictions of the movement. Men are rarely, if ever, completely conscious of the social roots of their own ideology. The fact that certain principles, at a given time, should appear to be so obvious, so eminently just merely on their enunciation, is frequently a reflection of the aptness of their time. If we fail to see that ideology is itself the product of real social conditions, then we may find ourselves subscribing to a kind of historical elitism which believes that one generation may actually be more "moral" or more "just" than another.

It is precisely the union between historical necessity and the ripened conditions for social change which gives rise to the zeal, to the absolutist principles, to the energy and forms of organization which make that change possible.

End of the Compromise on Slavery

In 1856, these inexorable social forces began to come together. The time for adjustment, compromise, conciliation was running out. Too much was at stake for those who had a vested interest in the slave system to yield peaceably—and history was becoming impatient.

The energetic campaign of the Republicans in 1856 was reminiscent of 1840; songs, poetry, parades, banners, buttons, hats, rallies and a general crusading spirit. But unlike the Tippecanoe campaign, the Republican drive did not feel impelled to obscure principle with lyrical paeans to a hero-candidate—although in the great Whig tradition, a hero-candidate was found.

John Charles Frémont, the Republican nominee, wasn't one of those generals for whom some sobriquet could be devised to which the adjective "old" could be casually affixed. Forty-three years of age, vigorous, a romantic figure, an explorer of the Far West, Frémont symbolized a spirit which defied all odds, undertook impossible tasks, radiated energy and youthfulness and promised activity rather than lethargy. So the Republicans sang of Frémont and his running mate Dayton and also of Jessie, the "pathfinder's" young wife who was constantly invoked as a symbol of the new vigor of the new party.

Jessie Frémont, the candidate's wife, was the daughter of Thomas Hart Benton, senator from Missouri and one of the important political figures of his day. Benton was opposed to the romance between his daughter and Frémont, whom he considered little more than an adventurer, but the young couple eloped, adding to the romantic aura which came to surround their life together. The title of the song, "We'll Give 'em Jessie," was a popular slang expression of the day meaning "We'll give 'em hell!" "Jessie" was also a play on words, based on the fact that Frémont's initials were "J. C."

The song "We'll Give 'em Jessie" incorporates several highlights of Frémont's career. "The mighty hills, 'twixt East and West the bars," mentioned in the song, are the rugged Sierra Nevadas, which Frémont crossed in dead of winter in 1844. Frémont's earliest fame came as a western explorer. He undertook several transcontinental trips in the early '40s accompanied by Kit Carson. The song also makes mention of Frémont's role in bringing California into the Union. In 1846, the intrepid explorer blazed a trail to Monterey and San Jose, then still under Mexican rule, and daringly raised the American flag over the area. Frémont was elected the first senator from California after the "El Dorado" state's admission into the Union.

WE'LL GIVE 'EM JESSIE

Tune: "Wait for the Wagon"

Ye friends of Free-dom, ral-ly now, And push the cause a-long; We have a glo-ri-ous can-di-date, A plat-form broad and strong; "Free speech, Free Press, Free Soil, Free Men, Fre-mont," We have no fears with such a bat-tle cry, but that we'll beat the Bu-chan-iers.___ We'll give 'em Jes-sie, We'll give 'em Jes-sie, We'll give 'em Jes-sie, When we ral-ly at the polls.___

Our leader scaled the mighty hills,
'Twixt East and West the bars,
And from the very topmost peak
Flung out the stripes and stars;
Nor cold, nor heat, thirst, hunger, naught
Of horror moved his fears;
With such a captain can we fail
To beat the Buchaniers?

In after time his dauntless arm
Unlocked the Golden Gate;
His eloquence to Freedom gave
The El Dorado State.
In every word, in every deed,
Such manliness appears,
Frémont's the man to lead us on
To beat the Buchaniers.

Where e'er clear heads and gallant hearts
Are wanted, foremost he;
And ever true in word or deed,
He's proved to Liberty.
Survey him every way you will,
The noble man appears,
So shout Frémont and Liberty—
Down with Buchaniers!

Then rally, rally, every man
Who values Liberty,
Who would not see our fair land given
To blighting Slavery.
Our cause: "Free Speech, Free Press, Free Soil,
Free Men"—So now three cheers
For the people's candidate, Frémont,
Who frights the Buchaniers.

From *The Freemen's Glee Book.*

The songs of the new party were characterized by an outburst of optimism. It was a heady spirit which was not dependent on victory at the polls for its sustenance. To the Republican partisans, it was clear that with the emergence of their party, the conflict with slavery had finally been joined. No longer would the slogans and songs hide behind meaningless rhetoric. The issues were out in the open now and, for the first time, a mass base for the antislavery forces had appeared. Its echoes could be heard in the self-confident songs of the Frémont campaign. To the tune of "Pop Goes the Weasel," the Republicans sang:

> What's the noise that goes about?
> What's the great commotion?
> Here and there and everywhere
> The people are in motion.
> Ho my friends, I tell you true
> Here's the agitation,
> 'Tis for FREEmont and Jessie, too,
> Glory to the nation!

> From "Freedom, Freemen, Frémont," rallying song of the Chelsea Frémont Club, pub. George P. Reed & Co., Boston, Mass., 1856.

Other Republican songs not only lauded freedom and Frémont but reviled the "doughfaces," a popular term of opprobrium for Northern politicians who did not oppose slavery in the South or its extension. During the Civil War it came to be used as a term for pro-Confederate Northerners. John Randolph, himself a Southerner, is said to have used the term first in political debate, so categorizing his northern "allies" who voted with the South for the Missouri Compromise. As an expression in general use it came to mean a person singularly lacking in character. The *New York Tribune* (1845) put it this way: "The genuine Doughface never alludes to the sad accident which deprived him of the use of his backbone." This song was to the tune of "Old Dan Tucker."

> The millions heard the thrilling cry,
> It warmed the blood, it fired the eye:
> "Free Speech, free pen, free soil want we—
> And FREMONT to lead to victory!"
>   Out of the way, Old Buchanan!
>   For we have out an honest man on!
>   Out of the way, each wriggling doughface,
>   Freedom's car will knock you no place.

> From "The March of Freedom," *The Republican Campaign Songster.*

All the excitement of new times and new prospects infected the Republican glees. Free soil with its promise of a nation of homesteaders as opposed to the mammoth plantations of the slave South evoked an image of hard-won wealth untarnished by the decadence and slothfulness of a slave system. The westward motion of America, symbolized by the gold of California and the virgin territories of the Great Plains, seemed to be carried on the wings of the new plans for a transcontinental railroad, a dream associated with Frémont. The most important element in the national mood—the key to it all, in fact—seemed to be the new willingness to finally confront the enormous blot of slavery, no matter what the price. The age of compromise was past and the future was waiting to be unlocked by the young, the daring and the principled. All this found its way into the songs the Republicans sang that fateful year.

HUZZA FOR THE RAILROAD!

Tune: "Wait for the Wagon"

The cars will soon be on the track, the locomotive screaming,
Across the continent and back, the trains will soon be steaming;
With Frémont for our engineer, and Dayton by his side,
We'll jump into the railroad cars and all take a ride.

Chorus:
Huzza! for the Railroad!
Huzza! for the Railroad!
The great Pacific Railroad
Upon which we'll all take a ride.

We'll bind the Union firmer, by the modern iron rail,
For Frémont, our young candidate, knows no such word as fail;
Then fling our banner to the breeze, and on its folds inscribe,
"THE GREAT PACIFIC RAILROAD!" upon which we'll take a ride.

And when our banner floats aloft, we'll publish to the world,
That freedom's hosts are marshaling, that freedom's flag's unfurled,
And waves above a gallant band of men of every station,
Who advocate *"Free Speech, Free Soil, all over God's creation!"*

From *Frémont & Dayton Campaign Songster.*

If songs alone could win, the Republicans would not have had to wait four years more. For they sang and they sang, attempting to accelerate the motions of history with song. They sang that "the slave reign is o'er" and advised old Uncle James (Buchanan) to "lay down the fiddle and the bow, take up the shovel and the hoe." They sang:

Our platform is *Freedom for Kansas!*
Our motto: *"Free homes for the Free!"*

From "Buck Shooting," *The Republican Campaign Songster.*

In 1856, the tide seemed inevitable and none knew the terrible price which history would exact for the struggle still to come. For the moment, the Republicans could adapt the melody of one of the popular favorites of the time, "Few Days," and sing that "we can't be kept back longer." They sang of "ten-cent Jimmy," reminding the voters that Buchanan had suggested that ten cents a day was a fair wage for workingmen. They jeered at Old Buck's bachelorhood, and if Senator Benton chose to endorse Buchanan, why the senator's daughter had preferred Frémont. They might gloss over Frémont's birth (as well they might, since he was born illegitimate) in Savannah, referring to it as "down thar" and mock the Democratic vice-presidential nominee, John C. Breckenridge.

The campaign of '56, for all its excitement and enthusiasm, was merely prelude. It was indeed but a few days until the campaign songs would be replaced by marching songs. There were still heroes and martyrs who would loom larger than John C. Frémont and James Buchanan when the final reckoning was made. The nation's time had come.

FREMONT AND FREEDOM
Tune: "Few Days"

A song I've got my friends for you, Few days, few days, The tune and style will
mont and free-dom is our word, Few days, few days, We've nailed our flag and

please you too For we're go - ing home. Fre -
drawn our sword, For we're go - ing home.

Chorus:
For there's the White House yon - der, Few days few days Fre - mont and

Day - ton's bound there, we're going home. We can't be kept back lon - ger

Few days, few days, Ev - 'ry day we're grow - ing stron - ger, we're going home.

Old ten-cent Jimmy is no go!
Few days, few days,
And Breckenridge is far too slow,
We're going home.
They both endorse weak Pierce's reign,
Few days, few days,
Which on our country leaves a stain,
We're going home.

Old Benton says he's out for Buck,
But his finger on his nose is stuck.
Frémont's the man, he surely knows,
Or if he didn't, his daughter does.
Old Bachelors are low in rate,
They'd never populate a state.
The White House parties must not drag,
And what could Bucks be but a Stag!

Though Frémont he was born down *thar,*
He's strong as his Rocky Mountain b'ar.
He made our California state,
It's made us rich—we'll make him great.
And now my friends, we vote a health,
To our first choice—the nation's wealth.
Frémont and freedom is the word,
We've nailed our flag and drawn our sword.

The dramatic growth of the Republican Party and the intensifying domestic conflict over the slave system clearly foretold the future course of events. But the Democrats sensed that the nation still hungered for one more chance to keep the Union together. Once again they strove for a momentary accommodation of North and South, utilizing their favorite political formula—a Northern man with Southern principles. This time he was James Buchanan, former secretary of state under President Polk, one-time senator from Pennsylvania, and most recently the American ambassador to Great Britain. As with such Democrats as Franklin Pierce and Lewis Cass, he confined his antislavery sentiments to a matter of personal taste, but made it clear that he fully supported the Compromise of 1850, vigorous enforcement of the Fugitive Slave Law and states'

rights. He was, in short, precisely the kind of "antislavery" man the South could and did support. His running mate, John C. Breckenridge, a Kentucky congressman, was even more acceptable to the South. In fact, he was the Southern Democrats' presidential nominee in 1860.

To a troubled North, increasingly opposed to the slave system but fearful over the prospect of civil war, Buchanan seemed to be one of those "last chance" candidates which a hysterical press is constantly proclaiming as the only alternative to the Final Cataclysm.

For the Democrats it was a negative campaign. Their theme was fear—fear of abolition, disunion, black republicanism and civil war. Their strength, outside the South, still rested with the big city political machines and the foreign-born vote. To many, the Democrats were still the party of Andrew Jackson, the workingman's party, the party of the poor immigrant Irish who comprised such a huge proportion of the newly emerging urban proletariat.

And so, with an irony of which they could not be aware, Democratic partisans could sing their opposition to "bigots" while yet proclaiming:

Come Democrats and listen,
While I sing to you a song,
'Tis all about the Nigger-Worshippers,
And it will not take me long.

Frémont is on their platform,
And their principles endorse,
To worship Niggers night and morn,
And ride the Woolly Horse.

Free speech, free niggers, and Frémont,
Now seems to be the go. . . .
But these crazy Nigger Worshippers
The Union would destroy.

For there's balm in Gilead,
We hear the people say—
With Buchanan and with Breckenridge
We will surely win the day.

From "Empire Club Song," *The Campaign Democrat,* July 30, 1856.

The "Woolly Horse" of the song was one of the Democrats' favorite campaign gibes against Frémont, because it was associated with a hoax. The great impressario, P. T. Barnum, ever alert to topicality, claimed to have in his possession in 1849 a "woolly horse," made up of one part each of antelope, camel and buffalo, which supposedly had been captured by Frémont's exploring party while they were lost in the Rocky Mountains. Barnum subsequently offered the creature to public view at twenty-five cents a head.

For the Democrats, the theme was Union. Only Buchanan could keep the Union together, they said. The others—Frémont and the Republicans, Millard Fillmore and the Know-Nothings—were "fanatics" prepared to sacrifice the Union for lesser causes. Stephen Foster, a life-long Democrat himself, typified that approach which, while not directly enjoying the benefits of the slave system, had its perception of the world shaped by the consciousness to which slavery gave rise. The racial stereotypes in the lyrics of Foster's greatest contributions to American music—"My Old Kentucky Home," "Old Black Joe," "Massa's in de Cold, Cold Ground," "Old Folks at Home" and many others—are indeed appropriate reflections of their era.

For all that, Foster's Union principles, like Buchanan's, were sincere. When the Civil War broke out, Buchanan became a Union Democrat, offering support to Lincoln. Foster wrote several war songs for the Union, including a setting of that popular poetic response to the outbreak of hostilities, "We Are Coming, Father Abraham, 300,000 More."

But in 1856, Foster was still writing of "The Great Baby Show or The Abolition Show," a lampoon of a Republican political demonstration in Pittsburgh, concluding with:

> They called it a Council of Freemen, you know,
> But I told you before, 'twas a great baby show,
> For when they had met, they had nothing to say,
> But "Poor Bleeding Kansas" and "Ten Cents a Day!"

"Bleeding Kansas" referred to the minor civil war in that territory in preparation for a vote on the question of whether or not slavery should be permitted in the new state. It was the first test of the doctrine of "popular sovereignty," and its violence shocked the nation into the realization that the normal course of law was not going to work in the antislavery struggle.

Even more to the point was another Foster campaign ditty:

> Let all our hearts for Union be,
> For the North and South are one;
> They've worked together manfully,
> And together they will still work on.
>
> Then come ye men from every State,
> Our creed is broad and fair;
> Buchanan is our candidate,
> And we'll put him in the White House chair.

From "The White House Chair," quoted in "Stephen Foster, Democrat," by Fletcher Hodges, Jr., the *Lincoln Herald*, June, 1945.

Not many campaign songs deal as specifically with the "issues" of the election as did this one on behalf of Buchanan.

BUCHANAN AND BRECKENRIDGE

Tune: "Star-spangled Banner"

Oh! say, brothers, say, are we not in the right,
When we proudly stand by our beloved Constitution,
And swear by each star and vow by each stripe,
We will never look on and see its pollution?
God grant, by the blood which our forefathers shed,
That union and peace o'er our fair land be spread,
And long may our stars and our stripes proudly wave
O'er the land of the free and the home of the brave.

On the shore, dimly seen, are the foes fast approaching,
With envy and strife and disunion at heart;
Be up and be doing, for now is the day-spring,
Our watchword is "Union," this brothers impart.
East state shall be free its own laws to enact,
And all shall unite in one glorious compact.
And thus, only thus, can our stars and stripes wave
O'er the land of the free and the home of the brave.

America now is the home for oppressed,
And thousands on thousands we daily receive;
They call us the land of the free and the blest;
The stranger and homeless pray never deceive.
But teach them, pray teach them, with banner in hand,
That "Union's" the password to save our fair land;
Old Buck is the man for freeman and slave,
"United We Stand" while our stars and stripes wave.

The tocsin now ring and the ball keep in motion,
Let not the usurpers with vaunting pretend
That they are the party to rescue the nation,
That they are the party the slave to defend.
We alone are the party the Constitution to save,
To protect the oppressed and cheer on the brave!
Three cheers, three times three, that our flag long shall wave
O'er the land of the free and the home of the brave.

From *The Campaign Democrat,* July 30, 1856.

The Democrats proclaimed themselves the party of "Union" and of the foreign-born—especially if he was a voter. The nativist strain in the Whig Party had not found a home with the Republicans, who, representing a burgeoning economic force, could not relate to the primitive antiforeignism which arrayed itself against the new source of labor. But anti-Catholicism and nativism were still virulent currents in the 1850s, representing the outmoded consciousness of a significant sector of the population whose once orderly world had been disrupted by the new social reality of a society on the verge of a massive plunge into the industrial revolution.

"No Irish need apply" became a phrase in the language of the era, while primitive fears were stoked by ancient legends of popish knavery. The political force which represented this current called itself, appropriately its adherents thought, the American Party, although they have been preserved in historical memory by their better-known title of the "Know-Nothings." Like their latter-day descendants, the Ku Klux Klan, the Know-Nothings were a semisecret organization, their title deriving from their custom of professing ignorance of the group's existence except to each other. Rebuffed by the Republicans and naturally antagonistic to the Democrats, the Know-Nothings surfaced in 1856 and fielded their own presidential ticket, nominating ex-President Millard Fillmore for the presidency and a one-time protégé and namesake of the former president, Andrew Jackson Donelson, as his running mate. They proclaimed themselves the guardians of both "Union" and "Freedom," but their nativist bigotry was the very fiber of their unity. One song, after attacking the "Woolly Horse" and his "woolly-headed clan," then let fire at the Democrats:

On the other side we see, how the foreign voters come,
From the banks of the Liffey and the Shannon—
And they swear by the powers of whiskey and of rum,
That their candidate is "Ould Buchanan."

From "The Union Course," *Fillmore and Donelson Songs for the Campaign.*

In the official Fillmore and Donelson campaign songbook we find advertisements for those fear-mongering penny dreadfuls of the day which exposed the secret horrors of Catholicism. Such titles as "The Escaped Nun; or, Disclosures of Convent Life" and "Awful Disclosures of the Hotel Dieu Nunnery, Montreal" were offered to the party faithful, along with more "learned" works such as Thomas Whitney's "A Defence of the American Policy, As Opposed to the Encroachments of Foreign Influence, and Especially to the Interference of the Papacy in the Political Interests and Affairs of the United States."

Other "Know-Nothing" songs threatened physical violence against any Irishman who might dare show up at the polls on election day.

WIDE-AWAKE YANKEE DOODLE

Words: William C. Marion
Tune: "Yankee Doodle"

> Come Uncle Sam, be "Wide Awake,"
> Too long you have been sleeping,
> Be on your guard to crush the snake
> That round you has been creeping.
> For it has almost charmed your eyes,
> To such imprudent blindness,
> That it could take you by surprise,
> And crush you for your kindness.
>
> Yankee Doodle, Wide Awake,
> Be silent you should never,
> Until you drive the popish snake
> From off the soil, forever.
>
> Americans should be "Wide Awake,"
> For surely you must know,
> That for our country's own dear sake,
> Each man his worth must show.
> For we are free and won't submit
> To intolerance and aggression,
> From papists who, from foreign lands,
> Come here to rule this nation.
>
> From a campaign broadside.

For the Know-Nothings, the campaign of '56 was the high-water mark. Their ideological influence was felt for decades to come, and clearly they were in the long line of traditional American bigotry which has been a part of our politics for well over 150 years. In 1856, Millard Fillmore polled some 900,000 votes and carried the state of Maryland. The Know-Nothing vote was a combination of nativism and a yearning for a simpler way of life which was no longer relevant to American reality. In trying to revive a dead past, the Know-Nothings invoked the names of earlier heroes, both Democrat and Whig. It was a gesture appropriate to both their conservatism and their futility.

THE UNION WAGON

Tune: "Wait for the Wagon"

> There's right and wrong in parties,
> And the Right is on our side,
> So we will mount the wagon, boys,
> And let the nation ride!
> The Union is our wagon,
> And the People are its springs—
> And every true American
> For Millard Fillmore sings.
>
> *Chorus:*
> Wait for the wagon,
> Wait for the wagon,
> Wait for the wagon
>   And we'll all take a ride.
>
> This wagon is a noble one,
> 'Twas made in '76,
> 'Twas driven by George Washington
> Through stormy politics.
> With western oak and eastern pine
> And northern ash 'tis bound,
> Palmetto, cypress, cotton-wood,
> In spokes and wheels are found.
>
> The Mill-boy of the Slashes, boys,
> Our gallant Henry Clay,
> Once sat within this wagon,
> As we're sitting here today.
> He drove the road of Compromise,
> By Constitutional charts,
> And held the reins of Union
> All around the people's hearts.
>
> In this, our glorious wagon,
> With the nation at his side,
> Through all the troubled elements
> Our Jackson once did ride.
> And now we keep his memory green,
> And hail his noble name;
> For Andrew Jackson Donelson
> A seat with us may claim.

When Webster shook the friendly hand
With noble-souled Calhoun,
'Twas here upon our wagon-box,
They sat in close commune.
Our Millard drove the wagon, then,
And Clay was at his side,
And never did the nation take
A safer Union ride!

From *Fillmore and Donelson Songs for the Campaign.*

Lincoln and Liberty

*Songs of the Four-Way Race of 1860
and the Wartime Contest of 1864*

There are those who feel that the American Civil War was really a "senseless" conflict, an "unnecessary" blood-letting which could have been avoided. They blame "sectionalism" and "short-sighted" men for allowing the forty-year dispute which had racked the country over the slave system to degenerate into the costliest and bloodiest war in American history.

Others believe that such a view, passed on with the benefit of elapsed decades, fails to comprehend the social reality which it purports to study. This "irrepressible conflict" had been delayed for forty years while the national political superstructure painfully struggled to adapt the external institutions of American society to an outmoded system. The most astute minds of two generations attempted to rationalize the accelerating contradictions posed by the continued existence of the slave system. In the end they "failed" because the power of the social energies dammed up by the resistance to historical necessity finally exploded with an urgency which defied containment.

Up until 1856, the unified structure of the country rested on the ability of the political parties to find a sufficient accommodation with the slave system to keep the restless forces of social development in check. But time was running out. Westward expansion meant that new states were getting ready to come into the Union—and with them, the balance of political power would shift from the slave-holding South. With the continued existence of slavery proving itself a brake on social development, a new consciousness of the "moral" evils of the slave system arose, and with it a greater reluctance to help the slave-owners support their "peculiar" institution. In practical terms, this meant that the northern states were on the verge of becoming sanctuaries for runaway slaves. The implications of such a development were too enormous for the slavocracy to consider with anything but the greatest disquiet.

All of these factors led not only to the growth of the Republican Party but to the disintegration of the Democrats. The leading representative of the Democrats' northern wing, Stephen Douglas of Illinois, was destroyed by his inability to serve two constituencies growing further and further apart. The Dred Scott Decision of 1857[1] and the struggle over the admission of Kansas to the Union underscored the dilemma of those who, like Douglas, attempted to appease the demands of the slave power while still retaining sufficient credibility with the northern electorate.

And so, when the Democrats met for their convention in Charleston, South Carolina in 1860, they were forced to adjourn without nominating a candidate. Another Democratic convention was called for Baltimore, and this time, with some of the seceders refused admission, Douglas was nominated. The southerners then went to another hall and nominated Buchanan's vice-president, John C. Breckenridge, for the presidency.

Meanwhile the Republicans, sensing that 1860 was the year of destiny, met in Chicago and chose carefully. Their nomination of Abraham Lincoln was both popular and astute. Lincoln was of the Party's "moderate" wing. A former Whig, staunchly anti-slavery in his sentiments, a westerner who exuded integrity and the "common touch," Lincoln was no "fanatic" on the question of abolition. He opposed the extension of slavery but made clear that he had no intention of interfering with the slave system where it already existed. (It was his personal belief that the slave system was doomed by its own internal failings and would eventually be eliminated by both attrition and law.) Two years earlier, in his race for the Senate seat from Illinois, Lincoln had captured the national imagination with his dramatic series of debates against Douglas. Despite his loss in that election (Lincoln actually outpolled Douglas but was defeated by an "elector" system in the Illinois legislature), he had already won a reputation as a "giant-killer"[2] and promised to be precisely the kind of unifying figure the new Republican Party required.

The other important political tendency in the country was the American (Know-Nothing) Party. After the election of 1856, the Know-Nothings had explored the possibility of reuniting with their former Whig associates in the Republican Party to present a united front in 1860. But John Brown's raid on Harper's Ferry panicked them away from a party which contained, even though in the minority, elements which supported Brown. And the Republicans were rapidly building a base among the German immigrants of the Midwest, a development which pushed that party even further away from the bigoted nativism of the Know-Nothings. Accordingly, these elements organized the Constitutional Union Party and nominated John Bell of Tennessee for the presidency.

The Campaign of 1860

The campaign itself was both heated and intense but, strangely enough, lacking in the flamboyancy and hoopla of the Tippecanoe and "Woolly Horse" campaigns. The more ardently antislavery elements of the Republican Party added Lincoln verses to their abolitionist songs and engendered most of the musical excitement of the times. Other Republicans borrowed a leaf from the Know-Nothings of 1856 and organized them-

---

1. The Supreme Court ruled that a slave-owner might take his "property" into a "free" territory without losing ownership of that "property." The Court ruled that Congress had no right to ban slavery from the territories. From a strictly legalistic point of view, the Supreme Court was acting logically on the basis of both precedent and the practical power relationships. But it was a fatal blow to the notion that there was any "legal" way to curb the slave system.

2. Douglas was popularly known as the "Little Giant." Physically, he was quite short, but he had the self-confidence and articulative ability of the born extrovert, as well as a keen mind and a shrewd tongue.

selves into "Wide-Awake" brigades to rouse the nation on behalf of the Republicans. But the tone, in general, was serious. Great decisions were being made; decisions which were only being effectuated in part at the ballot box.

The Lincoln songs of 1860 reflected a new mood in the country. Never before had a major party can-didate been supported with such forthright and mili-tant sentiments. Kansas had destroyed the notion that compromise with the slave system was still pos-sible, and the Republican stand on slavery was not to allow its extension into existing "slave" states or into new states and territories.

FREEMEN WIN WHEN LINCOLN LEADS   Tune: "Lutzow's Wild Hunt"

Oh, tell me what spir-it sweeps o-ver the land, U-nit-ing and rous-ing our num-bers? And why does the North in full pan-o-ply stand, Like a gi-ant a-roused from long slum-bers, Like a gi-ant a-roused from long slum-bers?

'Twas a cry for aid that o'er__ us swept.__
They were murd-'ring Kan-sas while__ we slept.__

But the North will not always submit to a wrong;
Once roused from her sleep, she ne'er falters.
To Kansas, despite the whole South, shall belong
Free soil and free speech and free altars—
Free soil and free speech and free altars.
The cry of Freedom each free man heeds,
And our cause must win, for Lincoln leads.

From *Hutchinson's Republican Songster for the
Campaign of 1860.*

The crusading spirit of the '56 campaign still un-derscored the Republican rhetoric. But this time it was tempered with the realization that the responsi-bility of administering the Republic in its most anxious hour was the price of electoral victory. Perhaps no one in the North believed that secession really would occur; or else, they could not imagine that the South would have the resources to conduct a long and costly struggle. In any event, the prospect of a final locking of horns with the slave system did not curb the resolution of the Lincolnites.

HAVE YOU HEARD THE LOUD ALARM?

Tune: "The Old Granite State" (after the Hutchinson Family Singers)

From the green hills of New England,
From the Western slopes and prairies,
From the mines of Pennsylvania,
  Have you heard the loud alarm?
For the war note has been sounded,
And the Locos stand astounded,
While their rule, in ruin founded,
  Sinks before the people's arm.

Steeped in infamous corruption,
Sold to sugar cane and cotton,
Lo! a nation's heart is rotten,
  And the vampires suck her blood;
O'er our broad and free dominions
Rules the cotton king whose minions
Clip our fearless eagle's pinions,
  And invite Oppression's reign.

We have chosen us a leader,
And with "resolute endeavor,"
Let us strike at once—or never,
  For the land we love so well;
With a victory before us,
And a stainless banner o'er us,
Let us shout the joyful chorus,
  Ringing loud the Freedom bell.

We believe as did the heroes
Of our noble Revolution,
That our noble constitution
  Is the guide to Liberty;
And we go for non-extension,
In the field, as in convention,
And rejoice in the declension
  Of the curse of all the free.

With a patriot heart to guide us,
All the *railing* accusations,
Honest Abraham occasions,
  Greet our ears as pleasant chimes;
For a son of honest labor,
Calling every man his neighbor,
Grasping Freedom's trenchant saber,
  Stands the hero of his times.

Come, then, friends of working classes—
Every State beneath its banners—
And with shouts and loud hosannahs
  Raise the people's standard high;

Roll along the mighty chorus,
And the reeling foe before us
Never more shall triumph o'er us,
  For a brighter day is nigh.

From *Hutchinson's Republican Songster
for the Campaign of 1860.*

Not all the songs for Lincoln and his running mate, Hannibal Hamlin, former U.S. senator from Maine, were so politically staunch. The Republicans of 1860 were part of a tradition dating back to Tippecanoe and the heroic campaign of 1840. And as with Harrison, the party propagandists found a handy designation for Lincoln. He was the "rail-splitter" candidate, an image which appears over and over again in Republican songs and campaign literature of the period. And of course there were the usual songs to "Honest Old Abe of the West" and the perennial pleas to "Strike for the Right." One campaign song invoked the old Whig spirit to the tune of "Rosin the Beau":

Every friend of our own "Gallant Harry,
The Star of the West," has declared,
The coming election they'll carry,
For every true man is prepared.

For Lincoln the Party's united,
For Hamlin the people are true,
The watch-fires all have been lighted,
As once for "Old Tippecanoe."

Then bring out the music and banners,
The "fence rails" and orators too,
And we'll teach Loco-focos good manners,
As we did with "Old Tippecanoe."

From *Hutchinson's Republican Songster
for the Campaign of 1860.*

If there were those in Republican ranks who still fought the battles of other years, the spirit of the country was less concerned with past glories than with the issues of the moment. But while Lincoln's supporters stressed the slavery question, they did not neglect more traditional forms of politicking. In this song, Jesse Hutchinson drew upon the migrations of the Lincoln family to instill a sense of "native son" pride in the voters of three states. Lincoln was born in Hardin County, Kentucky; his family lived in Indiana from 1816 to 1830, and his political career had been based in Illinois, whose citizens were known as "Suckers." (For some of the explanations of this obscure term, see B. A. Botkin, *A Treasury of Mississippi Folklore,* pages 507-09.)

LINCOLN AND LIBERTY

Words: Jesse Hutchinson
Music: "Rosin the Beau"

> Hurrah for the choice of the nation!
> Our chieftain so brave and so true;
> We'll go for the great Reformation—
> For Lincoln and Liberty too!
>   We'll go for the son of Kentucky
>   The hero of Hoosierdom through;
>   The pride of the Suckers so lucky
>   For Lincoln and Liberty too!
>
> Our good David's sling is unerring,
> The Slaveocrat's giant he slew;
> Then shout for the Freedom-preferring
> For Lincoln and Liberty too!
>   We'll go for the son of Kentucky
>   The hero of Hoosierdom through;
>   The pride of the Suckers so lucky—
>   For Lincoln and Liberty too!
>
> They'll find what by felling and mauling,
> Our railmaker statesman can do;
> For the people are everywhere calling
> For Lincoln and Liberty too.
>   Then up with our banner so glorious,
>   The star-spangled red-white-and-blue,
>   We'll fight till our Cause is victorious,
>   For Lincoln and Liberty too!
>
> From *Hutchinson's Republican Songster
> for the Campaign of 1860.*

Republican rhymesters attacked Douglas with a vigor and wit which belied the fact that of all the candidates in the field his position was the closest to Lincoln's. They blasted away at the old "plow hoss" whose

> . . . legs was short, but his speeches was long,
> And nothin' but hisself could he see,
> His principles was weak, but his spirits was strong,
> For a thirsty little soul was he.
>
> From O'Sullivan, *Political Songs in America.*

To the lilting melodies of such popular minstrel songs of the day as "Camptown Races" and "Boatman's Dance," they sang:

> Little "Dug" can never win,
>   Du da, du da,
> That Kansas job's too much for him,
>   Du da, du da day.
> His legs are short, his wind unsound,
> His "switch tail" is too near the ground.
>
> From "We're Bound to Work All Night,"
> *Wide-Awake Vocalist.*
>
> Hurrah! hurrah! did you hear the news?
> At Baltimore they got the blues,
> Because our leader is the best
> And tallest man in all the west.
>   Then dance, freemen, dance,
>   Oh, dance, freemen, dance,
>   We'll dance all night till broad daylight
>   To the polls with a vote in the morning.
> "High Old Abe" shall win,
> Split the rails and fence them in.
>
> From "High Old Abe Shall Win," *Wide-
> Awake Vocalist.*

And to the tune of "Nelly Bly," Republicans called attention to the fact that Douglas had compromised himself beyond redemption on the slavery question in his famous debates of 1858 with Lincoln. In the wake of the Dred Scott decision, which had nullified the Compromise of 1850, advertised by the Whigs as a check to slavery, Douglas fell back on the scheme of "squatter sovereignty," meaning that the citizens of a new state would decide for themselves whether or not they wanted to have slavery. It was a "dodge" which Douglas hoped (in vain as it turned out) would give him the support of Southern Democrats in 1860.

> Once we had a Compromise,
> A check to Slavery's wrong,
> Douglas crushed the golden prize,
> To help himself along.
> Then the North and then the West,
> Arose with giant power;
> Pierce succumbed to the South's behest,
> But Douglas had to cower.
>   Hi! Douglas! sly Douglas!
>   A Senator would be;

So he tried the "squatter dodge,"
And went for Kansas free.

From "The People's Nominee," *Hutchinson's Republican Songster for the Campaign of 1860.*

The Republican campaign song "Lincoln and Hamlin" dismissed the Know-Nothings' convention in Baltimore as a conclave of old fogies, and, according to the description of one commentator, they were quite correct. He characterized the convention as "a gathering of graybeards," mostly old-time political figures who hadn't had a new thought in their heads since the days of Clay and Webster. They expanded their view to go beyond the antiforeign bigotry of their '56 campaign, appealed for support to southern conservatives who still wanted to save the Union, changed their name to the Constitutional Union Party, nominated John Bell of Tennessee and Edward Everett of Massachusetts (later known as the man whose lengthy address preceded Lincoln's at Gettysburg) and managed to add a degree of confusion to an already fragmented election. However, although the Republican songwriters disparaged the Know-Nothings, they appropriated the "Wide Awake" label from the '56 Know-Nothing campaign and applied it to their own followers.

LINCOLN AND HAMLIN

Tune: "Wait for the Wagon"

Come, all ye friends of freedom,
And rally in each State,
For honest Old Abe Lincoln,
The people's candidate!
With Lincoln as our champion,
We'll battle for the Right,
And beat the foes of Freedom,
In next November's fight.

Chorus:
Hurrah! boys, for Lincoln!
Hurrah! boys, for Lincoln!
Hurrah! boys, for Lincoln!
Hurrah! for Hamlin, too!

The people want an honest man—
They're tired of fools and knaves;
They're sick of imbecile "J.B.,"
That in the White House raves.

They want a man for President
Of firm, unyielding will,
That is both honest, brave and true,
And Old Abe fills the bill!

Old Fogies down at Baltimore
In solemn conclave met,
The "Union Saving" farce to play,
With Bell and Everett.
But the people next November
Will put them all to rout,
And make them long remember
That the Fillmore game's "played out."

The Democrats are in a "fix,"
No wonder that they shiver;
For they all feel it in their bones,
That they're going up Salt River.
With their party split asunder,
The truth is plain to all,
That though united once they stood,
Divided, now, they fall.

Oh, Douglas, you can't win this race,
You'd better clear the way—
Your humbug doctrines won't go down,
At home you'll have to stay.
The Wide-Awakes are on the march
O'er all our hills and vales—
Our Giant-Killer's after you
With one of those old rails.

And Breckenridge will soon find out
The people he can't fool;
They've had enough, these last four years,
Of Democratic rule.
But Lincoln is their favorite,
And he is bound to win—
When Buck steps out next 4th of March,
Old Abe will then step in!

From a campaign broadside published by
H. De Marsan of New York City.

But there were other voices, too. The Republicans, like their Whig forebears, may have had a corner on most of the campaign songs, but partisans of the Little Giant in the North, and Breckenridge and Bell supporters in the South, had a few rhymes of their own. For the Douglas men, Lincoln was, of course, the prime target. In view of history's subsequent deification of Lincoln, it comes as something of a shock to realize that few men in

American public life have ever been so personally vilified in their own time. The attacks on Lincoln in later years, during the war and the 1864 election, were presaged in 1860 by newspaper editorials, cartoons, and songs like this Douglas ditty:

> Tell us he's a second Webster,
> Or, if better, Henry Clay;
> That he's full of gentle humor,
> Placid as a summer day.

> Tell again about the cord-wood,
> Seven cords or more per day;
> How each night he seeks his closet,
> There alone to kneel and pray!

> Any lie you tell, we'll swallow—
> Swallow any kind of mixture;
> But, oh don't, we beg and pray you—
> Don't, for land's sake, show his picture!

Quoted in "Campaign Songs of a Century," *New York Evening Post,* March 16, 1912.

Douglas' only chance for victory lay in the possibility of convincing the Northern voters that the traditional path of conciliation would be able to ensure both the sanctity of the Union and the gradual erosion of the slave power. It was the theme which had won for Pierce and Buchanan before, and Douglas partisans were still trying to adapt it to the changed circumstances of 1860.

The following song, in which the last two lines of each stanza are taken directly from "The Star-spangled Banner," reveals Douglas's campaign strategy. Like Douglas, the song attacked both Lincoln and Breckenridge—the latter for his support of William Lowndes Yancey, an Alabama legislator who was one of the mainstays of the secessionist movement and the Confederacy—but not Bell. Douglas's supporters hoped that their man would win the North over Lincoln and Bell would win the South over Breckenridge so that the two could form an alliance which would deliver the presidency to Douglas.

STAND BY THE FLAG

Tune: "Star-spangled Banner"

May patriots defend our flag to the last,
As proudly it streams from the national mast;
And ages to come, as it gracefully waves,
May no star e'er be lost 'mid the storm that it braves;
Against foreign foes ever gallantly borne,
By the hand of a traitor, let it never be torn.
  Come freemen, then rally, to the flag let's be true,
  'Gainst the treason of Lincoln, and Breckenridge too.
  "And conquer we must, for our cause it is just,
  And this be our motto: *In God is our Trust.*"

Let Lincoln proclaim "the irrepressible" fight,
To spread o'er his country its withering blight,
And water the soil with the blood of her sons,
By myrmidons shed, with knives, pistols, and guns.
Let us swear the blest Union we'll bravely defend,
And assassins in flight to their holes we will send.
  Come freemen, then rally, to the flag let's be true,
  And beat down the treason of Lincoln's black crew;
  "And conquer we must, for our cause it is just,
  And this be our motto: *In God is our Trust.*"

Let Breckenridge follow where Yancey may lead,
That Douglas may be crushed and his country may bleed;
Let him take his command from a traitorous mouth,
And his party betray for revolt in the South;
Still as patriots we'll move in an unbroken band,
Our standard to guard, and to save the dear land.
  Come freemen, then rally, to the flag let's be true,
  'Gainst the treason of Lincoln, and Breckenridge too;
  "And conquer we must, for our cause it is just,
  And this be our motto: *In God is our Trust.*"

Brave Douglas shall bear our banner on high—
The flag of the Union, let the people draw nigh;
From the North and the South, the blest Union to save,
He will rally a band with hearts honest and brave;
And sectional factions, North and South in dismay,
He'll scatter in shame on the next voting day.
  Come freemen, then rally, to the flag let's be true,
  We'll save the dear Union, and whip traitors too;
  "And conquer we must, for our cause it is just,
  And this be our motto: *In God is our Trust.*"

From *The Democratic Campaign Songster.*

When Douglas won the Democratic nomination in 1860, the proslavery faction held their own convention and nominated two ardently secessionist candidates, Vice-President John C. Breckenridge, and Joseph Lane, southern-born senator from Oregon. Lane, like so many other presidential candidates of the nineteenth century, was a military hero. He won promotion to the rank of major general in the Mexican War. The Breckenridge and Lane campaign was, in effect, the opening battle of the Civil War.

The song "Breckenridge and Lane" aimed its shafts at many targets besides Lincoln: the Republican Convention held in Chicago; William Seward, governor of New York, dubbed by the songwriter as "William, King of York"; Simon Cameron, one of the leading contenders for the Republican nomination and subsequently secretary of war in the Lincoln cabinet after a deal made at the Republican Convention, who was lampooned as "Old 'Wigwag,' the great Financier"; and Douglas, called the "Squatter King" because he championed the principle of "squatter sovereignty" as a means of deciding the slavery question in states newly admitted to the Union.

BRECKENRIDGE AND LANE
Tune: "Yankee Doodle"

Father and I went down to see
The Chicago Convention,
And there we saw more mimicry
Than it would do to mention.

Chorus:
With Breckenridge to take the lead,
And General Lane to help on,
Our num'rous foes we will oppose,
As in the days of Jackson.

The friends of William, King of York,
Were there, quite confidential,
Brains were much needed by the crowd,
But could not claim attention.

Old "Wigwag," the great Financier,
Had many good advisers,
Who found at last, without a tear,
He was 'mong the outsiders.

Knowledge is Power, and Gold is God,
So says the ancient maxim,
But both here on a *Rail* were rode,
In spite of this good axiom.

The friends of "Honest Uncle Abe,"
Had the records been o'erhauling,
And found by making one grand strike,
They could give their foes a mauling.

So we may talk just as we choose
About qualifications,
If mauling rails or towing boats
Makes rulers for great nations.

Our friends have met in Baltimore,
And made their nomination,
And Breckenridge, of Kentucky,
Receives our approbation.

The Squatter King should join with us,
Against the nation's foemen,
Instead of kicking up a fuss,
'Bout niggers 'mongst our Yeomen.

The *Lane* is long which has no turn,
And though foes beset us fiercely,
We'll foster principles that live,
And march straight on to victory.

From a campaign broadside, published
by Johnson's, Philadelphia, Pa.

Among the stranger developments in the strange campaign of 1860 was the appearance of the Constitutional Union Party and its candidates, John Bell and Edward Everett. They were, in essence, an anachronistic amalgam of southern Whigs and northern Know-Nothings whose one political theme was sung to the tune of the recently composed "Dixie's Land":

UNION DIXIE

We'll __ put down the pow-er of __ dis - so - lu - tion, By ral - ly - ing 'round our
In __ do - ing __ so, 'tis __ our in - tent To __ make __ John Bell our

Con - sti - tu-tion,} Right a - way, right a - way, Right a - way, right a - way.
Pres - i - dent,__}

Chorus:

That's the way we'll fix 'em, Oh, oh; Oh, oh. With our

lit - tle band we'll take our stand, And guard our homes and free - dom's land. Oh,

yes! Oh, yes! That's the way we'll fix 'em. Oh, fix 'em.

Of platforms let 'em make a fuss,
But our Constitution's enough for us,
    Right away, etc.
For Bell and Everett, let's give three cheers,
And the Union's safe for the next four years,
    Right away, etc.

From "We Are Bound to Fix 'Em," *Bell &
Everett Songster.*

The Bell and Everett men, partial inheritors of the Whig legacy, outsang the Douglas and Breckenridge supporters, but their old-fashioned platitudes were no longer enough. If the Lincoln campaign songs encapsulated the bursting energy of the future, the Bell and Everett ballads were echoes of an era which had vanished, the last testament of antebellum America.

CAMPAIGN RALLY SONG

Tune: "Boatman's Dance"

E - lec - tion Day is com - ing fast, And the Un - ion flag's nailed to the mast; Our
cause is on - ward, just and free, Our lead - er's Bell of

Ten - ne - see. Ad - vance, boys, ad - vance, Ad - vance, boys, ad - vance, Ad vance.

Fight for our cause and our Un - ion's laws, 'Twill be all right in the morn - ing.

Hi! Ho! Let 'em know, For Bell and Ev - er - ett we all go. we all go.

With Bell and Everett in the field,
Our Constitution we will shield;
No traitor or disunion foe
Can ever to the White House go.
    Advance, boys, advance, etc.

They talk of Lincoln splitting rails,
And pushing mud-scows without sails,
But our Union rail he cannot split,
For it's mighty tough and hard to hit.
    Advance, boys, advance, etc.

From *Bell & Everett Songster.*

Another Bell and Everett song pins the "woolly-head" label on the Republicans, not only to recall the association in the public's mind between Frémont and P. T. Barnum's hoax but also to appeal to prejudice against the blacks, who were called "woolly-heads" because of their kinky hair. The song is also a good example of the punning often indulged in by nineteenth-century popular poets and creators of campaign songs. The lines, "There's another *Bell* whose mighty tongue/Speaks 'The Union' now, where *ever it's* rung," not only associated the candidate, John Bell, with the Liberty Bell but also managed to incorporate a pun on the name of his running mate.

GET OUT OF THE WAY

Tune: "Old Dan Tucker"

Have you heard the news of late,
Resounding now from state to state,
For Bell and Everett lead our band,
With the Constitution in their hands.

Chorus:
Get out the way now, all seceders,
And woolly-head Disunion leaders.

You laugh, and call our party small,
And say we've got no chance at all;
But November next old Doug and Abe
Will find the boot on t'other leg.

There's a Bell in Independence Hall,
Which in Seventy-Six rang for us all;
There's another *Bell* whose mighty tongue
Speaks "The Union" now, where *ever it's* rung.

Your platforms now will soon break down,
And lay there useless on the ground:
While the Union Party's platform stands—
The Constitution of our land.

From *Bell & Everett Songster.*

The Campaign of 1864

If war is, as Von Clausewitz's classical aphorism informs us, the conduct of politics by other means, then the election struggle of 1864 must be viewed as but one front in the momentous Civil War which had wracked the North American continent for four years. In essence, the election was a referendum on the war—on both its conduct and its objectives. Lincoln's victory over McClellan at the polls was the American people's final confirmation that there would be no compromise with the slave system, that the Union would be restored only on the basis of the complete, total and final abolition of slavery throughout the United States. Despite the Republican Party's own vacillation on the issue in 1860, the cause of Union and Emancipation had become inseparable.

The Democrats remained a divided party. One wing, which favored a rapid end to the war based on concessions to the South, was called "Copperhead." This term, which came to be applied to all pro-Southern Northerners during the Civil War, had been used politically ever since 1831 to denote traitors to any cause who disguised their true convictions and struck without warning, as the copperhead snake does. Some Democratic Copperheads even supported an acceptance of the reality of secession and a complete abandonment of the war effort.

The other faction of the Democratic Party, composed of traditional Northern Democratic elements, largely based in eastern cities, was critical of Lincoln's conduct of the war and generally played on the widespread war weariness to undermine the Administration. While Copperheads chanted, "The Constitution as it is, the Union as it was, and the Negroes where they are" in a classically doomed effort to reverse the historical process, other Democrats sang:

> Honest old Abe, when the war first began,
> Denied abolition was part of his plan;
> Honest old Abe has since made a decree,
> The war must go on till the slaves are all free.
> As both can't be honest, will someone tell how,
> If honest Abe then, he is honest Abe now?

> From an anonymously printed broadside of
> the period.

Judging by their rhetoric, the two factions seemed to have vastly differing programs, but they were able to unite on a candidate for the '64 election. He was General George B. McClellan, one-time Commander of the Army of the Potomac, removed by Lincoln for his singular lack of enthusiasm in the conduct of the war. It may be that McClellan was merely an over-cautious soldier; but there were many at the time who felt that McClellan's reluctance to engage in battle had political roots, and that his failure to pursue the struggle had as much to do with his own ambivalence about the aims of the war as it did with military considerations.

For the Democrats, McClellan's availability was a godsend. He had some of the trappings of a popular hero and he was bitterly opposed to Lincoln. Even though "Little Mac" eventually renounced his own party's campaign platform, which pronounced the war a failure and proposed a "peace at almost any price" solution, the Copperhead faction had no difficulty in supporting him. If history will judge it ironic that the former head of all the Union forces should have his praises sung by those who bitterly opposed the war effort, the irony is compounded by the blatantly racist, proslavery ideology enlisted on behalf of the Democratic nominee. The following Democratic song attacked Lincoln for freeing the slaves and suspending the writ of *habeas corpus* during the war.

WHITE SOLDIERS' SONG

Tune: "John Brown's Body"

> Tell Abe Lincoln that he'd better end the war,
> Tell Abe Lincoln what we all came out here for,
> Tell Abe Lincoln 'twas the Union to restore,
>   As we go marching on.

> Tell Abe Lincoln to let the nigger be,
> Tell Abe Lincoln that we don't want him free,
> Tell Abe Lincoln that to this he did agree,
>   As we go marching on.

> Tell Abe Lincoln, the Constitution is our guide,
> Tell Abe Lincoln by the laws he must abide,
> Tell Abe Lincoln to let his proclamation slide,
>   As we go marching on.

Tell Abe Lincoln and his woolly-headed crew,
Tell Abe Lincoln his suspension writ won't do,
Tell Abe Lincoln we are going to put him through,
    As we go marching on.

Tell Abe Lincoln of Antietam's bloody dell,
Tell Abe Lincoln where a thousand heroes fell,
Tell Abe Lincoln and his gang to go to hell,
    And we'll go marching home.

From *Copperhead Minstrel.*

Copperhead songs and poetry flourished with the virulence of smallpox. Slander, calumny, lies and virtual calls to treasonous action were spewed forth by those who were, consciously or not, the propaganda agents for the slave system. To the melodies of such popular songs as "Wait for the Wagon" and "Lucy Long," they appealed to prejudice against blacks. Besides the Emancipation Proclamation, the following song attacked one of the many acts of Congress which resulted in a gradual recruitment of many tens of thousands of black soldiers for the Union Army.

I calculate of darkies we soon shall have our fill,
With Abe's Proclamation and the Nigger Army bill;
Who could not be a soldier for the Union to fight?
Now, Abe's made the nigger the equal of the white.
    Fight for the nigger,
    The sweet-scented nigger,
    The woolly-headed nigger,
    And the Abolition crew.

If ordered into battle, go in without delay,
Though slaughtered just like cattle, it's your duty to obey;
And when you meet the rebels, be sure and drive them back,
Though you do *enslave* the white man, you must *liberate* the black.

From "Fight for the Nigger," *Copperhead Minstrel.*

Another Copperhead song, employing minstrel "Negro" dialect, appealed to white fears by brandishing the menace of bloody slave revolts such as had frequently occurred in Santo Domingo, the "Sangomingo" of the song.

Oh, de Sangomingo darkeys had a standard which dey bore,
'Twas a pretty little baby's head, all dripping in its gore!
And if we understand aright de President's Proclaim,
He tells de Dixie niggers dey may go and do de same!

Oh, de Sangomingo darkies, dare old Massas took and tied,
And den dey got de handsaw and sawed 'em till dey died!
And after dey had sawed 'em till dey sawed away dare lives,
You may bet dey had a good time a-kissin' ob dare wives!

From "De Serenade," *Copperhead Minstrel.*

It was no easy matter for McClellan to maintain that he could simultaneously achieve military victory, restore the Union, and bring immediate peace. His speeches and documents tried to skip over this fundamental contradiction, and so the Democratic campaign was one which concentrated on attacking Lincoln and his administration at every opportunity. Thus, McClellan supporters would criticize the draft, decry Lincoln's ineptitude, castigate the Emancipation Proclamation, charge corruption in both Army and government, and hold Lincoln personally responsible for the havoc of the war. While one McClellan song proclaimed, "The Rebels'll catch in McClellan their match,/And we'll soon have peace with glory," down in Kentucky, William Shakespeare Hays, author of the vastly popular sentimental war song, "The Drummer Boy of Shiloh," wrote a campaign song which promised a peace based on accommodation with the South rather than military victory. Hays's song also attacked war profiteers in the North. "Shoddy," as used in the song, was a wartime term which denoted businessmen who made fortunes through fraudulent practices—particularly by peddling shoddy goods to the Army.

McCLELLAN IS THE MAN

Words and music: Will S. Hays

Corruption sits in places high,
And Shoddy rules the roost;
"Fight on!" is still Corruption's cry,
"More spoils!" is Shoddy's boast.
But we, the people, sovereigns all,
Declare our righteous cause;
"The Constitution as it is,
The Union as it was."

This cruel war will never cease
Until the South comes back;
The only man to do the work
Is glorious Little Mac.
Then let us put him in the chair,
And he will give us peace;
For "Peace in Union" is his aim,
And war's alarms will cease.

Let's heal dissensions and unite,
Then, stronger than before,
We'll bear our banner through the world,
The flag our fathers bore.
Its sunny stripes and golden stars
Shall give the people ease;
And all th'oppressed of every clime
Will hail our happy peace.

The hot-heads South cried, "Let's secede,"
But find it doesn't pay;
The hot-heads North cried "Confiscate,
And then we'll have our way."
But both have failed, and always will,
There is a better plan,
We'll choose a righteous President—
McClellan is the man!

From the original sheet music, published by William McCarrell, Louisville, Ky., 1864.

McClellan is the man! It was the theme of a campaign designed to appeal to all who had suffered any loss from the war or who nursed any dissatisfaction with the state of affairs. But behind the rhetoric was the promise of a white knight, one who would restore the Union as it was, reaffirm white supremacy not only in spirit but in law and social practice, and re-establish the former social order which had been so rudely broken off by the Republican triumph of 1860. To be sure, even a victorious McClellan could not have turned back the historical process at that point. But in 1864, the songs which attempted to sing McClellan into the presidency were laced with the ambiguities of Democratic politics. The following song offered the South "fair terms of peace," while Lincoln had pledged, in Grant's words, "Unconditional Surrender!"

SOON WE'LL HAVE THE UNION BACK

Tune: "The Hunters of Kentucky"

Good people all, both great and small,
I sing a tale of pity;
My hand I fling across the string,
And waken up the ditty.
A ruined land that once was grand,
Is not a joking matter—
Though Abe we know, the more our woe,
The more his jokes he'll chatter!
    Oh, McClellan,
    Georgie B. McClellan,
    Shall we have the Union back?
    Tell us "Mac"—McClellan!

All evil sure we could endure,
Thrice all the ills we suffer,
Could we but glance on any chance
Our Union to recover.
There gleams one way, a flash of day,
But one bright bow of promise,
Good Lord, alack! Just give us "Mac,"
And take Abe Lincoln from us!
    Oh, McClellan,
    Georgie B. McClellan,
    The one to bring the Union back
    Is only "Mac"—McClellan.

Then not a rag of our old flag
Should ever part asunder!
"Fair terms of peace if you will cease—
If not, we'll give you thunder!"

A million swords to back our words
Beneath McClellan gleaming,
And soon, ye know, Jeff D. and Co.
For France they would be steaming!
    Oh, McClellan,
    Georgie B. McClellan,
    Soon we'll have our prisoners back
    Under "Mac"—McClellan.

The people all, both great and small,
Except the sons of Shoddy,
Are on the track for "Little Mac"—
They're with him soul and body;
For well they know the nation's woe
Can never be abated,
Till in command of all the land
Our Chief we have instated!
    Oh, McClellan,
    Georgie B. McClellan,
    The Union will come leaping back
    Under "Mac"—McClellan.

From Campaign Document No. 19.

The following song is taken from an odd little songster, *The McClellan Campaign Melodist*, consisting solely of songs composed by its editor, Sidney Herbert, who described his folio as "a collection of patriotic campaign songs in favor of the Constitution and the Union, the election of General McClellan, the restoration of the Federal authority, and the speedy extermination of treason."

LITTLE MAC SHALL BE RESTORED

Words: Sidney Herbert
Tune: "Auld Lang Syne"

Shall brave McClellan sink in shame,
With all his deeds denied?
Shall slander rest upon the fame
Of one so true and tried?
Shall he be cast aside in doubt,
And wield no more the sword?
Rise, then, and turn his scorners out,
And "Mac" shall be restored.

Let all the young men say the word,
And help us in the fight;
McClellan wields a trusty sword,
And he'll defend the right.

Come then and join our Club tonight,
And battle for our Flag,
We never will desert the right,
Nor hail the "Rebel rag!"

Brave "Mac" is bound to win the day,
And our good cause to save,
Though jealous hatred dares to lay
Its hand upon the brave.
Oh, then, lift up the song of praise
For him who leads us on,
And let us hope for brighter days,
When Vict'ry shall be won.

The popular American composer Stephen Foster wrote both words and music for the following song supporting McClellan and his running mate, George Hunt Pendleton, Democratic congressman from Ohio. It is unlikely, however, that this version of the song is exactly the way the composer wrote it, since Foster died in January of 1864 and the Republicans did not select Andrew Johnson as their Vice-Presidential candidate until June, 1864. The publisher probably updated the lyrics after the Republican nominations.

LITTLE MAC! LITTLE MAC! YOU'RE THE VERY MAN

Words and music: Stephen Collins Foster

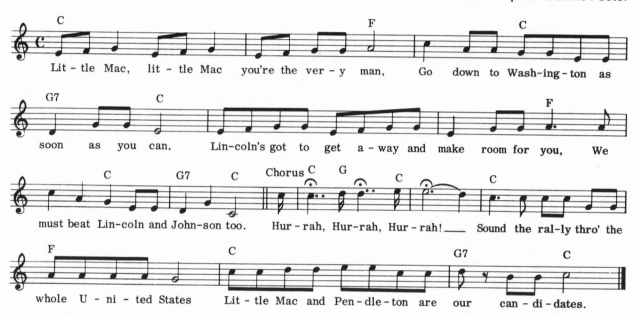

Lit-tle Mac, lit-tle Mac you're the ver-y man, Go down to Wash-ing-ton as soon as you can. Lin-coln's got to get a-way and make room for you, We must beat Lin-coln and John-son too. *Chorus* Hur-rah, Hur-rah, Hur-rah!___ Sound the ral-ly thro' the whole U-ni-ted States Lit-tle Mac and Pen-dle-ton are our can-di-dates.

Democrats, Democrats, do it up brown,
Lincoln and his niggerheads won't go down,
Greeley and Sumner and all that crew,
We must beat Lincoln and Johnson too.

Abraham the Joker soon will diskiver,
We'll send him on a gun-boat *Up Salt River*,
Scotch caps and military cloaks won't do,
We must beat Lincoln and Johnson too.

Southern men come again, Little Mac's a trump,
He'll restore the Union with a hop, skip and jump,
With nigger proclamations full in view,
We must beat Lincoln and Johnson too.

The "Scotch caps and military cloaks" of which Foster's song makes mention referred to a disguise reportedly worn by Lincoln when he went to Washington in 1861. According to a widespread Civil War legend, Lincoln wore a military cloak and Scottish plaid cap as a disguise in order to thwart possible assassination attempts. The story became the subject of many newspaper cartoons, designed, in most cases, to depict the President as a coward. Despite elaborate security precautions, as well as the discovery of a very real plot to assassinate Lincoln, there seems to have been no substance to the story. Carl Sandburg, in his massive Lincoln biography, asserts that the tale was started by a *New York Times* reporter frequently given to inventing hoaxes or embellishing on the facts in order to make for a more colorful story.

Just as Lincoln's most effective campaign appeal turned out to be Sherman's capture of Atlanta in September of '64 and Grant's pursuit of Lee in Virginia, so the best Republican campaign songs were those stirring ballads and hymns to which millions of young Americans had gone marching into battle. "Battle Hymn of the Republic," "The

Battle Cry of Freedom" and "Marching Along" were songs which clearly identified the national purpose with the president.

The expected "rally, freemen, rally" songs made their appearance in 1864, but who would sing them when songs like "We Are Coming, Father Abraham, 600,000 More" were already in the popular consciousness?

More interesting were the campaign parodies. George F. Root's "Battle Cry of Freedom" was the favorite and, as the first great inspirational song of the War, naturally lent itself to the purpose. Scores of ditties were written to the melody, and McClellan partisans used it as well. Here are two of the better Lincoln versions:

RALLY 'ROUND THE CAUSE, BOYS   Words: E. Mason, Jr.   Tune: "Battle Cry of Freedom"

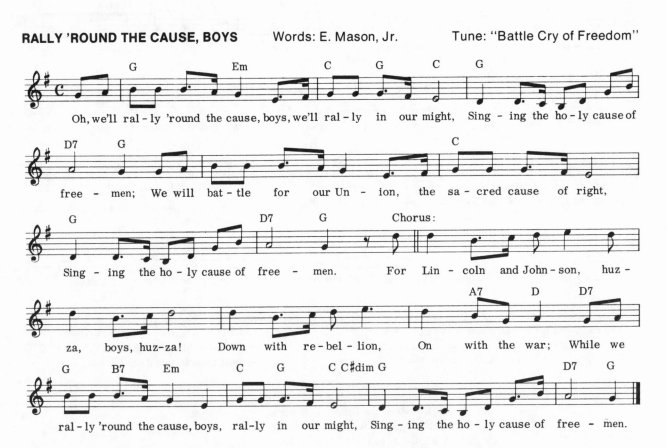

To reunite the States
We have got a *General Grant,*
Singing the holy cause of freemen,
We are sick of cries for "peace,"
And other rebel cant,
Singing the holy cause of freemen.

We will rally 'round our banner, boys,
And long may it wave,
Singing the holy cause of freemen,
And when Secession dies,
We will gather 'round the grave,
Singing the holy cause of freemen.

Then rally, "Wide Awakes,"
We will try it once again,
Singing the holy cause of freemen.
Beneath the Stars and Stripes
Our duty's very plain,
Singing the holy cause of freemen.

One hundred thousand more
Will finish up the strife,
Singing the holy cause of freemen.
We will stand by our Union
While heaven gives us life,
Singing the holy cause of freemen.

From *Lincoln Campaign Songster.*

RALLY FOR OLD ABE

Words: Enos B. Reed
Tune: "Battle Cry of Freedom"

Let's rally for "Old Abe," boys,
Let's rally once again,
Fighting for our homes and our Union,
We will cast our votes for "Abe," boys,
And cast them not in vain,
Fighting for our homes and our Union.

Chorus:
It's "Old Abe," forever, hurrah, boys, hurrah!
We are no traitors—all for the war;
Then we'll rally for "Old Abe," boys, rally once again,
Rally for "Old Abe" and for freedom.

He has done the best he could, boys,
The best could do no more,
Fighting for our homes and our Union,
And he'll fight the battle through, boys,
Until the fight is o'er,
Fighting for our homes and our Union!

We want no traitors' aid, boys,
But only ask the brave
To fight for our homes and our Union,
And in the land of freedom
We do not want a slave,
Then fight for our homes and our Union.

Then we'll rally for "Old Abe," boys,
Come, rally once again,
Fighting for our homes and our Union;
We'll try him once again, boys,
And try him not in vain,
Fighting for our homes and our Union.

From *The Republican Campaign Songster for 1864.*

While the Democrats chanted that "McClellan was the Man!", Lincoln supporters sang:

Oh, Patriots! Oh, Patriots!
Don't vote for craven Mac,
But cast your votes for Abraham,
He's on the Union track.

From "Cast Your Votes for Abraham," *Lincoln Campaign Songster.*

And in the style of the blackface minstrel songs of the period, to the tune of Henry Clay Work's "Kingdom Coming," they sang of Union, freedom and Lincoln. A later generation may well wince at the condescension towards blacks underlying such songs, but that, too, is a part of history, enabling us to understand, perhaps, that the struggle against slavery was only incidentally a struggle for such concepts as "justice" and "freedom," words which are always evoked by historical necessity.

UNION COMING

Tune: "Kingdom Coming"

Say, brudders, hab you seen McClellan,
Wid de sour look on his face,
Go down de road toward Salt Ribber,
Like a man dat's run his race?
He heard a sound all too de country,
Where the Union voters stay;
He says to Pen, we had better leab sudden,
While we both can get away.

Chorus:
For Maine has said, Ha! Ha!
Vermont she say, Ho! Ho!
We'll sing de song ob Union eber,
From Maine to Mexico!

Mac may be smart, but Lincum's smarter,
And de people tink so, too,
And on de eight' ob next November
I can tell you what dey'll do.
Dey'll fix de flint ob all de traitors
Who would hab us compromise,
And hoist de flag ob glorious Union
Till it reaches to de skies.

De Copperheads dey feel so lonesome
On de norf ob Dixie's line,
Dey all should move across de ribber
Whar Jeff Davis wants ter shine.
We've Abe and Andy and de Union,
And de ole flag tried and true;
We don't tink we'll be confed-e-ra-ted
By de rebel grayback crew.

De doughface tries to help Jeff Davis,
And he dodge around de stump,
We'll put him yet where he'll hab to holler,
Wid he head beneath de pump.
Their day is past, de word am spoken,
In de Union all am free;
We're good enough, smart enough, all to hab Union
From de lakes to gulf and sea.

From *The President Lincoln Campaign Songster.*

Republicans All

*Campaign Songs of the Postwar Era,
When Republicans Reign Supreme*

The Civil War is the Great Divide of American history. The War not only ended the slave system, it broke the South's political grip on the nation, unleashing forces of industry, commerce and expansion which the battle over slavery had held in check. But with the destruction of Southern political power, the real power of the North (industry, finance, trade) no longer had any concern with the newly emancipated blacks.

The so-called "drama" of Reconstruction is largely a myth. Despite differing views on how the Southern states should be reintegrated into the Union, few wielders of political power had any real concern with the fate of the ex-slaves. Every four years, Republican ballad-mongers renewed hostilities with the Confederacy, but during each successive Republican administration, decisive steps were taken to implement a new kind of structure, based on blacks as "free" labor, in the southern states.

The few politicians of the period who envisioned a genuine Reconstruction based upon complete equality for blacks and a form of indemnification ("forty acres and a mule") were denounced as wild-eyed radicals. In time, these "radicals" were either isolated or bought off by the "responsible" elements, who now took complete control of the Union. But for a few heady years, when Congress came within a single vote of impeaching Andrew Johnson, it almost seemed as though a second revolution, more sweeping than the one which had swept slavery away, might actually take place.

However, Johnson's vetoes of Congressional measures to extend the life of the wartime Freedmen's Bureau and of a civil rights bill giving citizenship to blacks seemed to jeopardize the very heart of the country's war aims. Actually, Johnson represented the classic political anomaly of many southern Democrats before and since. Opposed to the power of the eastern banking establishment, responsive to the needs of a small farmer constituency, Democrats like Andrew Jackson, Johnson, William Jennings Bryan, and George Wallace have all had a strong current of populism in their appeals. For the most part, they have also reflected the racist ideology of their constituencies.

Johnson went on a long campaign swing during the summer months of 1866 in an effort to secure election of a favorable Congress. The trip proved disastrous as the president, not at his best in extemporaneous speechmaking, managed to stir up hostile crowds in several cities. Johnson's "swing around the circle" (his trip took him to Chicago and back) was a *cause célèbre* of the time.

JUST BEFORE ELECTION, ANDY

Tune: "Just Before the Battle, Mother"
(Quoted in "Campaign Songs of a Century,"
New York Evening Post, March 16, 1912.)

Just be-fore e-lec-tion, An-dy, / We are think-ing most of you,

While we get our bal-lots read-y— / But be sure they're not for you!

No, dear An-dy, you'll not get them, / But you'll get what you de-serve— Oh,

yes, you'll get your leave of ab-sence / As you "swing a-round the curve!"

Chorus:

You have swung a-round the cir-cle, / That you ought to swing, 'tis true;

Oh, you tried to ve-to Con-gress, / But I guess we'll ve-to you!

Hail the Conquering Hero!

It was little wonder that the Republicans refused to renominate Johnson and turned to the popular Union general Ulysses Simpson Grant instead. Indeed, the president had no political base whatsoever. A Democrat elected on a Republican ticket, Johnson was anathema to both parties.

Grant was considered presidential timber since the early days of 1864 and by the time the nominating conventions of 1868 rolled around, the general was the overwhelming popular choice. He won the Republican nomination without a contest. Indiana congressman and speaker of the House of Representatives, Schuyler Colfax, was nominated for the vice-presidency, and the team was serenaded to a victory at the polls in November with campaign songs composed by some of the most popular wartime songsmiths.

J. P. Webster, famous for his setting of one of the great hit songs of the period, "Lorena," and composer of the melody for one of the all-time favorite hymns, "Sweet Bye and Bye," wrote the music for "Hurrah for General Grant" and "For President: Ulysses Grant, A-Smoking His Cigar." W. O. Fiske, C. L. Abdill, William Seibert and the prolific Mrs. Emily Parkhurst all composed Grant campaign songs. Among the best of the songs for Grant was a ballad by a famous song-writing pair, George

Cooper and Henry Tucker. Cooper had been a long-time lyricist for Stephen Foster ("For the Dear Old Flag I Die," "Willie Has Gone to the War," etc.), while Tucker had composed two of the war's most popular songs, "Weeping Sad and Lonely" ("When This Cruel War Is Over") and "Dear Mother, I've Come Home To Die." In later years, this team would collaborate on another all-time favorite, "Sweet Genevieve."

The entry of the professionals into the campaign songs sweepstakes introduced a considerable amount of verbal by-play into election verse. In this song, Tucker gets a free plug for one of his songs in the chorus and quotes from the candidates start appearing. Here one of Grant's most widely quoted statements, "I purpose to fight it out on this line if it takes all summer," is squeezed into the last verse. The original appeared in a letter from Grant to Secretary of War Stanton on May 11, 1864, after the bloody victory at Spotsylvania.

GENERAL GRANT'S THE MAN (A Song and Chorus for the Times) Words: George Cooper
Music: Henry Tucker

1. O! "re-con-struc-tion" is the rage— All o-ver this fair land,— And— in the game it's ver-y clear That all should take a hand; We— want a brand new Pres-i-dent— And on-ly one will an-swer But sure as guns he'll take the chair, For Gen-er-al Grant's— our man, sir.

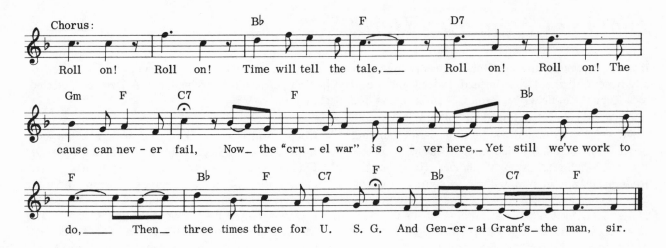

Chorus:

Roll on! Roll on! Time will tell the tale,___ Roll on! Roll on! The cause can nev - er fail, Now_ the "cru - el war" is o - ver here,_ Yet still we've work to do,___ Then_ three times three for U. S. G. And Gen - er - al Grant's_ the man, sir.

Our candidate has never "ran"
For office, that we know,
And certainly he's never "run"
From any mortal foe!
The "boys in blue" will tell the tale
Whene'er they get the chance, sir,
They won't forget the days of old,
And General Grant's the man, sir.

He'll make the nation brighten up,
Just like his own segar,
And all "discordant elements"
He'll quiet, near and far;
So "on this line we'll fight it out!"
It's sure to be our plan, sir,
Then "three times three" for U.S.G.,
Oh! General Grant's the man, sir.

From the original sheet music,
pub. by William A. Pond Co., New
York, 1868.

The Civil War, with its outburst of popular piano music, stimulated the growth of the music publishing industry. Firms like Lyon & Healy, Oliver Ditson Company, S. Brainard's & Sons and many others established themselves as highly profitable enterprises. One of the most successful, Root & Cady, was founded by George Frederick Root, whose wartime compositions, "Battle Cry of Freedom," "Tramp, Tramp, Tramp," "Just Before the Battle, Mother" and "The Vacant Chair," among many others, were the most widely sung in the country. From the end of the War until the turn of the century, it was these music publishers who were the main disseminators of campaign music.

With the memory of Grant's triumph over Lee fresh in the popular mind, and with the melodies of the Civil War marching songs still being sung, dozens of campaign parodies to the wartime songs burst forth. The ever enterprising publishers, Root & Cady, put out a collection of Grant campaign ditties, most of which were set to those Civil War airs copyrighted by that company.

Tune: "Tramp, Tramp, Tramp"

We are coming to the fight,
With our leader at our head,
And we know his heart is true—his arm is strong.
We will struggle for the right
As we did when first he led,
And the "Battle Cry of Freedom" was our song.

Grant! Grant! Grant! the land is calling,
Good-bye Andy, you may go,
We will place him at our head,
Who our bannered host has led,
And to whom a traitor ever is a foe.

Tune: "Kingdom Coming"

Come brave men, true men, all get ready
For the coming 'lection day,
We'll fight anew our country's battles,
And our country's call obey.
Our sword shall be the freeman's ballot,
And our field the ballot-box,
And I tell you what, we'll give the Andy's
Some pretty stiff hard knocks.

Hurrah, hurrah for Grant;
For Grant, for Grant hurrah!
Now wake up, boys, for 'lection's coming,
For 'lection, boys, hurrah!

Tune: "Battle Cry of Freedom"

We're going to Election, boys,
We're going there to vote,
Hurrah for the ballot-box of Freedom!
And we'll thrust their boasts and vauntings
Down each rebel-traitor's throat,
Hurrah for the ballot-box of Freedom!

Ulysses forever! hurrah, boys, hurrah!
Down with the traitor and up with our Star!
For we're going to Election, boys,
We're going there to vote,
Vote in the ballot-box of freedom.

Tune: "When Johnny Comes Marching Home"

Oh! hearken to the glorious news,
    Hurrah! hurrah!
The rebels all have got the blues,
    Hurrah! hurrah!
The people all are turning out,
With drum and banner, song and shout,
    And the Ku Klux Klans are
    A-trembling in their shoes.

The Ku Klux Klan, mentioned in the last song, was organized by ex-Confederate soldiers in 1866. Its main activity at this time consisted in intimidating the newly enfranchised blacks from enrolling in the Republican Party and from voting in elections.

In 1868, the Democrats selected their most reluctant candidate ever, ex-Governor of New York State, Horatio Seymour. A popular wartime governor, he had shown his independence of Lincoln by opposing many of the repressive war measures instituted in the North. Republicans called him a "Copperhead," which was clearly untrue, but the actual political alignments of the times made him acceptable to the southerners in the party and laid the basis for what was, in effect, a racist campaign. General Francis P. Blair, one-time Free Soil congressman, a Lincoln supporter who broke with the Republicans in the postwar period, was nominated for the vice-presidency by the Democrats.

Typical of the racist songs in the 1868 campaign was "The White Man's Banner." There were at least two compositions with this title. In addition to political considerations, there seems to have been some businesslike competition at work. The version printed here was published in New Orleans by the South's leading music publisher, A. E. Blackmar, who had been imprisoned during the Union occupation of New Orleans for continuing to circulate the original "Bonnie Blue Flag" after General Butler had banned it. A second New Orleans publisher, Louis Grunewald, put out another version of "The White Man's Banner" with slight changes in the lyrics and a somewhat altered melody.

THE WHITE MAN'S BANNER   Words: Anonymous   Tune: "Bonnie Blue Flag"

Raise high the white man's ban-ner, Let it float up-on the air,____ Fling to the breeze the hon-or'd names of Sey-mour and of Blair;____ Of Sey-mour, who a states-man is, of Blair, the he-ro bold,____ And let the lau-rel wreath sur-round these bla-zon'd names of gold!____

Chorus: Hur-rah!____ Hur-rah!____ for Sey-mour and Blair Hur-rah!____ Hur-rah! for the white man's flag, With ev-'ry state a star!____

With names like these to rally 'round,
The foe will find us strong
In vindicating every right,
In crushing out each wrong.
Come then, all free-born patriots,
Join with a brave intent
To vindicate our Fathers' choice,
A White Man's Government!

No Carpet-bag or Negro rule
For men who truly prize
The heritage of glory from
Our Sires, the true, the wise.
Let Grant and Colfax fight beneath
Their flag of sable hue,
The White Man's Banner we will raise
And conquer with it, too!

The following comic broadside, lampooning Grant as a dupe of the Radical Republicans and a potential military dictator, was given wide circulation by the Democrats. The song also exploited Grant's well-known fondness for the bottle. Interestingly enough, the three major figures in the 1868 election—Grant, Seymour and Johnson—were all criticized for an overly friendly attitude towards John Barleycorn. Grant's "drinking problem" had almost become a wartime scandal, occasioning Lincoln's famous remark that if he could find out where Grant got his liquor, he would order a supply from the same source for the other Union generals. Seymour was attacked for having, as governor, vetoed a prohibition law. Johnson had a reputation for being a frequent imbiber and on at least one occasion, in his opening address to the Senate upon becoming vice-president, was obviously under the influence.

CAPTAIN GRANT OF THE BLACK MARINES

Tune: "Captain Jinks of the Horse Marines"

I am Captain Grant of the Black Marines, The stupidest man that ever was seen I make no speech that's what I mean But I cut a swell in the army. I teach the taxpayers how to dance, how to dance, how to dance, I teach the taxpayers how to dance, For I'm the pet of the army.

Chorus:
I'm Captain Grant of the Black Marines, I go it blind for all extremes, I have no policy as it seems, But go with the Radical Army.

I smoke my weed and drink my gin,
Paying with the people's tin,
And if the White House I get in,
I'll still stay in the Army.
All the people think it strange,
Think it strange, think it strange,
All the people think it strange
That I don't resign from the Army.

[Spoken] *Well, I don't care if they do. I'm not a fool to give up a sure thing. I'm boss and Congress has got to fix matters to suit.*

For President my name they run,
But I, for one, don't like the fun,
For Seymour'll beat me two to one
Although I'm Head of the Army.
When the people find us out,
Find us out, find us out,
When the people find us out,
They'll disband the Black Marine Army.

The song's prediction of a majority for Seymour at the polls was wide of the mark. Grant outpolled Seymour by more than 300,000 votes out of some 5.5 million, winning the electoral vote 214 to 80.

Not all the Democratic songs were that "political." There were the usual pseudopoetic paeans to the candidate's glorious character:

Horatio Seymour, brave, honest and true,
Who deserves the support of the jackets of blue;
His bosom is free from intrigue, guile or art,
'Tis the shrine of that treasure—the patriot's heart.

From "Song for the Sailors," *Seymour & Blair Song Book.*

The cleverest of the Democratic songs flaunted an outrageous rhyme ("buy 'em" and "Hiram") on Grant's baptismal name and was a parody to the just composed "Not for Joseph," by the English comic songwriter, Arthur Lloyd. It was a tune which would show up in election campaigns for the next 40 years.

NOT FOR GRANT

Tune: "Not for Joseph"

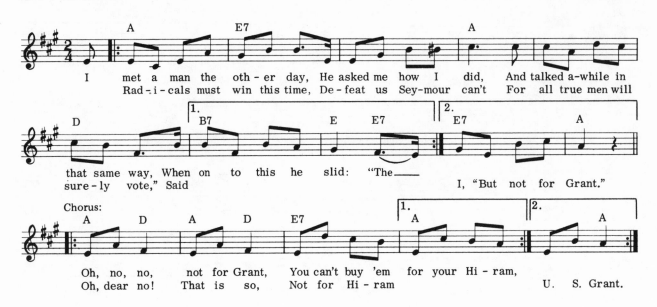

A man was spouting politics
Before a little crowd,
So I just stopped to listen,
He talked so very loud;
When he turned to me and shouted,
"Beat us! Why Seymour can't,
For all the honest people vote"—
Said I—"But not for Grant."

I went to hear friend Horace speak,
Before a Colfax club;
He told them Grant would surely win,
And that without a "rub,"
"For over all the land," said he,
"Our flag they'll proudly plant,
And men who love the truth will vote"—
Said I—"But not for Grant."

I heard Dan Sickles tell the boys,
The boys who wore the blue,
That Grant and Colfax were the men
To whom they must be true;
That all the soldiers of the land,
Whose hearts for freedom pant,
Would vote for men with whom they fought,
Said I—"But not for Grant."

Now I'm a boy who wore the blue,
And fought through all the war;
I did my duty to the last,
And bear the wound and scar;
But I shall cast my vote for one—
Though Sickles says I can't—
Who bravely led the "boys in blue,"
But 'tis not U.S. Grant.

From *Seymour & Blair Song Book.*

The "Horace" who predicted victory for Grant was Horace Greeley, who, strangely enough, became the opposition candidate against Grant in 1872. The "Dan Sickles" of the song was Major General Daniel Edgar Sickles, a colorful figure in New York politics for fifty years, congressman and diplomat. Presumably, the Union commander lauded in the last stanza was Blair, who served as a major general in the Union Army.

Grant Again in '72

It is conventional to characterize the eight years of Ulysses S. Grant's Administration as one of the most "corrupt" periods in American political life. That bribery, pocket-lining, conflicting interests, and the spoils system were operating on an unprecedented scale seems unquestionably true. But all too often, historians of the period have contented themselves with describing the surface reality of events, implying that the "corruption" of the era was somehow the result of personal weakness on Grant's part. Such an explanation is conveniently simplistic, for it disposes of much thornier questions without confronting them.

It should be noted that the country was going through an expansionist boom in industry, trade and transportation which the political structure had not developed the wherewithal to rationalize. The old structure, that precarious balance of sectional interests, had been destroyed by the Civil War. In its place remained the Republican Party, the agency of the new northern business interests, arrayed against a mangled and divided opposition. The result was a massive exploitation of the fruits of office. Much has been made of Grant's nepotism, of his cronyism, of his personal style of administration and the way in which political subordinates could manipulate him to their own advantage. But the real "corruption" of the era was much larger, much more ambitious in scope.

For this was the era of the great "robber barons," the Vanderbilts and Jay Goulds, who were allowed to loot the public domain with a rapaciousness rarely matched in a political system so responsive to the needs of giant corporations. The air of aggrandizement which surrounded the Grant Administration was a part of the general tone of the country at large, where no force existed capable of curtailing the demands and excesses of the empire-builders.

It was in this atmosphere that a group of Reform Republicans—many of them from the staunch old idealistic wing of the Party's earlier crusading days—banded together to challenge Grant's bid for a second term. Meeting in a special convention in Cincinnati, these motley dissidents, including many a crafty office-seeker who had been frozen out by the Administration, produced a platform calling for significant reforms in government, among them the establishment of a civil service system and economy in government financing. And then, in one of the strangest developments in the history of American politics, they nominated a man who had never held political office in his life, a curmudgeon whose personality and biting pen had created at least as many enemies as friends, the editor of the *New York Tribune,* Horace Greeley.

Greeley's nomination was even stranger, considering that he was a high tariff man, while most of the reformers who chose him as their candidate favored lower tariffs. The tariff question became one of the great continuing issues of the nineteenth century, largely a conflict between industrial interests which wanted protection against cheaper foreign imports, and consumer and mercantile interests who favored a free trade policy. In general, the country was committed to protecting native manufacturing, although concessions were made from time to time, until, in the twentieth century, the balance of world trade operated to reverse this pattern. During Grant's Administration, the tariff was a particular sore spot because some of the customs houses (notably the one in New Orleans) became centers for bribe-taking and thievery. With Greeley heading their ticket, the reformers compromised on the tariff issue and adopted a platform plank which actually leaned in both directions.

The office-hungry Democrats, out of power for twelve years, followed the proceedings of the dissident Republicans' convention with great interest, bided their time and then finally cast their lot with the Liberal Republicans by endorsing Greeley and his running mate, B. Gratz Brown, at their convention, held in Baltimore, July 9, 1872.

The Liberal Republicans tried to characterize Grant as a military dictator by referring to him as a "man on horseback." The phrase had been in use in American politics for at least a dozen years, but it seems to have stuck to Grant more than anyone else.

Greeley's campaign, quite naturally, focused on charges of corruption in the Grant Administration. It was the main theme of the Greeley songs, which all seem to be just on the verge of catapulting the movement to the level of a crusade but never quite making it.

The following song bears down heavily on

Grant's nepotism and the graft in his Administration. The song contains references to Frederick T. Dent, Grant's brother-in-law and military secretary to the President, one of the most powerful men in the government; and Thomas Murphy, a Republican wardheeler in New York City and political crony of Republican boss Roscoe Conkling, whom Grant appointed Collector of the Port of New York, which position he utilized as a source of party patronage and personal profit. The substitution of "Useless" for "Ulysses" was probably the Liberals' chief literary contribution to the campaign.

To the tune of "Not for Joseph," which had provided Seymour with a melody four years earlier, the Greeleyites sang:

> When Useless came to Washington
> He wore a jaunty plume,
> The Dents and Murphys crowded in
> And drove him to his doom.
> His nephews and his cousins all
> Came up to win the race,
> And every man who gave a dog
> Was sure to get a place.
>
> Down with Grant, Useless Grant!
> Up with Greeley, good old Greeley!
> Down with Grant, Useless Grant!
> Hurrah for Greeley! Old White Hat!
>
> From *The Farmer of Chappaqua Songster.*

Grant's primitive nepotism was of a piece with the age, and probably his loading the government payroll with relatives did less harm than his appointments of various friends and associates from Army days, scores of whom were eventually exposed as having had their hands buried deep in the public till. But the "nephews and cousins" helped illustrate the reformers' charges, and by contrast, the Liberals could promise

> Horace and no relations
> To fill the public stations.

No, Horace Greeley wouldn't bring his relatives to the White House; just his old white hat and his old white coat. Investing Greeley with all the phrases used to elect the Whigs of by-gone days, the Liberals celebrated his famous attire and sang of "Doctor Greeley," who could heal "the sickened body politic," "Farmer Greeley" (he maintained a summer home and farm at Chappaqua, N.Y.), "The Sage of Chappaqua," "Father Greeley," and many others.

"Farmer Greeley" was sung to the tune of "Champagne Charley." The original "Champagne Charley" was the creation of an English vaudevillian and music hall singer, George Leybourne, who also wrote the lyrics for "The Daring Young Man on the Flying Trapeze." The tune was by Alfred Lee.

The song depicted the Democratic candidate as the public's watchdog in matters of morality in government and an exemplar of the simple virtues and plain, wholesome living. In particular, the lyrics called attention to Greeley's vegetarianism and teetotalism.

FARMER GREELEY   Tune: "Champagne Charley"

There is a chap at Chap-pa-qua who lives up-on his farm And rais-es beets and cab-ba-ges to keep his soul from harm. He feeds on mush and milk and sich, and nev-er takes a dram; But strange to say, he keeps him-self as hap-py as a clam.

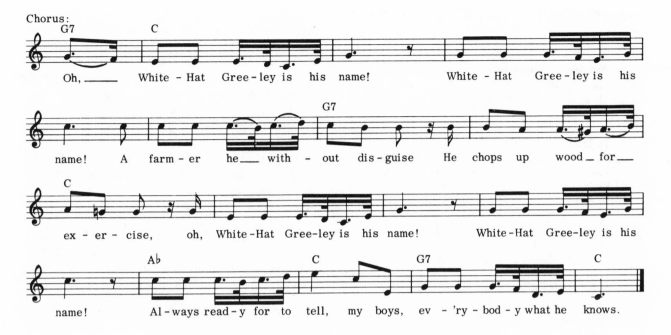

Chorus:

Oh, ___ White – Hat Gree – ley is his name! White – Hat Gree – ley is his name! A farm – er he ___ with – out dis – guise He chops up wood ___ for ___ ex – er – cise, oh, White – Hat Gree – ley is his name! White – Hat Gree – ley is his name! Al – ways read – y for to tell, my boys, ev – 'ry – bod – y what he knows.

He wears a pair of cowhide boots, because they're good and strong,
And stuffs his trousers in the tops whene'er they are too long;
And while he hoes his row, he thinks of strawberries and things,
Of how to manage cabinets, and presidents, and kings.

Some fools deride that old white hat, nor think that it contains
The head of a philosopher whose phosphorescent brains
Have presidents and parties made, and forced them both until
They listened to the people's voice, obeyed the people's will.

Between his farm and Uncle Sam's this farmer goes about,
And in the field of politics he is good at weeding out.
No buzzards light at Chappaqua on carcasses to prey,
And from the farm of Uncle Sam the thieves he drives away.

From *Greeley & Brown Campaign Songster.*

The Liberal Republicans tried to appeal to a great variety of constituencies. For the traditional antislavery elements in the Republican Party, they sang in minstrel dialect:

Tune: "Kingdom Coming"

Oh! Massa Greeley he lubbed de nigger,
And he lubbed him mighty well,
When he was no broader and no bigger
Dan de clapper of de bell.
He said de nigger should be free,
And, glory! here we am!

O, golly! he made de darkey happy
As a quart of apple jam.

From *Greeley & Brown Campaign Songster.*

Other songs addressed themselves to workers (referring to Greeley as "the poor mechanic's friend"), Civil War veterans, the poor, the South, and the foreign-born, most especially the Irish. The following song even claimed that Greeley was of Irish ancestry, although the first American Greeley was Zaccheus Greeley, who came from England in 1640.

THEN IT'S IRISHMEN, WHAT ARE YOU DOING?

Tune: "Rosin the Beau"

Then it's Irishmen, what are you doing?
Wid' laggin' and hangin' around,
Can't yer see that it's ould Horace Greeley
That's onward to Washington bound.

Chorus:
To Ireland he's always been friendly,
None more so in this mighty land,
Then, Irishmen, rally around him,
Let's turn to and give him a hand.

It's not long ago, ye remimber,
When Ireland was starved by a drought,
In all the whole land not a pratie
To put in the poor children's mouth. *(Cho.)*

Who was it that called to the Yankees,
To send them a bountiful store,
'Twas the noble old man of Chappaqua,
That sent over food to each door.

A ship, it was filled with provisions,
And o'er the broad sea it set sail,
'Twas the words of the man of Chappaqua,
For suffering never did fail. *(Cho.)*

Come rally a stroke for old Greeley,
A stroke 'g'in corruption and fraud,
Let Irishmen rally forever
For Greeley, it's all come aboard.

When Horace is sated so snugly,
Way down in the White House away,
Should England git up on her ugly,
You mind it, she'll just hev to pay. *(Cho.)*

No blood of the Cockney's in Greeley,
His ancestors are Irish clean through,
They've entailed a love for bright honor,
Though born 'neath the red, white and blue.

Then, once again, Irishmen, rally,
United, my boys, just for fun,
We cannot elect a poor paddy,
But only his gallant grandson.

Final Chorus:
Then rally, come Irishmen, rally,
And vote for old Ireland's best friend,
If ever again she is starving,
Another good ship he will sind.

From *The Horace Greeley Campaign Songster.*

The Democratic Party had gone for Greeley, not without much anguish considering his past hostility, but not all Democrats accepted the decision. One group of dissident Democrats, unhappy with the selection, met in Louisville under the aegis of the "Straight-Out Democrats" and nominated a slate of Charles O'Conor and John Quincy Adams. Despite the refusal of the nominees, the ticket appeared on the ballot in twenty-three states, although in no case did they draw enough votes to affect the outcome. Among the few mementoes of that abbreviated undertaking was the following campaign song, which dismissed Greeley's followers as soreheads. "Sorehead" was a term generally applied to party bolters. Free-Soilers had the label in 1848, and it was a natural to apply to the Liberal Republicans of 1872, who were accused of refusing to accept the majority decision of their party.

STRAIGHT-OUT DEMOCRAT

Tune: "Rosin the Beau"

We never took stock in H. Greeley,
Though Baltimore took him in tow,
We heard that our leaders had sold us,
But we never took stock in that "show."

Chorus:
The ticket that's honest we'll honor,
And that's the straight ticket, you know,
We would like to have Charley O'Conor,
For O'Conor and Adams we'll go.

'Twas said the old party no longer
Was worthy of having a head,
But we'll show the sick soreheads we're stronger,
When Liberals and soreheads are dead.

Then let Greeley go to the dickens,
We'll show him he's on the wrong track;
Too soon he has counted his chickens,
For Louisville hurts Chappaquack.

We will never desert the great party
That stands for Democracy true;
We'll vote on the 5th of November,
For Charley and John Quincy, too.

Quoted in Spaeth, Sigmund, *Read 'Em and Weep,* Halcyon House Publishers, New York, 1926.

Despite the defections and divisions, the Republican campaign strategists planned for the election with supreme confidence in Grant's continuing popularity. If corruption was in the air, so was prosperity, and the new leaders of the Republican Party had unlimited funds and the support of the biggest business interests to help them spread the word for Grant's re-election. In a time when memories of the war were still fresh, Grant still symbolized the Union cause and the legacy of Lincoln. Many a voter could easily echo the sentiments of this typical Grant refrain:

We'll vote for Grant again, my boys,
We'll vote for Grant again;
United North, South, East and West,
We'll vote for Grant again.

From original song, "We'll vote for Grant Again," by James F. Keegan and Arthur Percy, pub. by Oliver Ditson Co., Boston, 1872.

Greeley was a natural target for Republican satire, and the party lyricists enjoyed a field day at old Horace's expense. His personal habits were salaciously detailed in an effort to depict the man who was one of the foremost intellectuals of his day as some kind of quixotic faddist who probably wouldn't be able to find his way to Washington in the unlikely event of his election. And despite Greeley's record as an antislavery crusader from way back, he was labeled a "doughface" traitor and a friend of secession, largely because of his intercession on behalf of Jefferson Davis. In 1865, Greeley, along with some others, signed a $100,000 bail fund to secure the release from prison of Jefferson Davis. Greeley believed that the times required a spirit of reconciliation, which the continued imprisonment of Davis worked against. His action created a storm of controversy, hurt the circulation of the *Tribune*, and inspired demonstrations at which Greeley was hung in effigy.

Tune: "Kingdom Coming"

Say, Union boys, have you seen old Greeley
With the dough upon his face?
He has left the good old Union Party,
And taken Jeff Davis' place.
  The Union Greeley, ha! ha!
  The secesh Greeley, ho! ho!
The "Anything to Beat Grant" Greeley —
But he'll find he can't win so.

He went from New York on to Richmond
For to go Jeff Davis' bail;
He got hold then of the secesh feelings;
But the hold was on the tail.
  For a better hold, ha! ha!
  He had to bolt, ho! ho!
From the good and true old Union Party,
But he'll find he can't win so.

From *National Republican Grant & Wilson Campaign Song Book.*

The following song for Grant and his new running mate, Senator Henry Wilson of Massachusetts, attacked Greeley as a make-believe farmer, a foolish author, and an advocate of dangerous utopian schemes that would subvert society. Among Greeley's "causes" was his espousal of Fourierism, an early nineteenth-century scheme of utopian socialism based on the ideas of Charles Fourier, a Frenchman, who projected the model of a small commune. On the basis of these ideas, the experimental community, Brook Farm, was organized,

to which Greeley contributed money. Among the charges brought against the Farm were that members of its community practiced "free love." Some of Greeley's opponents even linked the settlement at Brook Farm with the radical communes organized in a number of French cities in the wake of the Franco-Prussian War. These local governments, strongly influenced by Marxist ideas, attempted a great variety of economic reforms and radical social changes before they were suppressed.

HURRAH! HURRAH FOR GRANT AND WILSON!

Tune: "John Brown's Body"

We'll hang the "Lib-'ral" Gree-ley on a so-ur ap-ple tree, Because he bailed Jeff Da-vis and he set the trai-tor free; He
nev-er can be pres-i-dent, as you can plain-ly see, As we go march-ing
on. Hur-rah! Hur-rah for Grant and Wil-son, Hur-rah! Hur-rah for Grant and
Wil-son, Hur-rah! Hur-rah for Grant and Wil-son, As we go march-ing on.

The Soreheads and Copperheads at Cincinnati quoth—
"We'll beat 'the man on horseback!'" and they sealed it with an oath;
But wait until November, and he'll surely beat them both,
    As we go marching on.

The Cincinnati thimble-riggers think they've hit the plan,
To cheat the common people into voting for their man,
But when the votes are counted, General Grant will lead the van,
    As we go marching on.

This Fourier-free-love Greeley, with his "triple sheet" Tribune,
A-blowing for "protection" and the wicked French Commune,
To win the votes of Democrats he must sing another tune,
    As he goes marching on.

He's a make-believe old farmer, and he wrote a foolish book,
Which now they say will win him votes from every farming nook—
They'll find the people never bite at such a naked hook,
    As they go marching on.

The people can't be cheated by the color of his coat,
He's sailing up Salt River since he fairly got afloat,
"The Cincinnati Platform" is the title of his boat,
    As he goes marching on.

From *National Republican Grant & Wilson Campaign Song Book.*

Greeley's durable trademark, the "old white hat," provided additional grist for the Republican mill.

OBITUARY FOR HORACE GREELEY

Tune: "Auld Lang Syne"

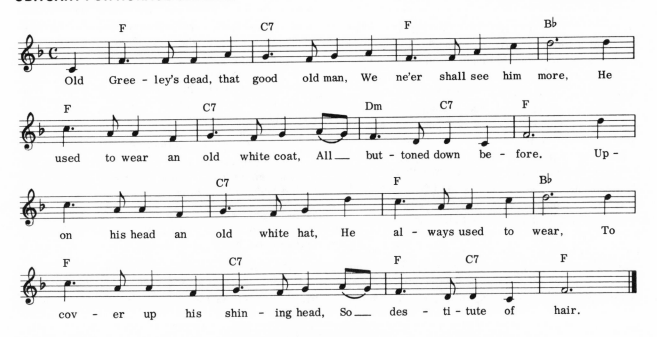

Old Greeley's dead, that good old man, We ne'er shall see him more, He used to wear an old white coat, All__ but-toned down be-fore. Up-on his head an old white hat, He al-ways used to wear, To cov-er up his shin-ing head, So__ des-ti-tute of hair.

A pair of massive spectacles
He wore upon his nose,
Which made him look benevolent,
As everybody knows.
He was a great newspaperman,
And published the *Tribune*,
And every day, or month, at least,
He always changed his tune.

From *National Republican Grant
& Wilson Campaign Song Book.*

The Long Count of '76

If the aroma of malfeasance pervaded the atmosphere of Grant's first term, his second four years in office reeked of corruption on a giant scale. Scandal after scandal, touching almost every member of the Administration, was revealed to a public whose sensibilities were likewise conditioned by an end to the "prosperity" of the earlier period. The collapse of Jay Cooke's financial empire which touched off the Panic of 1873 had ushered in a fierce depression. While the country agonized over lack of work, mortgage foreclosures and all the other effects of economic disaster, the revelations of the notorious Whiskey Ring in which the government had been defrauded of more than $4 million sent shock waves through the nation. One exposure followed hard on the heels of another. The secretary of war, General William Belknap, was shown to have amassed a fortune through the sale of army trading posts. The ambassador to Britain, General Robert Schenck, beat a hasty retreat from London after having publicly sponsored a fraudulent mining stock. The president's private secretary, Orville Babcock, narrowly escaped conviction on charges of having been the main organizer of the Whiskey Ring. And Speaker of the House James G. Blaine, involved in shady dealings with the Union Pacific Railroad, managed to escape exposure only by the most adroit oratorical legerdemain.

The depression and the scandals, plus the opportunistic Republican policy in the South designed as a maneuver to control the votes of the newly enfranchised ex-slaves, revived a Democratic Party which only four years before had been reduced to nominating one of its staunchest foes.

Rallying their ranks under the heady banner of Reform, the Democrats nominated two governors as their candidates—Samuel J. Tilden of New York and Thomas A. Hendricks of Indiana.

Tilden's credentials as a popular figure had not been put to many tests. Samuel J. Tilden, a multimillionaire whose fortune had been amassed in railroad manipulation, was a corporation lawyer and long-time power in New York Democratic politics. But he had played a leading role in exposing the machinations of the New York City Tweed Ring, on the strength of which he had won the governorship in 1874. As an exposer of corruption within Party ranks, Tilden was undoubtedly looked upon as one whose honesty could not be questioned and the one Democrat who could use even his own Party's shortcomings as an appeal—no mean accomplishment in conducting a reform campaign. Proclaiming that "Honest T. is the best Policy," Democratic supporters sang:

The night of gloom is gliding out,
Forth breaks the rosy day,
And Tilden is the sun of hope,
That lights the nation's way,
The Empire State will lead the van,
To clear the dismal storm,
For through the length of our proud land
Comes Tilden and Reform.

From original song, "Tilden and Reform," by William H. Long and J. G. Kuhn, pub. by H. T. Martin, Parkersburg, W.Va., 1876.

They sang the praises of "Honest Sam Tilden" and in one interesting song, even made out a case for the notorious Boss Tweed:

THE TIMES ARE SADLY OUT OF JOINT   Words: Samuel N. Mitchell   Music: H. A. Selington

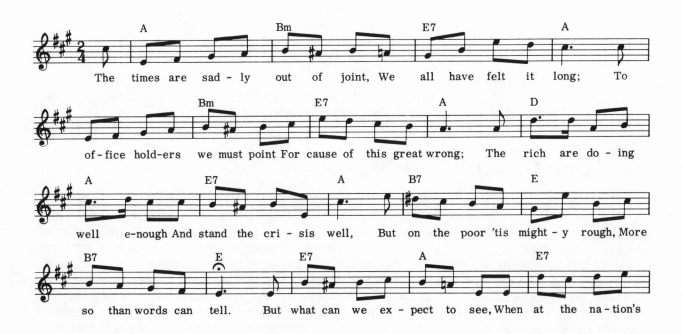

The times are sad-ly out of joint, We all have felt it long; To of-fice hold-ers we must point For cause of this great wrong; The rich are do-ing well e-nough And stand the cri-sis well, But on the poor 'tis might-y rough, More so than words can tell. But what can we ex-pect to see, When at the na-tion's

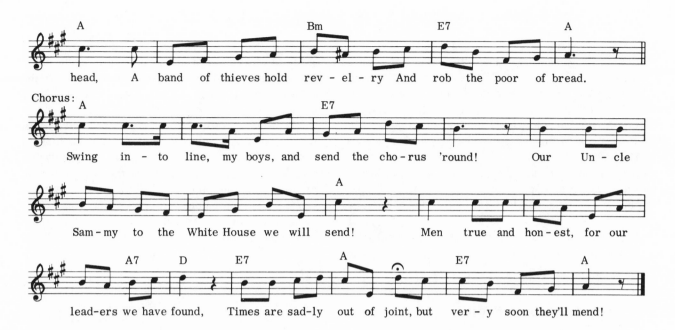

head, A band of thieves hold rev - el - ry And rob the poor of bread.

Chorus:
Swing in - to line, my boys, and send the cho - rus 'round! Our Un - cle

Sam - my to the White House we will send! Men true and hon - est, for our

lead-ers we have found, Times are sad-ly out of joint, but ver - y soon they'll mend!

The Whiskey Rings have flourished well
And made officials rich,
Belknap has nothing more to sell,
So he goes in the ditch;
Investigations are the rage
To find out what they can,
But all the wise men of the age
Can't tell an honest man.
The poor man has no chance at all
In this sad state of things,
He's pushed completely to the wall
By all these thieving rings.

Though Tweed did things we did not like,
He was the poor man's friend,
And when he ruled, men did not strike,
Nor ask his friends to lend.
He never stooped to offer men
One dollar-sixty a day,
But every honest lab'ror then
Was getting decent pay.
Now that the old man's on the wing,
We state this as quite sure,
Though he was boss of a bad ring,
He did not hate the poor.

As things look very bad indeed,
One course to us is clear:
Let none but true men take the lead,
And thieves send to the rear.
Our people are now quite intent
To make a change all 'round,
And have for our next President
A man that's pure and sound.
We want no one whose love of gain
Makes him accept the place,
And whose relations are a stain
And national disgrace.

From the original sheet music published
by J. L. Peters, New York, 1876.

There were, of course, other questions, but one can hardly blame the Democrats for pursuing the two—depression and corruption—on which their opponents were most vulnerable. The songs were simple and to the point. The best of them captured the spirit of the times and used melodies like "Hold the Fort," the recently composed and incredibly popular religious hymn. The hymn was composed in 1868 by an Illinois Sunday School teacher, Philip Paul Bliss. It was based on an actual incident from the Civil War in which Sherman had used the phrase. The song was popularized by the famous gospel singer, Ira D. Sanky. (For a more detailed account of the song's history, see the author's book, *Songs of the Civil War,* Columbia University Press, 1960.)

The following Democratic campaign song, to the tune of "Hold the Fort," focused on the corruption in the Grant Administration and pointed out, quite correctly, that honest officials who exposed government graft were dismissed from their posts. One such victim was Grant's secretary of the treasury, Benjamin H. Bristow, who was fired after he exposed the Whiskey Ring.

The song also trumpeted the personal integrity of the Democratic candidate and even tried to make a virtue of the fact that Tilden was a life-long bachelor. Why this should have, in the song's words, made him immune to "tempting women" bespeaks an incredible cynicism which could have been based only on the belief that the voting public was as naive as the literature it read.

HOLD THE FORT FOR TILDEN

Tune: "Hold the Fort"

See corruption boldly stalking
In our Congress Hall;
In our Presidential Mansion,
Tainting great and small.

Alternate Chorus:
"Hold the fort for we are coming,"
Hear the people cry;
"We will vote for Tilden, Hendricks,
Honest men we'll try."

See the rings, the combinations,
Whiskey, railroad, land;
Wicked schemes for 'peculations,
Rife on every hand.

See the shameful defalcations
In our savings banks,
Robbing poor men, widows, orphans,
By their thieving pranks.

See our commerce, credit sinking,
Factories are still;
Workmen idle, begging, starving,
Suffering every ill.

See our taxes, swelling, rising,
Money almost gone;
Produce falling, no one buying,
Farmers' faces long.

See the host of office-holders,
Honest be they can't,
For if honest, faithful, worthy,
They're turned out by Grant.

See the office-holders' ticket,
Running in Grant's track;
If elected, "no removals,"
No Reform in fact.

Come, then, voters, come go with us,
Vote for Uncle Sam;
He has throttled many evils;
Yes, he has, and can.

If you want to see times better,
Prosperous times again,
Rally 'round our Reform Banner,
Vote our Reform Men.

Uncle Sam is like Old Hickory,
Firm and true as steel,
His true heart it has no lover,
But our country's weal.

No seductive woman tempter
Can draw him aside,
His loved wife is our whole country,
She's his only bride.

Ho! Ye voters, pure and honest,
Rally with us then;
Vote for Tilden, vote for Hendricks,
Vote for honest men.

From *The Illustrated Campaign Tilden Song and Joke Book*.

While Tilden and his supporters shouted "reform," the Republicans reached back into their storehouse of political knowledge and "waved the bloody shirt." It was a phrase that would dominate the politics of the next two decades, a panegyric reminder of the agonies of the Civil War, a constant repetition of the charge that the Democratic Party was the party of "treason" and "rebellion." (For an interesting history of the phrase with many examples of its usage, see *Dictionary of American Political Terms*, Sperber and Trittschuh.)

The Republicans came up with a candidate untouched by the scandals of Washington, the innocuous Governor of Ohio, Rutherford B. Hayes ("a third-rate nonentity, whose only recommendation is that he is obnoxious to no one," according to Henry Adams). Dismayed at the Convention's choice, Joseph Pulitzer wrote in the *New York World:* "Hayes has never stolen. Good God, has it come to this?"

The answer is that it had. Clearly Republican hearts in '76 were with James G. Blaine, the Con-

gressional spellbinder who had literally orated his way out of serious charges of malfeasance in office. And Blaine almost got the nomination at that. But wiser heads, those more concerned with victory than personal loyalty, prevailed. Actually, Hayes had other "qualities" than his neuter image to recommend him. He had served in the war, and while his record was undistinguished, he wound up a Major General of Volunteers, no small asset in a campaign which would attempt to focus attention on past heroics rather than present embarrassments.

Song after song for Hayes and his running mate, William Almon Wheeler, a New York congressman, invoked the memories of '61. "The Boys in Blue" were serenaded as never before. Tilden was "Rebel Sam," while "Copperhead," "Confederate thieves" and "rebel traitor" were among the milder epithets applied to the Democrats. Such charges against Tilden were grossly unfair. The Democratic standard bearer had been opposed to the war, but once the fighting began, he gave unstinting support to the Union cause.

OUR WATCHWORD

Words: James Nicholson

Tune: "Hold the Fort"

See the Union ranks are moving
Over all the land,
In the front stand Hayes and Wheeler
Taking the command.

Chorus:
Loyal men throughout the nation,
Strike for Liberty;
Now the names of Hayes and Wheeler
Shall our watchword be.

Let our swords be turned to plowshares,
Let our sabres rust,
But the men allied with treason
We will never trust.

By the blood of half a million
Noble Union men,
We shall not resign the nation
To our foes again.

From *Hayes and Wheeler Song Book.*

Tune: "When Johnny Comes Marching Home Again"

We know in Eighteen-Sixty-One,
   Hurrah, hurrah!
The side that Tilden then was on,
   Hurrah, hurrah!
By orphans' tears and widows' sighs,
Freemen for Hays and Wheeler rise,
For Hayes and Wheeler—we are marching on.

From a campaign broadside.

"The Boys in Blue" not only "waved the bloody shirt" but turned the corruption issue around by reminding voters of the shady manipulations of two prominent Democratic politicos—William Marcy Tweed and John Morrissey. Tweed, head of the notorious "Boss" Tweed Ring in New York City, was the most powerful man in New York politics for two decades. The fraud and graft which the Ring perpetrated on the city has been estimated at no less than $30 million and as high as $200 million. The ring was broken in 1871 but its political reverberations were felt for many years. Morrissey, one-time claimant to the world's heavyweight boxing championship, was a legendary figure as a gambler, politician and prizefighter. He served two terms in Congress and became enormously wealthy as the result of financial speculation. He was a well-known "behind the scenes" power in New York politics.

THE BOYS IN BLUE

Words: T. K. Preuss

Tune: "Wearing of the Green"

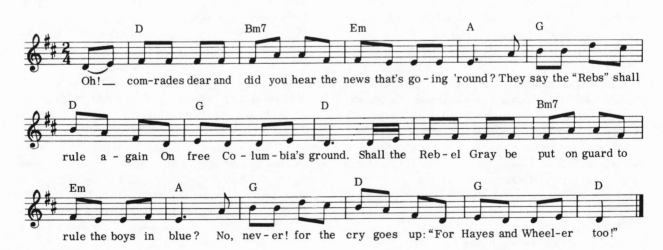

Oh!__ com-rades dear and did you hear the news that's go-ing 'round? They say the "Rebs" shall rule a-gain On free Co-lum-bia's ground. Shall the Reb-el Gray be put on guard to rule the boys in blue? No, nev-er! for the cry goes up: "For Hayes and Wheel-er too!"

Chorus (to the last eight measures of the verse):
For Hayes, and Wheeler too,
For Hayes, and Wheeler too,
We'll cast our vote—the *Boys in Blue*
For Hayes, and Wheeler too!

We staked our lives and fortunes
All for our country and its laws;
We fought the fight of Liberty,
And saved the Union cause.
We want no men to rule us now
But the loyal, staunch and true;
And "Hayes and Wheeler" is the card
To win the *Boys in Blue.*

We want no worn-out "party hacks,"
But men of spotless worth,
Whose record shines out clean and clear,
From their very day of birth.
No Tilden, Tweed or Morrissey
For the brave old *Boys in Blue;*
But every "mother's son" cries out
For Hayes and Wheeler too.

From a campaign broadside.

One somewhat desultory trend in campaign songwriting began to evidence itself in the 1876 campaign. With the growing involvement of professional songwriters in the campaign song market, a certain arch cuteness began to manifest itself, affecting the titles, the lyrics and even the musical style. In earlier campaigns, the songs had come largely from amateurs or from songwriters who were genuinely committed to their candidates. But the Civil War had shown that there was a healthy market in "political" and patriotic songs. Some songwriters began, as a matter of professional enterprise, to write songs for *both* candidates. Along with this trend, and likewise reflecting currents developing in popular song in general, there was a growing emphasis on puns, alliteration and other forms of word-play. Such songs as "We'll Go for Hayes! We'll Wheel 'er in on Time," gaily illustrated with Hayes perched on the front end of a wheelbarrow pushed along by Wheeler headed for the White House, were typical of the genre. "We'll Blow Our Horn for Hayes," proclaimed another of these, while a third labored over the image of an "honest load of Hayes" being rolled into Washington.

It was, in short, a campaign of the sheerest hypocrisy. The Republicans, caught in the public pocket almost to the man, waved the flag and sang the good old songs in a frank effort to divert attention from the real problems of the age. The Democrats, their own party dominated by the big city political bosses, yelled "Reform" and nominated a man accused of business manipulations that dwarfed the petty piracy of the Republican officeholders. It turned out to be the most disputed election in American history, Tilden's 250,000-vote popular majority negated by manipulation of the electoral college ballots to provide Hayes with a one-vote victory two days before his inauguration.

Garfield This Time

Rutherford B. Hayes had pledged himself to a single term in office, and much to everyone's relief, kept his word. He hadn't turned out quite as good a party man as the Republicans had hoped and had even made a few genuine efforts at reform. But time was running out on the Grand Old Party and the soberer political leaders realized that a juggling of faces would probably help the Republicans repair an image which daily grew more disreputable. And so they reached down into their storehouse of relatively untarnished political personalities and came up with James A. Garfield of Ohio, a genuine war hero and one-time major general in the Union Army. Garfield had been only slightly scarred by the scandals of the previous decade. In any event, he had a reputation for honesty and a fine war record, and he was a skillful politician from a key state, a good enough combination to renew Republican hopes after the near-disaster of 1876.

The Democrats countered with a military figure of their own, General Winfield S. Hancock, a hero of two (count them, two) wars and with no previous political experience.

It was a thoroughly predictable campaign, generating little excitement. The Republicans once again waved the bloody shirt, although with some dwindling enthusiasm, it must be noted, while the Democrats came out four-square against corruption.

The professional songwriters, reflecting the general amorphous air of the campaign, were more concerned with selling sheet music than electing a candidate. The busiest of the lot was Thomas P. Westendorf, somewhat better known as the composer-lyricist of "I'll Take You Home Again, Kathleen," who generously penned campaign songs for both Garfield and Hancock. "Beneath the Dear Old Flag Again" celebrated Garfield's war record, while "When Hancock Takes the Chair" did the same for the rotund old general. A little more pointed was Westendorf's minstrel dialect ditty, "Dey's All Put On De Blue," which made its contribution to the bloody shirt aspect of the campaign:

Marster he hab gone and jine a sort ob Yankee crowd,
Dat talks about de stars and stripes and hollers awful loud;
Dey calls demselves de Hancock men and says dey's veterans too,
And now in place of Rebel gray dey wears de Yankee blue.

Once again, the "good old bugle" was sounded, memories of "camp grounds" and the "march through Georgia" invoked. "To give the Solid South a chance of adapting a favorite air to modern circumstances," Republicans wrote:

Tune: "The Battle Cry of Freedom"

We'll repudiate our debts, boys,
We've borrowed from the North,
Shouting the battle cry of freedom,
We will burn the public schools
And we'll drive the niggers forth,
Shouting the battle cry of freedom.

'Tis slavery forever, hurrah, boys, hurrah!
Down with the Yankees, up with the bars;
While we ostracize the loyal and murder thousands more,
Shouting the battle cry of freedom.

From *Garfield and Arthur Campaign Songs.*

Another in a similar vein went:

ALL ARE READY FOR THE FRAY

Words: F. M. Clark
Tune: "Tramp, Tramp, Tramp"

In the Union ranks we stand
With our comrades brave and grand,
Touching elbow as we march upon the foe,
Every heart is light and gay,
All are ready for the fray,
That shall sweep the Democrats way down below.

Tramp, tramp, tramp, the boys are marching,
Onward for the cause of right,
And with Garfield at our head, we to victory are led,
While the rebel crew are beaten out of sight.

They now wear the "blue," we know,
But it is the same old foe,
That once fired upon our flag in Charleston Bay,
But that trick, it is too thin,
Like the ass in lion skin,
Their long ears stick out and give the thing away.

From *Garfield and Arthur Campaign Songs.*

The best song of this genre came from the singing of the Central Quartette of Chicago:

WHEN THE JOHNNIES GET INTO POWER

Words: Anonymous
Tune: "When Johnny Comes Marching Home Again"

When the Johnnies get into power again,
Aha! Aha!
When the Johnnies get into power again,
Aha! Aha!
Our laws they'll jeer, our flags they'll flout,
They'll turn our officers all out,
And we'll all wear gray
When the Johnnies get into power.

Oh, won't they hold a jubilee,
Aha! Aha!
The darkeys they'll no more be free,
Aha! Aha!
We'll pay their claims, we'll foot their bills,
We'll toe the mark or make our wills,
And we'll all wear gray
When the Johnnies get into power.

116

Jeff Davis' name they'll loudly praise,
　Aha! Aha!
And Lincoln's tomb will be disgraced,
　Aha! Aha!
Our nation's flag will lose its stars,
Its stripes they'll change to rebel bars,
And we'll all wear gray
When the Johnnies get into power.

You bet that day of jubilee,
　Hurrah! Hurrah!
The Johnnies never more will see,
　Hurrah! Hurrah!
We have the pluck, the Yankee wit,
We'll make the gray-backed rebels "git,"
And we'll all be born fools,
If the Johnnies get into power.

Then cheer for Garfield, three times three,
　Hurrah! Hurrah!
For Arthur, too, and victory,
　Hurrah! Hurrah!
We'll put them in, there is no doubt,
We'll keep the gray-backed Johnnies out,
And there'll be no day
When the Johnnies get into power.

From *Garfield and Arthur Campaign Songs.*

When they weren't waving the bloody shirt, Republican songwriters wrote scores of those innocuous paeans to "Garfield and Arthur, the People's Choice," the likes of which appear with cloying regularity every four years and which are hard-pressed to inspire even the most ardent of the party faithful. In the history of campaign song literature, it is hard to imagine a single candidate not celebrated as "brave," "true" or "honest." And when songwriters work that vein out, they all seem to switch to verses which invariably begin, "From Maine to San Diego," and after managing to bring in Florida, Texas, Oregon and various other geographical extremities collapse into a conclusion designed to convince the listener that only a handful of aliens and mentally deranged persons will fail to vote for the particular nominee. The Garfield literature was no exception to this trend, and most of the surviving examples are each as undistinguished as the other.

One interesting phenomenon, however, was the appearance for the first time, of campaign songs in a foreign language. The music publishing firm of Kunkel Brothers in Saint Louis, where a large German immigrant population had settled, produced a pair of bilingual songs, one for Garfield and the other for Hancock.

THE VETERAN'S VOTE
(DIE STIMME DES VETERANEN)

Words: I. D. Foulon　　　　Music: Charles Kunkel

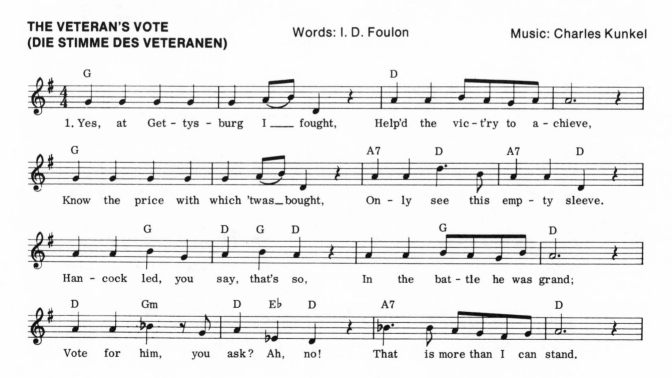

1. Yes, at Get-tys-burg I ___ fought, Help'd the vic-t'ry to a-chieve,
Know the price with which 'twas bought, On-ly see this emp-ty sleeve.
Han-cock led, you say, that's so, In the bat-tle he was grand;
Vote for him, you ask? Ah, no! That is more than I can stand.

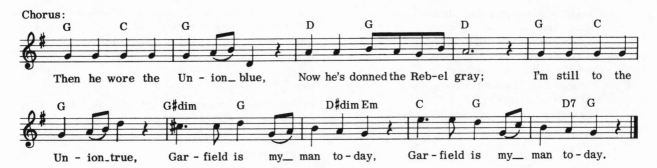

Chorus:

Then he wore the Un-ion blue, Now he's donned the Reb-el gray; I'm still to the

Un-ion true, Gar-field is my man to-day, Gar-field is my man to-day.

Ich in Gettysburg mich schlug,
Half erringen jenen Sieg,
Und die Kosten auch mit trug,
Wenn ich auch kein'n Nickel krieg.
Hancock fuehrte an, du sagst,
Im gefecht ein groser Mann,
Ob ich fuer ihn stimm', du fragst?
Nein, o nein, das geht nicht an.
Damals trug er Union Blau,
Jetzt liebt er Rebellen Grau.

Shortly afterwards, Kunkel Brothers came out with a "reply" to the above on behalf of Hancock:

THE SOLDIER'S VOTE
(DES SOLDATEN STIMME)

Words: M. Niedner   Music: Jacob Kunkel

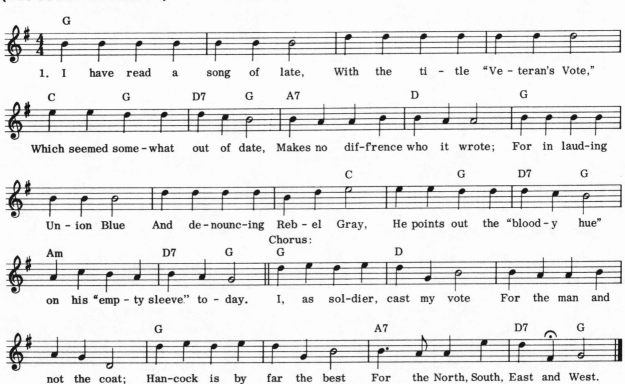

1. I have read a song of late, With the ti-tle "Ve-teran's Vote,"

Which seemed some-what out of date, Makes no dif-frence who it wrote; For in laud-ing

Un-ion Blue And de-nounc-ing Reb-el Gray, He points out the "blood-y hue"

Chorus:

on his "emp-ty sleeve" to-day. I, as sol-dier, cast my vote For the man and

not the coat; Han-cock is by far the best For the North, South, East and West.

Als ich juengst ein Liedchen lass,
"Stimm des Veteran" es hiess,
Dacht' ich, der die Zeit vergass,
Wer die Worte von sich liess;
Denn im Lob von Union Blau,
Schmoehen der Rebellen Grau,
Reisst er alte Wunden auf,
Giesst dann Vitriol noch drauf.
Als Soldat geh' ich fuer'n Mann,
Kehr' mich nicht an Rock und Ort;
Hancock Alles ein'gen kann,
Ost und West und Sued und Nord.

Considering that Charles Kunkel wrote the music for the Garfield song and Jacob Kunkel for the Hancock song, and that the Kunkel Brothers published both, one might infer some profound ideological split in the Kunkel family. It is doubtful, however, that any such high drama was involved. It is more likely that, in keeping with the custom of the day, local poets came to the Kunkels with their rhymes and engaged them to supply the tunes. Many music publishers provided just such a service, charging the lyricist for the work, and also arranging to have the song published and copyrighted by their own firm.

The 1880 campaign was also distinguished by being the first to employ Gilbert and Sullivan on behalf of political candidates in this country. *Pinafore* had premiered in the States in 1879, a year after its London stage debut, and almost overnight the whole country was familiar with the galaxy of songs which that operetta introduced. The author of the following parody is not known, but his sense of timing was clearly apropos:

NOW I AM THE LEADER OF THE DEMOCRACEE

Tune: "When I Was a Lad" from *H.M.S. Pinafore*

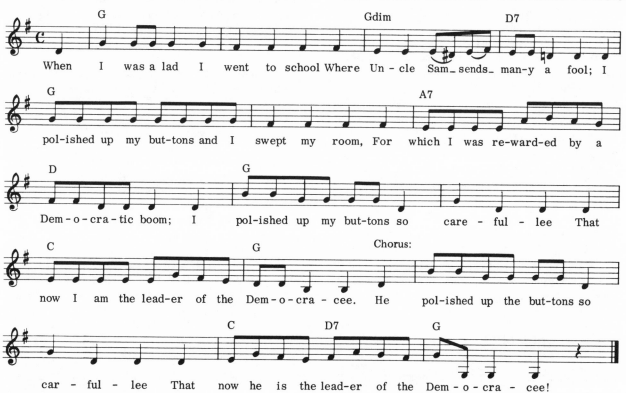

When I was a lad I went to school Where Uncle Sam sends many a fool; I polished up my buttons and I swept my room, For which I was rewarded by a Democratic boom; I polished up my buttons so carefulee That now I am the leader of the Democracee. He polished up the buttons so carefulee That now he is the leader of the Democracee!

In right-about-face I made such a mark,
That they gave me the post of an Adjutant's clerk,
I served the Ad. with a smile so bland,
And I copied all the letters in a big round hand.
In right-about-face I was so free,
That they made me the leader of the Democracee.

As a white cadet, I made such a name,
That a pet of the South I soon became;
I wore white gloves and a bran' new suit,
At the bottom of my class at the Institute.
So they dropped all their issues and nominated me,
And now I am the leader of the Democracee.

119

My political ignorance became so great,
That they took me up as a candidate;
So why shouldn't I obey the party's "call,"
Since I shall never have to think for myself at all?
I knew so little that they rewarded me,
By making me the leader of the Democracee.

Of civil life I knew no more
Than Tilden knows of military lore,
So they abandoned him and his great "reform,"
And fled to me—"any port in a storm!"
They abandoned all their leaders and begged of me
To come and be the leader of the Democracee.

In the Union war I fought so well
That my name is greeted with the "rebel yell."
Of a "man on horseback" they had such fear
That they nominated me—which is rather queer.
'Twas a right-about-face to nominate me,
And now I am the leader of the Democracee.

Now, Americans all, whoever you may be,
I'll give you a bit of strategee;
Never go to any but a military school,
And be careful to be guided by this Democratic rule:
Keep away from the polls, and let politics be,
And you all may be leaders of the Democracee.

From *Garfield and Arthur Campaign Song Book.*

Against the Republican charge that Hancock was a "southern" candidate, the Democrats responded with pleas for national unity. Hancock, they said, could unite the nation, since he had proven himself militarily as a foe of slavery and he had also held out the olive branch to the defeated South. Indeed, as military commander of Louisiana and Texas after the War, Hancock had demonstrated the most liberal policy of reconciliation of almost any Union administrator. His "forgiveness" of the rebels outraged blacks and Republican "carpetbaggers," who saw the old Democratic regime coming back to power with the connivance of the Union military forces.

In the campaign of 1880, the Democrats attacked the Republican "Stalwarts"—typified by Blaine, Grant and Garfield, among others—who continued to pursue a "hard" line against the South. The "bloody shirt" themes were, in general, ascribed to "Stalwarts," most of whom were motivated by opportunistic reasons, but who also reflected a widespread sentiment which genuinely feared (and with good reason) a resurgence of the Southern slavocracy. In the spring of 1880, the British magazine *Punch* carried the following limerick:

There was an old stalwart named Blaine,
Who hailed from the region of Maine.
    When he felt badly hurt
    He would cry "Bloody Shirt"—
And slay over the already slain.

Typical of the Democratic campaign songs summoning the party faithful to do battle against the "Stalwarts" was the following, written by George Hartwell:

Our Nation's laws we will obey,
And bury the bloody shirt;
Cement the Union north and South,
Sweep out the stalwart dirt.
We'll have no hatred in the land,
Nor strife of any form;
We'll rally round the dear old flag
For Hancock and Reform.

One popular Hancock song of the campaign directly addressed itself to the "bloody shirt" theme in the name of national unity:

THE BLEACHED SHIRT Words and music: William M. Pegram

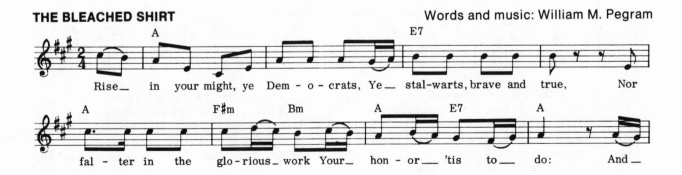

Rise in your might, ye Dem-o-crats, Ye stal-warts, brave and true, Nor fal-ter in the glo-rious work Your hon-or 'tis to do: And

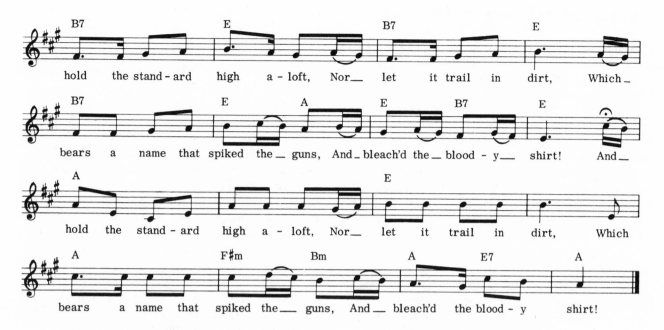

hold the stand-ard high a-loft, Nor— let it trail in dirt, Which—

bears a name that spiked the— guns, And— bleach'd the— blood-y— shirt! And—

hold the stand-ard high a-loft, Nor— let it trail in dirt, Which

bears a name that spiked the— guns, And— bleach'd the blood-y shirt!

No need have we to offer proof
Of that unsullied name,
The country, North, South, East and West,
Glows with its honored fame;
For perjury and jobs and bribes
It cannot be impeached,
One charge it owns, it spiked the guns,
The bloody shirt, it bleached.

The ruby ensign now no more
Republicans can wave,
Who, to attain ignoble ends,
Would rob the soldier's grave.
Instead of war's dread emblem now,
The flag of Peace we'll flirt,
Since Hancock's name has spiked the guns,
And bleached the bloody shirt!

No more we'll hear of "solid South"
Or "rebel brigadiers,"
They're "solid" for "one country,"
And of loyal men are peers;
The treasured goal for which they strove
At last, thank God, is reached,
For Hancock now has spiked the guns,
The bloody shirt is bleached!

From the original sheet music, pub. by Otto Sutro, Baltimore, Md., 1880.

Democrats may have hoped that the "war issue" had been bleached, but they were hardly prepared to stop waving their own banner of "reform" while charging the Republicans with the full litany of crimes of fraud, corruption, graft and thievery. The fact is, the partisans of both reform as well as the "shirt-wavers" were addressing themselves to real questions, no matter how opportunistic their reasons. Under the guise of national unity and reconciliation, a new political and social reality was emerging in the South which had already forestalled and diverted many of the possibilities opened up by the defeat of the slave system. Institutionalized segregation, the elaborate system of Jim Crow and black disenfranchisement, and the historic exploitation of the people and the land of the South by huge plantation owners and the northern financial interests to which they were beholden were the fruits of the betrayal of "Reconstruction" which had been agreed to by both major parties. And corruption, despite the relative integrity of the Hayes Administration, was still rampant in American political life, although more circumspect since the giant scandals of the Grant years. But it was a corruption which permeated both parties and the entire system of government at every level.

The petty and massive scandals of the era have been documented in great detail in subsequent histories of the period. A full recounting would provide eloquent testimony to the unbounded inventiveness of man when confronted with the opportunity for pecuniary gain. No matter what manner of business the government engaged in—whether collecting excise taxes or selling franchises for Indian trading posts—someone had figured out a scheme for lining his own pockets. And the exposure of each new scandal uncovered still others, as the culprits compounded their misdeeds with fresh maneuvers to hide their activities. The general cynicism was so widespread, in fact, that many of the swindles were performed openly. One such was the notorious "salary grab" act of 1873 in which the Republicans not only raised salaries of officeholders in the federal government at a prodigious rate; the congressmen, with undisguised

glee, made their own substantial raise of $2,500 a year each retroactive for two years.

It was in this atmosphere, therefore, that Democrats continued to pursue the assorted evils of past administrations. The following song, which almost achieved the status of an "official" campaign song for Hancock, called the voters' attention to a startling, albeit abortive, misadventure of the Grant Administration. Among the schemes which never materialized during Grant's presidency but which came to light afterwards was a grandiose imperialist plan for the annexation of the island of Santo Domingo. Many Republican politicians had made sizable investments in the island in anticipation of future developments. The Panic of 1873 and the ensuing depression forced Grant to hold off on the plan.

The song, however, did not confine itself to cataloguing Republican misdemeanors but glorified the military exploits of General Hancock, who had played a key role in stemming the rebel advance at Gettysburg and halted Lee's army when a rout was imminent.

HANCOCK IS COMING!

Words: Major M. P. Low   Music: J. N. Pattison

He seized all their cannon and silenced their thunder,
And scattered their armies and put them to rout;
And now he is coming to free us from plunder,
And all "loyal" swindlers will be "mustered out."

Chorus for remaining verses:
Soldiers and patriots, lustily shout,
For Hancock is coming to muster them out.

St. Domingo a wonderful story is telling,
Astonishing statesmen at home and abroad!
While fraud and corruption are steadily swelling,
And perjury meets with official reward.

"Visiting Statesmen" and "cabinet robbers,"
And "Carpetbag Gov'nors" must face, right about,
And "whisky ring" rascals and "wood pavement jobbers,"
"Safe burglars" and "Navy thieves" he'll muster out!

"Returning board dodgers" and "back-salary grabbers,"
With "Indian traders" and "Mobilier scouts,"
With "Custom House bummers" and "cotton blade knabbers,"
And all Public Robbers will be mustered out!

From the original sheet music, which carries the following
legend: "Recommended and endorsed by the National Democratic Committee," and lists the names and home states of the
Committee members. Published by J. N. Pattison, New York,
1880.

Time for a Change

The Cleveland Campaigns of 1884, 1888, 1892

After twenty-four years of uninterrupted Republican rule, the Democrats' turn finally came in 1884. Twice before they had come close: in 1876 when the "long count" turned Tilden's apparent victory into defeat, and in 1880 when Garfield nosed out Hancock by a mere 10,000 votes in the popular count.

But in 1884, the currents of history veered toward the Democrats. The Republicans, burdened with President Arthur, who hadn't turned out nearly as "cooperative" as the party bosses had hoped, dumped their chieftain and turned instead to the Party's most popular figure, James G. Blaine, the famed "plumed knight" of Maine—so often the bridesmaid but never the bride.

The designation of Blaine as "the plumed knight" was made originally by Colonel Robert Ingersoll in his nominating speech at the 1876 Republican Convention, referring to Blaine's famous "defense" against charges of corruption on the floor of Congress: "Like an armed warrior, like a plumed knight, James G. Blaine marched down the halls of the American Congress and threw his shining lance full and fair against the brazen forehead of every defamer of his country and maligner of its honor."

The Democrats, meanwhile, had managed to produce a genuinely popular figure from out of their ranks, Grover Cleveland, one-term Governor of New York who had risen to national prominence on the strength of battles with party bosses and his exposure of fraudulent practices in the city of Buffalo, where he had served as sheriff and then mayor. "Public office is a public trust," Cleveland is credited with saying, and if ever a time was right for the image of the incorruptible statesman, 1884 was it.

But other factors were at work, too. The agrarian/populist wing of the Democratic Party, so antagonistic to business interests, had been safely contained by the party bosses. Grover Cleveland could say with complete assurance, as he did, "No harm shall come to any business interest as the result of administrative policy so long as I am President." Civil Service reform, the great "issue" of the era, was clearly in the best interests of a rapidly growing capitalist class which required a stable and reliable political apparatus to regulate trade, taxation and public facilities. In the 1880s, American corporate interests were playing for bigger stakes than the hasty profits to be won from whiskey rings or the sale of trading posts, although the "spoils system" was not without a resilience of its own. But corporations were now concerned with "higher" matters—with "protection," land accumulation, the vast markets to the West and the even greater potential in the rest of the hemisphere.

Despite past differences and a fiery rhetoric, the platforms of the Democrats and Republicans in the 1884 campaign could have been exchanged and no one would have known the difference.

The Democrats Get Their Chance

But "change" was called for. The country was tired of corruption, graft and scandal. The Grand Old Party, in offering Blaine, was promising a dreary repetition of the past. Cleveland, and his running mate, Thomas A. Hendricks, Governor of Indiana, seemed to represent a fresh spirit, a chance for a new start. A Democratic campaign song touched on the popular mood:

LET'S HAVE A CHANGE   Words and music: Thomas P. Culiar

We have grown so sick and tired__ of Re - pub - li - cans and fraud, We've re -
solv - ed they shall be fired from the na - tion's bed and board, And a -
long with man - y thou-sands, we are pray - ing to the Lord to__ let us have a
change, __ *Chorus:* Do you won - der, Do you won - der Is the thing ab - surd or strange? Af - ter
twen - ty years of plun - der, We should want a lit - tle change.

They have robbed the nation's pocket book for nearly twenty years,
And they've grown so fat and saucy, now they haven't any fears,
Hear the many thousands crying through this awful veil of tears,
    Good Lord, let's have a change.

They will talk of rebel brigadiers and wave the bloody shirt,
And of the gallant boys in blue, they make a mighty spurt,
But of course such talk is nonsense, they are only throwing dirt;
    Good Lord, let's have a change.

We demand the rights of freemen, and we'll not be bluffed again,
We mean to seat our candidates in spite of scheming men,
With Democrats to rule the land, we'll all be happy then;
    Good Lord, let's have a change.

From *Cleveland and Hendricks Songster.*

Democratic songwriters dredged up every fraud and scandal of the previous twenty years and turned them into roaring ditties. Blaine, as the acknowledged source of power in the Republican Party, was a prime target—and his own ventures into shady schemes were mercilessly brought out. Resurrected were the details of the exposure in 1876 of Blaine's dealings with the Union Pacific Railroad, a charge which he demagogically circumvented in a famous speech on the floor of Congress, but which (quite rightly, as it turns out) always left a lingering doubt in the public mind. The Democratic slogan for the 1884 campaign was: "Blaine, Blaine, James G. Blaine,/The Monumental Liar from the State of Maine!"

To the tune of an old popular air, the Democrats recited a litany of Blaine's transgressions, beginning with his role in a railroad bond scheme from which he had derived enormous profits. The song sarcastically described Blaine as a "Man of Letters," referring to a packet of letters written by Blaine which clearly exposed the part he had played in this shady transaction. Blaine wrote these letters to a Boston stockbroker by the name of Warren Fisher, and damaging testimony concerning their contents was given by James Mulligan, a bookkeeper, before a congressional committee. As revealed in later years, these letters not only provided details on Blaine's involvement in the worthless bond scheme, they contained great infor-

mation concerning Blaine's steady services over the years to business interests. Blaine managed to get hold of the letters and in his famous speech before Congress, quoted from them selectively to give the impression that he had "nothing to hide." He managed to escape unscathed at the time (although it probably cost him the Republican presidential nomination in 1876), but the scandal caught up with him in due time. The most damaging line of all, appended to the bottom of one of the notes to Fisher, was "Burn this letter."

The reference in the song to Blaine's traffic in "Guano" concerned another one of his questionable business ventures. In 1882, while Blaine was secretary of state, a "Peruvian Company" tried to enlist the help of the U.S. government in a $500,000,000 claim against the government of Peru. It was a far-fetched scheme with little basis in fact, having to do with the "discovery" of rich guano and nitrate deposits years before in Peru. Blaine may have given the plan some encouragement.

The song also reminded the voters of the "Star Route" scandal, which broke during the early part of Arthur's tenure and involved fraudulent postal contracts. It was one of the most damaging to the Republicans since the Whiskey Ring was uncovered. One-time U.S. Senator Stephen Dorsey, also mentioned in the song, was a power in the Republican National Committee and one of the main culprits in the scandal.

MARY BLAINE   Words: Ben Warren   Tune: "Mary Blane"

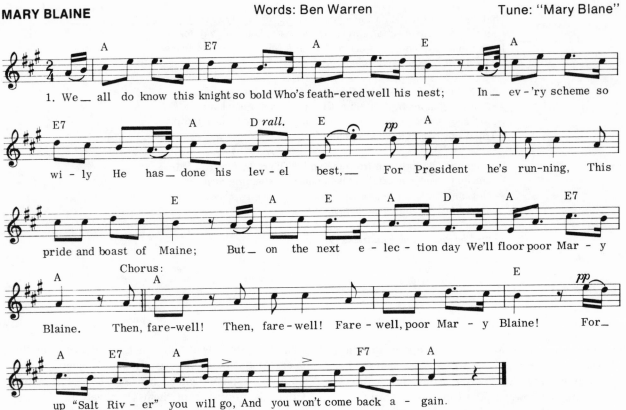

1. We all do know this knight so bold Who's feathered well his nest; In ev-'ry scheme so wi-ly He has done his lev-el best, For President he's run-ning, This pride and boast of Maine; But on the next e-lec-tion day We'll floor poor Mar-y Blaine.

Chorus: Then, fare-well! Then, fare-well! Fare-well, poor Mar-y Blaine! For up "Salt Riv-er" you will go, And you won't come back a-gain.

A "Man of Letters" is this knight,
You cannot this deny,
For Mulligan proclaims it,
And he shows the reason why;
With face as meek as Moses,
He tried hard to explain,
But votes will not be caught by chaff:
We'll swamp poor Mary Blaine.

His "fertile" brain is full of tricks
To fill his little purse;
To traffic in "Guano,"
This plumed Knight was not averse.
But "raising crops" of voters,
By this he'll try in vain,
For next November at the polls,
We'll shelve poor Mary Blaine.

Peruse the papers and they'll tell
About his "Peru" schemes;
To see his artful dodges,
How the Yankee Eagle screams!
Corruption and deception
The White House shall not stain!
We want an honest man this time,
And not poor Mary Blaine!

The Nation wants no hand unclean
To guide its mighty helm!
The people they have spoken
And their voice shall overwhelm!
By "star route" they will send you
Back to the State of Maine;
We won't endorse the "Dorsey" kind,
Not much, poor Mary Blaine!

We want a statesman that reproach
Could never dare assail!
No jobbing politician,
No Plumed Knight in rusty mail!
Corruption and its minions
Our votes defy in vain!
The tidal wave is sweeping on
To drown poor Mary Blaine!

From Maine to California,
A leader, staunch and true,
Shall rule this mighty Nation,
So, old fraud, good-bye to you!
Around our standard gather,
From mountain, vale and plain,
The honest-hearted voters who
Can't go poor Mary Blaine!

From the original sheet music, published by Hitchcock's Music Store, New York, 1884.

128

Song after song hammered away at the same theme. Credit Mobilier, the Whiskey Ring, the Fisher letters—the Democratic songsmiths came back to them over and over again.

A REPUBLICAN LETTER

Words: Dan Yell
Tune: "Wearing of the Green"

Oh, Jimmy dear, and did you hear,
The news that's going 'round?
They say, and truthfully, I fear,
Your record is not sound.
They even say you took some stock
In "Credit Mobilier,"
And what is more, they charge you, too,
With other things as queer.

From *Cleveland and Hendricks Songster.*

In the song which follows, the clever Democratic lyricist managed to revive memories of the infamous Whiskey Ring and appeal to the ethnic sensibilities of Irish voters with a single phrase, "No ringsters need apply!" From the 1850s onward, the phrase "No Irish need apply" was so widely used that it became a part of the slang of the day. Not the least of the struggles in the 1884 campaign was over the "Irish vote," and the Democrats' free use of the term here indicates, possibly, a closer affinity between them and the Irish.

NO RINGSTERS NEED APPLY

Tune: "Auld Lang Syne"

The people want a President,
And soon will choose a man,
But not by fraud or forgery,
Nor on the imperial plan.
One simple rule they will enforce,
With purpose stern and high,
That short and simple rule is this:
NO RINGSTERS NEED APPLY!

It matters not what foes may say,
About our chosen chief,
We know we've found an honest man,
And strong in this belief.
We'll win for him the people's trust,
And all his foes defy,
Enforcing this, the simple rule:
NO RINGSTERS NEED APPLY!

A brave, clear-hearted, truthful man,
Honest, and clear and fair,
Will be the people's choice to fill
The Presidential chair.
And when he scans the claims of men,
With clear and searching eye,
He will enforce this simple rule,
NO RINGSTERS NEED APPLY!

From *Cleveland and Hendricks Songster.*

WHERE REPUBLICANS MUST GO

Tune: "In the Sweet Bye and Bye"

There's a land that is hot-ter than this, It's a place where Re-pub-li-cans go; When the sins of their mis-deeds are known, And jus-tice from the peo-ple shall flow. They will fret, bye and bye, They will sweat in the tor-ments be-low; They will sweat, they will fret And will reap of the grain that they sow.

There are jobs, there are steals, there are thieves,
That have gone unmolested for years;
There are those who have been so unjust,
As to wring from the widow her tears.

From *Hamilton Democratic Glee Club Songster.*

It wasn't all just charges of corruption, though. The Democrats, too, were hungry for office, and with the smell of victory in the air could barely contain their enthusiasm. It was no small factor in getting the Party faithful out, not only to vote, but to watch the polls, pull other voters, and perform all the hundreds of ordinary tasks a successful campaign requires. And the "Good Democrats" responded.

To spur the Democrats on to greater efforts, the following song reminded them how they had been cheated of victory by the "long count" of 1876, in which Hayes prevailed over Tilden.

GOOD DEMOCRATS

Tune: "Maryland, My Maryland"

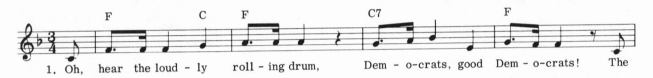

1. Oh, hear the loud - ly roll - ing drum, Dem - o-crats, good Dem - o-crats! The

time to right our wrongs has come, Dem - o-crats, good Dem - o-crats! Too

long have "rings" and fraud held sway, The sword of jus - tice hid a - way, 'Till

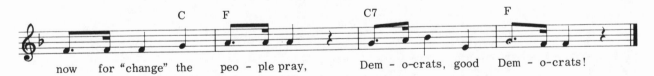

now for "change" the peo - ple pray, Dem - o-crats, good Dem - o-crats!

Our country calls on us tonight,
Democrats, good Democrats!
To battle bravely for the right,
Democrats, good Democrats!
Eight years ago we won the prize,
And then were robbed by tricks and lies,
Of Freedom's foes in friends' disguise,
Democrats, good Democrats!

In Freedom's cause we come again,
Democrats, good Democrats!
Our foes shall find their tricks in vain,
Democrats, good Democrats!
Our country's good we will maintain,
Our stolen rights we will regain,
And honest laws we will sustain,
Democrats, good Democrats!

Our gallant Cleveland is the man,
Democrats, brave Democrats!
To whip the whole Blaine-Logan clan,
Democrats, brave Democrats!
He is a statesman, brave and true,
He'll get the gray, he'll get the blue,
He's just the man for me and you—
Democrats, brave Democrats!

Yes Cleveland is of all the best,
Democrats, good Democrats!
He'll win the East, he'll win the West,
Democrats, good Democrats!
No treason stains fair Cleveland's skirt,
No rings have soiled his robes with dirt,
They'll wave no more the bloody shirt,
Democrats, good Democrats!

From *Cleveland and Hendricks Songster.*

But the "bloody shirt" was far from bowed. It was Blaine himself, after all, who had just about invented it by mounting a campaign against the then-helpless Jefferson Davis at the height of the exposures of Republican malfeasance. And although the passage of time had thrown a somewhat different light on the matter, Republicans assumed there was still some mileage to be gotten from the crimson garment, especially with the presence of a Union veteran, John Alexander Logan, on their ticket. Logan, a senator from Illinois, had risen to the rank of major general during the Civil War, commanding the Army of Tennessee during 1864, before being dismissed by Sherman because of an excess of political activity while in uniform. The Republicans didn't seem to have too much else besides the "bloody shirt" going for them that year—at least not at first. So the ever faithful Republican lyricists delivered themselves of the usual set of rhymes which spoke of treason, rebellion, slavery and Democratic "treachery." The following song personified the Democratic Party as a collection of Copperheads and Northern traitors:

It was just "befo' the wah," when our fight with him began,
He was faring very well under the Ad. of Jim Buchan,
And gave the South the muskets, the cannon and the grape,
To shoot our boys and trail the flag in South Car'lina State.

We'll stand by the party, the grand old party,
That stood by the boys who fought for the flag,
It saved the Nation's credit, we never can forget it,
Our zeal for it shall never, never lag.

From "Stand by the Grand Old Party," words and music by John H. Sarchet, pub. by George D. Newhall Co., Cincinnati, Ohio, 1884.

The "gray-haired boys in blue" were all supposed to be voting Republican still because they couldn't "forget the way our noble comrades died," and they weren't about to let any "traitor pen...write the laws to rule the boys in blue." Other songs recalled that it was the Democrats who "brought on the horrid war." But the old plea didn't have the effect it once did.

And then the Republicans were delivered a campaign issue which must have seemed like manna from heaven. A Buffalo newspaper exposed the fact that Cleveland had assumed responsibility for the illegitimate child of a Buffalo widow. Apparently the child's paternity was never established, but the bachelor Cleveland readily conceded that he "might" have been the father. The child had been born in 1874. The Republicans tried to make it the number one issue in the campaign. The tone was set by the song, which has come to signify the entire raucous and unscrupulous era:

MA! MA! WHERE'S MY PA?

Words and music: H.R. Monroe (probably a pseudonym for a popular songwriter of the period, Monroe H. Rosenfeld)

Lit-tle Tom Tid was a frol-ic-some kid, A cute lit-tle cuss, I de-clare, With eyes full of fun, And a nose that be-gun Way up in the roots of his hair.

Jol-ly and fat Was this frol-ic-some brat, As he played thro' the live-long day, But one eve, to his cost, His pa-pa got lost, And he and his ma sang a lay, Oh,

Chorus:

Ma! Ma! where is my Pa? Up in the White House, dar-ling,

Mak-ing the laws, work-ing the cause, Up in the White House, dear.

Ma! Ma! where is Pa-pa? Up in the White House, dar-ling:

Mak-ing the laws, work-ing the cause, Up in the White House, dear.

Once over a lawn that Tommy played on,
A bumble bee flew in the spring,
Said little Tom, "Hi! Tis a gay butterfly,
I'll catch him and pull off his wing."
Then with his cap, he struck it a rap,
That innocent, gay bumble-bee,
And puts its remains in the seat of his jeans,
And sang to his mama in glee, Oh— *(Cho.)*

So down on the green sat the little sardine,
In a style so strangely demure,
And said with a grin that was brimful of sin:
"I'll smash Mr. Butterfly sure!"
But soon with a cry that rose to the sky,
Up jumped Tommy Tid in the air.
And the welkin about rang out with a shout
Quite frightful to hear, I declare: *(Cho.)*

Poor little Tom Tid was only a kid,
Nor could you expect him to guess
What kind of a bug he was holding so snug
In the folds of his loose-fitting dress,
And he yelled in grief for a sweet relief,
And cried for his daddy in vain,
But no daddy was there, and oft through the air
Me-thinks I still hear the refrain: *(Cho.)*

From the original sheet music, published by
National Music Co., Chicago, 1884.

Strangely enough, the attack didn't work. It's safe to say that the whole affair won Cleveland at least as many votes as it lost him. Some may have voted for him out of sympathy; others simply because it became clear that the Republicans were working it for all it was worth in an effort to cover up their own peccadilloes. Charges that Cleveland had fathered an illegitimate child lost the Democratic candidate little support among the "Mugwumps," a group of reform Republicans who bolted the party in 1884 because they couldn't support Blaine. Carl Schurz, Charles Francis Adams, Jr., and Leverett Saltonstall were among the leaders of this group who eventually campaigned for Cleveland. A classic remark, attributed to a "Mugwump" leader, Moorfield Storey, may have summed up the way many people felt. Pointing out that accusations against Cleveland had to do with his private life and the charges against Blaine with his public life, Storey said: "We should elect Mr. Cleveland to the public office he is so admirably qualified to fill and remand Mr. Blaine to the private life which he is so eminently fitted to adorn."

Cleveland's frank admission of the truth in the charges actually won him a degree of support which helped to underscore the difference between his own candor and Blaine's ingenuousness concerning his own affairs.

Much more damaging in this tempestuous campaign was a statement made by a certain Rev. Dr. Samuel Burchard just a few days before election. Heading a delegation of Protestant ministers who called on Blaine at Republican headquarters on Oc-tober 29, Burchard won himself immortality as a footnote to history when he declared: "We are Republicans and don't propose to leave our party and identify ourselves with the party whose antecedents have been *rum, Romanism and rebellion."*

Historians have charitably noted that Blaine was exhausted from the long campaign and did nothing to disclaim the statement. By evening, Democratic newspapers in New York had spread the word throughout the city. The outraged Irish, against whom the remark was clearly directed, swung massively over to support the Democratic candidate, who went on to carry New York by a bare 1,200 votes. As it turned out, the election hinged on New York's electoral vote.

Accident? Perhaps. But Democrats had long since won the support of New York's Irish voters. In fact, that's what the good reverend was so upset about. Anti-Irish sentiment was rife in the ranks of the Republican Party, which had inherited the remnants of the Know-Nothings. Nativism was a strong ideological trend in America of the 1880s, and while wily politicians tried to keep it under wraps for fear of antagonizing the millions of newly enfranchised immigrants, it was nonetheless real—and strongest among the Republicans. The following campaign song of 1884, which purported to describe the unsavory career of an Irish hoodlum who hired himself out as a "repeater" (i.e., a voter who voted more than once), typified the feelings of many Republicans about immigrants "from the old sod."

I'M A ROARING REPEATER

Words and music: Thomas P. Culiar

1. My name is Mike Do-lan, I'm one of the boys, I'm fond of good whis-key and
plen-ty of noise; I'm a rare pol-i-ti-cian you'll free-ly ad-mit, Of
con-science and hon-or I have not a bit, I'm called a re-peat-er, but
that is my trade, I'm done with the pick-axe, the shov-el and spade, The
Dem-o-crat par-ty de-pends up-on me To give them a Pres-i-dent
now don't you see. I'm a roar-ing re-peat-er of Dem-o-crat fame, And
just from the state peni-ten-tia-ry I came, For when the e-lec-tion is
com-ing a-bout, The Dem-o-crats' Gov-ern-or par-dons me out.

I voted for Tilden from morning till night,
I killed a dutch tailor that day in a fight,
I scared the black nagers most out of their coats,
And so the Republicans lost all their votes.
While Johnny McReady, myself and Pat Flynn,
Stood close by the ballot-box, stuffin' them in;
But all of our labor went up in a blaze,
For blasted Republicans counted in Hayes.

Four years after that we had Hancock to lead,
Oh he was a jewel, a daisy indeed,
And though we repeated, we couldn't do much,
For we were outnumbered with nagers and dutch.
Our beautiful Solger was left in the lurch,
By a man from Ohio, a deacon in church;
And so they've defeated us year after year,
But sure there was plenty of whiskey and beer.

From *Blaine and Logan Songster.*

Republican songs in general, however, were a fairly tame lot in 1884. They sang of "Blaine, Blaine, Blaine of Maine," recalled past victories, and when they weren't waving the bloody shirt, they celebrated the white plumes of their shining knight.

THE PLUMED KNIGHT

Tune: "Battle Cry of Freedom"

> We will rally to the standard,
> We'll rally once again,
> Shouting the battle cry of vict'ry,
> Yes, we'll rally for the right, boys,
> And cast a vote for Blaine,
> Shouting the battle cry of vict'ry!

Chorus:
The Plumed Knight, forever, hurrah, boys, hurrah!
Stand by your leader, for honor and law!
Yes, we'll rally to the standard of Blaine and Logan true,
    Shouting the battle cry of vict'ry!

Yes, we'll gather 'round the Plumed Knight,
The friend of Garfield, too,
Shouting the battle cry of vict'ry,
For Republicans are faithful,
The country finds them true,
Shouting the battle cry of vict'ry. *(Cho.)*

From *Facts and Songs for the People.*

Caught up in the fervor of the moment was a thirty-year-old bandmaster, then conductor of the U.S. Marine Band, by the name of John Philip Sousa, one of whose first compositions was penned for the Blaine campaign:

WE'LL FOLLOW WHERE THE WHITE PLUME WAVES

Words: Edward M. Taber   Music: John Philip Sousa

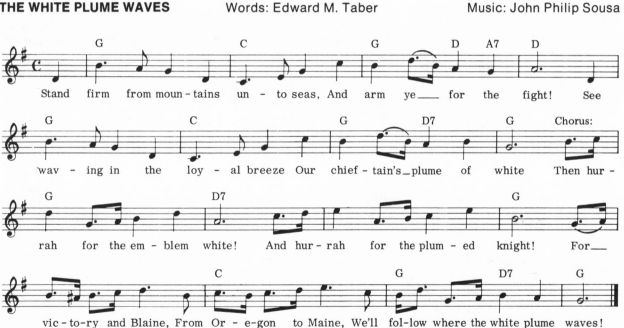

Stand firm from moun-tains un-to seas, And arm ye___ for the fight! See wav-ing in the loy-al breeze Our chief-tain's_plume of white Then hur-rah for the em-blem white! And hur-rah for the plum-ed knight! For___ vic-to-ry and Blaine, From Or-e-gon to Maine, We'll fol-low where the white plume waves!

Blaine's snow-white crest has never bowed
On legislative floor;
And Logan's voice rang clear and loud
Amid the battle's roar.

With Blaine of Maine we'll sweep the land,
As in the days of yore,
From old Atlantic's silver strand
To far Pacific's shore.

135

A million throats take up the strain,
Ten million hearts reply:
"With Blaine of Maine, the day we'll gain"
Is thundered to the sky!

And till the long campaign has ceased
Shall wave that snowy crest,
Above the statesman of the East,
The Soldier of the West.

From the original sheet music, pub. by
John F. Ellis & Co., Washington, D.C.,
1884.

The reference to Blaine as the "Soldier of the West" in the last stanza of "We'll Follow Where the White Plume Waves" was somewhat charitable. Having fallen into the habit of winning with Civil War heroes, the Republicans tried to spread the notion that Blaine had some kind of military record. Blaine's only connection with the nation's armed forces, however, seems to have been the three years he spent as a teacher at the Western Military Institute near Lexington, Kentucky in the late 1840s.

Once Again Tippecanoe

Somewhat numbed by the effect of losing their hold on the federal machinery for the first time in a quarter of a century, the Republicans approached the elections of 1888 with a renewed care. Having won with three generals and lost with a civilian, and sensing the need for a candidate who could not be attacked for his role in earlier scandals, the Republicans turned to the governor of Indiana, former Brigadier General Benjamin Harrison, a Party stalwart whose career had been safely spent a good distance from Washington—and who had the further distinction of being the grandson of "Old Tippecanoe," William Henry Harrison. The Grand Old Party gave the vice-presidential nomination to Levi P. Morton, New York congressman and banker, one of the important political figures in the Party.

Like every party out of power, the Republicans had the advantage of being able to exploit the usual blunders and *faux pas* of the incumbent. Grover Cleveland supplied them with a few while they found a few others ready-made. Among the "grievous sins" committed by the Cleveland Administration were the president's vetoes of a number of pension bills for Civil War veterans.

Cleveland's vetoes of the pension bills were a departure from tradition. Private pension bills had been regularly approved almost as a matter of course for almost twenty years. The president found that many of these petitions were based on fraud and misrepresentation and vetoed hundreds of them. He also vetoed a bill granting pensions to veterans who had suffered nonmilitary-connected disabilities. The Veterans of the GAR (Grand Army of the Republic) were outraged and actively participated in the campaign to unseat Cleveland.

Cleveland's alienation of the Union veterans made it easier for his political opponents to wave the bloody shirt, and they were helped by other items in the president's record: specifically, an Administration move, later withdrawn, to return captured Confederate battle flags to the Southern states and the fact that during the Civil War Cleveland had hired a substitute to serve in his place in the Army. The draft law provided that a man could pay $300 to hire a replacement, and the practice was widespread, but clearly no asset for one aspiring to public office.

So once again the "boys in blue" were exhorted into action, the good old tunes rang out and the quadrennial ritual of hanging Democrats in effigy began.

Tune: "Yankee Doodle"

When treason reared her horrid head,
And tried to trail our banner,
Then, by his love of country led,
This man from Indiana
He fought to keep the starry flag
Proud poised the Union over.
With dauntless heart he did his part,
But where, oh where was Grover?

From "Hip, Hip, Hurrah, Harrison!"
Harrison and Morton Campaign Songster.

The following song impugned the loyalty of the Democrats by linking them to the Copperheads and the many draftees who fled to Canada during the Civil War.

THE CANADA RESERVES

Tune: "Tramp, Tramp, Tramp"
(From *Acme Songs.*)

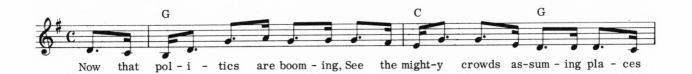

Now that pol - i - tics are boom - ing, See the might-y crowds as-sum - ing pla - ces

'mong the tramp-ers in the Grov - er line; And the Dem - o-crat - ic crew Have a

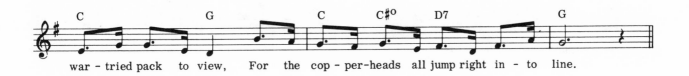

war - tried pack to view, For the cop - per-heads all jump right in - to line.

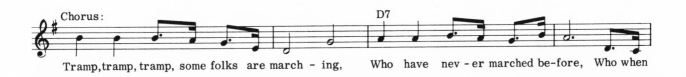

Tramp, tramp, tramp, some folks are march - ing, Who have nev - er marched be-fore, Who when

men in blue and gray were en-gaged in dead-ly fray Sly-ly skulked a-way to Can-a-da's safe shore.

Another Republican ballad attacked not only the president but also his chief political confidante, Daniel Manning, who served as secretary of the treasury until 1887, for their opposition to pension legislation on behalf of Union veterans:

GROVER'S VETO

Tune: "Tit Willow"

Oh, a fat man once sat in the President's chair, Singing veto, veto, veto; And his face was unwrinkled by sorrow or care, Singing veto, veto, veto. "I've no use for these pensioners, Daniel," said he, "For nine-tenths of their claims are all fiddle-de-dee, And this is the way I will fix them, you see, With a veto, veto, veto."

So he sat in his chair as the pension bills came,
Writing veto, veto, veto;
Regardless of merit, 'twas always the same,
It was veto, veto, veto.
For said he, "Had they followed my excellent plan,
And paid a small sum for a substitute man,
These bills would have never come under the ban
Of my veto, veto, veto."

But about next November the people will come
With a veto, *vote*, O, *vote*, O!
And say, "Sheriff Grover, you'd better go home,
With your veto, veto, veto.
For the sons of the thousands who suffered and died,
Will remember the trick and take a just pride,
In sticking right thro' your rhinoceros hide,
A veto, veto, veto."

From *True Blue Republican Campaign Songs.*

Benjamin Harrison's "virtues"—which seemed to consist mainly of his war record of twenty-five years earlier—were contrasted with Grover Cleveland's malfeasances by another Republican song. Here, the voters were reminded of Cleveland's "cowardice" and "Confederate sympathies," along with his girth and the fact that years earlier, as sheriff of Buffalo, he had actually participated in public executions of convicted criminals. "There are no flies on Harrison," they sang, utilizing a popular expression of the day connoting such boundless energy and activity by the person in question that he never stood still long enough to have flies settle on him.

THERE ARE NO FLIES ON HARRISON

Words and music: Aubrey De Vere

Oh! What's the matter with Harrison? Harrison?
Sure there can be no comparison
'Twixt a man who bares his breast to the foeman's
    deadly shot
And a man who's paid to tie the hangman's knot.
To be sure young Tip does not weigh a ton,
But a number six hat cannot cover his brain,
While Cleveland wears a shirt, that no matter which
    end's up,
Just fits him to perfection all the same.

Oh! What's the matter with Harrison? Harrison?
Sure, there can be no comparison
'Twixt the man who captured flags in the battle's
    blazing track,
And the cringing craven who would give them back.
For the boys in blue Mister Cleveland has no love,
Their loyalty he regards as a crime,
But for Rebs and Copperheads, he provides the softest
    beds,
And he draws his daily wages all the time.

From the original sheet music, pub. by Chicago Music Co., Chicago, Ill., 1888.

Having selected Tippecanoe's grandson for the nomination, Republicans were not about to overlook the advantages to be gained from history. Chauncey Depew, one of the powers in the Republican inner circle, reminded his associates that the election of 1840 had provided "one of the most picturesque campaigns in our history. There are enough survivors of that 'hard cider and log cabin' canvas to make an attractive contribution on the platform at every meeting." So many a Republican rally was reminded of the good old days with songs which attempted to revive the spirit of that earlier campaign.

Tune: "Tip and Ty"

> Oh, what has caused this great commotion
>   'motion, 'motion, all the country through?
> It is the ball a-rolling on
> For Tippecanoe and Morton, too,
> And with them we'll beat Mister Cleve,
> Cleve, Cleve must take his leave,
> And with them we'll beat Mister Cleve.

From *True Blue Republican Campaign Songs.*

Another song, which magnified the military feats of General William Henry Harrison, might have won more votes for "Old Tip" than for his descendant:

TIPPECANOE AND MORTON TOO

Words: William Marshall Cook
Tune: "Rosin the Beau"

> Now good people all give attention,
> And I'll tell you a story that's true.
> Of Harrison and his Grandfather,
> Some remember Old Tippecanoe.
>   The good and brave Tippecanoe,
>   That grand man, Old Tippecanoe,
>   And Benjamin's like his grandfather,
>   We will call him young Tippecanoe.
>
> In New York, Tip walloped the British,
> And he captured the whole dirty crew,
> And finally settled Tecumseh,
> Whom he routed at Tippecanoe.
>   At the Battle of Tippecanoe,
>   At the Battle of Tippecanoe,
>   In New York he walloped the British,
>   Won the Battle at Tippecanoe.

> Now Harrison is a brave soldier,
> And he fought in the ranks of the Blue,
> It's doubtful if any were bolder,
> In the days of Old Tippecanoe.
>   In the days of Old Tippecanoe,
>   In the days of Old Tippecanoe,
>   It's doubtful if any were bolder,
>   In the days of Old Tippecanoe.

From the original sheet music, published by Lee & Walker, Philadelphia, 1888.

And, of course, Grover Cleveland was one of the broadest targets—physically, that is—the Republicans had ever encountered. His running mate, a one-time Democratic congressman from Ohio, 75-year-old Allen Thurman, was a colorful character famous for taking a pinch of snuff and then hauling out a giant red kerchief to blow his nose. This "red bandana" became a Democratic campaign symbol.

Although many of their attacks were focused on the physical appearance and idiosyncrasies of the Democratic candidates, the Republicans did have some serious political charges to make against Cleveland. The president had announced his intention of overhauling the "spoils system" and extending civil service reform. But the obligations of party proved too much, although he was able to widen the coverage of Civil Service. Still, the great majority of Republican officeholders were swept out and replaced by Democrats.

The following Republican campaign song combined both personal and political attack on Cleveland:

THE COLLAR AND THE KERCHIEF

Tune: "John Brown's Body"

> Grover Cleveland is a collar of extraordinary size,
> So that many men mistake him for a corset in disguise,
> He standeth on his tip-toes and he looketh with surprise,
>   As we go marching on.

Chorus: Glory, glory hallelujah, etc.

When first he was invented for the Democratic shirt,
He was laundried by a mugwump who declared him free from dirt;
In spite of that, he's got to go, we might just here insert,
    As we go marching on.

The Muggies put about him for to keep him clean and warm,
A tie of beauteous colors that was called by them "Reform,"
But that was blown to glory in the office-seeking storm,
    As we go marching on.

Now the Democrats into his mammoth button-hole have tied
A dullish red Bandana that is very long and wide,
And have hung the two above them to excite the party pride,
    As we go marching on.

Against their mammoth collar, and their kerchief, too, of red,
We'll hoist the starry banner at our mighty column's head,
And never halt till Harrison to Washington we've led,
    As we go marching on.

From *The Harrison Log Cabin Song Book.*

Despite the usual inflated rhetoric, the perennial bloody shirt and the appeals to personality and prejudice, a genuine issue—of sorts—did emerge in the frenzied campaign of 1888. After years of careful straddling on the question of the protective tariff, Cleveland made a significant, albeit halting, step in the direction of "free trade" late in the days of his Administration. Largely impelled by a bloated treasury which was keeping money out of circulation and the pressure of certain "natural" social forces working against a tariff which had been kept high out of all proportion to the need for "protection," Cleveland made a historic speech to the nation in which he advocated a carefully planned program of selective reductions in the import duties.

Cleveland's cautious proposal was a far cry from the demands for "free trade" (no import duties) which many farmers and consumers were demanding. Its effect on domestic industrial interests would have been negligible. In fact, many quite conservative members of the financial community had long advocated similar reforms.

Cleveland's extremely limited plan was designed to curb the excesses of certain sectors of the corporate establishment in an effort to ward off the greater danger. In his message to Congress of December 6, 1887, Cleveland warned short-sighted business interests of the possible consequences of their opposition to tariff reform:

Opportunity for safe, careful, and deliberate reform is now offered; and none of us should be unmindful of a time when an abused and irritated people, heedless of those who have resisted timely and reasonable relief, may insist upon a radical and sweeping rectification of their wrongs.

But the American electorate had been carefully conditioned for more than thirty years to the belief that "protection" was the cornerstone of prosperity. And so, despite what amounted to little more than a reasonable and conservative reform, the Republicans mounted a fierce campaign against the menace of "free trade." For years they had tried to force the issue of "free trade" versus "protection" on the unwilling Democrats; now Grover Cleveland had obliged them and the pent-up rhetoric of decades was unloosed. "Protection" became the Republican watchword of the hour. Any suggestion of lower tariffs was equated with "treason," "rebellion" and connivance with the British, since the main exporter of goods to the United States was England. This fact also enabled the Republicans to make a determined bid for the Irish vote with a staunch anti-Anglo campaign, traditionally a favorite red herring of nineteenth-century elections and, oddly enough, actually used by the original Tippecanoe campaign strategists against Martin Van Buren—with as little justification, it must be added. Republicans issued booklets of "Protection" songs for the campaign, while soloists and quartettes sang such numbers as "Tippecanoe and the Tariff, Too," "Our Country and Protection," and "Down the Free-Traders." Here are some samples of the lyrical outburst occasioned by the cause:

Tune: "Yankee Doodle"

> John Bull is trying hard again
> To ruin this Yankee Nation,
> By forcing down our workingmen
> To foreign degradation.

Chorus:
Then freemen hear your Country's call,
Come forth from each direction,
And guard your Country's tariff wall,
That gives us all protection.

But Irish voters won't be fooled
By impudent free-traders—
Towards English schemes they're too well-schooled
To aid these sly invaders.

From "John Bull and the Free Trade Agitation," *Protection Campaign Songs and Recitations.*

Tune: "Wait for the Wagon"

Republicans are ready for the fight that is at hand,
Against established industries within their native land.
The Democrats to foreigners our ports would open wide,
They won't succeed, they cannot, against them is the tide.

Down the Free-Traders,
Down the Free-Traders,
Down the Free-Traders,
And come in with the tide.

From "Down the Free Traders," *Young Republican Campaign Song Book.*

Tune: "Tramp, Tramp, Tramp"

Fellow workers, would you know
Why some men would strike a blow
That would stagger all our industries at home?
They may not tell you so,
But 'tis English, don't you know,
This doctrine of free trade that's preached by some.

From "Fellow Workers, Would You Know," *Young Republican Campaign Song Book.*

Tune: "Jordan Is a Hard Road to Travel"

I looked to the East, and I looked to the West,
And I saw Ben Harrison a-comin',
With a terrible majority a-marchin' on before,
A-shoutin' and a-singin' and a-drummin'.

Then strip off your coats, boys, roll up your sleeves,
Free trade is a hard road to travel,
Then strip off your coats, boys, roll up your sleeves,
Free trade is a hard road to travel—I believe.

From "A Presidential Soliloquy," *Harrison and Morton Campaign Songster.*

Tune: Marching Through Georgia"

Rouse the good old tune again, we'll sing a campaign song,
Sing it with a spirit that shall start the world along,
The brave old party stands again ten million voters strong,
    Ready for the march in November.

Hurrah! Hurrah! We'll march to victory,
Hurrah! Hurrah! Free Trade can never be.
And we will vote "Protection" from Ohio to the sea,
    Marching on to vict'ry in November.

From "Republican Rallying Song," *Acme Songs.*

Traditional anti-British sentiment—a combination of hostility to British commerce and anti-monarchist levelism—made the following song a favorite of the campaign. It warned the working man of the threat to his wages represented by the proposed tariff reform bill's lowering or elimination of duties on goods imported from England and other Common-wealth countries such as Australia and Canada. The "Cobden cockade" of the song referred to Richard Cobden, a late British statesman responsible for many of the ideas associated with the free trade doctrine. He is supposed to have convinced Napoleon III of the desirability of free trade.

IT'S BRITISH, YOU KNOW

Words and music: John Gallaher

The next on the list is pure Liverpool salt,
It's British, you know, pure British, you know.
They're so fresh they'll need it when you call a halt,
That's Yankee, you're Yankee, you know.
They also want Canada timber in free,
And don't care a twig if it's you or it's me
Is hurt by the fall of our wages, you see—
It's British, so British, you know.

For roofs on their houses, they must have tin plate,
It's British, you know, so British, you know.
It's nothing for them, our American slate,
That's Yankee, pure Yankee, you know.
But sugar they would not reduce in the bill,
It would cripple the Trust to sweeten the pill
Of Free Trade as mixed up on Capitol Hill,
It's boodle they're after, you know.

It's too long a story to tell all their wants,
From Britain, you know, from Britain, you know.
When it rains in London, here they roll up their pants,
That's British, so British, you know.
American toilers, what do you say?
Are you ready to cast your birth-right away
To convicts and paupers who toil without pay?
You're Yankee, not British, you know.

Published by John Gallaher, New York, 1888.

It was a campaign in which the election song really came into its own. S. Brainard's Sons, one of the foremost music publishers of the era, issued both *True Blue Republican Campaign Songs for 1888* and *Red Hot Democratic Campaign Songs for 1888,* apparently hiring writers to pen them all. Philadelphia publishers Lee & Walker issued a plea for sales agents to "sell the most popular campaign and other music of the day."

Our catalogue of Campaign Songs is better, by far, than any other house in the country can offer. They are bright, stirring and catchy, solid and to the point. . . . Ladies make excellent agents in large towns and cities where there are many business houses and offices. . . . Good agents can make five dollars a day.

On the Democratic side, the 1888 campaign did not generate the same kind of excitement which had prevailed in 1884. The growing farmer discontent which would lead to the Populist revolt of 1892 was already widespread, while many of the reformers had become somewhat disenchanted with Cleveland's inability to substantially alter the spoils system. Many of the Cleveland songs seem to have been efforts by commercial music publishers to sell their wares rather than an outpouring of mass sentiment. Brainard's commissioned an anonymous writer in their stable to write a series of Democratic ballads under the pseudonym of "Yankee Free Trade." But such sentiments as "Board the free trade wagon and we'll all take a ride" probably did Cleveland more harm than good. One Democratic song, though, came from the heart and stands as a masterpiece of witty invective, a satiric verse which deserves enshrinement as one of the models of its genre:

HIS GRANDFATHER'S HAT

Tune: "Grandfather's Clock" by Henry Clay
  Work

(Quoted in "Election Songs of the United States," as sung by Oscar Brand, Folkways Records FH5280.)

His grand-fa-ther's hat is too big for his head, But Ben tries it on just the same. It fits him too quick, which has oft-times been said, With re-gard to his grand-fa-ther's fame. It was bought long a-go, and it made a pret-ty show In that jol-ly "hard ci-der cam-paign." But it don't fit e-ven a lit-tle bit on Ben-ja-min Har-ri-son's brain.

And one ambitious songwriter managed to get a good portion of the Party program into the following campaign ballad. Tax and tariff issues figured prominently in the song, which accused the Republicans of supporting measures which would reduce the prices of luxury items but make the necessities of life more expensive for the workingman. To drive home this point, the lyrics reminded voters that in the big tariff debate of 1888, the Republicans advocated removing the internal revenue tax on whiskey while refusing to accept the recommendation to lower the import duty on manufactured woolen goods. Nor did the song let voters forget one of the most telling arguments against the high tariff, namely, the whopping surplus in the Treasury, a matter of widespread concern to many in the financial community. It was estimated that this surplus amounted to some $140 million as of June 30, 1888, an astronomical sum for the times, representing ap-

proximately one-third of the nation's circulating capital. This was probably the foremost consideration in Cleveland's proposal to lower the tariff.

A special target of the Democrats, prominently mentioned in the song, was Congressman William "Pig-Iron" Kelley, one of the foremost proponents of protectionism. He authored the famous "Kelley Bill," which effectively sabotaged the recommendations of President Arthur's Tariff Commission in 1882 for a selective reduction in certain duties. Kelley was from Pennsylvania, home of the dominant figures of the American Iron and Steel Association, and hence the nickname.

The low tariff sentiments of the song, of course, did not appeal to everybody. Large numbers of manufacturers, concerned over Cleveland's seeming drift away from "protection," engaged in massive fund-raising for Harrison. One prominent leader of a high tariff association wrote: "I would put the manufacturers of Pennsylvania under the fire and fry all the fat out of them." A campaign fund acknowledged to be $1 million and more likely closer to $2 million was raised for the Republicans in 1888, largely from "frying the fat." The writer of the song, implying that the industrialists contributing to the Republican campaign fund were trying to buy the election, referred to them as "money kings with bar'ls" and tried to make them an issue in the campaign.

The song even worked in an appeal to ban Chinese immigration. The issue of ending Chinese immigration had become a "bloody shirt" cause of its own as exploited by certain Republicans (notably Blaine) who seized on it as an inexpensive way of winning labor votes. Eventually both parties went through the ritual of supporting Chinese Exclusion, culminating in an act to bar further immigration in 1882, after the railroads had completed their operations for which Chinese labor had been imported in the first place. Mentioning the question in the song

was a kind of gratuitous piece of racism just to keep the Exclusion franchise.

One of the interesting features of this Democratic campaign song is the attention which it paid to the Party's vice-presidential candidate and in particular to his legislative achievements, which emboldened the songwriter to liken him to the senators of ancient Rome. The song singled out Thurman's Sinking Fund Bill for special mention. This bill made an effort to get the railroads to repay some of the government money originally "borrowed" to build the transcontinental systems. The bill also restricted land grants to the railroads, thus making more land available for settlers.

Despite the prominence which the song gave to substantive campaign issues, however, the Democratic lyricist could not resist the nineteenth-century fondness for verbal cleverness. The " 'canoe'...full of holes" mentioned in the song was, of course, "Tippecanoe."

WAVE HIGH THE RED BANDANA   Words and music: Emma Washburn

Thur-man just as strong; And for the old De - moc-ra-cy Three times three if you have breath, And shout hur - rah! hur - rah! hur-rah!_ We'll be Dem - o-crats till death!

The 'Pubs are in the same old boat,
Their "canoe" is full of holes,
Their sanguinary sail is set,
And they're drifting on the shoals.
Their cry is still for help and aid
From the money kings with bar'ls,
But the more such freight they get aboard,
The greater are their perils.

On taxes and the tariff
They're senseless as a goat,
They'd take it off their whiskey
And leave it on our coat.
That's what they call protection,
Solid wisdom by the chunk,
But so clear is the deception
That they'll come down with a thump.

The taxes from the people wrung,
Must less and less be made;
We only need enough to run
And all just debts be paid.
The surplus in the Treasury
Is already much too big,
And we don't propose to make it more
To suit Bill Kelley's "Pig."

The railroads now must pay their debts,
The "Thurman Act" did that,
And we'll keep our lands for settlers
In spite of "Grandpa's Hat."
Monopolies must stand aside
And stop their thieving tricks;
John Chinaman must stay at home
To eat his rice with sticks.

Our party is the guardian
Of all who till the soil,
The true, firm friend of every man
Who earns his bread by toil.
The rights of these we will defend
'Gainst demagogues who prate,
The men of muscle and of brain
Vote Democratic straight.

So we'll whoop it up for Cleveland,
And will never let them rest;
Our cause is just and vict'ry sure,
Our ticket is the best.
Then all join in the chorus,
Let the cheers be loud and deep,
For our honest, able President
Another term will keep.

From the original sheet music,
copyright by the author.

But in 1888 the whoops were softer and the Republican "fat" did its job. Cleveland hadn't lost his popularity, winning a plurality of more than 100,000 votes; but they weren't distributed very strategically and little Ben Harrison won on the electoral count. The Democrats would have to wait four more years for that "other term."

Cleveland Again

In 1892, both the Republican and Democratic parties renominated their presidential standard-bearers of four years before. Harrison's running mate was Whitelaw Reid, successor to Horace Greeley as editor of the *Tribune* and a loyal Blaine man. The Democrats chose Adlai Stevenson as their vice-presidential candidate. Stevenson served as first assistant Postmaster-General in the first Cleveland Administration. Formerly he was a congressman from Illinois. He was put on the ticket largely as a concession to the "free silver" and "greenback" advocates, although he discreetly did little to push for these programs after his election.

As has happened so many times before and since, the real political drama of the 1892 campaign was not played out between the Republicans and Democrats. The agrarian revolt in the West (and portions of the South), combined with a growing labor agitation, reflected the reluctance of party government to curb the excesses of monopoly in the economy. With the emergence of the People's Party in the West and intensified union organization in the industrial East, a genuine popular upsurge was in the making.

The brutal Homestead strike/lockout of 1892 had dispelled the notion that labor was, in any way, the beneficiary of a "protectionist" policy. The squeeze on the small farmer from mortgage-holding banks and the railroads (who controlled freight rates) had engendered a mass disaffection from the normal workings of the system. Many "enlightened" representatives of the financial interests realized that a Democratic victory in 1892 might help allay the discontent. Lifelong Republicans like Henry Villard, president of the Northern Pacific Railroad and considered one of the most important railway promoters in the country, "switched" to Cleveland in 1892, saying, "Only a Democrat...could meet the emergency."

After Cleveland's victory, Andrew Carnegie's partner, Henry Frick, the man who had personally directed the effort to crush the iron worker's union at Homestead, wrote: "I am very sorry for President Harrison, but I cannot see that our interests are going to be affected one way or the other by the change in administration." To which Carnegie responded: "We have nothing to fear and perhaps it is best. People will now think the Protected Manu-facturers are attended to and quit agitating. Cleveland is a pretty good fellow."

The campaign itself was fairly uneventful. Republican efforts to repeat the "Free Trade vs. Protection" farce of 1888 found few supporters, although a handful of the Harrison campaign songs tried to stir up the question once again. In New Jersey, one campaign song which has survived from memory[1] was chanted by local Republicans to the tune of "Marching Through Georgia":

Up in Bergen County, where the old stone houses stand,
Silent, lasting memories of a brave and noble band,
Rally with your ballots, boys, defend our native land—
    Under the banner PROTECTION!

Chorus:
Hurrah! Hurrah! New Jersey must be won!
Hurrah! We'll show what Bergen County's done,
When we bring the good old state in line for Harrison,
    Under the banner PROTECTION!

Another Republican lyric, to the tune of "Yankee Doodle," recounted past victories and concluded with a verse for '92:

> With Harrison and Whitelaw Reid
> "Pure Coinage" and "Protection,"
> We'll rout the Democrats this time
> In every direction.
>
> From "Just Wait Until November,"
> by L. E. Meacham, published by
> Columbia Music Co., Chicago,
> 1892.

Some half-hearted efforts to stir up another Tippecanoe campaign didn't amount to much either, although they produced a few other Republican songs, the best of which was this one:

1. Sent to the author by Ava F. Collingwood of New York City, who writes: "The enclosed campaign song (was) written by my father (H.W. Collingwood), who at that time was living in River Edge, New Jersey. I have often heard my parents tell of touring the County during the campaign, a piano on a large wagon, a leader of the singing....My father (in later years) would remark wryly that actually Bergen County went Democratic that year by an unprecedented majority."

GRANDFATHER'S HAT

Words: D. E. Boyer

Music: "Rosin the Beau"

Ye jolly young lads of the nation,
And all ye sick Democrats, too,
Come out from the Free-Traders Party,
And vote for our Tippecanoe.
    And vote for our Tippecanoe,
    And vote for our Tippecanoe,
    Come out from the Free-Traders Party,
    And vote for our Tippecanoe.

Old Tippecanoe, in the forties,
Wore a hat that was then called the *bell;*
His grandson, our leader, now wears it,
And it fits him remarkably well.
    And it fits him, etc.

Our battle-cry still is protection,
Our flag is the red, white and blue;
We're marching straight forward to vict'ry,
Again with young Tippecanoe.
    Again with young Tippecanoe, etc.

Remember, November is coming,
Free-Traders begin to look blue;
They know there's no chance for Grover,
For grandfather's hat will sail through.
    For grandfather's hat, etc.

From *The Harrison Campaign Songster.*

The Democratic rhymesters did little better. Carefully forgotten were any intimations of "free trade" this time; that mistake (even in rhetoric) wasn't about to be repeated. The Democrats, instead, went back to their perennial theme of "reform," which had served them well enough in the past:

TURN THE RASCALS OUT   Words and music: Philip H. Bruck

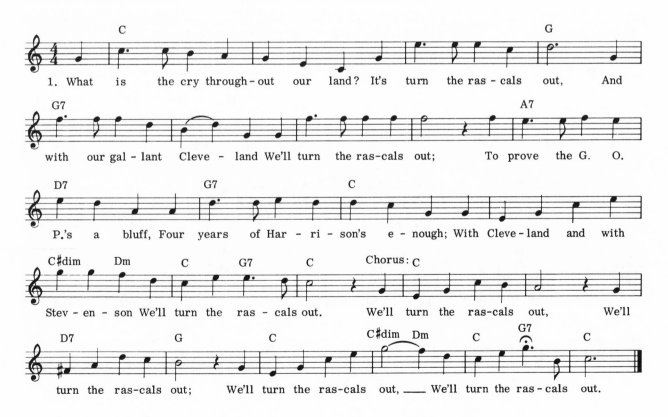

We want a man for President,
We'll turn the rascals out.
We want a head and not a hat,
We'll turn the rascals out.
Reform and honesty we want,
Not words deceptive full of cant;
With Cleveland and with Stevenson,
We'll turn the rascals out.

No Harrison nor Reid will do,
We'll turn the rascals out,
But Cleveland brave and Stevenson true,
We'll turn the rascals out;
So all you voters, workmen all,
Join hands and push them to the wall,
With Cleveland and with Stevenson,
We'll turn the rascals out.

What did we do in Eighty-four?
We turned the rascals out.
What will we do in Ninety-two?
We'll turn the rascals out.
Poor Ben can leave the White House then,
And Grover will move back again;
And Steve will run the Senate when
We turn the rascals out.

From the original sheet music, copyright 1892 by the composer.

The usual "Cleveland and Victory" and "Hurrah for Cleve and Steve" songs showed up, but there is little evidence that they roused any particular fervor for the Democratic cause. None of them went beyond the repetition of standard banalities. Typical of the lot, and bearing the marks of a higher grade of professionalism, was the following, the work of the man who had written such popular hits as "Little Old Log Cabin in the Lane," "Mollie Darling," and "The Drummer Boy of Shiloh," along with hundreds of other well-known tunes of the day:

CLEVELAND IS THE MAN   Words and music: William (Shakespeare) Hays

For honest Government we'll fight,
For all that's true and fair,
And Grandpa's hat will get mashed flat
When Grover takes his chair.
He ran this grand old Country once,
As President did reign,
As Democrats, let's put him back
To run it once again.

Let Democrats throughout the land
For gallant Cleveland shout,
From ev'ry throat and cast his vote
And man to man, turn out.
Let's win our cause, the world's applause,
And do all that we can,
Work day and night with all our might,
For Cleveland is the man.

From the original sheet music, pub. and
copyright 1892 by John F. Ellis & Co.,
Washington, D.C.

It was that kind of campaign.

Oh, the People's Ticket!

Songs of the Farmer and Labor Revolts from 1876 to 1892

The fierce contests between Democrats and Republicans from 1876 to 1892 seemed to many a poor farmer in the West and not a few poor workingmen in the East, a "sham battle." While Hayes and Tilden, Garfield and Hancock, Cleveland, Blaine and Harrison talked of reform, the tariff and the bloody shirt, a vast social crisis was overtaking the small homesteaders west of the Mississippi. Induced by the government and the railroads to buy cheap land in Kansas, Nebraska, Colorado and the Dakotas, these small, hard-working farmers gradually found themselves encompassed in an intricate network of mortgages, inflated freight rates charged by the railroads, monopolistic practices by the mills which bought their wheat, falling prices for their crops and rising prices on their purchases. Having contracted ten-year mortgages on their lands, they found that the combination of accumulating interest and a shortage of cash was wringing them dry.

Their response to these developing pressures began to manifest itself politically with the demand for "soft currency" and antimonopoly legislation. Occasionally forging a loose alliance with eastern workers and southern tenant farmers, these western agrarians tried to find a political vehicle through which to correct the situation. From 1876 to 1892 they tried various political organizations, culminating in the People's Party of 1892 (usually known as the Populists), whose broadly based support in the Plains states proved most alarming to eastern business interests. Eventually they cast their lot with Bryan and the Democratic Party in 1896 and soon disappeared as an independent force in American politics. But for some twenty years they participated actively in national election campaigns and at their high point they were the chief political entity in four western states.

Their songs, unlike the campaign ditties of the major party candidates, have the crusading fervor of a cause; only rarely do these songs focus on the personality of their candidates. These were not movements for political office, they were social upheavals, agonizing attempts by a sector of the population to direct the course of history towards a restructuring of society which, in its fullest implications, could not have been realized short of revolution. They fought against their immediate oppression, but their antagonists—the banks, the railroads, the giant monopolies and the government itself—never lost control of the situation. In the course of the struggle, these midwestern farmers enunciated a political philosophy as radical as any to grow out of the fertile soil of this continent.

The Greenback Party

The National Greenback Party was organized in 1878, but a slate of candidates running on a greenback platform had participated in the 1876 campaign, garnering a small but significant vote in several midwestern states. Their platform was simple. They wanted the government to issue more money (greenback notes), thereby devaluing the dollar and making it easier for the debt-ridden farmers to meet their obligations. They first emerged as a significant national force in the congressional elections of 1878, polling more than a million votes and sending 14 representatives to Congress. They mounted a substantial national campaign two years later, but the lack of a patronage system and old-party loyalties proved too strong, and their vote fell to some 300,000. Their message of an independent farmers' voice, however, was spread throughout the Midwest. Their candidate was General James B. Weaver of Iowa, a one-time Republican who had been elected to Congress on the Greenback ticket in 1878. B. J. Chambers of Texas was Weaver's running mate. The Greenback songs sang of cheap money, the rights and virtues of labor, the need for honest government and the betrayal of the old parties.

A NEW NATIONAL ANTHEM
Tune: "America"

> My country, 'tis of thee,
> Once land of liberty,
>   Of thee I sing.
> Land of the millionaire,
> Farmers with pockets bare,
> Caused by the cursed snare—
>   The Money Ring.
>
> Land where the wealthy few
> Can make the many do
>   Their royal will.
> And tax for selfish greed
> The toilers till they bleed,
> And those not yet weak-kneed,
>   Crush down and kill.

> Land once of noble braves,
> But now of wretched slaves,
>   Alas! too late!
> We saw sweet freedom die,
> From letting bribers high,
> Our unpriced suffrage buy,
>   And mourn thy fate.
>
> So when my country, thee,
> Which should be noble, free,
>   I'll love thee still.
> I'll love thy Greenback men,
> Who strive with tongue and pen
> For liberty again,
>   With right good will.

From *The Alliance and Labor Songster.*

THE GREENBACK TICKET
Tune: "Hold the Fort"

> Oh, ye people, see the signal
> Waving in the sky,
> Reinforcements now appearing,
> Victory is nigh.
>
> *Chorus:*
> Hold the fort for we are coming,
> Hear the people cry,
> We will vote the Greenback Ticket,
> Honest men we'll try.

See Corruption boldly stalking
In our Congress Halls,
In the Presidential mansion,
Tainting great and small.

See our commerce, Credit sinking,
Factories all still,
Workmen idle, begging, starving,
Suffering every ill.

See our taxes, swelling, rising,
Money almost gone,
Produce falling, no one buying,
Farmers' faces long.

Ho, ye Voters, true and honest,
Rally with us then;
Come and vote the Greenback ticket,
Vote for honest men.

From *National Greenback Campaign Songs.*

RALLY TO THE CALL, BOYS

Words: Mrs. Annie Sufficoal
Tune: "Battle Cry of Freedom"

Let us rally to the call, boys, rally to the call,
   Shouting the battle cry of freedom!
We're determined that the rule of oppression now must fall,
   Shouting the battle cry of freedom!

Chorus:
The greenback forever! hurrah! boys, hurrah!
Down with oppression, demand equal law;
So, we'll rally to the call, boys, rally once again,
Shouting the battle cry of freedom.

We are coming from the east, we are coming from the west,
   Shouting the battle cry of freedom!
All monopolies we'll hurl from their hold, too long possessed,
   Shouting the battle cry of freedom!

"In unity is strength," boys, then bravely march along,
   Shouting the battle cry of freedom!
Lay old party ties aside and for equal rights be strong,
   Shouting the battle cry of freedom!

From *National Greenback Campaign Songs.*

The following Greenback song of the 1880 campaign attacked both Hancock and Garfield, although the verses castigating Garfield are not included in those printed here.

CLEAR THE TRACK FOR GENERAL WEAVER

Tune: "Old Dan Tucker"

A plowboy, as he walked along,
Was singing to himself this song—
Oh, Hancock, you can never win,
With such a load of party sin.

Chorus:
Get out of the way, you base deceiver,
Clear the track for General Weaver,
Get out of the way, you base deceiver,
Clear the track for General Weaver.

Our Hawkeye hero's star is rising,
The vote he'll get will be surprising.
The law of right shall rule the land,
And oppression flee at its command.

The Southern palm and Northern pine
Their branches firm shall intertwine,
When the gallant gray and loyal blue
Shall rally for Weaver and Chambers, too.

From *The Political Catechism and Green-back Song Book.*

155

The following Greenback song protested the government's monetary policy and accused John Sherman, secretary of the treasury during the Hayes Administration, of being the culprit chiefly responsible for it. Sherman carried out the "hard money" policy of those years which increased the debt burden on the farmers.

AS WE GO MARCHING ON

Tune: "John Brown's Body"

When Greenbacks were abundant, our people lived at ease,
Prosperity on every hand as leaves upon the trees;
We demand their restoration or we'll raise a mighty breeze,
    As we go marching on.

Chorus:
Glory, glory hallelujah!
Glory, glory hallelujah!
Glory, glory hallelujah!
As we go marching on.

Corrupt John Sherman's policy brought misery to our land,
And wretchedness and poverty are seen on every hand;
This terrible contraction is more than we can stand,
    As we go marching on.

The morning light is breaking, the darkness disappears,
Old parties now are shaking with penitential fears;
Republicans and Democrats, we've got you by the ears,
    As we go marching on.

We'll rally to the ballot-box, proclaim that we are free,
Disperse the proud usurpers on the land and on the sea;
We'll burst the chains of bondage, proclaim the jubilee,
    As we go marching on.

From *National Greenback Campaign Songs.*

Anti-Monopoly Party

Disappointed with the decline of Greenback fortunes in the 1880 campaign, the debt-ridden farmers began turning toward the Democrats, hoping that the party of the "outs" might be able to do something practical for them. The old Republican "Radical," General Benjamin F. Butler, had been sent to Congress in the Greenback wave of 1878. In 1882 he won the governorship of Massachusetts as a Democrat, but failed of reelection a year later. Butler mounted a campaign for the Democratic nomination in 1884, but the southern wing of the party would have nothing to do with him and the party bosses had much more realistic plans.

A new Anti-Monopoly Party joined forces with the remnants of the Greenback Party to nominate Butler for the presidency. It was a development which the Republicans viewed with considerable interest and the historical evidence strongly suggests that Blaine's campaign managers helped finance the Ben Butler campaign in an effort to split the Democratic vote. Butler's appeal to the workingmen and farmers only drew about 175,000 votes and failed to stop Cleveland's election. But those who had forsaken the old party machinery had no place else to go.

BEN BUTLER SONG

Tune: "Oh! Susanna"

I dreamt a dream the other night,
When everything was still,
I thought I saw Ben Butler's boys,
Upon the White House hill.
The White House door was opened wide,
The porter, with a grin,
Just made a bow and stepped aside,
And Benjamin walked in.

Chorus:
Oh, Blaine and Cleveland,
Why did you ever try?
You might have known the workingmen
Would send you up sky-high.

Monopolists looked green and blue,
Land-grabbers' claims were sold,
The speculators bursted up,
Their corners wouldn't hold.
The frauds turned pale and skipped away
To England or to France;
They knew that Ben would make them pay
The piper for the dance.

The toilers flung their hats on high
And shouted loud and long,
Three cheers for Benny Butler, boys,
For he will right our wrong.
Three cheers for Benny Butler, boys,
For he is bold and true,
He'll give fair-play to the many, boys,
And not enrich the few.

From *John Swinton's Paper,* New York, Sept. 14, 1884.

Union Labor Party

The torch of third-party dissent was kept alive in the 1888 election by the short-lived Union Labor Party, which attempted to piece together a coalition from the remains of the Greenback and Anti-Monopoly parties and the new emerging labor groups in the eastern cities. Their candidate was Alson J. Streeter, of Illinois, who had been active in the Farmers' Alliance; and the bulk of their small vote (roughly 150,000) came from the same areas which had voted Greenback. But their songs revealed a new militancy, one which spoke of workers ruling the nation and putting monopolies to death.

LABOR'S YANKEE DOODLE

Tune: "Yankee Doodle"

We, toilers, have made up our minds
To have a revolution,
And make the "fighting dollar" soon
A standing institution.

Chorus:
Yankee Doodle, Banks and Bonds,
Yankee Doodle Dandy,
Bounce the banks and burn the bonds,
Yankee Doodle Dandy.

We'll make the Greenback crisp and new,
A lasting, legal tender,
For Labor and Bondholders, too,
And Gold-bugs shall not hinder.

And when our debts shall all be paid
In lawful greenback money,
Our country—Labor's promised land—
Shall flow with milk and honey.

Let honest homespun take the lead
Till Truth is resurrected,
And wealth gives place to honest worth
And Labor is respected.

For Labor's Party's in the field
For Labor's elevation;
We must put workers to the front
To rule the State and Nation.

From *Labor Songs.*

MARCH OF UNITED LABOR

Words: George Campbell
Tune: "Marching Through Georgia"

Come forth, ye toiling millions, and join our worthy band,
As on we pass to victory to free our native land.
Our glorious cause we will defend and equal rights demand,
   While we go marching to victory.

Chorus:
Hurrah! Hurrah! A shout of joyful glee!
Hurrah! Hurrah! We bring the jubilee!
The farms and labor shall unite and sweep from sea to sea,
   While we go marching to vict'ry.

The lords of mammon tremble when they hear our joyous shout,
As on we press to victory and put them all to rout,
The trusts and pools and money-kings—we'll turn the rascals out,
   While we go marching to vict'ry.

The toiling millions can't unite; that's what the bankers tell,
But hark! the tramp of millions and their chorus anthem swell,
They shout for home and country, and monopolies' death knell,
   While they go marching to vict'ry.

We'll raise our fathers' banner, boys, and spread it out on high,
Beneath these sacred stars and stripes, monopolies shall die.
We have the ballot in our hands, all traitors we'll defy,
   While we go marching to vict'ry.

Our weapon is the ballot and our word is "Right About!"
All hail the power in Union, boys, we'll give the word a shout;
The hand is writing on the wall: go cast the devils out!
   While we go marching to vict'ry.

From the manuscript collection of Richard Stephenson, University of Kansas.

Hayseeds Like Me

Of all the third-party campaigns in American history, with the possible exception of the George Wallace bid in 1968, none generated so much enthusiasm and concern as that aroused by the People's Party in 1892. And no similar effort has generated such a great body of song, although the Henry Wallace campaign in 1948 revived memories of earlier singing crusades. The songs of 1892 had been written over the course of the previous decade, just as the roots of the Populist movement went back to the Grange and Farmers' Alliance.

With the election of 1888 and the cynically cooperative role played by Cleveland and the Democrats, masses of western farmers simply gave up on the two-party system. Despite their very real complaints, their petitions and demands, and their abiding faith in both traditional virtues and the two-party system, they received no relief from the depredations of the railroads and the trusts. The dream of making the prairie a land of plenty had been dispelled by drought, grasshoppers, eastern moneylenders and the inexorable workings of an economic vise which found the frontier yeomen bound by the agents of often unscrupulous bankers, railroad monopolists and elevator operators. The two songs below, to the tune of a popular hymn, "Beulah Land," illustrate the contrast between the ebullient optimism of the Kansas farmers on first acquiring their land and the rueful second thoughts they came to have after tangling with the banks and corporations which kept them in debt.

I've reached the land of corn and wheat,
Of salt and coal and sugar sweet;
I got my land of Uncle Sam,
And am as happy as a clam.

Oh, Kansas land, sweet Kansas land,
As on its fertile plain I stand;
I look the pleasing landscape o'er,
For acres broad, I strive for more.
Till Gabriel's trump of loud command,
Says: you must leave your Kansas land.

From *The Alliance and Labor Songster.*

THE KANSAS FOOL

Words: C. S. Whitney   Music: "Beulah Land"

At first we made some money here,
With drouth and grasshoppers each year;
But now the interest that we pay
Soon takes our money all away.

The bankers followed us out west,
And did in mortgages invest;
They looked ahead and shrewdly planned,
And soon they'll have our Kansas land.

From *The Alliance and Labor Songster.*

The farmers of Kansas, Nebraska, Colorado and the Dakotas gave birth to a folk song literature which has lasted to this day—singing of their little sod shanties where they were "starving to death on my government claim," celebrating the hard-working farmer, "the man who feeds them all," complaining of the hard times and the chinch bugs and the injustices of an economic system that could not buy their produce while millions lived in poverty in the giant cities.

But in time the songs began to change, and instead of lamenting the loss of that "dear prairie home," they began to sing of organization, political action and a revolution at the ballot-box. In 1890, the farmers organized in the most serious and thorough fashion ever. They by-passed the old parties and in state after state throughout the South and the northern Midwest, under the auspices of the Farm-

ers' Alliance, they scored significant electoral victories. Governors, senators, a sizable bloc of representatives, and numerous state legislators were swept into office. Preparations began for the national elections of 1892.

At various Alliance meetings and farmer conventions from 1890 to 1892, a host of songs helped express the fervor of these agrarian radicals as they castigated the "old party bosses" along with the railroads and monopolies. Drifting eastward, this radicalism panicked the eastern financial interests. Especially did the attacks on the major parties seem to herald a possible breakup in one of the most reliable political institutions—the two-party system.

The sweeping Populist victory in Kansas in 1890 was ascribed largely to the persuasiveness of songs like the following:

GOODBYE, MY PARTY, GOODBYE   Tune: "Goodbye, My Lover, Goodbye"

I was raised up in the kind of school,
Good-bye, my party, good-bye,
That taught to bow to money rule,
Good-bye, my party, good-bye,
And it made of me a "Kansas fool,"
Good-bye, my party, good-bye,
When they found I was a willing tool.
Good-bye, my party, good-bye.

The old party is on the downward track,
Good-bye, my party, good-bye,
Picking its teeth with a tariff tack,
Good-bye, my party, good-bye,
With a placard pinned upon his back,
Good-bye, my party, good-bye,
That plainly states: "I will never go back."
Good-bye, my party, good-bye.

From *The People's Songster.*

THE HAYSEED

Words: Arthur L. Kellog
Tune: "Rosin the Beau"

I once was a tool of oppression,
And as green as a sucker could be,
And monopolies banded together
To beat a poor hayseed like me.

The railroads and old party bosses
Together did sweetly agree;
And they thought there would be little trouble
In working a hayseed like me.

But now I've roused up a little,
And their fraud and corruption I see,
And the ticket we vote next November
Will be made up of hayseeds like me.

From *The Farmers' Alliance* (newspaper), Oct. 4, 1890.

MY PARTY LED ME   Words: S. T. Johnson   Tune: "All The Way My Saviour Leads Me"

1. All the way my par-ty led me, And they robbed me ev-'ry day;
But I did not see my fol-ly Till my home was took a-way.
Mort-gaged farm-ers, wives and chil-dren, Ral-ly to the Al-liance call,
For, if you should long-er tar-ry, Mon-ey kings will have it all.
For, if you should long-er tar-ry, Mon-ey kings will have it all.

All the way my party led me, and these wrongs I helped to make,
For the Democrats I hated, when the bloody shirt they'd shake;
Oh, how true did Abe, the prophet, tell us of this troubled day!
How the money kings would rob us, take our liberties away.

All the way my party led me, I was blind and could not see,
When I halloed and I shouted over party victory.
In our victory was defeat, as we now can plainly see,
For we're on the road to slavery, and must fight if we'd be free.

All the way my party led me, led me to the fix I'm in;
But I will not longer heed them, a new life I'll now begin.
Oh yes, farmers, day is breaking, scales now from our eyes do fall,
For we see the great injustice that's been done to one and all.

From the manuscript collection of Richard Stephenson, University of Kansas.

THE INDEPENDENT MAN

Words: Mrs. J. T. Kellie
Music: "The Girl I Left Behind Me"

I was a party man one time,
The party would not mind me—
That's all for which I have to thank,
The party's left behind me.

Chorus:
An older, sadder, poorer man,
Sure every year did find me—
That's all for which I have to thank,
The party left behind me.

I asked that from the railroad's clutch,
A way out they should find me;
One party answered me, "not much,"
The other would not mind me.

I was to moneyed men a slave,
They said it was a fable;
One party would not try to save,
The other was not able.

A true and independent man,
You ever more shall find me—
I work and vote, and ne'er regret
The party left behind me.

From *The Farmers' Alliance* (newspaper),
Sept. 27, 1890.

As the election of 1892 approached, the Populists sounded more confident and even more militant. Their candidate was General Weaver, the one-time Greenback nominee, but it was hardly a campaign of personalities for the embattled farmers. For them, it was

. . . the People's ticket; oh the People's ticket,
People's ticket I'm going to vote because it am so true;
Oh, the People's ticket, oh, the People's ticket—
People's ticket I'm going to vote in the fall of '92.

From *The People's Songster.*

In "The People's Jubilee," the Populists waxed audacious in their egalitarian threats to established order:

THE PEOPLE'S JUBILEE　　Words: C. S. White　　Tune: "Kingdom Coming"

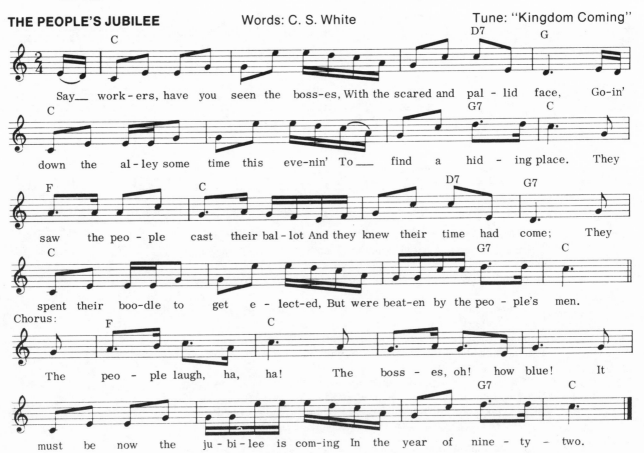

Say__ work-ers, have you seen the boss-es, With the scared and pal - lid face, Go-in'
down the al-ley some time this eve-nin' To __ find a hid - ing place. They
saw the peo - ple cast their bal - lot And they knew their time had come; They
spent their boo-dle to get e - lect-ed, But were beat-en by the peo - ple's men.

Chorus:
The peo - ple laugh, ha, ha! The boss - es, oh! how blue! It
must be now the ju - bi-lee is com-ing In the year of nine - ty - two.

The working people are getting tired
Of having no home nor land;
So now, they say, to run this government
They are going to try their hand.
There's gold and silver in the White House cellar,
And the workers all want some,
For they know it will all be counted out
When the People's Party comes.

From *The Alliance and Labor Songster.*

Of course, the jubilee did not come in 1892. The Populists polled more than a million votes and, for the first time since the Civil War, a "minor" party broke through the barrier of the electoral college, where Weaver received 22 votes. Two years later, the Populists would score even greater victories in the congressional elections, but 1892 represented a high-water point of nineteenth-century American radicalism. The Populists were never able to effect the farmer-labor alliance of their rhetoric and so were easily absorbed into old party politics via the Bryan campaign of 1896. If they had found the path to unity with workers in the industrial urban centers, American political history might have been far different.

But before we leave the Populists to the mercies of history, one curious musical sidelight must be added to the record. Colorado was one of the states which elected a Populist ticket in 1892, and so in the 1894 campaign appear a sheaf of Colorado Republican songs, among them this verse to the tune of "Oh, Dear, What Can the Matter Be?"

Dear, dear, what can the matter be?
Dear, dear, what can the matter be?
Dear, dear, what can the matter be?
Popguns are ruling the state.
Oh where are the good times with which we were baited?
Oh where are the wages we anticipated?
Just wait till November, you'll not hear it stated
That Popguns are ruling the state.

From *Republican Campaign Songbook.*

Gold Bugs and Silver Lions

The McKinley-Bryan Campaigns of 1896 and 1900

A Republican newspaper early in the year 1896 wrote: "The Republicans seem at present to have all the patriotic songs and to sing them also with a hearty good will as an expression of their political views and personal feelings, while the discordant and unhappy Democrats have very little to sing about."

And at the beginning of Cleveland's final year in the presidency, the Democrats did indeed appear a party in disarray. Their president seemed barely distinguishable from the Republicans, Populists were ready to displace them in the West and even threaten their grip on the South, while only Irish New York offered any hope for success in the East. But less than six months later, the Democrats were a vital, energetic organization with a dynamic new personality heading their slate. They had achieved a semblance of unity and rid themselves of the millstone of their own president.

What happened to achieve this state of affairs was an internal upheaval in the Democratic Party which resulted in a massive turn to the left heralded by the party's adoption of Free Silver (the unlimited coinage of silver) as its major theme and the nomination of one of its truly historic figures, William Jennings Bryan, for the presidency of the United States. William Jennings Bryan had served in the Congress as a Democrat from a traditionally Republican district in Nebraska for two terms after being elected in 1890. He was defeated in a campaign for the Senate in 1894 and served as editor-in-chief of the *Omaha World-Herald*. He was a Chautauqua lecturer and widely known as a free silver advocate at the time of the Convention.

The Cross of Gold

The "boy orator from the Platte" was only thirty-six years old when he delivered his electrifying speech to the Democratic Convention in 1896: "You shall not press down upon the brow of labor this crown of thorns. You shall not crucify mankind upon a cross of gold." But the moment which he personified had been in the making for two years, ever since the sizable Populist vote in the 1894 elections. Bryan and the other Silver Democrats had been working to absorb the Populist movement into their ranks. As early as the summer of 1895 they had met to plan their strategy, and by the time of the Convention they were able to upset the plans of the eastern bosses, adopt a platform which seemed outrageously radical for the day (in favor of the income tax, tariffs for revenue purposes only, against injunctions in labor disputes, in favor of Cuban independence, against a third presidential term, etc.) and name their own presidential ticket. But the heart of the platform was this: "We demand the free and unlimited coinage of both silver and gold at the present legal ratio of sixteen to one without waiting for the aid or consent of any other nation." It was a convention which put an end to that temporizing of twenty years which had made of the Democrats the mirror image of the Republicans.

To the financial community at large—including the Gold Democrats, who split off from the party and ran an independent slate in the election—it was a "leap into the foul pit of repudiation, socialism, anarchy, etc." Business interests and the eastern establishment rallied around the banner of the Republican standard-bearer, Congressman William McKinley from Canton, Ohio. But to the debt-ridden farmers of the South and West Bryan's candidacy was a dream come true, a genuine chance to fight for their own interests within the framework of the two-party system. The crusading fervor of the Populist campaigns poured into a Democratic Party suddenly revived. The Bryan candidacy touched off a wave of enthusiasm among tens of thousands who viewed it not so much as an election campaign as a religious movement, a sentiment which Bryan's own fundamentalism and silver tongue helped enhance. Mrs. May Kennedy McCord, who was a young girl then, recalls how a Silver Glee Club was organized in Stone County, Missouri, and a band of young folks would travel around the area trying to win votes for Bryan and free silver. One of the group, Sally Porter, wrote the words to their campaign songs:

GO TELL McKINLEY
Tune: "Go Tell Aunt Rhody"

Go tell Mark Hanna,
Go tell Mark Hanna,
Go tell Mark Hanna,
He's crazy in the head.

166

THE SILVER LION CAME TEARIN' OUT THE WILDERNESS

Tune: "Old Abe Lincoln Come Tearin' Out the Wilderness"

The Sil - ver Li - on came tear - ing out the wil - der - ness,
Tear - ing out the wil - der - ness, Tear - ing out the wil - der - ness, The
Sil - ver Li - on came tear-ing out the wil-der-ness, At six - teen to one.

William Bryan will be our next President,
Be our next President, be our next President,
William Bryan will be our next President,
We'll get Sixteen to One.

Tune: "John Brown's Body"

Hurrah, hurrah for William Bryan,
Nebraska's noble Silver Lion,
Never think the cause is dyin',
Free Silver's marching on!

All three songs from the singing of Mrs. May Kennedy McCord of Springfield, Mo., recorded in 1936 for the Library of Congress by Sidney Robertson Cowell.

Stirred by the opportunity to have a portion of their program enacted through a major party, the Populists endorsed Bryan on the basis of the silver issue. Bryan songs filled the pages of the Farmers' Alliance newspapers as Populist zeal embraced Nebraska's fair-haired son.

WE WANT NONE OF THEE   Words: Nellie Saunders   Tune: "My Bonnie Lies Over the Ocean"

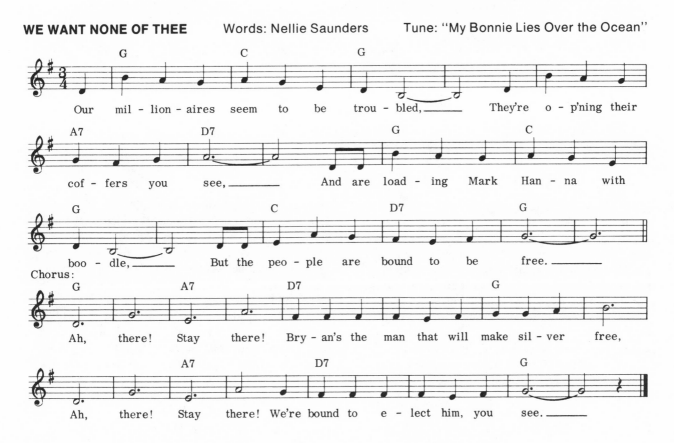

Our mil - lion - aires seem to be trou - bled,___ They're o - p'ning their
cof - fers you see,___ And are load - ing Mark Han - na with
boo - dle,___ But the peo - ple are bound to be free.___

Chorus:

Ah, there! Stay there! Bry - an's the man that will make sil - ver free,
Ah, there! Stay there! We're bound to e - lect him, you see.___

McKinley lives over at Canton,
He's backed up by the East, don't you see;
But the people will say in November,
Oh, Billy, we want none of thee.

Our hero, he comes from Nebraska,
He's the "orator boy of the Platte,"
He's offering relief to the poor man,
And I tell you we're voting for that.

From *Nebraska Folklore Pamphlets, #20.*

SILVER SONG

Tune: "Marching Through Georgia"

Sound the good old bugle with a bi-metallic ring,
Silver free from sea to sea with lusty voices sing,
Our banner with its silver stars to waiting breezes fling,
While we go marching to victory.

Chorus:
Hurrah! hurrah! we sing the Jubilee,
Hurrah! hurrah! our coinage ever free;
Let the nation hear us from the prairie to the sea,
While we go marching to victory.

Every Shylock in the land is trembling now with fright,
Lest the people break the chains of gold that hold them tight,
Now our silver bows we bend, the wily fox to smite,
While we go marching to victory.

United now we firmly vow to press this one appeal,
Until the pledge is plainly signed that silver's in the deal;
No longer to a golden calf shall freemen basely kneel,
Then forward, my boys, to victory.

Courtesy *The People's Songs* Library.

Phrases like "Sixteen to One" and "The Cross of Gold" made their appearance as song titles and on pamphlets and cartoons all across the country. Along with Populist sentiments came ancient prejudices, "explanations" of the troubles of the poor which avoided confronting the basic problems. A nascent anti-Semitism nurtured by time-worn stereotypes shows up in many of the songs of the time.

One such song was "How It Happened (or The Jew Of Lombard Street)" which inveighed against "wily" Jewish international financiers who had supposedly conspired—along with John Sherman, Secretary of the Treasury under President Hayes and a well-known advocate of "hard money"—to keep money dear. The "Lombard Street" mentioned in the song was famous in London as a center for financial business, especially moneylending, while Rothschild, of course, was Baron Lionel Nathan de Rothschild, head of his family's London banking house, the first Jewish member of Parliament and one of the handful of truly powerful international financiers. The House of Rothschild was one of the giant banking families of Europe.

HOW IT HAPPENED
(or THE JEW OF LOMBARD STREET)

Words: Charles F. Gilbert   Music: J. A. Parks

The deed was done in broad daylight and none but Sherman knew,
Except a few who followed and this wily London Jew;
The dollar of our fathers brave, that long had served us well,
Became a mere commodity for reasons none could tell.
At last the secret came to light, the truth dawned on us all,
That as the price of silver fell, all property must fall.
That as the dollars we may coin are plentiful or few,
So prices may be far advanced or almost cut in two;
That prices may be far advanced or almost cut in two.

For twenty years we've struggled hard 'gainst Rothschild and his gold,
We've suffered loss and poverty and misery untold;
The party of the bosses has proclaimed unto the world,
Devotion to the banner by this London Jew unfurled.
Then rouse ye sons of freedom all, and rout this alien band,
Whose treachery and bribery have blighted our fair land.
We'll coin the silver dollar in equality with gold,
And good times will come back again as in the days of old,
And good times will come back again as in the days of old.

Copyright 1896 by J. A. Parks Co., York, Nebraska.

But most of all it was Bryan, "The Silver Knight of the West," the people's champion who had, David-like, taken on the Goliath of Wall Street, the banks and railroads. He was:

> The noblest chief who ever broke
> From sons of toil a galling yoke.

Their cause was not that of the farmers alone, they said, but represented the needs of the poor and unrepresented everywhere:

> The cause for which we raise our voice
> When won, will make the world rejoice.

They sang, they marched, they pleaded, they reasoned, and they voted. In the end, their votes were not enough to carry their chieftain through, but their leveling Populist view became a part of the new political reality of the aborning twentieth century. They were absorbed by the system they set out to change, but in the process they won a small share of the rights for which Bryan led the way.

The Bryan campaign song below gleefully noted the defection of two silver Republicans from Republican ranks: Charles Arnette Towne, Minnesota congressman, and Henry Moore Teller, Colorado senator. Towne and Teller supported Bryan in 1896. In an optimistic vein, the chorus for the last two verses predicted the election results as follows: "The people on that day,/Will bury Bill McKinley,/And Bryan leads the way."

BRYAN LEADS THE WAY   Words and music: J. B. Babcock

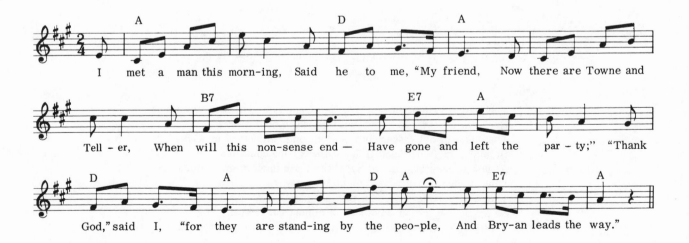

I met a man this morn-ing, Said he to me, "My friend, Now there are Towne and Tell-er, When will this non-sense end — Have gone and left the par-ty;" "Thank God," said I, "for they are stand-ing by the peo-ple, And Bry-an leads the way."

Bry - an, Bry - an, Bry - an leads the way, Bry - an, Bry - an, Bry - an leads the way, No - vem - ber third is com - ing, The peo - ple on that day, Will say, "We're for free sil - ver," And Bry - an leads the way.

The Democratic Party,
They, too, have left the track,
On Jefferson and Jackson
They now have turned their back.
"You're wrong again," said I, "they
Are not off it as you say,
The Democrats are on it
And Bryan leads the way."

"McKinley is my leader,
I'll follow him," said he,
"Now you may follow Bryan,
But Mac's the man for me;"
"Well, you may follow Mac," said I,
"He'll lead you far astray,
He'll never be elected,
And Bryan leads the way."

This man then lost his temper,
A foolish thing to do,
"Gold wins," he roared, "I'll wager
At odds of five to two."
Said I, "Don't get excited,
I have just this to say,
Sixteen to one it doesn't,
For Bryan leads the way."

Copyright 1896 by the author.

Bryan had the Populists and the songs and the fervor of a great moral crusade, but William McKinley had assets too—most notably, Mark Hanna. Marcus (Mark) Hanna was the prototype of the master politician, the first "national boss" of a political party. Active in Ohio politics for more than a decade, he became McKinley's particular patron, boosting him to the governorship and directing the effort for the Republican Presidential nomination and the election in 1896. He became chairman of the Republican National Committee in 1896 and invested that post with new importance. As director of McKinley's two campaigns and as a continuing behind-the-scenes influence in Washington, he was considered by many the most powerful man in the nation.

McKinley and the Republicans had songs, too. They had songs for Gold, for "sound" money, for Protection. They even had a song for Mark Hanna, possibly the only time a political boss has been so celebrated in melody and rhyme. The "extra bandana" was a reference to the Democratic trademark of Cleveland's ill-fated second campaign.

WHAT'S THE MATTER WITH HANNA?   Words: Henry Denver   Music: Bertha C. Marshall

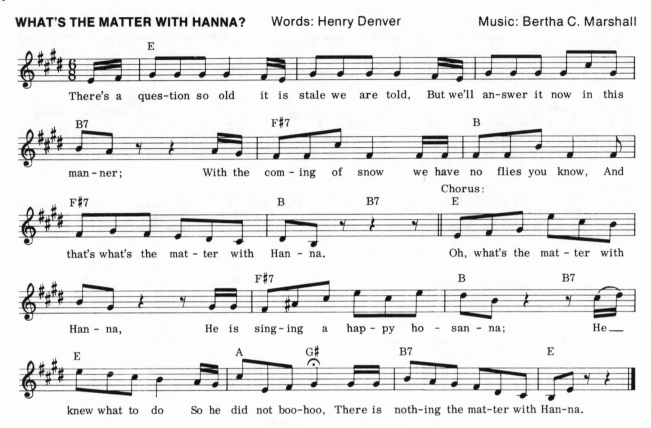

There's a ques-tion so old it is stale we are told, But we'll an-swer it now in this man-ner; With the com-ing of snow we have no flies you know, And that's what's the mat-ter with Han-na.

Chorus: Oh, what's the mat-ter with Han-na, He is sing-ing a hap-py ho-san-na; He— knew what to do So he did not boo-hoo, There is noth-ing the mat-ter with Han-na.

The fellows who kicked are sure to be licked,
And should carry an extra bandana;
They made a bad break and can't take the cake,
But that's not the matter with Hanna.

They had better go slow or a cyclone may blow,
If with silver they trim the old banner;
They will soon have enough of that bolt in a huff,
But all is serene with our Hanna.

Near the bright golden gate floats the good ship of state,
American patriots man her;
She is cleared for the fight, her crew is all right,
And that's what's the matter with Hanna.

From the original sheet music, copyright 1896 by
Edward H. Phelps.

As it turned out, the election of 1896 was no contest. To an electorate largely confused by the "money question," the Republicans skillfully managed to embellish their position with the rhetoric of traditional virtues and an appeal to the working class which, in effect, said that its best interests were bound up with the good fortunes of the companies which employed them. The appeal of "sound" money undoubtedly convinced many who associated the term with a "responsible" approach to affairs—as opposed to the "unsound" policies advocated by the Free Silver partisans. In Wilmerding, Pennsylvania, a barbershop quartet organized by members of the Young Men's Republican Tariff Club sang:

Free trade and free silver, free whiskey, free lunch;
Free love and free speech is their cry,
But when all our products are free as they wish,
Of whom will our customers buy.

Then bear well in mind, you shortly will find,
McKinley's the favorite son,
We'll beat Billy Bryan without even tryin',
And do it by Sixteen to One.

From the song, "Sixteen to One," words and music
by John H. Fullmer, copyright and published by
J. H. Fullmer, Wilmerding, Pa., 1896.

All the poetic virtues of gold were hauled out by
Republican songwriters to spread a halo of benevo-

lent optimism around McKinley and the Republican
Party. "Gold is the Standard to Win," wrote one,
"and the box that will hold American gold is made
of American tin." Another wrote:

The doctrine of "free silver" we believe to be a sham,
There's nothing like the *yellow dust* to brace up Uncle Sam,
And make his credit good world-wide, so do not be a clam,
But vote for "Gold, Protection and McKinley."

From the original song, "Prosperity, Protection and
McKinley," words and music by F. A. Blackmer, pub. and
copyright by F. A. Blackmer, Boston, Mass., 1896.

And who could resist the virtues of Honest
Money?

HONEST MONEY　　　　Words: E. W. Allen　　　　Music: W. S. Hawkins

1. The time has come to make a stand, Shoul-der to shoul-der and hand to hand, To
save our homes and save our land By a vote for hon-est mon-ey.

Chorus:
Gold, gold, we are for gold, We can't be bought, and we won't be sold; For a
dol-lar that's hon-est-ly earn'd and spent, And Wil-liam Mc-Kin-ley for Pres-i-dent.

We've had hard times, and we've had enough,
We don't believe in the silver bluff,
And we call on men of the true-blue stuff
To vote for honest money.

We want a chance to work and eat,
We want a "country that can't be beat,"
We want a man in the President's seat,
And we vote for honest money.

From the original sheet music, copyright 1896
by E. W. Allen.

Spreading fear of the wild-eyed "Popocrats" who were ready to destroy American institutions, the Republicans invoked radical and revolutionary wraiths. It was not the last time that visions of anarchist subversion would appear in a presidential election campaign. Some of the most fearsome figures of the age—James Kimbrough Jones, John Peter Altgeld, "Pitchfork" Ben Tillman—were invoked to tarnish Bryan as an associate of "radicals."

Jones was a Democratic Senator from Arkansas, a free silver advocate, and chairman of the Democratic National Committee in 1896; he was a leading figure in the revolt at the Democratic Convention which renounced the Cleveland Administration.

Altgeld, Democratic Governor of Illinois, had been denounced in the Republican press because he issued pardons to four of the Haymarket "conspirators" and declared that their trial was a miscarriage of justice, thus casting doubt on the entire affair in which seven men had been executed. He had protested at federal intervention in the Pullman strike of 1894 and was an ardent free silver advocate. He was generally considered the most "radical" political figure within the major party system.

Tillman was the most powerful leader of the southern wing of populism. Outspokenly racist, he never broke with the party system and kept the southern wing of the Democrats under his control as devoted to the poor farmer and against the blacks.

PAY NO HEED TO BILLY BRYAN

Tune: "Coming Through the Rye"

Pay no heed to Billy Bryan,
He's on treacherous ground;
See the company he's keeping,
None are safe or sound.
Jones and Altgeld are deceivers,
Pitchfork Tillman, too;
Many more we could well name,
But think this list will do.

From *Six Republican Songs for the 1896 Campaign.*

Another Republican campaign song verged on the hysterical in its dire warnings:

The Demo-Pop, Socialist yellers are yelling
Like French Revolutionists, Anarchist pitch;
And all their mad couplets in falsetto telling,
The Red Capper's anthem of "Down with the rich!"

From "Up with the Poor," by Nell Carpenter and J. B. Herbert, pub. and copyright by Fillmore Bros., Cincinnati, Ohio, 1896.

Other songs took note of Bryan's admitted gifts of oratory and tried to turn them back on the Democratic candidate:

SOUND MONEY AND PROTECTION

Words: "Zacheus"
Tune: "Battle Cry of Freedom"

We will welcome to our numbers all honest men and true,
Shouting sound money and protection,
And the rich and poor shall share in the wages when they're due,
Shouting sound money and protection.

Protection forever, hurrah! boys, hurrah!
Down with "free silver," and stop Bryan's "jaw,"
Then we'll rally 'round McKinley, we'll rally once again,
Shouting sound money and protection.

From *Three of the Greatest Republican Campaign Songs of the Season,* pub. by L. S. Lyman, New York, 1896.

MARCHING WITH McKINLEY TO VICTORY

Words: M. C. Dawsey

Tune: "Marching Through Georgia"

Young Bryan comes from out the west, a would-be "favorite son,"
With "popocrats" and "Silverites" who shout, "Sixteen to One!"
He comes with startling "metaphors" and with a "silver tongue,"
While we go marching to vict'ry.

"Free Silver" is Bill Bryan's text, he "spouts" from day to day,
His mouth and lungs and vocal chords all talk, but nothing say;
His "cross of gold" and "crown of thorns" are always in his way,
While we go marching to vict'ry.

McKinley is the magic name that sweeps the country through,
In time of peace, Columbia's friend, in war so brave and true,
He's bound to win in this campaign, and rule this country, too,
While we go marching to vict'ry.

From *Three of the Greatest Republican Campaign Songs of the
Season,* pub. by L. S. Lyman, New York, 1896.

The reference to McKinley as "Columbia's friend, in war so brave and true" harked back to his service in the Civil War. While not a general, like his Republican predecessors in the White House, McKinley had served in the 23rd Ohio Volunteer Infantry and, at the time of mustering out, had risen to the rank of major.

The Full Dinner Pail

McKinley's Administration was marked by a substantial easing of the economic crises of the early nineties. A sudden enlargement of the world's gold supply even brought a measure of relief to the farmers, so that by the time of the 1900 campaign, the burning issue of '96, "Free Silver," had become largely academic. Mark Hanna declared that the Republican slogan ought to be, "Let well enough alone," which finally was translated into the main Republican theme, "Four more years of the full dinner pail."

The Democrats nominated Bryan again, but much of the fervor of 1896 was gone. McKinley's adventures with Spain had unleashed a torrent of jingoistic pride and a vast sense of an America whose unbounded prosperity would be enhanced by a policy of expansion. To be sure, this new expansionist policy which saw the United States assume undisputed control of the Western Hemisphere along with the staking-out of an empire in Hawaii and the Philippines, was launched in the name of "anti-imperialism." Sympathies were enlisted on behalf of "poor Cuba" to justify American intervention in a revolution which some historians claim was on the verge of being won by the Cuban people themselves, and when that failed to raise sufficient public clamor for the use of troops, the U.S. battleship *Maine* was blown up under mysterious circumstances in Havana harbor. The American "hero" of the Cuban campaign, Theodore Roosevelt, swept into the governorship of New York on a wave of flag-waving hysteria, was induced to accept the Republican vice-presidential nomination.

Bryan, who had volunteered to serve in Cuba against the Spanish, expressed dismay at McKinley's blatant designs for the construction of an American empire in the Caribbean, Latin America and the Pacific. He tried to make it the Democrats' chief issue in the 1900 campaign, but the country at large had small concern for the realities of these issues, preferring to accept the Republican claim to be for both liberation and expansion. The lure of the "full dinner pail" was appealing.

THE FULL DINNER PAIL   Words: Henry Tyrrell   Music: Charles Puerner

1. There's a sound of march-ing mu-sic, and there's cheer-ing in the air, For the con-test now is read-y to be-gin. We've a tried and val-iant lead-er, and a stand-ard that is fair, And we hope the bet-ter man is going to win. There is Sil-ver Dol-lar Bry-an in the run-ning as be-

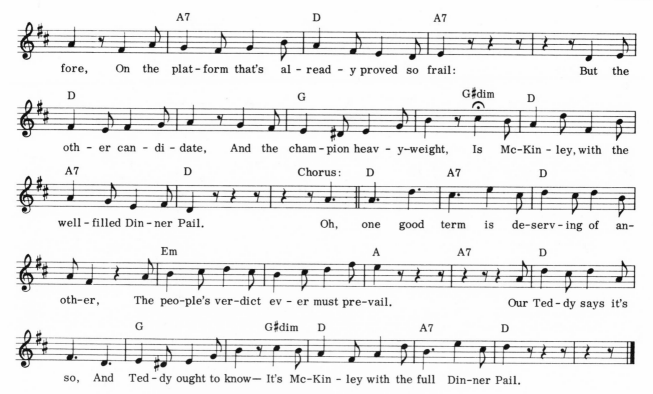

fore, On the plat-form that's al-read-y proved so frail: But the oth-er can-di-date, And the cham-pion heav-y-weight, Is Mc-Kin-ley, with the well-filled Din-ner Pail. Chorus: Oh, one good term is de-serv-ing of an-oth-er, The peo-ple's ver-dict ev-er must pre-vail. Our Ted-dy says it's so, And Ted-dy ought to know— It's Mc-Kin-ley with the full Din-ner Pail.

Oh, the Dinner Pail is ample, and it's made of honest tin,
But it stands for what is worth its weight in gold.
There are honor and prosperity all snug and tight within,
And the courage to achieve and have and hold.
There is Silver Dollar Bryan, with repudiation coin,
He's a Jonah, let us throw him to the whale!
For the man that we select, and the man that we elect,
Is McKinley with the well-filled Dinner Pail.

When the war with Spain awakened all our spirit, *not* our fear,
And there came a time for action to be done,
Then our Army and our Navy to the roll call answered, "Here!"
And McKinley was the Man Behind the Gun.
There is Silver Dollar Bryan, with his anti-everything,
And his policy to murmur and to wail;
But when all the strife is past, Bryan, too, may break his fast,
From McKinley's over-flowing Dinner Pail.

We remember, yes, remember, not so very long ago,
When the times were hard and work was scarce, at that,
Now, what brought about the happy change, right well we also know,
Democratic years were lean, but ours are fat.
Down with Silver Dollar Bryan, with his promises of wind,
And his bill of fare so meagre and so stale:
We're contented with our lot, and we want the man we've got,
That's McKinley with the well-filled Dinner Pail.

Published as a special supplement to *Judge* magazine,
No. 922, Oct. 20, 1900.

While Bryan charged the Republicans with following an imperialist policy, the Republican rhymesters replied that they were fighting Spanish imperialism. To a people whose country had seemingly forsworn "colonies," it seemed as though U.S. motives in the Caribbean and the Pacific must indeed be as noble as the State Department proclaimed them to be. And in 1900, the Republicans sang:

We cannot vote for Bryan with his imperialistic fad,
Oh no, we cannot trust him, he would make
    our money bad.
No Protection, no Expansion, while he seeks
    his own renown;
On Uncle Sam's New Islands, he would pull
    Old Glory down.

From "The Way We Vote and Why," by D. Oscar Loy and A. C. Wooyatt, orig. sheet music, copyright 1900, pub. at Atkinson, Ill. by D. Oscar Loy.

In another song, the new "expansion" poets urged:

. . . Don't give up the Philippines,
Give them full autonomy whenever right and best
    it seems;
And we will follow, brave and true,
The glorious flag from shore to shore.
Dispensing light and truth and freedom,
Till wrong and tyrants are no more.

From "We Are Ready, Mac and Teddy!" by W. W. McCallip, *The National Republican Song Book.*

The classic of the genre, however, may have been the following campaign ditty, which deserves some kind of award for jingoistic ingenuousness. The "base usurper, Aguinaldo" was Emilio Aguinaldo, leader of the original insurrection against the Spanish, who cooperated with the Americans during the war. Proclaimed first President of the Philippine Republic, Aguinaldo led a revolt against the American army of occupation when it became clear that the United States had no intention of leaving the Philippines. His troops were subsequently defeated by the American army. The "Mauser joys" incorporated a charge that Aguinaldo's men were equipped with Mauser rifles.

ANTI-IMPERIALISM

Words: Edwin A. Hartshorn
Tune: "On the Banks of the Wabash"

From the thralldom of Spain's cruel rule in Cuba,
Brave McKinley set the suffering people free.
He unfurled the Stars and Stripes in Porto Rico [*sic*],
Liberation and expansion—don't you see?
And in some distant isles of the Pacific,
The Spaniards pressed the Filipinos sore;
We sank their ships and swept Spain from those islands,
And she'll curse the Filipinos nevermore.

Chorus:
Yes, we shed our blood to save them from oppression,
And to free them from the cruel rule of Spain,
And we couldn't let the tyrant Aguinaldo
Curse the helpless Filipinos with his reign.

Whereupon the base usurper, Aguinaldo,
And his band began to kill our soldier boys,
Plotting wickedly to massacre our army,
And give us for our kindness Mauser joys.
Of course, we had to conquer Aguinaldo,
And scoop, *without consent,* his rebel band,
We didn't want to do it, but we had to,
For we couldn't let him loose to curse the land.

A better day has dawned upon the islands,
Since the Stars and Stripes, proud emblem of the free,
Floats o'er them, not for conquest, but for freedom,
Not for thralldom, but for priceless liberty.
To bless and not to curse the Filipinos,
We drove the Spanish tyrants from their shore;
In the Philippines, Old Glory, as in Cuba,
Floats to terminate oppression—nothing more.

From *Campaign Songs Written for the Cosmopolitan Male Quartet.*

Bryan was still a figure to be ridiculed, and the memories of '96 were invoked by attacks on the Popocrats, satires on free silver and Bryan's "silver tongue," while schoolchildren in the streets of New York sang, to the tune of "John Brown's Body," this song attacking Bryan and his running mate, Adlai Stevenson, vice-president under Cleveland.

To hell, to hell with Billy Bryan,
To hell, to hell with Billy Bryan,
To hell, to hell with Billy Bryan,
And Adlai Stevenson, too.

But for the most part, the supremely confident Republicans sang of their own candidates, the stalwart McKinley and the colorful Teddy Roosevelt. It was a flamboyant age, just discovering the infectiousness of ragtime, believing that there was no better place to be on all the earth than in America. Their slang was pungent, their politics straight, and they liked their song titles long. Nothing struck them quite so funny as a professional song-and-dance man, burnt cork covering his features, mouthing songs like "Hooray for Bill McKinley and that Brave Rough-Rider Ted" in an atrocious "coon" dialect. They liked songs with a bit of a twist to them:

> There'll be lots and lots of moving when the springtime comes once more,
> People will be changing houses as they have done the years before;
> But one family in the country then will not be moving—nay!
> The McKinleys of the White House, in the White House they will stay.
>
> From "McKinley of the White House (In the White House He Will Stay)," by George Newell Lovejoy, copyright by the author, Genesee, N. Y., 1900.

The best of these was a potpourri of flag-waving, slogans of '96, Roosevelt's war record and McKinley's program for prosperity, along with the standard clichés of candidate exaltation:

McKINLEY IS THE MAN!

Words: D. J. Muir   Tune: "Our Sailor Boys at Santiago"

For Teddy's brave and Teddy's true,
And he will serve us right;
You'll find that on Election Day,
Bill Bryan's out of sight;
For he may shout with frenzied gall,
And he may scheme and plan,
But Election Day will prove to all
McKinley is the man;
But Election Day will prove to all
McKinley is the man!

Ted helped to whip the treacherous foe,
And quickly it was done;
Bill Bryan only chewed the rag
And snarled, "Sixteen to one."
Mac's held to right, to stand or fall,
Since first his term began,
And Election Day will prove to all
McKinley is the man;
And Election Day will prove to all
McKinley is the man!

Our soldier boys love Teddy
And the farmers love him, too;
The business man says, he's all right,
He knows just what to do.
Mac's firm and true to duty's call,
We'll vote for him again,
And Election Day will prove to all
McKinley is the man;
And Election Day will prove to all
McKinley is the man!

Pub. and copyright 1900 by S.
Brainard's Sons, Chicago.

The Bryan campaign had two strains: the agitational class consciousness of '96 and the anti-imperialism of 1900. Given the heady combination of "the full dinner pail" and the greater glories of American jingoism, the Bryan partisans stood little chance. For despite their rhetoric, the class consciousness of the Democrats was rooted primarily in the small farmers of the Midwest rather than the workers of the industrial East. And their attacks on expansionism were based on such notions as justice and fair play, hardly a match for the "greater self-interest" espoused by the Republicans. (Could one expect that Bryan or the Democrats in 1900 would envision an alliance comprising Cubans, Filipinos and American farmers? Everything to its historical moment.)

One booklet of Bryan campaign songs, *Six Red Hot Songs Written and Composed Especially for the Campaign of 1900,* called on "those interested in aiding our just cause" to "assist in sending out as many quartets as possible, drilled on these songs, to help by their singing to seat our great leader and champion of the people's rights in the presidential chair." Among the songs which, it was promised, "are so worded and the tunes so inspiring that they will have the effect of awakening the sleepy and arousing the negligent and lazy to intense action and enthusiasm" was:

WHEN BRYAN IS ELECTED

Words: Will Hubbard Kernan
Tune: "John Brown's Body"

When Bryan is elected, as he certainly will be,
The Trusts will be demolished by a popular decree,
And Labor, re-endowed, will rise—strong, merciful and free,
    As we go marching on.

Chorus:
Cheers and a tiger for Bryan,
Cheers and a tiger for Bryan,
Cheers and a tiger for Bryan,
As we go marching on.

He will drive the hordes of Hanna into merited disgrace,
He will give the boon of freedom to the Philippino race,
And will grant the Cuban people all their proud and proper place,
    As we go marching on.

When Bryan is elected there will come a charming chill
To the Wall Street sharks and sharpers who now balk the public will,
And our Dr. Bryan will prescribe for them a drastic pill,
    As we go marching on.

For another declaration has been issued by our clan,
Setting forth in lines of fire all the regnant rights of man,
And the people have adopted it, with Bryan in the van,
    As we go marching on.

Another Democratic parody was even more direct
in its class point of view:

WHEN BRYAN COMES MARCHING IN

Words: Mrs. Bernard J. C. Abel
Tune: "When Johnny Comes Marching Home Again"

Hurrah for Bryan, we grip his hand,
    Hurrah! Hurrah!
He is the pride of all our land,
    Hurrah! Hurrah!
Though fight he must, he'll down each trust,
And never give up, though he should bust,
Till he gets for us, boys,
    A little bit off the top.

For Bryan we'll shout our song, hurrah!
    Hurrah! Hurrah!
The friend of right, the foe of wrong,
    Hurrah! Hurrah!
For William Bryan he makes no fuss,
And every mother's son of us,
Will see that he gets
    A little bit off the top.

From *Campaign Prize Songs.*

Democratic attacks on expansionism were by no means the unanimous sentiment of the Party. An anti-imperialist position was forced on the Democrats largely by Bryan, whose own constituency of midwestern farmers was traditionally isolationist and dubious of foreign adventures. They had also had some experience with the wealth-sharing promises of the trusts and were skeptical of a false prosperity to be earned from overseas adventures which would un-doubtedly benefit the huge corporations but which would cost the lives of American youth in the process.

While Republicans employed Paul Dresser's hit song of 1899, "On the Banks of the Wabash," to celebrate "liberation and expansion" (see the song "Anti-Imperialism" above), the Democrats used the same tune to champion the cause of Filipino independence:

AMERICA HAS SONS TO CRUSH OPPRESSION

Tune: "On the Banks of the Wabash"

Nobly did the mother bear the sudden parting,
Though her heart, indeed, was sorely racked with pain,
"Go, my only son, and fight as fought your fathers,
In the grand old cause of Freedom—fight 'gainst Spain."
In the front ranks fought the boy, but not 'gainst Spaniards,
For, forced to fight those Spain had long oppressed,
He did his duty, did it well and bravely,
And he died—a Mauser bullet in his breast.

Chorus:
Oh, the President sits smiling in the White House,
He is dreaming of a second term to stay,
But a mother's heart is filled with hopeless grieving
For her boy who lies lifeless far away.

Say the Filipinos, "Give us Independence,
This you promised us if we would help you fight,
By the Declaration of your great Republic,
It is ours to have by every sacred right."
'Tis a plea this great, big, self-respecting nation,
Must find an answer, yes, must give it heed,
America has sons to crush oppression,
But no blood to shed to help despotic greed.

From *The Democratic National Campaign Song Book for 1900.*

Another anti-imperialist song parodied Gilbert and Sullivan:

THE WHITE HOUSE TOM-TIT

Words: George S. Thompson
Tune: "Tit Willow"

On a tree near the White House, a little tom-tit,
Sang, "Willie, oh, Willie, oh, Willie.
You won't here much longer complacently sit,
No, Willie, no, Willie, no, Willie.

The blood of our soldiers you causelessly spill,
To govern a people against their free will,
Forgetful of Lexington and Bunker Hill—
Are you, Willie, come, Willie, say, Willie."

From *Campaign Prize Songs.*

In the style of the day, in which the dialects and cultures of all non-Anglo ethnic groups in America were fair game for the songwriter, another Democratic anti-imperialist song came out as a "stage Dutch" duet between "Hans and Uncle Sam."

VOT VOS YOU UP TO, UNGLE SAM?   Words: Ralph T. Butler   Music: Andrew J. Boex

(From *Campaign Prize Songs*)

There were, of course, the usual songs celebrating "William Jennings Bryan of Nebraska" and the candidate who was "A Democrat, A Soldier and a Man"—but the Silver Lion from the Platte was, to the country at large, just another politician. Back in Kansas and Nebraska, however, the farmer-poets were still making up rhymes and songs, some of which would drift into that word-of-mouth cultural heritage of the people we call folk song.

As the following song shows, the western farmers took special delight in the fact that Bryan's popularity forced even his political enemies in the Party, the big-city bosses of the East, to reconcile themselves to his nomination. One of these bosses was

183

David Hill, long-time leader of the Democratic machine in New York State, who had opposed Bryan's nomination in 1896. When Bryan won his party's endorsement that year, Hill remarked: "I'm a Democrat still—very still." But Bryan's appeal to the rank and file of the party was so great in 1900 that the old eastern bosses couldn't oppose him, and Hill actually participated in the nomination.

GET OUT OF THE WAY, YOU GRAND OLD PARTY

Tune: "Old Dan Tucker"

Voters come and hear my ditty,
What was done at Kansas City,
David Hill, the New York Lion,
Nominated Billy Bryan.

Chorus:
Get out of the way, you grand old party,
Get out of the way, you grand old party,
Get out of the way, you grand old party,
You're so old, you're getting warty.

For running mate there was a pull.
But 'twas no use, the woods were full.
And then and there to still the noise,
They gave the job to Illinois.

Still your boss is Mark A. Hanner,
He looks just like a stockyards tanner,
In the ring our hats we're shyin',
Whoop! hurrah! for Billy Bryan!

Keep the banners ever flyin',
Follow always Billy Bryan.
Onward now and all keep steady,
'Cause we're after Mack and Teddy.

From *Nebraska Folklore Pamphlets, #20.*

Teddy, Taft and Wilson—That's All!

The Ragtime Campaigns of the Early Twentieth Century

There never has been a Republican president (or candidate, for that matter) like Theodore Roosevelt. Picked for the vice-presidency by Republican party bosses who wanted to shelve the rambunctious Roughrider, Roosevelt ascended to the presidency after McKinley's assassination; and Mark Hanna wailed, "That damned cowboy is President of the United States!" If there ever was a ragtime Republican, it was Roosevelt, at forty-three, the youngest man ever to assume the presidency, a tempestuous, colorful figure who supervised an unprecedented American growth throughout the Western Hemisphere while proclaiming the need to "bust the trusts." At the top of his lungs, he shouted, "Speak softly and carry a big stick!" and introduced the notion of reforming some of the more blatant abuses of corporate capitalism into the body politic. The people loved him, the politicians respected him, and businessmen liked his achievements but were anxious about his style.

His campaign for re-election in 1904 was actually no contest and the Democrats didn't even try to make it one. After two tries with Bryan, they went back to an eastern conservative, Chief Justice of the New York Court of Appeals, Alton B. Parker, inspiring one Republican songsmith to write:

> Oh, I know our Billy Bryan, I went crazy for him twice,
> And yellow Billy Hearst, he's the man who has the price.
> I remember Grover Cleveland, too, with Wall Street for a barker,
> But what I really want to know is—Who is Parker?
>
> From "Who Is Parker? (as sung by the Old Democrat)," by
> James Valentine, copyright 1904 by J. V. S. Paddock.

The "yellow Billy Hearst" of the song was William Randolph Hearst, founder of a string of sensational newspapers and at that time a New York congressman, Parker's chief rival for the Democratic nomination.

The No-Contest Election of 1904

For the Democrats, 1904 was a holding action. They went through the motions, but no one had much heart for the fight. No one was about to beat Roosevelt. The party platforms were essentially the same, with the Democratic candidate retreating to the gold standard, although currency was hardly a big issue this time around. The only thing at stake, aside from who would fill the offices, was the personality of the candidates.

With no great issues being debated—or even obfuscated—the popular singing explosion of previous campaigns never materialized. For the most part, the campaign songs were the work of professionals who were more concerned with selling sheet music than winning votes. Paul Dresser, author of "On the Banks of the Wabash" and "My Gal Sal," poked some good-natured fun at Teddy, committed some atrocious puns, and did his bit for Parker. As a prominent Hoosier, Dresser no doubt carried out his task with special relish, since Indianans played such a conspicuous role on both sides in the campaign. Thomas Taggart of Indiana was chairman of the Democratic National Committee. On the Republican side, Senator Charles Fairbanks of Indiana was Roosevelt's running mate.

Dresser chose his words for maximum effect, even using one of the President's favorite expressions, "Deelighted!", to signify the people's reaction to a Democratic victory. And the composer-lyricist seized the opportunity to advertise his hit song, "On the Banks of the Wabash," in his line, "On the Icebanks of the Fairbanks of the Washbanks far away."

PARKER! PARKER! YOU'RE THE MOSES WHO WILL LEAD US OUT OF THE WILDERNESS

Words and music: Paul Dresser

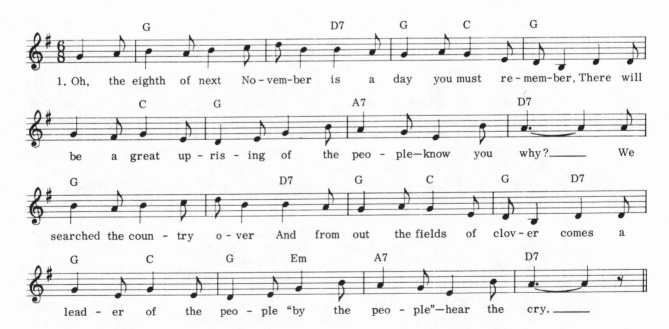

1. Oh, the eighth of next No-vem-ber is a day you must re-mem-ber, There will
be a great up-ris-ing of the peo-ple—know you why?_____ We
searched the coun-try o-ver And from out the fields of clov-er comes a
lead-er of the peo-ple "by the peo-ple"—hear the cry._____

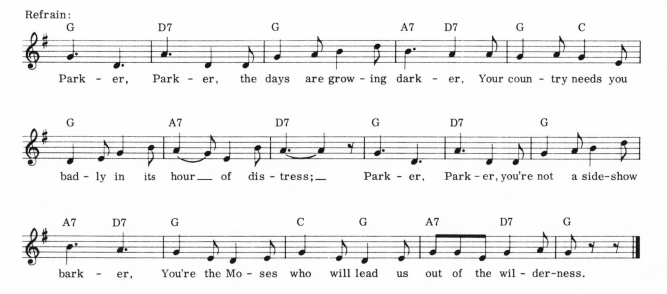

Refrain:

Park - er, Park - er, the days are grow - ing dark - er, Your coun - try needs you

bad - ly in its hour of dis - tress; Park - er, Park - er, you're not a side-show

bark - er, You're the Mo - ses who will lead us out of the wil - der-ness.

There will be no brag or bluster,
No military fluster,
No more mountain lion shooting, no more wild and wooly fun,
A Democracy united
Will see that things are righted,
Everyone will be *deelighted,* for we have them on the run.

There will be a great hosanna
When New York and Indiana
Go Democratic, it will be a case of hip hooray!
So up and down the middle
Taggart has them on the griddle,
On the Icebanks of the Fairbanks of the Washbanks far away.

From the original sheet music pub. 1904 by James H. Curtin,
New York.

John W. Bratton, a popular composer responsible for the music to such hits as "Henrietta, Have You Met Her?" and "Isabelle, Belle of the Season," along with lyricist Paul West, waxed a little more optimistic over Parker's prospects than even the Democratic orators. In the time-honored tradition of countless American campaign songs, the Democratic candidate was depicted as a plain, outspoken farmer with his "hand upon the plough" at his farm near Esopus, New York. The song's char-acterization of Parker as a man who insisted on win-ning the presidency by stating the truths in which he believed had its basis in a telegram which the judge sent to the Democratic Convention after it had nominated him and before it adjourned. Parker an-nounced for the gold standard and offered to withdraw from the race if the Convention felt that this position would make him unacceptable. Bryan attacked Parker, but the Convention was too far committed and let the nomination stand.

GOOD-BY, TEDDY, YOU MUST MARCH! MARCH! MARCH!

Words: Paul West
Music: John W. Bratton

We are cheer - ing for a man that's safe and sane, For a

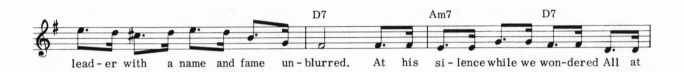

lead - er with a name and fame un-blurred. At his si - lence while we won-dered All at

once a na - tion thun-dered At the flash - ing of the light-ning of his word.

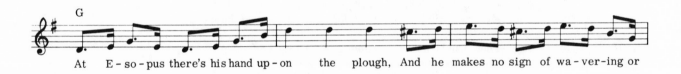

At E - so-pus there's his hand up - on the plough, And he makes no sign of wa - ver-ing or

doubt. Farm - er, judge, no man de-ceiv-ing, Plain the truths that he's be-liev-ing, And on

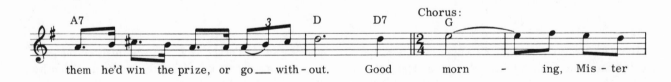

them he'd win the prize, or go __ with - out. Good morn - ing, Mis - ter

Roose - velt, ____ per - mit ____ us to pre - sent, ____ Just the

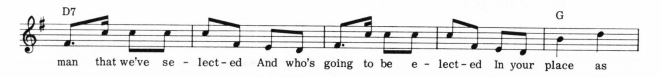

man that we've se - lect - ed And who's going to be e - lect - ed In your place as

Pres - i - dent.___ Go wash ___ the White House chi - na ___ and ___

all ___ the lin - en starch ___ Have a clev - er met - al mark - er Stamp the

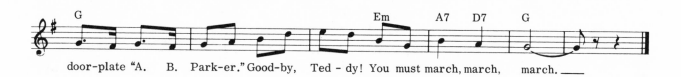

door-plate "A. B. Park-er." Good-by, Ted - dy! You must march, march, march. ___

To his party's call he answers, prompt and true,
For he hears behind the call his country's plea.
There are mischiefs that are brewing,
It's an hour for steadfast doing,
For the good ship, *Constitution,* "all at sea."
So with cheers and votes and gladsome heart and mind,
When November brings Election Day around,
We'll be booming things for Parker
And the Presidential marker
Will observe that Teddy's margin can't be found.

From the original sheet music, published by
the *Sunday World,* New York, 1904.

On the Republican side of the campaign hustings, songwriter Gus Edwards, composer of "Schooldays," "In My Merry Oldsmobile" and "By the Light of the Silvery Moon," contributed the following song. Its lyrics called attention to dissension in the Democratic ranks. Much of this dissension was caused by Parker's stand on the gold standard. After Parker's gold standard telegram to the Democratic Convention, Bryan accused David Hill, still head of the New York Democratic organization, of playing "peanut politics." The "Grover" mentioned in the song was, of course, Grover Cleveland, who enjoyed a short boom for the Democratic nomination before withdrawing his name.

WE WANT TEDDY FOR FOUR YEARS MORE

Words: Frank Abbott   Music: Gus Edwards

There's a hot time com-ing soon, There'll be blood up-on the moon And the
good old Yan-kee Ea-gle will scream.____ There will be a grand earth-
quake That is ver-y sure to wake The Dem-o-crat-ic Don-key from its
dream.____ And the peo-ple of this land, They will shout to beat the band The
oth-er na-tions all will hear the roar.____ We will make the wel-kin
ring When this song we loud-ly sing: We want Ted-dy for_ four years more.

Chorus:

We want Ted-dy the brave____ Our____ ban-ner to wave ____
We want free-dom ____ from shore to shore.____

It will be an awful fall
For dear old Tammany Hall
When the honest voters rise in their might;
All the grafters soon will prance
And good men will get a chance
For this is to be a real finish fight.
So in spite of all their tricks
And their Peanut Politics,
The Republican flag will proudly roar:
Lift your voices on high
In this great battle cry,
We want Teddy for four years more.

There will be a wild alarm
On that quiet Esopus farm
Where Chief Justice Alton Parker resides.
And to David Bennett Hill
It will be a bitter pill
That will put a kink in his insides.
He will pack his bag of tricks
Full of bunco and gold bricks,
And join our old Grover on the shore.
While that monumental "shine,"
Mister William Jennings Bryan,
Will stop talking for four years more.

From the original sheet music, published
by M. Witmark & Sons, New York, 1904.

But the most well-known piece of Roosevelt campaign music was a ragtime march, "A Hot Time in the Old Town Tonight," a jazz tune associated originally with a famous Saint Louis brothel. Whether or not the band actually played that piece as Teddy's Roughriders made their famous charge up San Juan Hill, as legend has it, is of little moment. The tune was indelibly associated with Roosevelt, although in later years he tried to discourage its use. But if Teddy was somewhat embarrassed by this raucous, earthy jazz lyric (popularized in typical "darkey" dialect), a team of black vaudeville songwriters helped to make up for it all with a typical ragtime Teddy number.

The songwriting team of Cole and Johnson consisted of Robert Cole and a number of different Johnsons. Cole and Billy Johnson, who may have written the original "Boola, Boola" song as well as such atrocities as "The Wedding of the Chinee and the Coon," worked together before the turn of the century. The team was reorganized in 1901 and this time Johnson was a pair of brothers, James Weldon and J. Rosamond, each of whom achieved fame on his own as poet and singer-musician respectively. In later years, it was this team which composed the famous "Under the Bamboo Tree." But in 1904 they collaborated on:

YOU'RE ALL RIGHT, TEDDY

Words and music: Cole and Johnson

The coun - try calls a - gain_____ For true and hon - est men To
let us all u - nite,_____ And cast our bal - lots right For

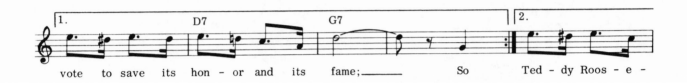

vote to save its hon - or and its fame;_____ So   Ted - dy Roos - e -

velt the man we name.   Oh! you are all right, Ted - dy! ____

You're the kind that we re - mem - ber; Don't _____ you wor - ry! We are

with you!   You're all right, Ted - dy! _____ And we'll prove it

in No - vem - ber, Ted - dy! We're going to keep you in the White House.

Oh, Teddy is a man,
That's built upon a plan
To make the hearts of plucky men rejoice;
For when the game begins,
He goes right in and wins,
And that is why he is the people's choice.

Oh! you're a man indeed,
The kind of man we need,
The kind of man we need to hold the gap;
You've steered the country straight,
You've made the country great,
In fact, you've put the country on the map.

And when the country's cry
For men to fight and die
Resounded through the land from Washington,
Then Teddy didn't balk,
He didn't stop to talk,
But went and did his work at San Juan.

When Europe raised a fuss,
And tried to say to us:
"What? Dig through Panama, you never shall!"
Our Teddy said: "All right!
I'll think it over for a night."
Next day we got the Panama Canal.

From the original sheet music, pub. by Joseph
W. Stern Co., New York, 1904.

Get on the Raft with Taft

William Howard Taft may not have been the best president this country ever had but he was the biggest. Weighing in at some 326 pounds in the altogether—a condition he was not likely to be found in—Taft, although the protégé of Roosevelt, looked like that father image so many political figures try to cultivate.

Given Taft's enormous size, one can only admire the optimism of the various songwriters who, finding "raft" an admirable rhyme for "Taft," invited the public to board such a slight craft with their candidate. But it was that kind of election—one given to the echoes of political confrontation rather than its substance.

Both candidates were, in effect, stand-ins; Taft for Roosevelt, and Bryan (nominated for the third time) for the "boy wonder" who had stirred such enthusiasm twelve years earlier.

Roosevelt's reforms had moved the Republican Party significantly away from its old conservative image. Bryan's years and the continuing stability of the Democratic Party had managed to absorb the Populist radicalism and remove its sting. (The radicals were going elsewhere, to Eugene Debs and the suddenly vitalized Socialist Party, which was building towards a significant peak in 1912.) Again, the party platforms could have been readily exchanged with each other, except for the self-congratulatory rhetoric of the Republicans and the factional attacks of the Democratic "outs."

The paucity of campaign songs is revealing. That outpouring of parodies and jingles which is usually a sign of popular sentiment is barely to be found. And even the professionals are noteworthy for their absence from the campaign, their merchandising antennae undoubtedly telling them that it wasn't a good year for the campaign song trade.

The perennial amateur songwriters showed up with such enterprises as "Our Good and Honest Taft" and "The Man of the Hour," but there is no evidence to suggest that any of these received much circulation. The best songs of the year's paltry fare belonged to Taft and were clearly derivative of then-popular musical numbers. "B-I-Double L-Bill," the work of Monroe H. Rosenfeld, was so obviously patterned after George M. Cohan's "Harrigan" that it was a wonder that its author didn't run into a copyright infringement suit. Rosenfeld seemed to lead a charmed life, however. One of the authentic characters of the popular show business world of the time, Rosenfeld is credited with inventing the name "Tin Pan Alley." If so, it's about the only original idea he ever had, but he was moderately successful with a long string of popular songs almost all of which bore striking resemblances to either older numbers or contemporary popular hits.

193

B-I-DOUBLE L-BILL

Words: Monroe Rosenfeld   **Music: Rosie Lloyd**

Guitarists: Capo on 3rd fret—play chords in parentheses

Thro' the land, ring-ing grand, Is a name known to fame, that we all love, so dear! And we stand, hand in hand, at his loy-al com-mand, his no-ble cause to cheer! So for our states-man let us all fall in-to line, He's the man that we want in Nine-teen-Nine! And we'll sail on the raft, crowd-ed down fore and aft, For our good Bill Taft!

Chorus:

B - I - Dou-ble L - Bill! Good, old, hon-est Bill! He's the Bill to start each mill, And we'll have him, yes, we will! He'll get in for the next four years, Let's all give him three heart-y cheers! B - I - Dou-ble L - Bill, Taft's no coun-ter-feit Bill!

March along to the song,
That will ring with a swing,
For our good, big Bill!
With a cheer, far and near,
That the nation may hear!
He is the People's will!
He is our leader and our country's worthy pride,
And we'll rally in triumph to his side!
Let us sail on the raft, crowded down fore and aft,
For our good Bill Taft!

Copyright Edward B. Marks Music Corporation.
Used by permission.

Another pair of journeyman songwriters latched onto the Taft-raft rhyme, threw in some graft and wound up with this bid for popular acclaim, sheet music sales and support for Taft and his running mate, James Sherman, a New York congressman for twenty-two years.

GET ON THE RAFT WITH TAFT   Words: Harry D. Kerr   Music: Abe Holzman

The greatest man that ever ran
The greatest land on earth,
Is Teddy R. whose shining star
Is only in its birth.
We'd like some more of Theodore,
But Theodore has said,
That Taft was meant for President
To follow in his stead.

His running mate's from New York State,
We'll all give him a hand;
Our votes he'll get, and you can bet
The second place he'll land.
Jim Sherman's square and always fair,
In due respect to him,
All Democrats must doff their hats
To dear old "Sunny Jim."

Of Bryan's bluff we've had enough,
He'd talk you deaf and blind,
The million trusts he's goin' to bust
Are only in his mind.
Seems he has run since Washington
First started in the game,
If his legs were gone, he'd keep right on
A-running just the same.

While Republican songwriters seemed to be trying to float Taft into the White House, Democrats were trying to rekindle some of the enthusiasm of earlier Bryan campaigns. For the most part, it was a thankless task. The only old-time note of the hour was struck in a parody by an E. J. Foster, to the tune of "John Brown's Body." The song appealed to the workingman by pointing out that tycoons like John D. Rockefeller, Edward H. Harriman and J. P. Morgan were supporting Taft and presenting Bryan as the candidate of the people.

Then there's John D. and Harriman and Jimmy Morgan, too,
And each trust and grabbing syndicate is wheeling in to view,
Let them vote for Taft and Sherman, but consider what we do,
As the voting time comes on.

Bryan! Bryan! Hallelujah!
Bryan! Bryan! Hallelujah!
Bryan! Bryan! Hallelujah!
The voting time comes on.

From the original sheet music, "The People's Inning."

For the most part, though, the songs were of that brand of doggerel in which a change in name might have enlisted them on behalf of almost any candidate of any party at any time.

LINE UP FOR BRYAN Words and music: George W. Gale

Like the rol - ling of the thun - der ech - oes loud the bat - tle song, 'Tis

sung through-out the na - tion with a cho - rus good and strong, We are

com - ing from the moun - tain and we're com - ing from the plain, From

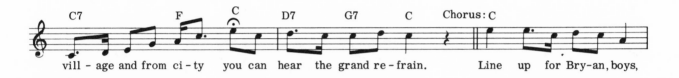

vill - age and from ci - ty you can hear the grand re - frain. Line up for Bry-an, boys,

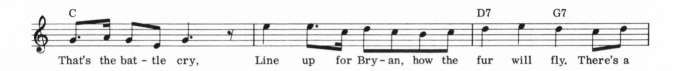

That's the bat - tle cry, Line up for Bry-an, how the fur will fly. There's a

hot time com-ing in the sweet bye and bye, When we line up for Bry-an in the morn - ing.

We are marching on to victory, there's music in the air,
We'll place our gallant leader in the Presidential Chair,
We are ready for the battle now, we're waiting for the day,
We'll fall in line for Bryan, boys, Hip, hip hooray!

From the original sheet music published by the Gale and
Mullane Music Co., 1908.

A pair of Chicago songwriters, composer W. R. Williams and lyricist Jeff T. Branen, saw the campaign of 1908 as a battle of East versus West. They liked Bryan, the man from "dear old Lincoln, N.E.B.," but didn't care for either Tammany or Teddy. Song lyrics for which Branen seems to have been responsible were "You're An Indian," "Somebody Lied," and (wisely reversing his name to Jeff T. Nenarb) "She's the Daughter of Mother Machree." Williams was a pen name for Will Rossiter, who as both music publisher and songwriter was one of the great influences of his day. Among Rossiter's own famous compositions was "Meet Me Tonight in Dreamland," while as publisher, he was responsible for launching such favorites as "Let Me Call You Sweetheart" and "Some of These Days." Rossiter also published the following song.

197

WOULD YOU RATHER BE A TAMMANY TIGER OR A TEDDY BEAR?

Words: Jeff T. Branen
Music: W. R. Williams

For years the elephant has been
The whole menagerie,
The tow'r of strength and emblem of
The mighty G.O.P.,
But now, perhaps, the end has come
Of Teddy Bear commands,
And Uncle Sam awakes to find
An elephant on his hands.

When Uncle Sam goes scouting,
He's the daddy of them all,
For Uncle Sammy never shoots
That something doesn't fall,
So listen for the awful crash
When he brings down that pair,
Ohio's baby elephant
And New York's Teddy Bear.

The Bull Moose Campaign

The story of the 1912 campaign is the story of the man who wasn't supposed to be there—Teddy Roosevelt. Having announced in 1904, after his election, that he would not run for a third term, Roosevelt had stuck to his word and transferred title on the White House to Taft. But Taft's politics matched his girth—labored, slow-moving, unimaginative. Once again the Republican Party receded into its traditional conservatism.

Roosevelt, meanwhile, still young and energetic, had embarked on a trip around the world which included some big-game hunting in Africa, an exploit which seems to have captured the public imagination. As the stodgy politics of the Taft Administration dampened the country's enthusiasm, a genuine yearning for the good old days of Roosevelt began to express itself. The professional songwriters, ever in tune with popular sentiment, began composing "Teddy" songs in 1910. A pair of Tin Pan Alley pros, Seymour Brown and Nat Ayer, wrote "When Yankee Doodle Teddy Boy Comes Marching Home Again"; while out in Chicago, Irving Lee and Will Rossiter, under his pen name of W. R. Williams, worked the theme of "When Johnny Comes Marching Home Again" into this song, which—like so many others—capitalized upon Roosevelt's experiences in hunting big game.

WHEN TEDDY COMES MARCHING HOME   Words: Irving B. Lee   Music: W. R. Williams

Chorus:

smile in the beak of the Eag - le____ There's a grin in the bill of the stork____ It com - men - ces a - way out in Fris-co____ And it stretch-es a - cross to New York____ Oh there's not as much game in the jun - gle____ As there is round the Cap - i - tol dome.____ And__ North and South and__ East and West, There'll be no sleep, and there'll be no rest: When Ted-dy comes march - ing home.____

He great a man like Chris Colum,
Says Pedro to Antone,
A smarter man like Solomon,
Says Silverstein to Cohn.
You'll see it, there shall be
A reg'lar jubilee
When Teddy comes marching home again,
   Hurrah! hurrah!
Dot Teddy is von fighter yet,
Says Schultz to Guggenheim;
There's Irish blood in him, I'll bet,
Says Casey to O'Brien.
There'll be a hot old fight
In Washington, the night
When Teddy comes marching home again,
   Hurrah! hurrah!

From the original sheet music, pub. 1910
by Will Rossiter, Chicago, Ill.

Another song which was popular then was Vincent Bryan's "Theodore," written originally in 1907, but revived during the bleak Taft years, while this frank plea for Teddy's return undoubtedly echoed a widespread sentiment:

TEDDY, COME BACK

Words: W. D. Nesbit   Music: R. N. Lombard

Guess we've got the sleep-ing sick-ness since you went, ___ For it don't seem like when you were Pres-i-dent; ___ So we send this C. Q. D. to wher-ev-er you may be, And be sure that ev-'ry word of it is meant: ___

Chorus:
Ted-dy, come back! Come and take up the slack, You can wake us up and shake us up And put us on the track. We miss your nerve, we miss your smile, We miss your dar-ing, dash-ing style, So Ted-dy, oh Ted-dy, come back! ___

Used to be that every day you swung your stick,
Making some bold grafter feel almighty sick;
Can't you hustle back and bust every high and mighty trust,
We'll be standing at your back through thin and thick.

Let the lions and the tigers roam the earth,
Come and tighten up your old rough-rider girth;
We are waiting here for you, and we need you P.D.Q.,
So come back and pitch right in for all you're worth.

From the original sheet music, pub. 1910 by New York and
Chicago Music Publishing House.

But if there was popular sentiment running high for Roosevelt's return, it was not shared by President Taft and the Republican hierarchy. Perhaps Roosevelt thought that all he had to do was announce his intentions and the nomination would be his. His announcement, "My hat's in the ring," touched off a wave of excitement and inspired a song of that title by a team of Tin Pan Alley tunesmiths: Harry Williams, Egbert van Alstyne and James Brockman. But after a bitter convention battle in which the machine men simply overrode the claims of the Roosevelt delegates, Taft and his running mate, James Sherman, were renominated.

Roosevelt's announcement had inspired much more than a potential political campaign, however. A staunch coterie of "Progressive" reformers had been won to the Roosevelt cause, and were determined to continue the fight. They organized the Progressive Party, nominated Roosevelt and California Governor Hiram Johnson, and in a great outburst of fervor and song, launched the most spirited third-party campaign in American history. Scores of Roosevelt songs were written, and some of them enjoyed considerable popularity; but the real theme songs of the campaign were "Onward Christian Soldiers" and "The Battle Hymn of the Republic," both of which had the solemnity and spiritual commitment which were such an indelible part of the movement. Popular parodies, hard to find since the heady days of Bryan's earlier crusade, once again appeared:

OUR VICTORY BANNER

Tune: "Marching Through Georgia"

Bring out Progressive banner, boys, and wave
    its colors high,
Listen to the chariot wheels of freedom rolling by,
While a nation's mighty voice mounts upward
    to the sky,
    As we go marching to vict'ry.

Hurrah! hurrah! then rally for the fray!
Hurrah! hurrah! Democrats, clear the way!
Trusting in the Voters' strength, we'll surely
    win the day,
    As we go marching to vict'ry.

Now the gathering boom rolls onward
    from the Empire State,
Making Eastern hearts rejoice and
    Western hearts elate,
Roosevelt for our President, Governor Johnson
    for his mate,
    As we go marching to vict'ry.

Come, my fellow voters, let's hasten to the poll,
For Roosevelt and Johnson, too, we will
    our names enroll.
Prosperity is our watchword, we'll defend it
    heart and soul,
    As we go marching to vict'ry.

From *Up-to-Date Progressive Party Campaign Songs.*

The first verse of the following song for Roosevelt and Johnson was taken from a Lincoln campaign song of 1860.

WAIT FOR THE WAGON

Words: C. H. Congdon
Tune: "Wait for the Wagon"

Where the Mississippi's rolling
Like a silver belt along,
Where Niagara shouts for freedom
In the thunder of the song,
Where the avalanches tumble
From the lofty mountain side,
They jump into the wagon
And will all take a ride.

Chorus:
Wait for the wagon,
Wait for the wagon,
Wait for the wagon,
And we'll all take a ride.

The people own the wagon,
And they own the horses, too,
And it's time they had a driver
Who can drive the horses through;
So they've chosen for their leader
A man already tried,
But the bosses are against him
For he will not let them ride.

In far off California
Beside the Golden Gate,
He found in Hiram Johnson
A noble running mate;
They shook hands across the continent
And now stand side by side,
So we'll jump into their wagon
And we'll all take a ride.

But it wasn't just amateur night for the Bull Moose candidate. The professional songwriters did their bit for Teddy, too, although their work was not, on the whole, terribly inspiring. The best of the lot was this one by Alfred Solman and Harry D. Kerr. Solman was a fair songwriter whose popular numbers included such period pieces as "The Bird on Nellie's Hat" and "You Splash Me and I'll Splash You." Kerr was a lyricist who didn't play favorites. In 1908 he wrote the words for "Get on the Raft with Taft."

WE'RE READY FOR TEDDY AGAIN

Words: Harry D. Kerr Music: Alfred Solman

Our Coun-try's need at last we heed, and choose a man we know,___ Who's

al - ways stood for ev - 'ry good for the peo - ple high and low;___ He

needs no friend to re - com-mend, he's been there once be - fore;___ He's

on the track and go - ing back, this man called The - o - dore.___ Once

more, once more we want our The-o - dore! We're read-y for Ted-dy a -

gain, boys, for the pres - i - dent - ial chair;___

Come lift your voice for the peo - ple's choice, A real man to do and

dare.___ Root stead - y for Ted - dy a - gain boys,

With all your might and main;___ The time is right for a

man to fight, We're read-y for Ted - dy a - gain.___

The trusts will go, and all the dough
That they will have to spend,
Shall not defeat, nor tend to beat
This man whom we defend.
He pleads for all, the just recall,
Of men who prove untrue,
This candidate the Bosses hate,
Will stand for me and you.
Once more, once more
We want our Theodore!

All party ties and party cries
Have failed to down our man,
The issue's plain, we ask again
To let the people plan;
Progressive deeds, progressive needs
And equal rights for all;
We'll now begin to fight and win
For Teddy in the fall.
Once more, once more
We want our Theodore!

Much that has been written and said about the Bull Moose movement tends to suggest that it was largely an extension of Roosevelt's personality. But while Teddy clearly personified the movement, the campaign was a reflection of an intense current for reform in American life at the time which found its most volatile expression in Roosevelt. What inspired the social reformers, woman suffragists and the other thousands of political amateurs who formed the party and worked for it tirelessly was not so much the Teddy of big-game hunts and flamboyant style as the realities of a program which called for major political reform (initiative, referendum, recall of elected officials and judicial decisions, direct primaries, direct election of senators, woman suffrage, etc.), strict regulation of big business, tariff reduction, taxation of the rich (through income and inheritance taxes), and various forms of social security, old age pensions, and protective legislation for workers. It was a far cry from the socialism its opponents charged. It embodied the most realizable goals of the Populists and anticipated the program of another Roosevelt twenty years later.

The division in Republican ranks was, of course, of the utmost interest to the Democrats, who smelled the chance of victory after sixteen years of defeat. The contest boiled down to one between Champ Clark of Missouri, speaker of the House of Representatives, and the recently elected governor of New Jersey, Woodrow Wilson. Clark was the popular figure and the preconvention favorite. His campaign song, "You Gotta Quit Kickin' My Dawg Around," was known throughout the country. But in a last-minute switch, Bryan threw his support to Wilson and after forty-six ballots the governor won the nomination.

The Wilson campaign represented "moderate" reformism, as contrasted with the "progressivism" of Roosevelt and the conservatism of Taft. The Democrats favored many of the governmental reforms associated with Roosevelt (although not woman suffrage) and also made certain concessions in the direction of proposing the regulation of big business. It was not an inspiring platform, nor was Wilson an inspiring figure. But both represented the kind of cautious liberalism which could win the huge middle of a divided electorate. Wilson's final vote was 1.5 million less than the combined Taft-Roosevelt vote (Taft was a poor third), but it is doubtful that either Republican could have polled the combined total. Many a Roosevelt voter would have gone for Wilson in preference to Taft, and many Republicans would have preferred the cautious New Jersey governor to the wild man from Oyster Bay.

A handful of songwriters found inspiration in Wilson's campaign, although there doesn't seem to have been any particular public clamor for their work. One Wilson song was called "Bust the Trusts," which may have seemed somewhat presumptuous in view of Roosevelt's origination of the slogan. Another promised that

. . . it will not cost us half so much to eat,
And the very clothes we wear
Will be cheap they all declare
After Woodrow Wilson takes his seat.

From "After Woodrow Wilson Takes His Seat," by J. Fred DeBerry, pub. by the author, Tampa, Fla., 1912.

But the most popular Wilson song of all was indebted to the currency of an advertising slogan for a blend of whiskey. "Wilson—That's All!" was a household phrase, and it was no surprise that a pair of imaginative songwriters should find a way to turn it into a best-selling campaign song.

Ballard MacDonald, lyricist of "Wilson—That's All!", is also remembered for writing the words to "Rose of Washington Square," "The Trail of the Lonesome Pine," "Beautiful Ohio," and, to George Gershwin's music, "Somebody Loves Me."

WILSON—THAT'S ALL! Words: Ballard MacDonald Music: George Walter Brown

Billy Taft had his steam-roller,
Teddy's hat was in the ring,
Clark came to town with his darn houn'
But Wilson kicked it all aroun';
Billy Bryan he made speeches,
Not a delegate would fall,
Till someone sang, "How dry I am,"
And the crowd began to call—

The third man in the race, and almost forgotten in the uproar, was the president of the United States, William Howard Taft. The bolt of the Progressives made his situation impossible, and it is doubtful that many of his partisans had any great hopes of his winning. Taft also ran a poor third in campaign songs, although a few from 1908 were revived and we know that there was a 1912 version of "Get On the Raft With Taft." There were actually three kinds of Taft songs: anti-Democrat, anti-Roosevelt and the traditional "hail to the candidate" doggerel. Following is one example of each.

"Taft and Sherman" attacked the Democrats, including not only Wilson but also two of his principal rivals for the Democratic nomination: Champ Clark and Governor Judson Harmon of Ohio. In particular, the song took the Democrats to task for championing free trade. It blamed the Panic of 1893 on free trade agitation, and the "Wilson Bill" mentioned in the lyrics was probably the Wilson-Gorman Tariff Act of 1894, which lowered the tariff on many goods.

TAFT AND SHERMAN

Words: George E. Fairbanks
Tune: "Yankee Doodle"

Now let the people come to town
And hear the news that's going,
For Teddy he has lost his hat,
But still he keeps a-crowing.

Chorus:
Yankee Doodle, whoop her up,
Teddy he will hear us,
Democrats are standing near
And hear the people cheer us.

We've started in the fight to win,
And this shall be our sermon,
That every man that knows what's right
Will vote for Taft and Sherman.

Goods from abroad will never bring
Good wages for our people.
It may be you would hurt yourself
By jumping from a steeple.

Remember well in 'ninety-three,
When Cleveland was the leader,
When they commenced to talk free trade,
It was a panic breeder.

The Democrats we do not want,
With Wilson, Clark and Harmon,
So we shall do our very best
And vote for Taft and Sherman.

I knew a man in Cleveland's time
Who had hearty supper,
Who when they passed the Wilson Bill,
His bread it had no butter.

That man today will tell his friends,
And do his best to stir them,
So when it comes election day
They'll vote for Taft and Sherman.

*From Fairbanks' Republican Campaign
Songs.*

TEDDY MUST BE KING

Words: George E. Fairbanks
Tune: "Just Before the Battle, Mother"

Just before the battle, brother,
We are planning what to do.
With the G.O.P. before us,
With their statesmen tried and true.
We must smash them all to pieces,
Teddy he will tell us how,
We must know no other leader,
Simply to his plans we bow.

Chorus:
Let us then be up and doing,
Father every plan they bring,
Smash the poor old Constitution,
Teddy he must be our king.

We are thoroughly progressive,
Running after Teddy's hat;
Though it's kicked and punched and sat on,
Till it's tattered, torn and flat.
Still we're crying—down the bosses!—
Teddy's boss enough for us,
Any other that would dictate
Simply seeks to make a fuss.

Trusts are bad, but some are good ones,
You can tell them if you will;
All the good ones very freely
Put their money in our till,
So that we can buy the people,
They will get it by and by,
Simply when election's over,
They will price their product high.

There's no need of legislatures,
And the courts are out of date,
You will know by asking Teddy
And you will not have to wait.
When we have one with such wisdom,
Who can tell us everything,
There can be no earthly reason,
Why he should not be our king.

From *Fairbanks' Republican Campaign Songs.*

TAFT THE LEADER   Words: M. Strauss   Music: P. Fox

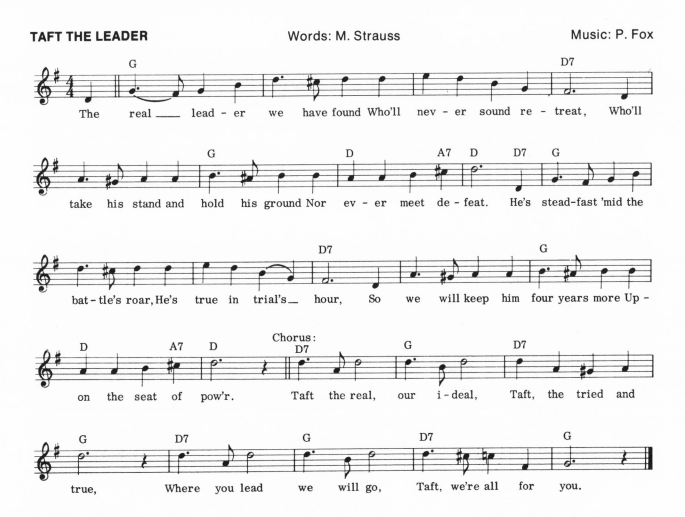

The real ___ lead - er we have found Who'll nev - er sound re - treat, Who'll
take his stand and hold his ground Nor ev - er meet de - feat. He's stead-fast 'mid the
bat - tle's roar, He's true in trial's ___ hour, So we will keep him four years more Up -
on the seat of pow'r. Taft the real, our i - deal, Taft, the tried and
true, Where you lead we will go, Taft, we're all for you.

Oh, statesman of the winsome smile,
We're happy, for we feel
We'll sail with you for many a mile
Upon an even keel.
The whole world hails you as a man
And wise, not over-bold,
A stalwart true American
Of patriotic mold.

A man of peace you are, oh yes,
You'd put an end to war,
And have us grow in happiness
With no wild strife to mar.
But we'll back you for vigor true
To riddle every sham,
They cannot honey-fugle you,
Staunch son of Uncle Sam.

From the original sheet music, published by the Willis Music Co., Cincinnati, Ohio, 1912.

During this time, Tin Pan Alley was enjoying a vogue of "jungle" songs—a reflection, no doubt, of that primitive ethnocentricity which has always made of the culture and customs of the nonwhite world a convenient objectification in U.S. mass culture. "Congo Love Song," "Aba Daba Honeymoon," "Under the Bamboo Tree" and "Down in Jungletown" were among the hits of that simplistic era. In 1909, A. Seymour Brown and Nat Ayer collaborated on "Moving Day in Jungle-town," which had some clever references to Teddy Roosevelt's hunting trip. For the 1912 campaign, Brown teamed up with another composer, Bert Grant, to create a "jungletown" nonpartisan commentary in which all the important figures of the 1912 election appeared: Taft as a "baboon," Roosevelt as "another monkey," Clark as the leopard who was "speaker of the house," Bryan as "the lion...from the plains," and Wilson as the "kangaroo."

THE ELECTION IN JUNGLE TOWN

Words: A. Seymour Brown   Music: Bert Grant

And in the other party, too,
Dissension started in to brew,
Which made the donkey sore.
The leopard argued with the mouse
And said, "I'm speaker of the house,
So I should have the floor."
Then the lion came from the plains,
With flowing mane, to explain,
Said, "If I will only use my brains,
I'll be President."
The elephant began to shake

And called upon his aide, the snake,
To see what he could do.
Then the tiger said, "There is a course,
We'll pursue it as a last resource,
Make the kangaroo our old dark horse,
And he'll hop right in the chair."

Go Right Along, Mister Wilson

Judging by the songs, the 1916 election should have been a landslide for Woodrow Wilson. While songs for Charles Evans Hughes that year were scarcer than Republican votes in Georgia, Tin Pan Alley did its best by Wilson. In retrospect, it seems to have been another one of those campaigns in which the outcome made little difference. Wilson campaigned on the slogan, "He kept us out of war," and promptly brought the country into World War I within a month of his second inauguration.

As it was, the election turned out a cliff-hanger with a tiny majority in California supplying Wilson's margin of victory. But in terms of songs, it was all Wilson. As might have been expected, someone came up with the not-so-original idea to "Never Swap Horses When You're Crossing a Stream," while another pair of songwriting pros proposed that "Four Years More in the White House (Should Be the Nation's Gift to You)" in celebration of Wilson's marriage to Edith B. Galt in 1915. Perhaps the most extravagant of the Wilson songs was this one:

I THINK WE'VE GOT ANOTHER WASHINGTON (AND WILSON IS HIS NAME)

Words and music: George Fairman

1. When Yan-kee Doo-dle came to town, He brought a man of great re-nown and called him Georg-ie Wash-ing-ton. In his-to-ry I'm told, He proved a he-ro bold By win-ning vic-to-ries un-told.___ Con-di-tions are a-bout the same to-day.___ And I'm might-y proud to say.___ I think we've got an-oth-er Wash-ing-ton, Some-one who's just as good as he can be,___ He's called the man of Peace___ no mat-ter where he goes.___ He's just the one for me,___

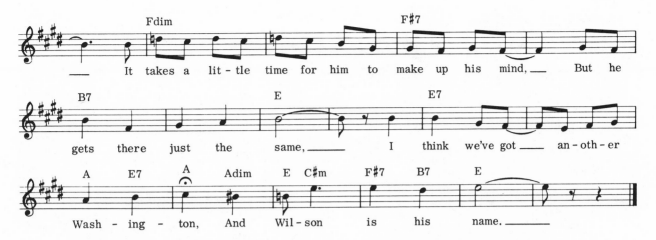

It takes a lit-tle time for him to make up his mind, ___ But he gets there just the same, ___ I think we've got ___ an-oth-er Wash-ing-ton, And Wil-son is his name. ___

I can't forget George Washington,
The things that he has said and done
Have all gone down in history;
And how they treated him,
With cheers they greeted him,
It must have been a sight to see.
I must admit that was some time ago,
But I want you all to know:

From the original sheet music,
published by Kendis Music Co., New
York, 1915.

The war in Europe, of course, was on everyone's mind. The theme song of Wilson's campaign was a popular hit of 1915, "I Didn't Raise My Boy to Be a Soldier." This ragtime number was also enlisted for Wilson's re-election:

WE'RE GOING TO CELEBRATE THE END OF THE WAR IN RAGTIME
(BE SURE THAT WOODROW WILSON LEADS THE BAND)

Words and music: Coleman Goetz and Jack Stern

Ev-'ry-bod-y's ask-ing when ___ we will be at peace a-gain, ___ Ev-'ry-bod-y wants pros-per-i-ty, ___ I hear man-y peo-ple say, ___ "Lay the sword and gun a-way," ___ But still they're fight-ing 'cross the sea, ___ The end must come, it's true, ___ That's why I say to you: ___

Chorus:

We're going to cel-e-brate the end of war in rag-time, Ev-'ry nation soon will sing in rag rhyme, Eng-land, France and Ger-ma-ny, __ E-ven folks from It-a-ly, __ The A-ris-to-crats, And the Dip-lo-mats, March-ing arm in arm, See them tip __ their hats To __ a rag-gy mel-o-dy __ (so pret-ty,) Ev-'ry-where there's har-mo-ny, __ So when we cel-e-brate __ the end of war in Rag-time, Be sure that Wood-row Wil-son leads the band. _____

Everyone will feel so gay,
There'll be one long holiday,
When each nation claims neutrality,
There'll be lots of waving flags,
Waving to the raggy rags,
Each one will have their liberty;
With peace in every land,
I trust you'll understand:

Copyright © Shapiro, Bernstein & Co.,
1915. Used by permission.

A combination of jingoism, preparation for war and the spirit of hail-to-the-chief went into this Wilson re-election song by Seymour Brown, who had written "Teddy" songs just a few years earlier:

GO RIGHT ALONG, MISTER WILSON (AND WE'LL ALL STAND BY YOU)

Words and music: A. Seymour Brown

Guitarist: Capo on 3rd fret and play chords in parentheses

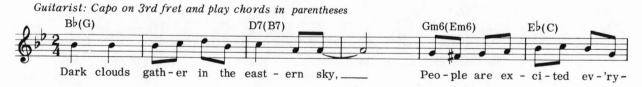

Dark clouds gath-er in the east-ern sky, ____ Peo-ple are ex-ci-ted ev-'ry-

213

Those who lose upon the battlefield,
Never will return to us again;
Wilson knows the sorrows of a war,
And he's trying to spare us the pain.
But even he may have to call on you,
And so prepare to play your part:
Polish your gun while you pray for peace,
And say to him with all your heart:

"Go Right Along, Mr. Wilson" (Brown).
© 1915 by Jerome H. Remick & Co.
Copyright renewed. All rights reserved.
Used by permission of Warner Bros.
Music.

The 1916 campaign marked the end of an era. At the least, it was the last campaign of innocence. The war, a carnage without precedent and on a scale hitherto unimagined, together with the world's first successful communist revolution, were the real birth pangs of the twentieth century. The men and elections up until that time in the United States were still of the nineteenth century. And with the end of innocence, the campaign song which had evolved in an almost unbroken line from "Tippecanoe and Tyler Too" to "We Want Wilson In The White House Four Years More" also came to an end.

The campaign of Charles Evans Hughes, Associate Justice of the U.S. Supreme Court, was, in its own way, a herald of campaigns to come. And the few songs which paid their tributes to Hughes were likewise forerunners of a newer and even more innocuous brand of election song which, with a few notable exceptions, came to be the dominant style of such music up until today.

CHARLES E. HUGHES, THE AMERICAN   Words and music: William H. Pease

The na-tion calls for one to lead, An A-mer-i-can tried and true.___ One that has done his du-ty well, The hon-or comes to you.___ As Gov-er-nor of the Em-pire State, Hon-est gov-ern-ment you did give.___ Put to the test, you gave your best. Your hist-'ry long will live.___

Chorus:
Mis-ter Hughes, we're glad you were se-lect-ed,___ For you are an A-mer-i-can thru and thru.___ The rea-son we be-lieve you'll be e-

lect - ed, _____ Is you have been tried and al - ways found true blue. _____ We know you did not look for this great hon - or, _____ But re - spond - ed on - ly to your na - tion's call. _____ You're the can - di - date for me, You'll pre - pare on land and sea. We need a true A - mer - i - can, that is all. _____

At no time in our history,
Have we needed men so, that's true,
Like Lincoln you only know the right,
No boss can get near you.
In politics you have played no tricks,
You have done your duty well.
Your honest name has brought you fame
Election Day will tell.

From the original sheet music published
by North Eastern Music Co., New York,
1916.

Despite such singular lack of imagination, Charles Evans Hughes gave Wilson quite a run for the money. In the end, it was a few thousand votes in California which saved the day for the Democrats, inspiring a pair of top-notch professional tunesmiths to try their luck with the little number below.

Andrew B. Sterling, who wrote the words of the song, was one of the most successful lyricists of his era. One of Harry von Tilzer's main collaborators, he wrote the words to such von Tilzer hits as "Wait Till the Sun Shines, Nellie," "On a Sunday Afternoon," and "Rufus Rastus Johnson Brown." With other composers Sterling provided the lyrics for "Meet Me in St. Louis (Louis)" and "When My Baby Smiles at Me." Robert A. Keiser, who com-posed the music for the Wilson song, was one of the most prolific tunesmiths of Tin Pan Alley, under a variety of pseudonyms, for some fifty years. Most of his compositions were under the name of Bob King, although he also wrote under the names Mary Earl and Kathleen Roberts. While highly successful as a journeyman popular composer, few of his compositions are remembered today.

The song by Sterling and Keiser gave some credit to woman suffrage as well as California for electing Wilson. The western states were the first to pass woman suffrage laws. California in 1911 and Washington in 1910 were among the most recent. All of the states west of the Dakotas went for Wilson in 1916.

BE GOOD TO CALIFORNIA, MR. WILSON (CALIFORNIA WAS GOOD TO YOU)

Words: Andrew B. Sterling　　　　　　　　　　Music: Robert A. Keiser

From Maine to California they went rolling on with Hughes,
And we waited for the news,
For we knew we couldn't lose.

The answer will go thund'ring down the corridors of fame,
California's answer: "Wilson is his name":

Copyright 1916 by Shapiro, Bernstein Music Publishers. Used by permission.

What a Weapon Is the Ballot!

Songs of Parties with a Cause

From the Free-Soilers of 1848 to the American Party of George Wallace in 1968, third parties have been a recurring feature on the American political scene. From time to time, such parties have managed to significantly affect the outcome of an election—1912, for instance—and in a few other cases, such as the 1968 campaign, they have amassed a really significant vote. But for the most part, these parties have lasted for one or, at the most, two elections, and then vanished. Usually their programs have been sufficiently absorbed by one of the major parties so that most of their supporters have found it to be more practical to work for their goals within the two-party structure.

Three movements of social reform which played a significant and sustained role in American political history in the period from 1865 to 1920 were prohibition, woman suffrage and socialism. In time, all three were absorbed into the political mainstream. The prohibition and woman suffrage amendments to the Constitution, passed in 1919 and 1920 respectively, effectively brought those movements to a close. The socialism of Eugene Debs eventually found most of the short-term reforms it proposed for the country incorporated into Franklin Roosevelt's New Deal.

But in the course of their many decades of agitation and electoral campaigning, all three of these movements produced a lively body of song which is an indispensable part of the history of campaign singing in the United States. Unlike the major party songs which were, as a rule, couched in the vaguest of generalities or concentrated on the personalities of the candidates, the songs of these movements are clearly "cause" songs—consciously viewed as educational concerning the issues as well as (hopefully) an inspiration to voting a particular way. With a few exceptions, the songs are a humorless lot (although an occasional didactic satire may be found), because the people who were attracted to these movements were quite solemn in their commitments. Rarely are they as slick or polished as the "best" of the major candidate songs, but they frequently compensate in intensity for whatever they may lack in superficial gloss.

Marching Through Rum-Land

The Prohibition Party was organized in 1869 after nonpolitical temperance societies had failed to make any impact towards legally outlawing the manufacture, sale and distribution of alcoholic beverages. Largely religious in orientation, prohibitionists reflected both a strong "moral" view of life along with a very real concern for the human waste which frequently ensued from the use of liquor. The central contradiction of their politics was that they were trying to save someone else—not themselves; and so, while they were ardent crusaders for their cause, their own lives were not defined in the same ways as those they were trying to "save."

Starting in 1872, Prohibitionists ran candidates in every presidential election. At first their vote was so infinitesimally small that it was rarely even tabulated. But in the election of 1884, their candidate, John P. Saint John, polled some 150,000 votes nationally and 25,000 votes in New York State, which was probably the crucial factor in losing New York and the election for James G. Blaine. Not so coincidentally, the first temperance songs which dealt directly with the question of the ballot appeared about the same time. In 1888, the party drew a quarter of a million votes, and its high point was reached in 1892 when John Bidwell received 265,000 votes for president. Bryan brought many of these into the Democratic Party and some of the militants moved leftward to a form of Christian socialism which went beyond but incorporated temperance. The party's vote stayed around the 200,000 mark for the next several decades, but with the adoption and subsequent repeal of the Prohibition Amendment, it has largely lost whatever mass character it once had.

Its songs are a reminder of a certain single-minded fervor in American life which has frequently been able to wield an influence out of proportion to its actual numbers. The writers of songs like "Marching Through Rum-Land" obviously regarded the struggle to outlaw liquor as a crusade and compared it to the crusade against slavery represented by the Civil War. The Prohibitionists insisted, however, that the weapons they used in their holy war would be ballots and not bullets.

The Prohibitionist song below inveighed bitterly against James G. Blaine, the Republican presidential candidate in 1884. Prohibitionists, most of whom would ordinarily have been Republicans, were particularly incensed at Blaine because the Republican Convention had made short shrift of a temperance petition. Although they left Republican ranks, Prohibitionists invoked one of the favorite catchwords of the Republican Party, "protection." "Home-Protection" was a Prohibitionist rallying cry in an era which, as the result of the tariff debates, was very much "protection" conscious.

The song as it appears here is actually a composite of "Our Next Campaign, Boys" and "Marching Through Rum-Land," both by Horace B. Durant and from his *Prohibition Party Campaign Songs,* published in 1884.

MARCHING THROUGH RUM-LAND

Tune: "Marching Through Georgia"

We have stood in battle, boys, when bullets fell like hail,
Now we meet another foe, our courage shall not fail;
Forward! then, we'll conquer rum, the liquor-lines assail,
    As we go marching through Rum-land!

Chorus:
Hurrah! Hurrah! We march to victory;
Hurrah! Hurrah! From rum we shall be free;
From hill, plain and valley, from the mountain to the sea;
    As we go marching through Rum-Land!

Why Blaine should be President, it would be hard to say,
He has served the liquor-trade, 'tis true, and made it pay,
And the homes he has betrayed, we now behold today;
    As we go marching through Rum-Land!

He will get the whiskey vote—of course, his party's, too,
They have common interest in rum-made revenue,
Boasting loud of "temperance," but we'll expose the crew—
    As we go marching through Rum-land!

Both old parties are accursed with all the crimes of rum,
But the Prohibition Party, their stern judge, has come;
Guilty, self-convicted, they bow in its presence dumb!
    As we go marching through Rum-land!

Ballots now, not bullets, boys, not bayonet and gun,
Not the roar of deadly strife, from rise to set of sun;
Yet the vict'ry shall be greater when the field is won,
    As we go marching through Rum-land!

Rally to our standard, boys, that stainless greets the light—
Prohibition Home-Protection leads us in the fight,
God and home and native land, inspire our souls with might,
    As we go marching through Rum-land!

The Prohibitionists made it abundantly clear that Republican proposals for a set of licensing codes which would regulate liquor traffic rather than abolish it did not satisfy them. As the temperance crusaders never tired of pointing out, government at all levels was deeply implicated in the manufacture and sale of alcoholic beverages. The following song reminded voters that whiskey taxes were a prime source of income for the federal government and that local governments used liquor revenue to pay for education. Indeed, the fact that liquor taxes paid for education was a favorite argument of the anti-Prohibition forces. The Prohibitionists, however, abhorred the use of whiskey-tainted money even for worthy purposes; and they insisted that they would be able to abolish the demon rum if, as Christians, they voted just as they prayed.

VOTE FOR OUR PARTY

Tune: "Wait for the Wagon"

Six hundred thousand victims
Drink yearly binds in chains,
That deadly still and dram-shop
May reap their guilty gains!
We want no license party,
A bloody flag that waves,
O'er sixty thousand drunkards,
It yearly sends to graves!

Chorus:
Then vote for our party!
Then vote for our party!
Then vote for our party!
And we'll put rum away!

Away with party boasting
Its crime-cursed revenue,
That costs its countless millions
For every million due!
We are determined fully
That rum no more shall rule,
And that its crime-cursed money
Shall not support the school.

Hurrah, for Prohibition!
We'll put this rum away,
If we go grimly forward,
And vote just as we pray;
Hurrah! the mighty ballot
Is never known to fail!
Then sturdily we'll wield it,
And over rum prevail.

From *Prohibition Party Campaign
Songs.*

The following Prohibitionist song minced no
words in declaring the aim of the Party:

HURRAH FOR PROHIBITION

Tune: "Yankee Doodle"

The Temp'rance folks are waking up
Throughout the Yankee nation,
To put the liquor traffic down,
And drive it from creation.
The stills and drinking dens are doomed
To lawful demolition;
For all good men are going in
For legal Prohibition.

Chorus:
Prohibition is the song,
We'll shout it thro' the nation;
Prohibition to the wrong
Is right through all creation.

Too long King Alcohol has reigned,
All moral suasion scorning,
Too long his murd'rous savages
Have filled the land with mourning.
Rum-sellers care not for our prayers,
Or tears, or admonition;
But there's a pow'r can make them quake,
'Tis legal Prohibition.

No scoffs or foes or doubts of friends
Shall weaken our endeavor
To brand the traffic with disgrace
And wipe it out forever!
Right on shall go the noble work
Until its full completion;
We'll "fight it out upon the line"
Of total Prohibition!

From *The Prohibition Songster.*

One should not discount a strong streak of nativism which ran like a thread through Prohibition sentiment. The whiskey-drinking Irish and the beer-drinking Germans were constant targets (usually for ridicule) in Prohibitionist songs. The chorus of one such musical tract, after commenting on the "temperance" sentiments of a Republican preacher and a Democratic deacon, protests:

But he votes with Jimmy Doolan, Paddy Ryan
     and Teddy Flynn,
All saloonists, and his ballot counts and helps
     these men to win.

Fillmore's Prohibition Songs.

Blaine obviously blundered in 1884 when he failed to disassociate himself from the famous "Rum, Romanism and Rebellion" charge, but the fact is that a significant temperance bloc *did* lump all three together. A "stage Irish" dialect ballad, "The Happy Irishman," makes much of the incongruous rarity of a Hibernian teetotaler, while in "Murphy's Song," an Irish saloon-keeper celebrates the inconsistency of "temperance folks [who] are all a hoax" because "they vote our way." A German saloon-keeper, "Yakob Schneider," boasts in "Dutch dialect" verse, "mit my saloon, I git reech soon." And in the style of the era, scores of dialect "coon" songs were employed by the Prohibitionist versifiers.

During the campaign of 1900, while Bryan and the Democrats were attacking McKinley's imperialist adventures in Cuba, Puerto Rico and the Philippines, Prohibitionists were also concerned with these "foreign entanglements." Their solicitude, however, was not over the involvement of the United States with other peoples, but a warning against allowing the "beneficiaries" of American "civilization" to drink liquor.

They are semi-savage now, but we will show them what they need,
We must civilize the Philippines, you know;
There'll be sure to be a harvest when we once have sown the seed,
We must civilize the Philippines, you know.
We will send our civilization to them o'er the ocean wide,
She will lift them up and teach them to our boundless joy and pride,
And the blessings of enlightenment shall 'round about them flow,
As we civilize the Philippines, you know.

From "Civilize the Philippines," *Fillmore's Prohibition Songs.*

So went one verse of a song called "Civilize the Philippines," popular with Prohibitionists at the time, which then went on to bemoan the fact that "our civilization's married, she is now the bride of rum." Another such might well have been sub-titled "The (Dry) White Man's Burden":

Over the sea in their ignorant blindness,
Dwell the poor heathen 'mid darkness and night.
We in the homeland with brotherly kindness,
Reach out with longing to send them the light.
So o'er the ocean our good ships are speeding,
Gladly to bear them the tidings of cheer;
But side by side with the word of God—think of it!
Travels its foe—our American beer.

Bibles and beer! what a strange combination!
Whoever heard of the like in creation?
Mustn't the heathen consider us queer?
Sending them cargoes of bibles and beer?

From "Bibles and Beer," *Fillmore's Prohibition Songs.*

As with all third parties, the Prohibitionists had to refute the charge that their supporters would be "wasting their votes." So they had songs, probably borrowed from the Populists, which said "Good-by, Old Party, Good-by" and celebrated the virtues of "The Prohibition ballot, corruption's mighty foe." This one tackled the question head on:

IT IS NOT THROWN AWAY   Words: Mrs. Ida M. Budd   Music: J. H. Fillmore

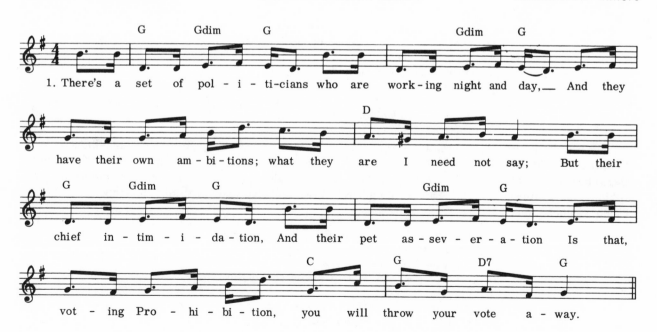

1. There's a set of pol-i-ti-cians who are work-ing night and day,— And they have their own am-bi-tions; what they are I need not say; But their chief in-tim-i-da-tion, And their pet as-sev-er-a-tion Is that, vot-ing Pro-hi-bi-tion, you will throw your vote a-way.

Chorus:

But you nev - er need be - lieve them, for, no mat - ter what they say, Not a
vote for right and jus - tice ev - er yet was thrown a - way; Truth is
strong - er still than er - ror, Wrong from right shall flee in ter - ror, And our
cause shall sure - ly tri - umph: Has - ten on the glo - rious day.

One, perhaps, his man approaches in a confidential way,
And the subject mildly broaches of how best a vote will pay;
Then his arguments arraying,
He will clinch them all by saying,
"You will never be so silly as to throw your vote away."

Haply then comes by another, with his speech all learned by rote,
Of the first a worthy brother, and he sounds the self-same note;
With his sophistries he'll ply you,
(If he dared, he'd try to buy you),
And he taunts you with your folly if you throw away your vote.

So just keep your headpiece level and to such advisers say,
You're no partner with the devil and you'll not accept his pay;
Then, no matter who repels you,
Put your vote where conscience tells you,
And ere long you will discover that it was not thrown away.

From *Fillmore's Prohibition Songs.*

But it wasn't all just cold logic in the Prohibition camp. The crusade against drink had its analytical side, to be sure, but the songs which really expressed Prohibitionist sentiment were those grand old ballads of pathos which painted lurid pictures of the human wreckage resulting from the uninhibited use of alcohol. These were the songs which helped fill the collection plate and provided the emotional framework for the songs of valor and voting:

Once he was so light and fair, glad and light and free,
Filled my soul with peace and joy, life was dear to me,
But he took the fatal glass, 'twas a fleeting joy,
Drank, and lo!, the hand of death, grasped my darling boy.

From "Save the Boy!" by Mrs. C. S. Ellsworth and
W. Warren Bentley, *The Prohibition Songster.*

Tune: "Old Folks at Home"

From the bar-room, drunken laughter sounds on the night,
While across a little death-bed falls the moonbeam cold and white;
Go search for father where the wine is red,
Tell him how our hearts are breaking, tell him little Lou is dead.

From "Tell Him Little Lou Is Dead," *Fillmore's Prohibition Songs.*

. . . sad is our home and the story I tell,
How brightness was turned into darkness and gloom,
For father's a drunkard, his manhood all gone,
He left love and home for the licensed saloon.

From "The Licensed Saloon," *Fillmore's Prohibition Songs.*

Where is my wand'ring boy tonight?
Down in the licensed saloon....
Learning new vices all the night long,
Tempted to all that's sinful and wrong,
Listening to the harlot's foul song,
Down in the licensed saloon.

From "Down in the Licensed Saloon," *Fillmore's Prohibition Songs.*

THEN AND NOW   Words: Palmer Hartsough   Tune: "My Old Kentucky Home"

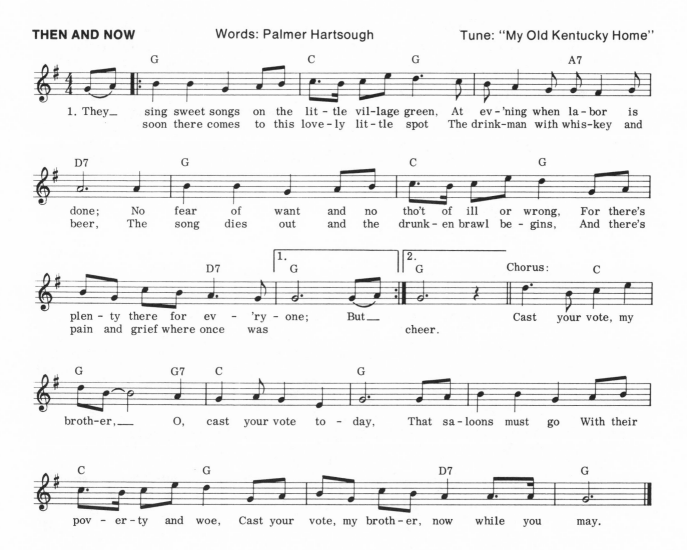

1. They sing sweet songs on the lit-tle vil-lage green, At ev-'ning when la-bor is
   soon there comes to this love-ly lit-tle spot The drink-man with whis-key and

done; No fear of want and no tho't of ill or wrong, For there's
beer, The song dies out and the drunk-en brawl be-gins, And there's

1. plen-ty there for ev-'ry-one; But—
pain and grief where once was
2. cheer.
Chorus: Cast your vote, my

broth-er,— O, cast your vote to-day, That sa-loons must go With their

pov-er-ty and woe, Cast your vote, my broth-er, now while you may.

The drink-man hangs on the wall of his saloon
A writing most precious and rare,
And safe is he with this license o'er his head,
For it bears Columbia's seal so fair;
He leads young men in the path of sin and shame,
And mothers and maidens must weep,
He breaks great hearts and he wrecks the brightest homes,
Yet serenely on his way will keep.

The drink-man rules for in caucus he is king,
His bidding his tipplers all do,
And good men vote with the party and the ring,
So the drink man's schemes are carried through;
The time comes fast when beneath the tyrant Rum
The nation must bow as a slave,
Stand, patriots, then for the cause of truth and right,
And your colors fly, ye freemen brave.

From *Fillmore's Prohibition Songs.*

Hail the Social Revolution!

The ideas of Karl Marx had a degree of currency in America for more than half a century before national organizational forms developed which based themselves to any appreciable extent on socialist ideology. Various brands of utopian socialism had surfaced from time to time, usually resulting in short-lived experiments in communal living by a handful of the faithful whose commitment was more religious than political. A more materialist view of socialism was brought to the country by German and Jewish immigrants of the 1880s and 1890s, but it wasn't until the railway strike of 1893 and the subsequent radicalization of America's first important socialist spokesman, Eugene V. Debs, that the cause began to develop roots within the American working class.

In terms of presidential politics, the Socialist Party's greatest influence came over the course of two decades from 1900, when it was known as the Social Democratic Party, to 1920. In five of the six elections in that period, Debs was the standard-bearer of the Socialist Party. A summary of the Party's popular vote over that period is instructive:

1900	94,864
1904	402,460
1908	420,820
1912	897,011
1916	585,113
1920	919,799

The Socialist vote dropped in 1916 because Debs refused to run and the developing war fever caused some Socialist supporters to defect from the Party because of its opposition to the war. Allan Benson was the Socialist candidate in 1916. Debs was in jail during the election of 1920 on charges growing out of his antiwar activities.

Socialist politics was an odd blend of Christian morality and Marxian economics—and no one summed up that combination better than Debs, who right up to the time of his death in 1926 projected to the American people the image of a "good" man. Because of this, historians have tended to paint Debs as something of a political innocent, a kindly and naive intellectual lightweight. In reality, Debs's knowledge of socialist theory was much more extensive than he has generally been given credit for; in fact, his understanding of Marxian ideas was so deep that he was able to forgo the usual rhetoric we have come to associate with such beliefs and use the kind of language that American workers could understand, which may be why some have doubted his capacity.

But it would be wrong to assume that the socialist movement in America was dependent on the personality of Debs. Like the prohibitionists and the populists, the socialists advanced their cause much more than the man. The party literature was more concerned with the ideas of socialism than with the figure of Debs. And in the socialist songs of the period, it was ideology much more than the candidates that inspired the party faithful.

The spirit of militant Christianity is a recurring theme of the socialist songs. To the tune of "John Brown's Body," they sang of Jesus, Marx and "overthrowing the system."

OUR CAUSE IS MARCHING ON

Words: Rev. M. A. Smith
Tune: "John Brown's Body"

We know the workers now can forfeit nothing but their chains,
We've nothing to reward us now for all our toil and pains;
However hard we labor with our muscles and our brains,
But still keep marching on.

Chorus:
Glory, glory hallelujah,
Glory, glory hallelujah,
Glory, glory hallelujah,
Our cause is marching on!

The parasites oppose us both with cunning and with stealth,
But we will stand for Jesus whether sickness or in health,
Until we meet in our cooperative commonwealth,
We'll still keep marching on.

We'll overthrow the system that's upheld by thieves and knaves,
That dooms our precious children to the life of toiling slaves;
And sends the plundered workers prematurely to their graves,
We'll still keep marching on.

From *Socialism in Song.*

One could quote from many socialist songs to show the strong religious strain running throughout, but equally revealing is the fact that so many of the songs are written to church tunes. "Stand Up For Jesus," "Onward Christian Soldiers," "The Ninety and Nine"—these were the tunes with which socialists were familiar. While the campaign melodies for Roosevelt, Taft, Bryan and Wilson ran the gamut from ragtime to martial, the socialist music was, for the most part, fairly stern and straight-laced. And while the rhetoric of the Socialists was forthright and militant, their faith seemed to reside in the possibilities of the electoral system for achieving socialist goals.

WHAT A WEAPON IS THE BALLOT

Words: Rev. M. A. Smith
Tune: "What a Friend We Have in Jesus"

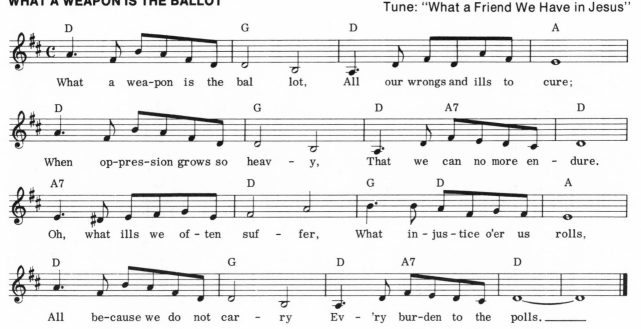

Are you homeless, poor and wand'ring,
Tho' you've toiled throughout the year?
Are your wife and children needy?
Is the future dark and drear?
Has your labor naught relieved you?
Are there landlords grasping tolls?
You should never be discouraged,
You can right it at the polls.

From *Socialism in Song*.

Although the songs of the socialists stressed ideology more than their party's nominees, many did mention the candidates. Debs, as the perennial Social-ist candidate, appears again and again. But there was also Job Harriman, Debs's running mate in 1900, a lawyer, and one of a group of "kangaroos" who jumped from Daniel De Leon's Socialist Labor Party to join with Debs in forming the new Social Democratic Party; and Ben Hanford, nominated for Vice-President at the second national convention of the Socialist Party held in Chicago on May 1, 1904. Hanford, who was to run again with Debs in 1908, was a socialist newspaperman, best known for being the creator of the mythical "Jimmy Higgins," the rank-and-filer who did all the unsung jobs of the revolution.

HAIL THE SOCIAL REVOLUTION

Tune: "John Brown's Body"

We are coming, Debs and Harriman, one million voters strong,
We come from shops and mines, from fields and plains with joy and song,
We'll teach the ruling class a point on how to right the wrong
While we are marching on.

Chorus:
Hail the Social Revolution!
Cheer the peaceful Revolution!
Speed the coming Revolution!
The Brotherhood of Man.

From Lakes to Gulf we'll work and vote for Debs and Harriman,
From East to West, let Labor shout, "We come to free the land!"
Wage slavery must cease and men be free throughout the land,
For we are marching on.

From the Socialist newspaper, *The Advance*, San Francisco, Oct. 27, 1900.

OUR JUBILEE

Words: Harvey P. Moyer
Tune: "Kingdom Coming"

Say, comrades, have you seen our master,
With a big scare on his face,
Go down the street sometime this morning,
Like he's going to leave the place;
He dropped into the Chicago Convention,
Where the Socialist force held sway,
But he took his hat and left very sudden,
And I guess he's run away.

Chorus:
The capitalist runs, ha, ha,
The Socialist laughs, hee, hee;
It must be now the Kingdom's coming
And the Year of Jubilee.

He's six foot one way, three foot t'other,
And he weighs three hundred pound,
He lived so long on the labor of others,
That he thought his claims were sound;
But he heard them tell of a world-wide movement,
Labor's plans to keep its own,
And the news of a million class-conscious voters
Made him take the first train home.

226

He heard them tell of a good time coming
When the people should be free,
No need to beg for work or rations,
No wrong, no misery;
When all the earth'd be common treasure,
And its wealth we all should share;
He'd get his equal share with others,
If he'd do his best while there.

Three cheers for Debs! three cheers for Hanford!
Our standard-bearers grand,
Let all who freedom's cause hold dearest,
On our glorious platform stand;
To all the world proclaim our mission,
Let all the people see,
To work and vote for the Socialist Party
Will bring true liberty.

From *Songs of Socialism.*

The following song, from the 1912 campaign, lumped Teddy, Taft and Wilson together, along with a backhanded reference to Champ Clark (the "yaller houn' ") and the popular song associated with his unsuccessful bid for the Democratic nomination, "You Gotta Quit Kickin' My Dawg Around."

VOTING FOR LABOR

Words: James R. Townsend
Tune: "Marching Through Georgia"

Comrades, it is time for us to sing another song,
Sing it with a courage that will sweep the world along.
Sing it from the heart, oh comrades, sing it loud and strong;
Labor shall now vote for Labor!

Chorus:
Hurrah! Hurrah! We'll bring the jubilee!
Hurrah! Hurrah! The workers shall be free!
Life and Love and Truth shall reign instead of property,
For Labor is voting for Labor!

Dividends have long been paid from Labor's weary toil,
To idlers who despise a brother marked with Labor's soil;
Soon we'll tell those idlers their own dinner pots to boil,
For Labor is voting for Labor!

The Democratic teeter-board long worked up and down,
And Tammany is riding there, likewise the "yaller houn',"
But they are now no longer kicking Labor votes aroun',
For Labor is voting for Labor!

The elephant has a big fat man who makes a mighty load,
'Tis Teddy's fault the elephant was ever thus bestrode;
But Teddy, Taft and Wilson now are on Salt River road,
For Labor is voting for Labor!

Oh, yes! and there are Union men, Eugene V. Debs is one!
His genial face is shining like the early morning sun,
And in the White House race Eugene will show them how to run,
For Labor is voting for Labor!

From *The California Democrat,* Aug. 29, 1912.

I'm a Suffragette

When Margaret Brent appeared before the Maryland House of Burgesses in the year 1647 and demanded the right to vote, she may have earned the honor of being the first woman suffragist in North America. The struggle for the ballot for women dates back at least that far, although Anne Hutchinson's battle with the elders of the Bay Colony for a voice in church affairs ten years earlier was also, in effect, a suffrage demand. More than 100 years later, in the early days of the American Revolution, Abigail Adams wrote her husband, John: "In the new code of laws which I suppose it will be necessary for you to make, I desire you would remember the ladies and be more generous and favorable to them than your ancestors....If particular care and attention is not paid to the ladies, we are determined to foment a rebellion, and will not hold ourselves bound by any laws in which we have no voice or representation."

Widespread agitation for woman suffrage did not really begin, however, until immediately after the Civil War. The first organized campaign took place in 1867 in Kansas, where a referendum was placed on the ballot which would have given women the vote in that state. The proposal was defeated by a margin of more than two to one, but the campaign helped to highlight the issue of woman suffrage. Playing an active role in the campaign was one of the great crusading singer-songwriters of the era, John W. Hutchinson, who collaborated in composing the following, undoubtedly the oldest English-language woman suffrage song:

KANSAS SUFFRAGE SONG

Words: P. P. Fowler and John W. Hutchinson
Tune: "Old Dan Tucker"

Oh, say what thrilling songs of fairies,
Wafted o'er the Kansas prairies,
Charm the ear while zephyrs speed 'em,
Woman's pleading for her freedom.

Chorus:
Clear the way, the songs are floating,
Clear the way, the world is noting;
Prepare the way, the right promoting,
And ballots, too, for women's voting.

We frankly say to fathers, brothers,
Husbands, too, and several others,
We're bound to win our right of voting,
Don't you hear the music floating?

We came to take with you our station,
Brave defenders of the nation,
And aim by noble, just endeavor,
To elevate our sex forever.

By this vote we'll rid our nation
Of its vile intoxication.
Can't get rum? Oh, what a pity!
Dram-shops closed in every city.

Fear not, we'll darn each worthy stocking,
Duly keep the cradle rocking,
And beg you heed the words we utter,
The ballot wins our bread and butter.

All hail, brave Kansas, first in duty,
Yours the need of praise and beauty,
You'll nobly crown your deeds of daring,
Freedom to our sex declaring.

Quoted in *History of Woman Suffrage*, Vol. 2, edited by Elizabeth Cady Stanton, Susan B. Anthony and Matilda J. Gage, Charles Mann Inc., Rochester, N. Y., 1887.

But while the Hutchinsons sang of "women's voting," others were bemoaning the dire fate of those of the "fair sex" who were willing to despoil themselves by association with the ballot-box. R. A. Cohen of Saint Joseph, Missouri was neither the first nor the last misogynist, but he may have been the first man to construct a song specifically directed *against* woman suffrage, an act inspired, undoubtedly, by the women's rights agitation in Kansas.

FEMALE SUFFRAGE

Words: R. A. Cohen   Music: A. J. Phelps

1. You may wear your silks and sa-tin, Go____ when and where you please, Make em-

broi-der-y and tat-tin', And____ live quite at your ease. You may

go to ball and con-cert, In gau-dy hat and coat— In

fact, my charm-ing crea-tures, Do ev-'ry-thing but vote.

Chorus:

You may vis-it ball and con-cert, In gau-dy hat and

coat, In fact, my charm-ing crea-tures, Do ev-'ry-thing but vote.

You may seek for health and riches,
And marry at your will,
But man must wear the breeches,
And rule the household still;
For nature so designed it,
And so our fathers wrote,
And clearly they defined it,
That man, alone, should vote.

But when from her position,
A careless woman's hurled,
She's the loathing of our manhood,
The scorn of all the world;
She loses her identity,
With all that's noble, then,
And seeks the common level
Of the commonest of men.

Then mothers, wives and sisters,
I beg you keep your place;
And remain what nature made you—
The help-meets of our race.
Let no temptation lead you,
Nor any wily fox,
To descend unto the level
Of the nation's ballot-box.

You wish to be our equal,
We prize you something more,
And proudly look upon you
Than angels little lower.
We would not have you equal,
But superior to us;
A something we can idolize,
Though fashioned out of dust.

I have given my opinion,
And I hold that it is true—
What would strengthen politicians
Would tend to weaken you.
It would bring you to its level,
In spite of all that's said,
And political corruption
Would show its hydra-head.

Published by P. L. Huyett & Son,
Saint Joseph, Mo., 1867.

229

The women lost in Kansas, but in distant Wyoming, not yet a state, the sparsely settled territory enacted the first woman suffrage legislation in 1869, leading to a spate of songs which managed to rouse enthusiasm in the ranks but little else.

> In Wyoming, our sisters fair,
> Can use the ballot well;
> Why can't we do so everywhere,
> Can anybody tell?
>
> From "A New Suffrage Song,"
> *Suffrage and Temperance Melodies.*

The chief opponents of woman suffrage were the liquor interests. For a variety of reasons, the cause of prohibition and women's rights were joined together for more than half a century, and the greatest fear of the distilleries was that woman suffrage would immediately swing the tide toward a ban on alcohol. This is not to minimize the strength of entrenched male supremacist attitudes, but without the material support of the liquor manufacturers and similarly concerned sectors of business, it is safe to say that woman suffrage could have been won much earlier.

But the woman's movement made no secret of its intentions to use the ballot for social and moral reform, as this song *circa* 1884 reveals:

OH, DEAR, WHAT CAN THE MATTER BE?
Words: L. May Wheeler

GOING TO THE POLLS
Words: Julia B. Nelson
Tune: "Coming Through the Rye"

> If the men should see the women,
> Going to the polls,
> To put down the liquor traffic,
> Need it vex their souls?
> If we're angels, as they tell us,
> Can we once suppose
> That all the men would frown upon us,
> When going to the polls?
>
> *Chorus:*
> We love our boys, our household joys,
> We love our girls as well,
> The law of love is from above,
> 'Gainst that we ne'er rebel.
>
> No discharge have Christian women
> From the war with sin;
> At the polls with Gog and Magog
> Must the fight begin.
> Since we've Bible-marching orders,
> Need it fright our souls,
> Though all the men should on us frown
> When going to the polls.
>
> From *Suffrage and Temperance Melodies.*

Much more pointed, and with an undertone of bitterness, was this suffrage song of the same period:

Tune: "Oh, Dear, What Can the Matter Be?"

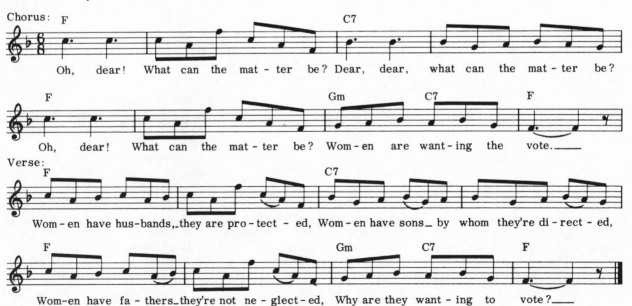

Chorus:
Oh, dear! What can the matter be? Dear, dear, what can the matter be?
Oh, dear! What can the matter be? Wom-en are want-ing the vote.____

Verse:
Wom-en have hus-bands, they are pro-tect-ed, Wom-en have sons_ by whom they're di-rect-ed,
Wom-en have fa-thers_they're not ne-glect-ed, Why are they want-ing to vote?____

Women have homes, there they should labor,
Women have children, whom they should favor,
Women have time to learn of each neighbor,
Why are they wanting to vote?

Women can dress, they love society,
Women have cash, with its variety,
Women can pray, with sweetest piety,
Why are they wanting to vote?

Women are preaching to sinners today,
Women are healing the sick by the way,
Women are dealing out law as they may,
Why are they wanting to vote?

Women are trav'ling about, here and there,
Women are working like men everywhere,
Women are crowding—then claiming 'tis fair,
Why are they wanting to vote?

Women have reared all the sons of the brave,
Women have shared in the burdens they gave,
Women have labored *your* country to save,
That's why we're wanting to vote!

Oh, dear, what can the matter be?
Dear, dear, what can the matter be?
Oh, dear, what can the matter be?
When men want every vote?

From *Suffrage and Temperance Melodies.*

Every revolution invokes the rhetoric and spirit of previous upheavals. The women's movement found not only logic in the struggles of their colonial ancestors against King George, they may even have been implying a lightly veiled threat of using some of the same tactics in this suffrage song:

THE TAXATION TYRANNY   Words: General E. Estabrook   Tune: "The Red, White and Blue"

That one man shall not rule another,
Unless by that other's consent,
Is the principle deep underlying
The framework of this government.
So, as woman is punished for breaking
The laws which she cannot gainsay,
Let us give her a voice in the making,
Or ask her no more to obey.

From *Manual for Political Equality Clubs.*

The turning point came in 1890 when Wyoming was admitted to the Union and became the first state with woman suffrage. Colorado, Idaho and Utah followed suit during the next few years, but it wasn't until 1910 and 1911 that California and Washington adopted woman suffrage. By 1912, votes for women had become one of the central political questions of the day. The suffragists were becoming increasingly vocal; some engaged in civil disobedience while others concentrated on mass organizing. Still others worked for an explicit amendment to the Constitution. But it was one struggle and the songs reflected both a growing militancy (as in "The Taxation Tyranny") and also a broader base of popular support.

WINNING THE VOTE

Words: Mrs. A. B. Smith
Tune: "Not for Joseph"
[*To be sung as a duet*]

> *Boys:*
> I've been down to Madison
> To see the folks and sights;
> You'd laugh, I'm sure, to hear them talk
> About the women's rights.
> Now 'tis just as plain as my old hat,
> That's plain as plain can be,
> That if the women want the vote,
> They'll get no help from me.
>
> Not from Joe, not from Joe,
> If he knows it, not from Joseph!
> No, no, no, not from Joe,
> Not from me, I tell you no!
>
> *Girls:*
> Say, friend Joseph, why not we
> Should vote as well as you?
> Are there no problems in the State
> That need our wisdom too?
> We must pay our taxes same as you,

As citizens be true;
And if some wicked thing we do,
To jail we're sent by you.

Yes we are, same as you,
And you know it, don't you Joseph?
Yes you do, yet you boast,
You'll not help us win the vote.

Boys:
But, dear women, can't you see,
Your home is your true sphere?
Just think of going to the polls
Perhaps two times a year!
You are wasting time you ought to use
In sewing and at work,
Your home neglected all those hours—
Would you such duties shirk?

Help from Joe? Help from Joe?
If he knows it, not from Joseph;
No, no, no, not from Joe,
Not from me, I tell you—No!

Girls:
Joseph, tell us something new,
We're tired of that old song;
We'll sew the seams and cook the meals,
To vote won't take us long.
We will help clean house, the one too large
For man to clean alone,
The State and Nation, don't you see,
When we the vote have won.

Yes we will, and you'll help,
For you'll need our help, friend Joseph;
Yes you will, when we're in,
So you'd better help us win.

Boys:
You're just right, how blind I've been,
I ne'er had seen it thus;
'Tis true that taxes you must pay
Without a word of fuss;
You are subject to the laws men made,
And yet no word or note,
Can you sing out where it will count—
I'LL HELP YOU WIN THE VOTE!

Yes I will. [*Girls*]: Thank you Joe.
[*All*]: We'll together soon be voters;
Yes we will, if you'll all,
Vote "Yes" at the polls next fall.

From the original sheet music, pub. by Busy World Publishing Co., Madison, Wisc., 1912.

Not every man was as easily persuaded as Joseph. Many found the suffrage agitation a singular cause for amusement. In "Your Mother's Gone Away to Join the Army," a pair of songwriters, Thomas Gray and Raymond Walker, told this "sad" tale:

A little lad with curly hair stood by his father's knee,
You could see that he was crying, he was sad as he could be;
He sobbed and said, "I feel so blue," as tears ran down his cheeks,
"Oh, father, where is mother? She has not been home for weeks."

His pa said, "Lad, the tale is sad, she's down at Suffrage Hall,
She's gone to fight for women's rights, why there's their bugle call.
Hear the tramp of their feet as they come down the street,
Gee, those girlies look sweet, they're all dressed up so neat—

Your dear old ma just took a fighter's place,
She likes the smell of powder 'cause it's always on her face;
There's no rats in her hair, you can see she don't care—
Holds her head in the air, Gee your mother's a bear!"

Tramp, tramp, tramp the girls are marching—
"Your mother's gone away to join the army!"

Perhaps they were, in some ways, laughable. Surely their sublime belief that woman suffrage would become a great instrument for social reform seems naive in retrospect. Their frequent assertions that they would not neglect "women's work" while taking on "man's" undoubtedly seems today like a needless concession to male prejudice and oppressive social roles. But in the context of their time, given the social hostility and the moral codes of the era, they were indeed a fearless band trying to direct the course of history in a time when most women dared not dream of directing the course of their own lives. Their slogans and their songs are, of course, relics of the past; but they are, at the same time, keepsakes of courage, reminders of a tradition which is being reinvigorated in our own time by a new upsurge of the women's liberation cause.

I'M A SUFFRAGETTE

Words: M. Olive Drennan   Music: M. C. Hanford

My papa does the voting
While mama does the work,
And when there is any shirking,
He is the one to shirk.

And the children growing up,
Are starting in to school,
If the teacher's a gentleman,
They have to "mind the rule."

Oh, the men make all the laws,
Which do we women fret,
But you should see those laws when we
At last our suffrage get.

I have a dandy little beau,
He lives down in the town,
And when he asks me to "be his,"
I'll look at him and frown.

Final chorus:
Yes, papa votes, but mama can't,
Oh no, not yet, not yet,
But I'll not marry any man
Till I my suffrage get.

From the original sheet music,
copyright 1912 by M. Olive Drennan.

The Republican Twenties

After the War and Before the Depression

The Great War—World War I—marked the end of one era and the beginning of another. One of the most significant changes was the revolution in communications. The modern tabloid newspaper and the mass circulation magazine came into their own in this era, which also saw both radio and film develop into important molders of consciousness. The continental land mass of the country had been consolidated into a nation and the new perspective of a virile American colossus radiating out to a waiting world began to dominate the national awareness.

But the war had changed much more than technology. The Bolshevik Revolution of 1917 in Russia had fundamentally altered the political realities of the planet. Communism was no longer the theory of a handful of agitators; it had suddenly become a real power in the affairs of mankind.

The cultural changes in America which the twenties could not deny were far-reaching and profound. Horatio Alger and O. Henry were replaced by F. Scott Fitzgerald and Ernest Hemingway, while the period saw such diverse phenomena as the first Miss America contest, the first transcontinental air mail service, the founding of the American Communist Party, and the development of mass spectator sports. The census of 1920 revealed that the country had passed the 100 million mark in population. Enrico Caruso made his farewell appearance at the Metropolitan Opera and, a few years later, Victor Herbert passed into legend while the country discovered the music of George Gershwin and Cole Porter. If songs like "Daddy Has a Sweetheart—and Mother Is Her Name" were typical of the prewar era, "I Wish I Could Shimmy Like My Sister Kate" typified the new age. Women voted, jazz replaced ragtime, and the great political leaders of the recent past— Wilson, Bryan, Roosevelt, Taft—either died or slowly faded into oblivion. In the election of 1920, radio station KDKA in Pittsburgh, for the first time, broadcast election returns.

Among the casualties was the old-fashioned political campaign; and with it, the traditional campaign song.

To be sure, the passing into history of campaign singing did not signify the death of the campaign song. Songwriters, both amateur and professional, continued hopefully to launch new musical manifestoes by way of sheet music and popular parodies, but these ventures were, for the most part, largely in-effectual. Occasionally a song would become part of the identifiable decor of a political candidate— "Sidewalks of New York" for Al Smith, "I Like Ike" for Eisenhower—but in general there was no market for such material and little inspiration.

The songs which follow are, nonetheless, interesting artifacts of their time. They tell us something about the way people looked at their politicians and occasionally they reveal a groundswell of momentary enthusiasm. So far as campaign songs are concerned, the twenties and thirties represent not so much oblivion as the twilight years. The songs are still there and attempts continue to be made to use them in the new media of phonograph and radio. And every once in a while we even come across a song which would seem to have deserved a better fate than the premature obscurity which engulfed it.

Back to Normalcy

If a novelist wanted to find a model for what popular culture has conceived of as the "typical" American presidential election, chances are he would turn to the campaign of 1920. On the Republican side, all of the stock elements were there: the "dark horse" candidate, the astute campaign manager, and a campaign which managed to successfully straddle every issue and obfuscate every source of potential disruption of the smoothly-running machine. And there was a real, honest-to-goodness "smoke-filled room" with its assiduous selection of a man for reasons of geography and availability. Harry M. Daugherty, Harding's campaign manager, is generally credited with having predicted some five months before the convention that there would be a deadlock and that the final choice would actually be made "in a smoke-filled hotel room about eleven minutes after two o'clock" one morning by the real decision-makers of the party. And, as it turned out, this was pretty much what happened.

That was just the Republican side. The Democrats came up with a deadlocked convention requiring forty-four ballots and the nomination for the vice-presidency of the most attractive new face in either party—Franklin Delano Roosevelt.

As befits a campaign with so predictable a scenario, the handful of songs enlisted in the respective causes were monuments to innocuousness. At that, Warren Harding had the better of it, simply because the tide was clearly running his way; and if a war-weary nation could be induced to buy anything in the way of campaign music, it wouldn't be Democratic.

One of the most popular show business stars of the day, Al Jolson, better known for his singing than his songwriting, created "the official Republican campaign song" of 1920:

HARDING, YOU'RE THE MAN FOR US

Words and music: Al Jolson

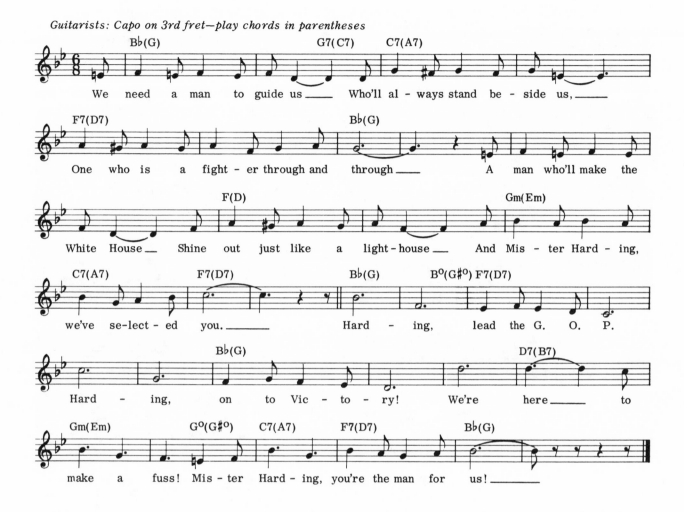

Guitarists: Capo on 3rd fret—play chords in parentheses

We need a man to guide us ___ Who'll al - ways stand be - side us, ___

One who is a fight - er through and through ___ A man who'll make the

White House ___ Shine out just like a light-house ___ And Mis - ter Hard - ing,

we've se - lect - ed you. ___ Hard - ing, lead the G. O. P.

Hard - ing, on to Vic - to - ry! We're here ___ to

make a fuss! Mis - ter Hard - ing, you're the man for us! ___

We know we'll always find him
With Coolidge right behind him,
And Coolidge never fails, you must agree,
We know he will be guarding
The Nation just like Harding
When they are both in Washington, D.C.
Harding, Coolidge is your mate,
Harding, lead the ship of state,
You'll get the people's vote,
And you'll also get the Donkey's goat!

Copyright 1920 by Al Jolson.

A little slicker musically but just as bland in its rhetoric was this one which bore the inscription, "Endorsed and approved by the Republican National Committee."

237

MR. HARDING (WE'RE ALL FOR YOU)

Words and music: John L. McManus

From the town of Ma-ri-on, O-hi-o, _____ Comes a man A-mer-i-can right through; _____ He's the man for us be-cause we know him _____ Cour-a-geous, strong and true. _____ Oh, Mis-ter Hard-ing, _____ You're the man of the hour. _____ Oh, Mis-ter Hard-ing, _____ you will soon have the pow'r _____ With Cal-vin Cool-idge _____ in an A-mer-i-can way _____ To serve the good old U. S. A. _____ The Na-tion's lead-er _____ You will ver-y soon be, _____ As Pres-i-dent we'll see you through _____ For you there's on-ly one right _____ house, And that is the White _____ House, Mis-ter Hard-ing _____ we're all for you. _____

From the Good old state of Massachusetts,
Calvin Coolidge comes as running mate.
He and Harding into port will steer us
Aboard the Ship of State.

[*In second chorus sing following for last three lines*]:
You know the people all need you,
The whole world will heed you,
Mister Harding, we're all for you.

The Glee Club of the Republican League of Massachusetts showed a little more initiative and composed several parodies which they presumably inflicted upon the voters during the campaign with no discernible difference in a marked proclivity for the vacuous generality. There was, however, a new element in these songs—exhortations to women voters. The national campaign of 1920 was the first in which women had the vote; hence the frequent references to both sons and daughers in both of the following songs.

THE CAMPAIGN HYMN OF THE REPUBLIC

Tune: "John Brown's Body"

America is calling: Sons and Daughters brave, arise!
And defend your Nation's glory every loyal heart must prize,
Pledge your deepest pure devotion to the fairest flag that flies,
   As we go marching on.

Chorus:
Cheer for Harding and for Coolidge,
Cheer for Harding and for Coolidge,
Cheer for Harding and for Coolidge,
As we go marching on.

There's a solemn referendum we are eager to decide,
And with Lincoln and with Roosevelt, brave, our country's course to guide;
We will keep the Grand Old Party still the Nation's hope and pride,
   As we go marching on.

Our sons and daughters crossed the sea to battle for the Right,
And to keep the victory they won, we loyally unite,
While we cast our ballots solemnly as God shall give us light,
   As we go marching on.

THE LITTLE SNUG OLD WHITE HOUSE IN THE LANE

Tune: "Little Old Log Cabin in the Lane"

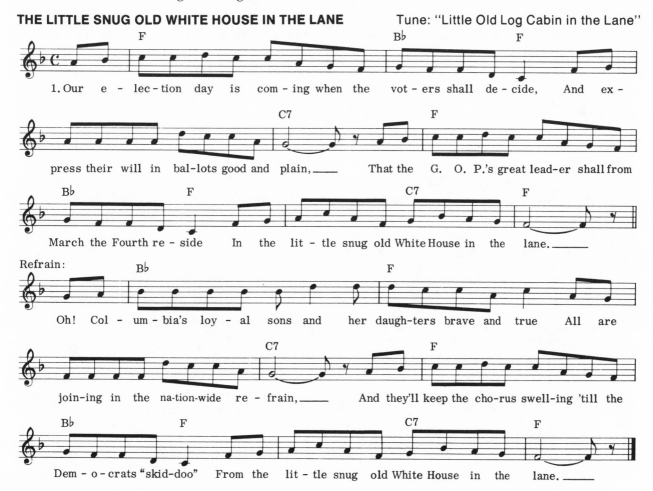

1. Our e - lec - tion day is com - ing when the vot - ers shall de - cide, And ex - press their will in bal - lots good and plain,_____ That the G. O. P.'s great lead - er shall from March the Fourth re - side In the lit - tle snug old White House in the lane._____

Refrain:
Oh! Col - um - bia's loy - al sons and her daugh - ters brave and true All are join - ing in the na - tion-wide re - frain,_____ And they'll keep the cho - rus swell - ing 'till the Dem - o - crats "skid-doo" From the lit - tle snug old White House in the lane._____

With wise Harding for our leader and with Coolidge for his mate,
They will guide our land a-right with heart and brain;
We'll have one who has the wisdom to direct the Ship of State
In the little snug old White House in the lane.

For the most part, the Democratic songs were equally vapid. "Jimmie Cox Will Win the Day" and "Gov'nor Cox You'll Surely Do" were distinguished by such lines as:

> Election day will soon be here,
> Let's shed our coats and never fear,
> The man we have has oft been tried,
> Like Washington, he's never lied.

A little more interesting was one entitled "Who Wrecked the League of Nations?" which, at least, tried to focus on one of the real political questions of the day. It accused Harding and the Republicans of being opposed to the League, despite a rather general campaign plank which seemed to favor it—a charge which seems to have been confirmed by the policies of the new administration. The song also commented on the "smoke-filled room" and Colonel George Harvey, a one-time Democrat and close associate of powerful financial interests, in whose hotel suite the famous room was located.

> Now Lodge and Harvey after midnight as you all do know,
> Met in the room of some hotel and there framed up the show.
> And when the great convention met, their Harding then was named,
> But with a handicap so great, he'll ne'er attain the game.
>
> From "Who Wrecked the League of Nations?", words by A. J. Kiser,
> music by Edouard Hesselberg, Colorado Springs, Colo., 1920.

About the only Democratic song which seems to have enjoyed any circulation at all, however, is this "Democratic Campaign March Song" which was printed up and distributed by the Indiana State Committee of the party.

THE TIE THAT BINDS
(or JIMMY IS THE MAN FOR US) Words and music: Roy L. Burtch

Our peo - ple love their Coun - try, For its hon - or they will fight___ Both
day and night, the U. S. A. Holds proud her Stars and Stripes.___ This
fall the man who rules our land, Clear from coast to coast,___ Must be
firm and strong, to make right, all wrongs, On "Jim - my's" name we boast.___ The

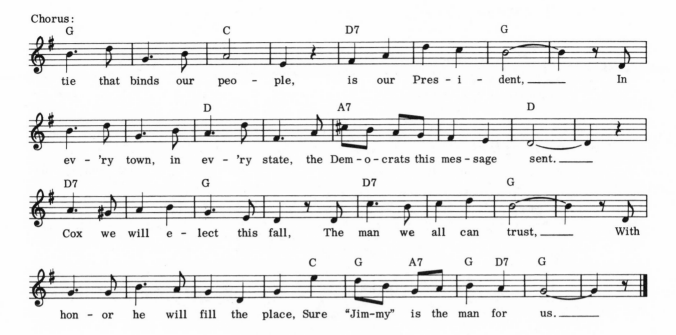

Chorus:

tie that binds our peo - ple, is our Pres - i - dent, _____ In
ev - 'ry town, in ev - 'ry state, the Dem - o - crats this mes - sage sent. _____
Cox we will e - lect this fall, The man we all can trust, _____ With
hon - or he will fill the place, Sure "Jim-my" is the man for us. _____

Our great and glorious nation
Stands for liberty—that's right.
We want new laws to serve our cause,
Election Day looks bright.
High cost of living must come down,
Prices on the square,
We all want good times, so just get in line,
Put Jimmy in the chair.

Published by Halcyon Music Co.,
Indianapolis, 1920.

Keep Cool and Keep Coolidge

The man whom H. L. Mencken described as a "second-rate provincial," Harding, had presided over an administration in which ineptitude and corruption contended with each other for predominance. With two of Harding's cabinet up to their necks in the Teapot Dome scandal, the Democrats had a natural issue on which to campaign; and unlike the election of 1920, there were some real questions in the political arena—including the growing influence of the Ku Klux Klan in national affairs, the failure of prohibition, and the League of Nations.

But Harding died in 1923 and Calvin Coolidge, the man whom the party bosses added to the ticket in 1920 for his popular appeal, became president. Cool, conservative, unimpeachably honest, Coolidge had no need to run on his predecessor's record. The sorry tale of Harding's tenure in office was buried with him and Coolidge single-handedly managed to salvage the Republicans' fading image. No wonder a grateful party made its campaign slogan for 1924: "Keep Cool and Keep Coolidge!"

241

KEEP COOL AND KEEP COOLIDGE   Words: Ida Cheever Goodwin   Music: Bruce Harper

In a quaint New Eng-land farm-house on an ear-ly sum-mer's day, A farm-er's boy be-came our Chief in a home-ly sim-ple way, With neith-er pomp nor pa-gean-try, he firm-ly met the task, To keep him on that job of his, Is all the peo-ple ask.

Refrain:
So "Keep cool and keep Coo-lidge" is the slo-gan of to-day, "Keep cool and keep Coo-lidge" for the good old U. S. A. A lot of pol-i-ti-cians can-not do a thing but knock, But Cal-vin Coo-lidge is a man of ac-tion and not talk, So just "Keep cool and keep Coo-lidge" in the White House four years more, We have a chance to do it in this year of "twen-ty - four," He's been tried, he's nev-er want-ing, He is giv-ing of his best, "Keep cool and keep Coo-lidge" is our coun-try's might-y test.

With a private life of virtue and a public record clean,
He stands upon the summits with a countenance serene,
Defender of the righteous and a juggernaut to wrong,
We'll make him stay in Washington—a hundred million strong.

Described as "the official campaign song of the Home Town
Coolidge Club of Plymouth, Vermont."

A few others made attempts to launch Coolidge campaign songs, but none became popular. "Coolidge and Dawes for the Nation's Cause" struck no sparks, nor did any of the others.

The Democrats did no better in the musical department and a lot worse in the election. After a knock-down convention battle between Al Smith of New York and William McAdoo of California, the Democrats picked a comparative nonentity, John W. Davis, former congressman from West Virginia, one-time ambassador to Great Britain and a Wall Street lawyer, on the 103rd ballot. The theme was reform and the slogan was "Remember the Teapot Dome!"

Teapot Dome was an oil reserve unit in Wyoming under control of the United States Navy. Harding's Secretary of the Interior, Albert B. Fall, leased the reserve to the Mammoth Oil Company without competitive bidding. Harding's campaign manager, Harry M. Daugherty, then Attorney-General, was also involved in the scandal. Subsequent investigation revealed that it was part of a pattern of bribery and collusion between government and big business which resulted in the dismissal and indictment of most of the key figures.

JOHN W. DAVIS
(REMEMBER THE TEAPOT DOME)

Words: J. J. Carney
Music: P. B. Story

John Dou-ble-u Da-vis is the name we shout, The Old Re-pub-li-can Par-ty we'll show "this way____ out"____ This last ad-min-is-tra-tion Just sur-prised our dear old Na-tion, Re-mem-ber the Tea-pot dome.____

Chorus:
Hur-ray, Hur-ray, we'll have good times once more,____ When Da-vis gets be-hind the White House door.____ When we're un-der hon-est rule, And no Pol-i-ti-cian's

243

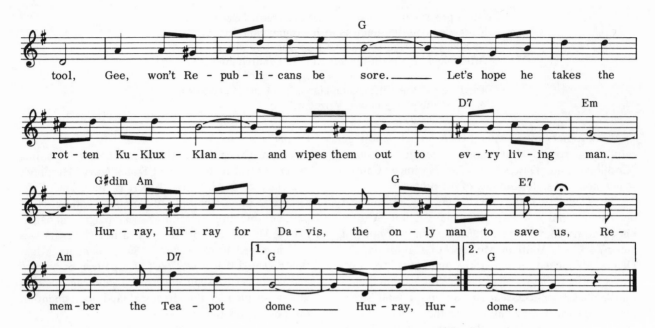

tool, Gee, won't Re - pub - li - cans be sore.___ Let's hope he takes the rot - ten Ku - Klux - Klan___ and wipes them out to ev - 'ry liv - ing man.___ ___ Hur - ray, Hur - ray for Da - vis, the on - ly man to save us, Re - mem - ber the Tea - pot dome.___ Hur - ray, Hur - dome.___

John W. Davis the choice to make,
And we will never regret it for our welfare's at stake,
We need his good protection and insist on his election,
Remember the Teapot Dome!

Our Davis upholds all that is good and true,
West Virginia says, "We are proud of you,"
Our Nation's losses he'll retrieve,
He'll spurn all bribes, he'll not deceive,
Remember the Teapot Dome!

John W. Davis without spot or stain,
Will help to get all the Navy oil lands back again,
He'll win in this election,
And through his wise direction,
He'll save the Teapot Dome!

Published by J. J. Carney, New York, 1924.

Despite the campaign ammunition they were furnished by the Teapot Dome affair, the Democrats were hampered by divisions within their party. Chief among these was the antagonism between big-city Catholic voters of the North and anti-Catholic southerners. The southern wing would not tolerate the nomination of Al Smith, who was a Catholic. The northern city politicians, who had largely Irish and Italian working class constituencies, were insistent on the Party having an explicit denunciation of the Catholic-baiting Ku Klux Klan in its platform.

The considerations which went into the Democrats' choice of Davis as their presidential candidate were pretty well summed up in the "Democratic Victory Song," written by a pair of Oklahomans, T. J. Nicholson and Lillian Green:

He's the most Southern Northern man,
He's the most Northern Southern man;
He's neither Catholic or Klan,
He's just a Presbyterian;
Some wanted Smith, some wanted McAdoo,
But the people wanted a man between the two.
He's an every-day, all around, high grade American!

"The Slogan of the Day" was a Democratic attempt to reply to the "Keep Cool and Keep Coolidge" phrase, while "A Democrat Is Going to the White House" was a lot more optimistic than the facts warranted. But the song which tells the most about the fine art of campaign music was the production of Charles K. Harris, composer of such all-time classics as "After the Ball Is Over,"

"Break the News To Mother" and "Hello Central, Give Me Heaven." In addition to his songwriting talents, Harris was also a music publisher, and early in the year 1924 dug an old piece out of his files called "The Teddy Roosevelt March to the White House in 1904," a venture which had never achieved the success Harris thought it so richly deserved. Harris tried to interest the Republicans in adopting it and even tacked Calvin Coolidge's name to the last line. But the Republicans were not impressed; so Harris tried the Democrats instead. The original, apparently, was written by a songwriter since claimed by obscurity, Rudolph Aronson; so Harris decided to put his own name on it, figuring, quite correctly, that this might have some selling power. A young Democratic campaign publicity worker by the name of Claude G. Bowers, later a widely respected historian and diplomat, was won over and with Davis' name now hopefully added to the ending, the song became an official song of sorts. (The whole incident is related in delightful detail by one of the participants, James J. Geller, in an article in *The New Republic* [Oct. 15, 1956] called "Mayhem in Three-Quarter Time.")

MARCH TO THE WHITE HOUSE Adapted by Charles K. Harris

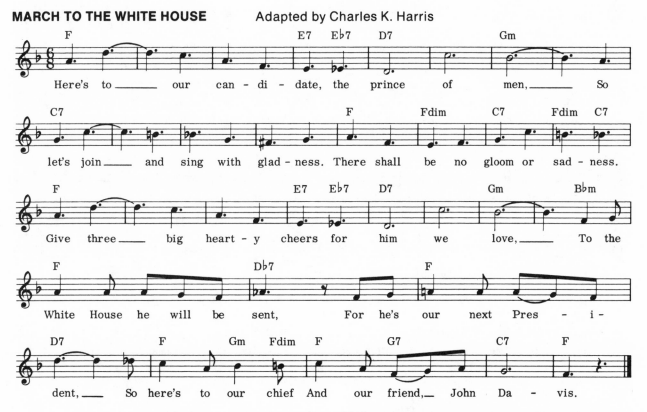

Here's to our candidate, the prince of men, So let's join and sing with gladness. There shall be no gloom or sadness. Give three big hearty cheers for him we love, To the White House he will be sent, For he's our next President, So here's to our chief And our friend, John Davis.

The nomination of a staunch New England conservative and a Wall Street lawyer by the Republicans and Democrats respectively caused a great dismay in the liberal wings of both parties. A "progressive" revolt had been brewing for some time in the Midwest; and with Coolidge and Davis as the choice, many of these dissidents came together and nominated Senator Robert La Follette of Wisconsin for the presidency. His candidacy drew the support of many liberals and independents; and the Socialists, who had polled almost a million votes in 1920, threw their support to the Wisconsin maverick.

La Follette actually polled a sizable vote, more than four million; but the Progressive Party of 1924 was not organized with a long-range prospect in view, and with the death of La Follette in 1925, the party disappeared almost as suddenly as it had emerged. In its brief and turbulent career, the party left behind some memories of militant political independence and one more vain effort to beat the two-party system. And it also bequeathed us a campaign song:

ROBERT LA FOLLETTE IS THE MAN OF MY HEART

Words and music: Robert Stagg

There is a man in Wis - con - sin, The fin - est in the na - tion, A man that's shown a lev - el head And kept cool like a man. He's fought for the peo - ple's rights, on ev - er - y oc - ca - sion Hur - rah for Rob - ert La Fol - lette, He's the man of them all. For

Chorus:

There goes a man, He's a cred - it to our na - tion, There goes a man, That can take his own part, He's fit for a Pres - i - dent or an - y - thing cre - a - ted, Rob - ert La Fol - lette, He's the man of my heart.

He's over there in Washington,
Fighting for the people,
He's progressive and up to date,
Deny it if you can.
He's shown up all corruption
In the last administration,
Hurrah for Robert La Follette,
He's the man of them all!

Published and copyrighted by
the author, New York, 1924.

246

The Great Engineer and the Happy Warrior

A slight revival in the fortunes of campaign music marked the 1928 campaign, largely due to the personal popularity of the Democratic candidate, Governor Al Smith of New York, with the songwriting fraternity of Tin Pan Alley. Smith, the first Catholic to receive a major party nomination for the presidency, was the product of the rough-and-tumble ward politics of New York City. He was a colorful personality, largely without precedent in national politics. Smith represented a kind of rough-hewn egalitarianism reinforced by his down-to-earth argot and his anti-establishment stance. He was, for his time, prolabor, and his strong stand against prohibition endeared him to hundreds of thousands who were but dimly aware of the puritanical elitism which had fathered the Eighteenth Amendment. For all this, Smith had the respect of the financial community, which recognized that his "fairness" was a far cry from revolution and that his commitment to the status quo was unquestioned. Still, many who in earlier years had voted for the left-liberal Progressives of 1924 or the socialism of Debs were to be found in the Smith ranks in 1928.

Denied the nomination in 1924 as the result of a vicious campaign of prejudiced innuendo, Smith's personal popularity grew in the intervening four years. The "happy warrior" whom Franklin Roosevelt had nominated in a memorable speech in 1924 was selected by an overwhelming vote in 1928, and almost immediately the whole country was singing and whistling the Al Smith version of "The Sidewalks of New York," adapted from the original, written by Charles B. Lawlor and James W. Blake in 1894:

AL SMITH   Campaign chorus: Al Dubin   Tune: "Sidewalks of New York"

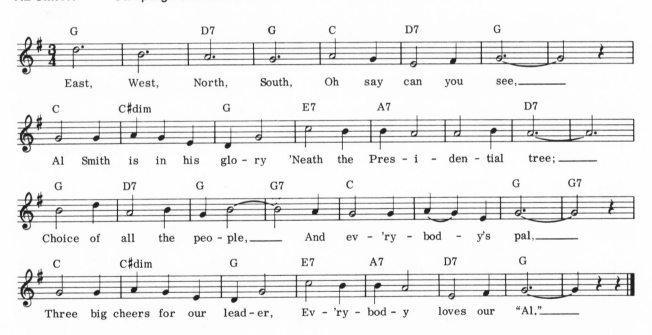

A more ambitious musical enterprise was the work of Edward Laska, an occasional lyricist for Jerome Kern, who wrote the words for "Goodbye Cal, Hello Al—C from Cal leaves Al." Laska managed to get his composition sung at the Democratic National Convention and issued an elaborately designed piece of sheet music, but it was no competition for the old favorite. Another Al Smith song was the work of a pair of old pros, A. Seymour Brown and Albert von Tilzer. Von Tilzer's brother Harry was an even more successful songwriter and publisher. Albert's biggest hit was "Take Me Out to the Ball Game." He also wrote "Put Your Arms Around Me, Honey." Brown was an old hand at campaign songs, having written the words for "The Election in Jungle Town" (1912) and the words and music for "Go Right Along, Mister Wilson" (1916). Von Tilzer and Brown managed to mix snatches of "Sidewalks of New York," "Yankee Doodle" and "Auld Lang Syne" into their song, which was launched by Frank McCormack in a Broadway musical of the year, *Anvil Chorus*.

HE'S OUR AL   Words and music: Albert von Tilzer and A. Seymour Brown

Born obscure, of parents poor,
He struggled through his youth,
His guiding light to make the fight
Was decency and truth.
Doing big things modestly,

His greatness common sense,
Until his name has reached its fame
Through love and confidence.

© 1928 and 1955 Broadway Music
Corp. Used by permission.

The most optimistic note of the campaign was sounded by one of the country's most popular songwriters, Irving Berlin, who was swept up in the heady atmosphere of that inflated prosperity which had given the era much of its cultural style.

(GOOD TIMES WITH HOOVER)
BETTER TIMES WITH AL

Words and music: Irving Berlin

Good times with Hoover,
BETTER TIMES WITH AL;
Blue skies with Hoover,
BLUER SKIES WITH AL.
They tell us that the future will be rosy and bright,
But they don't have to tell us, we admit that they're right.
That we'll have good times with Hoover,
BETTER TIMES WITH AL!

"Better Times with Al" by Irving Berlin. © Copyright 1928 by Irving Berlin. © Copyright renewed 1955 by Irving Berlin. Reprinted by permission of Irving Berlin Music Corporation.

While "Sidewalks of New York" and "He's Our Al" characterized the Smith campaign in most of the country, down in the Kentucky and Tennessee hills they were singing a different kind of Al Smith election song. The song below favored Smith for President because he supported the repeal of prohibition, which would enable people to buy legal whiskey and not just "moonshine" and which would end the abuses of illegal liquor production and consumption.

AL SMITH FOR PRESIDENT

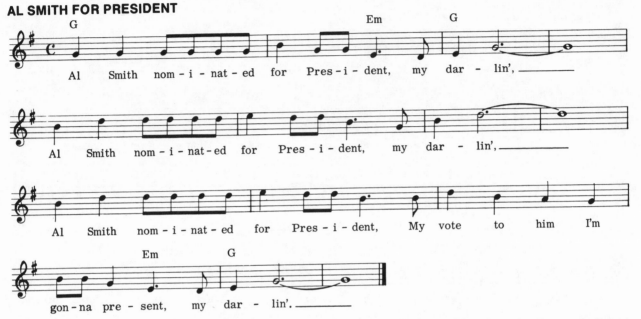

Al Smith is a mighty fine man, my darlin', etc.
He wants to be president of this land, my darlin'.

Al Smith is a-getting on a boom, my darlin', etc.
He don't favor the old saloon, my darlin'.

Smith wants everything to be just right, my darlin', etc.
The law's gonna get you if you get tight, my darlin'.

Moonshine's been here long enough, my darlin', etc.
Let's all vote right and get rid of such stuff, my darlin'.

From the singing of Tom Paley of the New Lost City
Ramblers, Folkways Record FH5263, "American
Moonshine and Prohibition Songs."

In the early, heady days of the 1928 campaign, it may indeed have seemed that "everybody loved our Al." But the Republicans were no slouches at the electoral game, and when "Silent Cal" managed to talk himself out of a third term with one half-considered statement—"I do not choose to run"—the GOP did not hesitate. It gave the nomination to the man who was probably the country's most popular and well-respected Republican, Herbert Hoover. Political legend has not dealt kindly with Hoover, who has come to be identified with "head-in-the-sand" conservatism and last-ditch opposition to the social reforms of the thirties. But in the decade before his nomination, Hoover had won an enviable reputation as a crackerjack administrator. His work in food relief during and after the war was widely hailed as a model of efficiency. He never held elective office before 1928, but as secretary of commerce under both Harding and Coolidge, he was probably the dominant public figure of both administrations. Graduated from Stanford University as a mining engineer, Hoover seemed to represent the new "technocratic" approach to government, somehow removed from the taint of politics.

With one exception, the songs for Hoover and his running mate, Charles Curtis of Kansas, Majority Leader of the Senate, were largely an undistinguished lot. "Hoover Is the Man," "We Want Hoover," "We're for Hoover and Curtis" and others in a similar vein were typified by such original sentiments as:

H-double O-V-E-R spells Hoover,
He's rough and ready from the Golden West,
Just like Teddy, for the job he's best.

From "Hoover! We Want Hoover!" Pacific Music Pub., San Francisco, 1928.

He's the man to head our nation,
Build her up and make her grand,
He's the man to save our country
From the unrest in the land.

From "Hoover Is The Man," by B. J. McPhee, Louis H. Ross Music Co., Boston, Mass., 1928.

Hoover—you are the nation's pride,
Curtis—you're right there by his side.

From "We're for Hoover and Curtis," by Albert Gould and Tom Shane, M. Witmark & Sons, copyright 1928.

But at least one Hoover song was both original and inventive. It may have been the first "endorsement" song in the history of campaign singing—excepting, of course, the almost pro-forma endorsements of ex-Presidents for members of their own party.

IF HE'S GOOD ENOUGH FOR LINDY (HE'S GOOD ENOUGH FOR ME)

Words and music: Of unknown composition

Charles Lind-bergh flew his plane all the way to France.
Most of the way he flew by the seat of his pants.

Good old A-mer-i-can know-how, that's the right way to be, and if he's good e-nough for Lind-bergh, he's good e-nough for me.

Chorus (to the same melody as the verse):
If he's good enough for Lindy, he's good enough for me,
If he's good enough for Lindy, he's good enough for me,
If he's good enough for Lindy, he's good enough for me.
Herbert Hoover is the only man to be our nation's chief.

Charles Lindbergh flew his plane to France to see what he could see,
Now that he's back he's looking at our old country;
And what he has to say stands out in bold relief,
Herbert Hoover is the only man to be our nation's chief.

Now you all remember Hoover, back in the war,
He saved us from the Kaiser, now he'll give us something more;
He'll serve as the President of the land of the free,
If he's good enough for Lindy, he's good enough for me.

From *Sing Out!*, Vol. 14, No. 5, as transcribed from the singing of Oscar Brand.

A "nonpartisan" musical colloquy, in the "Gallagher and Shean" style of the period, provides a fitting summary to this last campaign before the Great Depression. Robert A. Keiser, who wrote the music to "Be Good to California, Mr. Wilson," also composed this song, but under the pen name of Robert King.

MR. HOOVER AND MR. SMITH
Words: Herb Magidson   Music: Robert King

I had a dream the oth-er night, I saw two fam-ous men, They met each oth-er on the street, Shook hands a-while and then They start-ed talk-ing in a friend-ly way.___ And here's ex-act-ly what I heard them say:___

Chorus:

Who's the grand-est great-est man this coun-try ev-er knew? Oh! it's you, Mis-ter Hoo-ver No, it's you, Mis-ter Smith. Ex-cept-ing Georg-ie Wash-ing-ton, he was a good man, too He's not run-ning, Mis-ter Hoo-ver, What a break, Mis-ter Smith. Are you dry?___ you can't re-mem-ber!___ But you'll know know know in No-vem-ber?___ Well, an-y-how you'll get one vote, be-cause I'll vote for you. Be your-self, Mis-ter Hoo-ver, Keep the change, Mis-ter Smith.

I've heard politicians say that you have got technique.
What's technique, Mister Hoover?
It's the bunk, Mister Smith.
Why don't you bring your family to visit me next week?
Great idea, Mister Hoover.
Bring your lunch, Mister Smith.
Do you trust in your supporters?
I did once, but now I use garters.
I'm feeling kind of hoarse today,
Why I can hardly speak,
Try some oil, Mister Hoover,
No, I'm cured, Mister Smith.

This dream was such a funny sight,
It certainly was queer,
I watched but neither cracked a smile,
For they were both sincere.
I listened and I didn't miss a word,
Now here's some more of what I overheard:

How will you treat the farmers if they put you in the chair?
Once a week, Mister Hoover;
Applesauce, Mister Smith.
I think you'll like the Capitol, they'll give you lots of air,
Hot or cold, Mister Hoover,
Just hot air, Mister Smith.
Oh! I hear you're from the East Side,
No, you're wrong, old top, it's the WET side;
What will we give the people who have done more than their share?
Vacuum cleaners, Mister Hoover?
Why not cough drops, Mister Smith?

I've got some new ideas that I'd like to use next fall,
Hope you do, Mister Hoover,
Yes, you do, Mister Smith.
I hear you've got some wrinkles up your sleeve, and that ain't all,
Lots of wrinkles, Mister Hoover,
Press your pants, Mister Smith.
You look swell in your brown derby,
Shows I'm not high-hatting you, Herbie.
Well anyhow, I've got to go, I hear my Party call,
Reservoir, Mister Hoover,
Skip the gutter, Mister Smith.

The Roosevelt Years

The New Deal
Becomes a Revival

There has never been a period in American political history like the Roosevelt years. Never did one man so dominate the American political scene—not only in an unprecedented and unduplicated series of triumphs at the polls, but in a continuing influence over the course of events for two decades to follow.

Franklin Delano Roosevelt was a remarkable man but his influence was much more than the vigor of a particular personality. In retrospect we can see how this scion of wealth and power was the instrument whereby the political energies of the American working class were simultaneously released and absorbed into the system. That product of the sidewalks of New York, Al Smith, could only warn in 1932, at the height of the depression: "This is no time for demagogues. At a time like this, when millions of men, women and children are starving throughout the land, there is always a temptation to some men to stir up class prejudice, to stir up the bitterness of the rich against the poor, and the poor against the rich. Against that effort, I set myself uncompromisingly."

But Franklin Roosevelt, hand-picked by Smith for the New York governorship, somehow understood that the economic crisis ushered in by the stock market crash of 1929 was no ordinary event. The very life of the free enterprise system itself was threatened by the worldwide economic crisis. Roosevelt understood that only extraordinary measures, designed to rationalize the vast output of the huge corporate technology, would prevent the system from self-destructing. Not that Roosevelt's "New Deal" was as elaborately thought out as all that. But the young governor with the magic name projected a sense of imagination and flexibility in confronting the country's most severe economic crisis.

Happy Days Are Here Again

Herbert Hoover's promise of "a chicken in every pot" was not very credible in 1932, but when partisans of Roosevelt sang the Democratic theme song of the year, "Happy Days Are Here Again," it seemed as though change was possible.

The issues in 1932 seemed reasonably clear-cut after a decade in which the most controversial question had been the religion of one of the presidential candidates. A program of relief and reform to cope with the depression, repeal of prohibition, a new policy for the sorely pressed farmers of the Midwest and a new spirit of internationalism characterized the Democratic platform of 1932.

With unemployment reaching staggering proportions and with money extremely scarce, the campaign song market didn't seem to offer much hope for the professionals of Tin Pan Alley. The creators of pop culture found they could do better by taking people's minds off their troubles rather than focusing on them. "Forty-Second Street" was the hit show of the year, contributing a number of songs towards diverting the country's state of despair—although "Brother, Can You Spare a Dime?" tapped another strain in the national mood. Eddie Dowling and J. Fred Coots contributed "Row, Row, Row with Roosevelt (On the Good Ship U.S.A.)" to the political campaign while a team of Chicago tunesmiths produced "Everything Will Be Rosy with Roosevelt"; but most of the other songs were either nonpolitical melodies like "Happy Days" or the work of amateurs and less successful pros.

ON THE RIGHT ROAD WITH ROOSEVELT
Words and music: Robert Sterling
(Copyright 1932 by J. M. Novelty Co., New York)

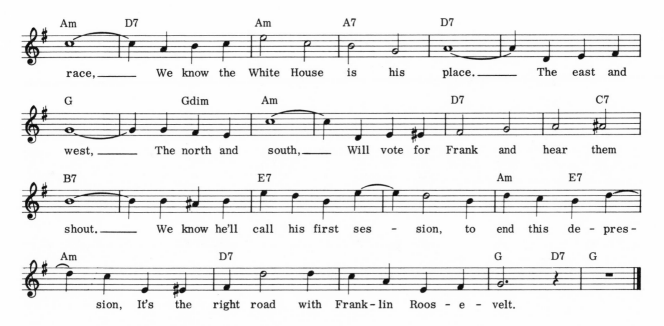

race, _____ We know the White House is his place. _____ The east and
west, _____ The north and south, _____ Will vote for Frank and hear them
shout. _____ We know he'll call his first ses - sion, to end this de - pres -
sion, It's the right road with Frank - lin Roos - e - velt.

The revived concern with issues is reflected in the following campaign song, whose printed cover highlights the following questions, one on each corner of the page: Repeal, Employment, State Rights, Tariff Adjustment. The repeal of the Prohibition Amendment was an especially potent issue, but the Republicans straddled it, some of them advocating a rather involved plan called "resubmis-

sion," which would allow each state a certain "local option" while keeping certain restrictions in the hands of the federal government. In "We Want a Man like Roosevelt," the Démocratic candidate was depicted as a man of action who would end unemployment and not equivocate on the issues, most especially Repeal.

WE WANT A MAN LIKE ROOSEVELT   Words and music: Kenneth Wardell

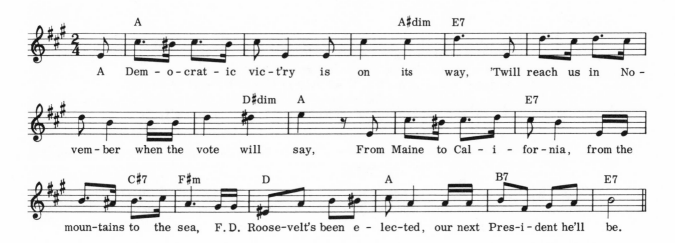

A Dem - o - crat - ic vic - t'ry is on its way, 'Twill reach us in No -
vem - ber when the vote will say, From Maine to Cal - i - for - nia, from the
moun - tains to the sea, F. D. Roose - velt's been e - lec - ted, our next Pres - i - dent he'll be.

Chorus:

We want a man like Roose - velt, We want a man that knows, _____ How to pull the coun - try from de - press - ion's pit, How to fur - nish work for men who crave for it. We want a man like Roose - velt, One with prov - en grit and cour - age rare, _____ He'll knock out pro - hi - bi - tion with re - peal, not re - sub - mis - sion, When he's seat - ed in the Pres - i - den - tial chair. _____

Throughout our glorious nation a sign appears,
It tells of want and hunger and our children's tears,
But greed will soon be routed and the poor forgotten man
Will have all that God intended when our new chief drafts his plan.

Copyright by author, 1932. Sold through Charles Coleman, Brooklyn, N.Y.

The "forgotten man" phrase was taken from one of Roosevelt's preconvention campaign speeches in which he had referred to the unemployed and the aged as the "forgotten man."

Perhaps the best songs of the campaign were a group of parodies which emphasized the glories of Repeal and employment.

KISS YOURSELF GOODBYE!

Words: Wallace Le Grande Henderson
Tune: "Coming Through the Rye"

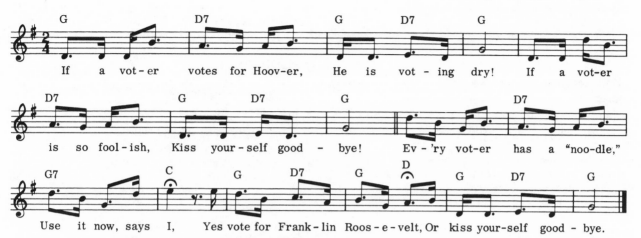

If a vot-er votes for Hoov-er, He is vot-ing dry! If a vot-er
is so fool-ish, Kiss your-self good-bye! Ev-'ry vot-er has a "noo-dle,"
Use it now, says I, Yes vote for Frank-lin Roos-e-velt, Or kiss your-self good-bye.

> If you want some decent wages,
> What's the use to sigh?
> You can't turn tears into dollars,
> No matter how you try!
> Every voter gets a ballot,
> Mark it right, says I,
> Make Roosevelt your President,
> Or kiss yourself goodbye!

GONE ARE THE DAYS

Words: Wallace Le Grande Henderson

Tune: "Old Black Joe"

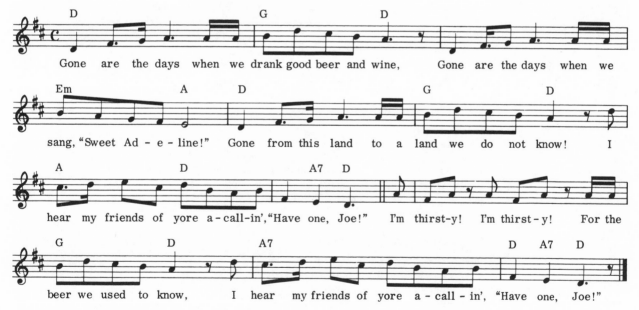

Gone are the days when we drank good beer and wine, Gone are the days when we
sang, "Sweet Ad-e-line!" Gone from this land to a land we do not know! I
hear my friends of yore a-call-in', "Have one, Joe!" I'm thirst-y! I'm thirst-y! For the
beer we used to know, I hear my friends of yore a-call-in', "Have one, Joe!"

Gone are the days when we had good jobs and "kale,"
Gone are our friends to Prohibition jail!
Gone from our homes like the bums of long ago,
I hear the sheriff's voice a-callin', "Out you go!"

I'm starving, I'm starving, no matter where I go!
I'd like to hear my old friends calling, "Eat some, Joe!"

Meanwhile, in the cultural underground of children's rhymes and chants, seven- and eight-year-olds in New York City were singing

We want Hoover, we want Hoover,_
With a rope around his neck!

But there were indeed some who really wanted Hoover again, and some of these wrote songs. Without exception, they were a pathetic lot, occasionally rising to such poetic heights as

Forget the depression and give it the air,
The good times are coming, let us all prepare,
So rally back to Hoover and the G.O.P.,
Come sailing back again to prosperity.

From "Hoover for President, the Hope of Our Nation," by Anna Lifter and Anthony La Paglia, pub. New York, 1932.

. . . for after all is said and done,
He's got depression on the run,
So we're gonna keep Mister Hoover in the White House Chair.

From "We're Going to Keep Mr. Hoover in the White House Chair," by James Wright, pub. Paterson, N.J., 1932.

A pair of Republican parodies reveal the fact that never was a cause so hopeless but that some optimist could not be found who would compose a song capable of defying the coldest reality. Indeed, so optimistic was the lyricist of the first song below that he predicted 23 million votes for Hoover, which turned out to be just about the total number of votes that Roosevelt received (22,809,638). Hoover received some 15,750,000 votes.

WHOOP IT UP!

Words: W. Hartley Gay
Tune: "Hold the Fort"

Rally to our Grand Old Party,
Boost it to the sky!
Do not rest a single moment,
Victory is nigh!

Chorus:
Whoop it up for Herbert Hoover,
He's our leader, strong;
Hoover stands for saner freedom,
Triumph over wrong.

Ho! ye young men and ye old men,
Noble women, free;
Cast your votes for Herbert Hoover—
Twenty million, three!

Hoover-Curtis, that's the ticket!
Statesmanship is rare.
Voters put them in the White House
And will keep them there!

From the Music Division, Library of Congress.

BATTLE HYMN OF THE REPUBLICAN PARTY

Words: Alfred J. Thieme
Tune: "John Brown's Body"

Mine eyes have seen the glory of the man, our president,
He typifies the things for which our precious blood was spent;
His loyalty, fidelity, his deeds will never die,
His fame is marching on.

Chorus:
Hoover, Hoover, we need Hoover,
Hoover, Hoover, we need Hoover.
Glory, glory hallelujah,
Our country's marching on.

When foreign desolation brought disaster to our shore,
He stood there like Gibraltar, as did Washington before;
He fought to save our nation from destruction and despair,
His faith is marching on.

When the war's intense expansion brought depression in our land,
He mobilized our forces, far and wide on every hand;
He battled hard to save the things that made our country great,
His work is marching on.

The battle now is almost won, depression's in retreat,
Let's stand behind our President, there can be no defeat;
God gave us Herbert Hoover, let us vote to keep that trust,
His truth is marching on.

From the Music Division, Library of Congress.

As Maine Goes, So Goes Vermont

Rarely has there been an American political campaign in which the mass media were so heavily on the side of one candidate and the voters on the side of the other as in 1936. While with historical perspective it is possible to see that Franklin D. Roosevelt was the best friend the business system ever had, a majority of the businessmen and stockholders in the country in 1936 didn't see it that way. Trying to update the country in a few short years, Roosevelt had managed to enact the most massive array of social reform legislation in history. Between the emergency steps he took to relieve the suffering caused by the depression and the more ambitious plans to get the system running again, he amassed on behalf of the federal government, particularly the executive, a degree of power without precedent in American history. At the same time, he set in motion the legal and judicial machinery which made possible the biggest organizing drive in the history of the American labor movement. The organization of the CIO and the various industrial unions attached to it undoubtedly created more anxiety in the board rooms of big business than all the alphabet soups which Roosevelt's "Brain Trust" was so adept at cooking up.

The fortunes of the GOP were at their lowest ebb since the Party was founded in 1854. Roosevelt's massive electoral victory in 1932 and the congressional elections of 1934 had destroyed the Republican hold on almost every branch of government. What had really happened, which no one understood yet, was that the number of registered Democratic voters had come to exceed the number of registered Republican voters—a situation which, despite the subsequent election of Eisenhower in 1952 and Nixon in 1968, prevails to this day.

Not the least of the Republican troubles was the lack of a popular candidate. While there may have been some sentiment in the ranks for Hoover, the party bosses weren't having that millstone around their neck; and Democratic triumphs in the Congress had made it almost impossible to find a likely figure in either the Senate or the House. The best prospect for the GOP turned out to be the governor of Kansas, Alfred M. Landon, a singularly colorless, old-fashioned midwesterner who, the party hoped, would seem to represent the old-fashioned virtues. Undoubtedly he did. Unfortunately, it was hardly the time for anything old-fashioned—even virtue.

Republicans tried to whip up a storm of enthusiasm for their unlikely candidate. So deep was their hostility to "that man in the White House" that they emphasized everything about Landon which would seem to be different from Roosevelt. In the process they did something of a disservice to the Kansan, who was far from being the hide-bound conservative which the stalwarts of his party so ardently painted him to be.

261

HORSE AND BUGGY WAYS   Tune: "Jingle Bells"   (From *Campaign Songs for Landon & Knox*)

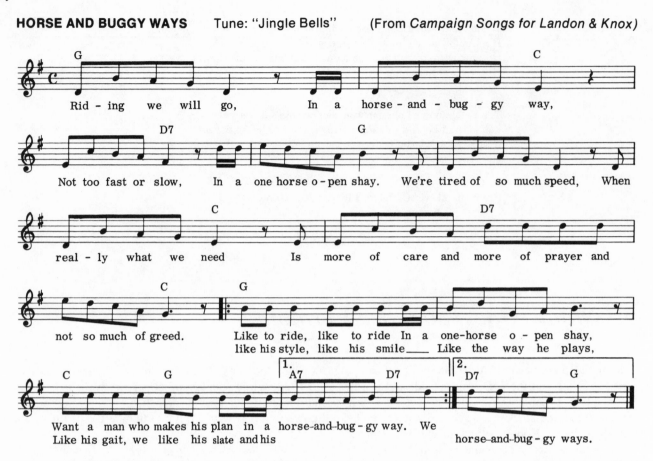

Rid - ing   we will   go,   In   a   horse - and - bug - gy   way,

Not too fast or slow,   In   a   one horse o - pen shay.   We're tired of   so much speed,   When

real - ly   what   we need   Is   more   of   care   and   more   of   prayer and

not   so much of greed.   Like to ride, like to ride In   a   one-horse   o - pen   shay,
like his style,   like his   smile___ Like the   way   he plays,

Want a man who makes his plan in a horse-and-bug-gy way.   We
Like his gait, we like   his slate and his

horse-and-bug-gy ways.

The 1936 Republican Convention was more like a one-song hootenanny than a political meeting. The song was Stephen Foster's "Oh! Susannah," which, by actual count, was played some 1,800 times during the course of the proceedings. A trio of singers introduced a Landon version of the song; and while these particular words didn't last the rigors of the campaign, the song itself became identified with the Republican cause.

LANDON, OH, LANDON   Tune: "Oh! Susannah"

Our___   Ship of State is   on   the rocks   And soon   it   will   be   sunk,   It___
wan - ders to   the right and left,   It floun - ders all   a - round,   It___

has · no   pi - lot   at   the wheel,   But   re - gi - men - ted   Bunk.   It___
needs a   cap - tain on   the bridge Whose reck - on - ing   is

sound. Lan - don, oh, Lan - don Will lead to vic - to -
ry, With the dear old Con - sti - tu - tion And it's good e - nough for me.

The alphabet we'll always have,
But one thing sure is true,
With Landon in, the raw deal's out,
And that means P.D.Q.
Alf Landon learned a thing or two,
He knows the right solution,
And in the White House he will stay
Within the Constitution.

In this New Deal of Alphabets
That runs from "A" to "Z,"
You've only had experiments,
All full of lunacy.
And if at first they don't succeed,
They try and try again,
While out of work you still can find
About twelve million men.

We've had enough emergency,
Enough experiment—
We've seen the money go all right,
But don't know where it went.
If Roosevelt could have his way,
We'd all be in his grip,
And soon he'd change the Ship of State
To his Dictatorship.

As quoted in the *New York Times,* June 8, 1936.

As part of the process of generating enthusiasm for the campaign, William Randolph Hearst, an ardent Landon supporter, instituted a song contest in his newspapers in fifteen cities. The Hearst papers invited their readers to submit parodies to "Oh! Susannah" and offered a prize of $10 to a daily winner and a grand prize of $1,000 at the end of the contest. Rarely have American newspapers so blatantly promoted the fortunes of a political candidate. This comment from the *New York American* of September 20, 1936 was typical:

Daily entries for the Landon Campaign Song Contest of the New York American increased yesterday. They came from all parts of the New York metropolitan area and from many distant States. This is taken to indicate Gov. Landon's campaign is taking on momentum everywhere, the entries appearing to represent a cross-section of the electorate. They come from workers, doctors, lawyers, ministers, housewives and professional women. Many of the women enclose with their entries notes explaining that they are university graduates, and are observing a growing sentiment for Gov. Landon among women who think through their own problems.

Here is a sampling of verses from among the $10 prize winners, the first one of which exhorted voters to follow the example of Al Smith, who endorsed Landon.

They spend our money right and left,
We take it on the chin;
Enough's enough, let's follow Smith,
Let's get Alf Landon in!
He'll show the way to save the day
And scrap all this relief,
He knows it's jobs the people want,
Not idleness and grief.

Oh! Alf Landon,
You're the one man we can see,
Who'll bring back peace and happiness
To this land of liberty.

Oh, he comes from out of Kansas
With a fervor good to see,
And he's going to the White House
With the help of YOU and ME.
He's not out to experiment,
He treads a well-planned path,
And for all those visionary schemes,
He has a sane man's wrath.

Oh! Alf Landon,
Just wait and you will see,
We'll put you in the White House
Where you really ought to be.

Oh, the good old Constitution
Always rides the stormy sea,
If it's good enough for Landon,
Then it's good enough for me.
It was good enough for Washington,
For Grant and Lincoln, too,
And for good old TEDDY Roosevelt,
So it's good enough for you.

Oh! Susanna,
Susanna, dry those tears,
For the Jubilee is comin'
After four long years.

From Maine to California
We've heard his battle call,
Come on, you staunch Americans,
And do your duty all!
Salute the Founding Fathers brave,
The legacy left me and you,
Let's save our menaced freedom
From Moscow's reddish hue.

Hurrah, for Landon!
Hail all his followers true!
He'll land on hand in Washington,
For the Red, the White and Blue.

And a charge of prescience might have been levelled against the author of this verse:

From the fertile State of Kansas,
There's a strong man we'll soon see,
A-sitting in the White House,
Where he really ought to be.
There's a landslide soon a-coming,
And we'll make the cow-bells ring,
When the nation's count is tallied up
We'll all stand up and sing.

With entries like these, it is clear that the distinguished judges who had to select a grand prize winner were not faced with an easy task. Among those who lent themselves to this enterprise were Dr. Sigmund Spaeth, a chronicler of American popular music and at that time the host of a popular radio program; Miss Dagmar Perkins, president of the National Association for American Speech; and Arthur Cremin, director of the New York Schools of Music. Dr. Spaeth, who served as chairman of the prize committee, commented that "the quality of the entries has so far been exceptionally high, and we have ample evidence that the contest has evoked the widest interest in all parts of the country."

Despite the flood of outstanding compositions, the prize jury finally did come up with a winner, Miss Violet E. Willoughby of Detroit, Michigan, described as "a housemaid." She was awarded the $1,000 first prize for the following song on behalf of Landon and his running mate, Colonel Frank Knox, publisher of the *Chicago Daily News*.

LANDON CAMPAIGN SONG

Words: Violet E. Willoughby
Tune: "Oh! Susannah"

O hear the cry, it's sounding high,
From every dale and hill,
It's heard upon the city streets,
In every roaring mill.
Our people now are calling for
A sturdy man to save
The heritage of Liberty
Our Founding Fathers gave.

Chorus:
Win with Landon,
The drive is under way,
He is our all-American
To make the running play!
Win with Landon,
His lineup spreads grim shocks,
He smashes with the ball held fast,
He'll score with Colonel Knox!

On every hand across the land,
We hear his praises sung;
His common sense and confidence
Lift hearts that have been wrung.
No foolish pride or pomp has he,
No silver tongue in cheek;
A man of deeds, not words, is he,
He'd rather serve than speak.

Come rally all, join in the call,
Swell up our battle cry,
To do our part with voice and heart
That Freedom shall not die.
Stand firm as offspring of our sires,
And let our challenge sound;
Have Landon lead the White House team
To sane and safer ground.

All of the Landon songs were not on such an exalted level, however. There was "Happy Days With Landon," which failed to stem the Roosevelt tide; while songs like the following may actually have cost the Republicans votes:

HAPPY LANDIN' WITH LANDON

Words and music: Jack Stern and Sid Caine

(From the original sheet music, pub. 1936 by Caine & Stern, Los Angeles, Calif.)

While Hearst was buying up Landon verses at $10 a day and the *Literary Digest* was predicting a Republican election victory, the voters were preparing to make the election of 1936 one of the most one-sided in history. Veteran newspapermen laughed when Democratic campaign manager James Farley predicted that Roosevelt would lose only Maine and Vermont; but when the voters delivered their verdict on election day, the wily Democratic chairman was proven right and the *Literary Digest* went out of business.

The enthusiasm for Roosevelt was heightened by

the obvious hostility which the representatives of the powerful and the wealthy had for him. It was only in later years that many of FDR's severest critics came to understand the real significance of these remarks made by Roosevelt during the 1936 campaign:

I believe, I have always believed, and I always will believe in private enterprise as the backbone of economic well-being in the United States. It was this Administration which saved the system of private property, the system of free enterprise, after it had been dragged to the brink of ruin by these same leaders who try to scare you.

As they were to do for every election of the next three decades, the Democrats of 1936 ran against Herbert Hoover and the Depression. It was a telling argument.

THAT'S WHY WE'RE VOTING FOR ROOSEVELT

Words: Thomas O'Dowd
Tune: "Marching Through Georgia"

Herbie Hoover promised us "Two chickens in each pot,"
Breadlines and Depression were the only things we got,
I lost my job, my bank blew up, and I was on the spot,
That's why I'm voting for Roosevelt.

Hooray! Hooray! Herb Hoover's gone away,
Hooray! Hooray! I hope he's gone to stay,
For now I'm back to work and get my three squares ev'ry day,
That's why I'm voting for Roosevelt.

My eyes are sore from searching for the "Grass on our Main Street,"
But honest men are smiling every time they chance to meet,
For green grass cannot flourish 'neath the tramp of busy feet,
That's why I'm voting for Roosevelt.

Hooray! Hooray! We know it won't be long,
Hooray! Hooray! You'll hear them shout this song,
From Portland, Maine to Frisco there's a hundred million strong,
Shouting and voting for Roosevelt.

They tell us Mr. Landon is a very clever gent,
He kids them out in Kansas, though he never spends a cent,
But Willie Hearst and Standard Oil are coughing up his rent,
That's why we're voting for Roosevelt.

Hooray! Hooray! They fooled me once before,
Hooray! Hooray! And was I feeling sore,
No G.O.P. can hoodwink me as in the days of yore,
That's why I'm voting for Roosevelt.

Wall Street sure is kicking for they know they're on the pan,
Franklin D. in Washington upset their little plan,
And now the one on top is that poor once forgotten man,
That's why we're voting for Roosevelt.

Hooray! Hooray! He banished all our fear,
Hooray! Hooray! Our banks are in the clear,
He brought us back prosperity, he gave us back our BEER,
That's why I'm voting for Roosevelt.

From *1936 Franklin Roosevelt Songbook.*

Dozens of avid amateurs penned songs for FDR. Songs like "Things Look Rosy With Roosevelt" and "Mr. Roosevelt's the Man" were hopefully launched and, despite the sometimes determined efforts of their authors, quickly forgotten. "Happy Days Are Here Again" still proved to be the most effective campaign song. There were "issue" songs which were quite specific in terms of the legislation of the first Roosevelt term; there were standard patriotics and personality songs, the kind in which one might have substituted the name "Harding" or "Cleveland" with damage to nothing but the rhyme scheme; and there were some which had not yet recovered from the long drought.

BYE-BYE LANDON, GOODBYE!

Words and music: James F. Kiely

(From the original sheet music, Library of Congress)

When Roose-velt beat Hoo-ver a few years a - go, We tho't we were thru with pro' - bi - tion you know, But the G. O. P. part - y, that's read-y to die,___ Sent out to Kan-sas and picked out a dry,___ They'll tell us pro' - bi - tion is no - ble and grand, but all of us know it's the curse of the land, Their false res - o - lu - tions will all turn to tears,___ For we'll e - lect Roose-velt an - oth - er four years!___ So Bye, Bye, Lan-don, good - bye,___ When you're beat there's no one will cry,___ We know we are thru___ with pro' - bi - tion and you,___

267

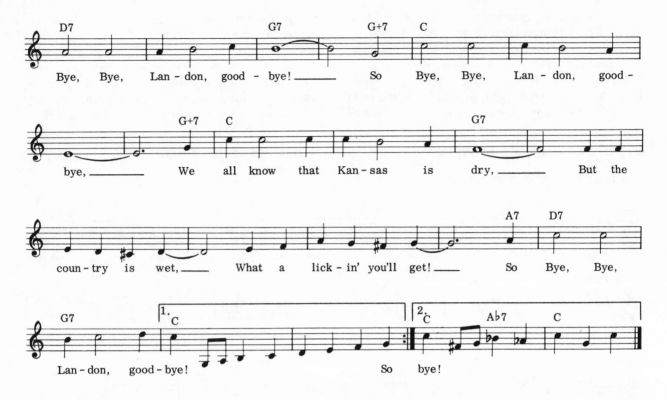

Bye, Bye, Lan-don, good - bye! _____ So Bye, Bye, Lan-don, good - bye, _____ We all know that Kan-sas is dry, _____ But the coun-try is wet, _____ What a lick-in' you'll get! _____ So Bye, Bye, Lan-don, good-bye! So bye!

During this time, various movements for social reform emerged. The suddenly burgeoning Communist Party helped found many organizations devoted to specific issues, such as the Workers Alliance, which based itself primarily on the unemployed. In different parts of the country, demagogues like Huey Long, Father Coughlin and Gerald L. K. Smith tried to turn the popular sentiment into various schemes of both personal aggrandizement and a Nazi-style political movement. Among the most interesting of the movements was the one organized by Dr. Francis E. Townsend of California, who came up with a plan for relief to the aged. The Townsend Plan would have provided for a monthly pension of $200 to be paid to all people over the age of sixty who did not work, provided they spent the money in the same month they received it. The idea, of course, was not only to provide relief to the elderly who had been particularly hard hit by the depression, but to use that relief as a stimulus to small consumer business. The Townsend Movement attracted tens of thousands of people to its cause. Townsend clubs were formed in hundreds of cities. Eventually, the Social Security Act stole most of the movement's thunder, but in its day it exerted a powerful appeal.

TOWNSEND PLAN SONG

Words: Judge John Carabine (Springfield, Mass.)

Tune: "Tramp, Tramp, Tramp"

Doctor Townsend has a Plan
That will banish poverty,
And restore prosperity to all mankind;
It will give the unemployed
Back the jobs they once enjoyed,
And the comforts of a home once more they'll find.

Chorus:
Work, work, work for Dr. Townsend,
With his Plan we all agree,
Twenty million more will join,
Congress will supply the coin,
And we'll all be marching on to victory.

How the aged will enjoy,
Spending their annuity,
As they mingle with the crowds in every store,
Merchants then will wear a smile,
As with goods their shelves they pile,
And we'll hear the word "Depression" nevermore.

From *Townsend Convention Songbook.*

The Third Term

No one knows for sure just when it was Franklin Roosevelt decided to break with historical precedent and run for a third term. The chances are that he considered the possibility fairly early in his second term. Clearly Roosevelt had learned the lessons of past two-term presidents who harbored secret hankerings for renomination. Teddy Roosevelt's declaration on the occasion of his inauguration that he wouldn't seek a third term had come back to haunt him eight years later. Calvin Coolidge's "I do not choose to run," as weak a denial of intent as any man had ever made, was enough to set the machinery in motion for all the other hopefuls. Neither by word nor deed did Roosevelt discourage any suggestions that he might run again. When the growing international crisis and the continued progress of New Deal reforms combined to make Roosevelt the only available Democrat, the thorny third term question simply vanished—at least so far as the Democrats themselves were concerned.

Roosevelt was a genuinely popular choice. The New Deal and his own reassuring personality had made of him an authentic folk hero. In the euphoria which swept the country after Roosevelt's re-election in 1936, a country singer by the name of Bill Cox struck a popular chord with a song which was recorded less than a week after that electoral landslide.

FRANKLIN D. ROOSEVELT'S BACK AGAIN   As sung by Bill Cox for Okeh Records

Just hand me my old Martin, for soon I will be startin' Back to dear old Charleston, far-away. Since Roosevelt's been re-e-lected We'll not be neglected, We've got Franklin D. Roosevelt back again.

Chorus:
Back again, Back again, We've got Franklin D. Roosevelt back again. Since Roosevelt's been e-lected, moonshine liquor's been corrected, We've got legal wine,— whiskey, beer and gin.

I'll take a drink of brandy
And let myself be handy,
Good old times are coming back again;
You can laugh and tell a joke,
You can dance and drink and smoke,
We've got Franklin D. Roosevelt back again.

Alternate Chorus:
Back again (back again),
Back again (back again),
We've got Franklin D. Roosevelt back again;
We'll have money in our jeans,
We can travel with the queen,
We've got Franklin D. Roosevelt back again.

No more breadlines we're glad to say,
The donkey won election day,
No more standing in the blowing, snowing rain;
He's got things in full sway,
We're all working and getting our pay,
We've got Franklin D. Roosevelt back again.

From *The New Lost City Ramblers Songbook*,
Oak Publications, New York, 1964.

When, in 1939, Jay Gorney, who wrote the music for "Brother, Can You Spare A Dime?", and Henry Myers collaborated on a musical plea to Roosevelt to run again, this was no mere campaign ploy. It reflected a sentiment widely felt and which, a year later, would produce still another overwhelming political victory.

MISTER ROOSEVELT, WON'T YOU PLEASE RUN AGAIN?

Words: Henry Myers
Music: Jay Gorney

(Copyright 1939 by Advance Music Inc. Reprinted by permission of the authors.)

rum - ti - did - dle - di - um - ti - um. A hun - dred mil - lion vot - ers, here they

come! ___ {For you're the hope ___ of all ___ A - mer - i - can wom - en and
If Hoov - er could last ___ one term ___ Then you are en - ti - tled to

men } Mis - ter Roose - velt, Won't you do it a - gain? ___
ten;}

Interlude:

"My friends," ___ he says, ___ And friend - ship trav - els far.

E - ven for - eign coun - tries love the voice of F. D. R. Does

ev - 'ry - one know what they want? Yes! Ev - 'ry - one know what they want? Right!

His - to - ry shows that ev - 'ry - one knows, {Ex - cept - ing Maine and Ver - mont!} Mis - ter
                                              {In - clud - ing Maine and Ver - mont!}

gain! ___

Republicans, who had gone into a state of shock after the 1936 debacle, began to stir themselves with the approach of the 1940 campaign. Significant reverses for the Democrats in the congressional off-year elections had helped bring the GOP out of its coma. Roosevelt's bid for a third term seemed to promise an issue which might be profitably exploited.

But if the Democrats had no alternative to Roosevelt, neither did the Republicans. The two most promising possibilities, Robert A. Taft of Ohio and Thomas E. Dewey of New York, were relative freshmen in the political wars. Neither would provide a match for the old campaigner. It was at this juncture that a political newcomer burst upon the scene, a corporation lawyer without any previous political experience, a plain-spoken folksy utilities magnate, a rags-to-riches child of the American Midwest—a man of whom practically no more than one-tenth of 1 percent of the people had ever heard just a few months earlier, Wendell L. Willkie.

On the strength of one of the shrewdest preconvention publicity campaigns ever launched, combined with a winning personality and a classical image of homespun honesty, Willkie erupted onto the national political scene, created a genuine groundswell of popular support, and overwhelmed the entire Republican Party machine to walk off with the party's presidential nomination.

It was a lively campaign, largely because Roosevelt evoked both enthusiasm and hostility. Republicans called Roosevelt a dictator because of the third term issue. Democrats called Willkie a third-rater in return. Republicans built up an image of Willkie as the Indiana farm boy, the man of the people. Salty old Harold Ickes, Roosevelt's Secretary of the Interior, responded: "Wendell Willkie is just a simple, barefoot Wall Street lawyer." And wherever Wendell Willkie went, the band played Paul Dresser's grand old tune, "On the Banks of the Wabash." Occasionally someone would sing these special campaign verses:

ON THE BANKS OF THE WABASH
(Wendell Willkie Version)

Words: John W. Bratton
Music: Paul Dresser

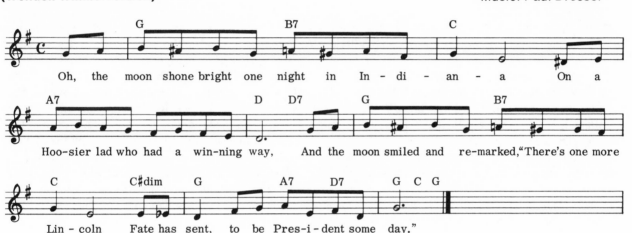

Oh, the moon shone bright one night in In-di-an-a On a Hoo-sier lad who had a win-ning way, And the moon smiled and re-marked, "There's one more Lin-coln Fate has sent, to be Pres-i-dent some day."

We will win with Willkie all along the Wabash,
Guiding all his footsteps from the milky way.
And to keep peace in this land the stars are saying,
"Carry on, Wendell, in the Willkie way."

We will win with Willkie all along the Wabash,
And where rivers run, through states both great and small.
On a tidal wave he'll glide o'er the Potomac,
Till he lands in the White House in the fall.

Farmers will be glad to plow the New Deal under,
When they vote November, north, south, east and west,
Farmer Willkie then will shout, "Let's get together;
All dig in and in happiness invest."

There's ten million unemployed on him depending,
And their future lies deep in his homespun heart;
All life long they know he, too, has been a worker;
And he'll work to give them another start.

There's a little town named Ipswich in New England,
And the switch school teacher used we can recall,
There's a railroad switch, a hair switch and some others,
But the big switch to Willkie beats them all.

Have you heard that mighty sound like magic music,
Spreading shore to shore across this continent.
It's the voice of "We, The People" loudly singing,
"We all want Willkie for our President."

When a harvest moon shines over the Potomac,
Next November down in Washington, D.C.,
Uncle Sam will hang this sign up in the White House:
"Welcome Home, Willkie and Prosperity."

The phrase "We, The People" in the song above was the title of a magazine article by Willkie in the April 1940 issue of *Fortune*. It had created quite a stir in the country. Willkie's campaign manager, Oren Root, Jr., had the article reprinted and circulated as a petition asking that Willkie be nominated. It was probably Willkie's most effective preconvention campaign tactic.

Although Willkie was a more attractive candidate than Landon, it was still more an anti-Roosevelt campaign than a pro-Willkie one. Again the newspapers overwhelmingly supported the Republican, although nothing quite as contrived as Hearst's "Oh! Susannah" contest appeared. The *Chicago Tribune,* ever an arch-foe of the New Deal, ran an anti-Roosevelt campaign song in its Sunday supplement every week for about a month until Election Day. One of these was called, "Elliott, I Wanna Be a Cap'n Too!" Elliott Roosevelt, son of the president, had been appointed a captain in the U.S. Army; and an attempt was made by Roosevelt's political opponents to prove that this was some form of nepotism. The Republican press gave it a lot of coverage, but the issue does not seem to have agitated too many others. The song contained such verses as:

I haven't had the courses, and I haven't made the grade,
I can't shoot a pistol; I can't pass on parade,
But father was the Chief and he knew his stuff,
He just whispered to "my friends" and my friends made the bluff.

I haven't been to Hyde Park, and I'm not known up there,
I have no pull in Washington, so a gun I'll have to bear.
My Congressman's not friendly, King Franklin doesn't care,
So I'll have to be a private, and the insult I must bear.

A songsheet from a campaign rally in New York City for Willkie and his running mate, Charles L. McNary of Oregon, Republican floor leader in the Senate, included a variety of parodies, the words for which were written by Alice Brockett, described as "Music Chairman, Women Workers for Willkie." Among the targets of the parodies were such famous Roosevelt trademarks as his "fireside chats" over the radio, which traditionally began with the phrase, "My friends"; his favorite sport, deep-sea fishing, and his family. The Roosevelt family was a perennial source for campaign attacks and satire. The President's wife, Eleanor, was probably the most activist First Lady in American history, while the Roosevelt children were also constantly in the news in their own right.

The following are typical:

Tune: "Oh, Dear, What Can the Matter Be?"

O, dear, what can the matter be?
O, dear, what can the matter be?
O, dear, what can the matter be?
Franklin's had more than his share.

He promised he'd balance the National budget,
He cannot get near enough even to nudge it,
He promised a lot—but just look what we got,
We are all of us living on air!

DO YE KEN F.D.?

Tune: "Do Ye Ken John Peel?"

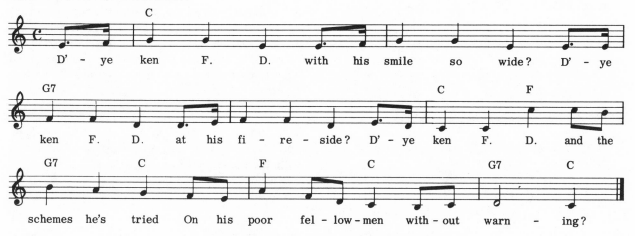

He had schemes for packing the Supreme Court,
He has schemes that are leaving the Treasury short,
He has dreams of making a Third Term port,
But he's got to wake up in the morning.

FARE YOU WELL

Tune: "Tavern in the Town"

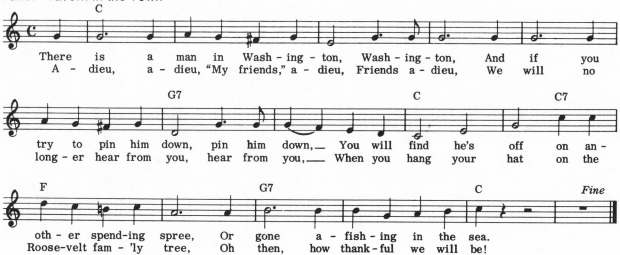

275

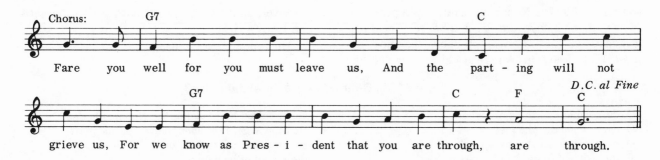

Fare you well for you must leave us, And the part-ing will not

grieve us, For we know as Pres-i-dent that you are through, are through.

And now, a man has come to town, come to town,
A man who'll never let us down, let us down.
And with Willkie we will win a victory,
We'll say goodbye to Franklin D.!

Radio, motion pictures and the phonograph record were making the old-fashioned campaign—and with it, the old-fashioned campaign song—

obsolete. But there was a role for music in the new era. Campaign sound-trucks would play records of music associated with their candidate over and over again, as part of a recorded message urging people to register, to vote, to campaign. Willkie sound-trucks played "On the Banks of the Wabash," and, in many cases, songs like the following, which was used extensively in New York City at the time:

WE'RE ALL GOING OUT TO VOTE FOR WILLKIE

Words and music: Jock McGraw and Mary Schaeffer

(Copyright 1940 by Red Star Songs Inc., New York. Copyright renewed by Mary Schaeffer and Tone Music. Used by permission.)

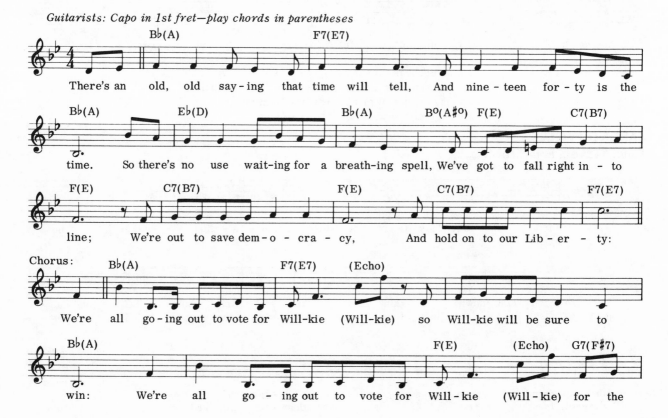

Guitarists: Capo in 1st fret—play chords in parentheses

There's an old, old say-ing that time will tell, And nine-teen for-ty is the

time. So there's no use wait-ing for a breath-ing spell, We've got to fall right in-to

line; We're out to save dem-o-cra-cy, And hold on to our Lib-er-ty:

Chorus:

We're all go-ing out to vote for Will-kie (Will-kie) so Will-kie will be sure to

win: We're all go-ing out to vote for Will-kie (Will-kie) for the

276

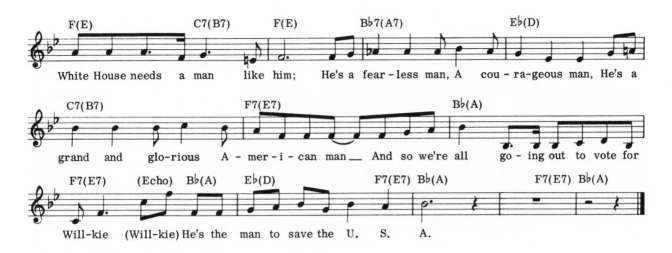

White House needs a man like him; He's a fear-less man, A cou-ra-geous man, He's a grand and glo-rious A-mer-i-can man— And so we're all go-ing out to vote for Will-kie (Will-kie) He's the man to save the U. S. A.

Never Swap Horses

After the tradition-shattering third term campaign, Roosevelt's decision to run for a fourth term was taken pretty much in stride by the nation as a whole. The Republicans, to be sure, charged "one-man rule" and "personal dictatorship," but such arguments never convinced anyone except the party faithful. More to the point was the Republican charge that the country was being run by "tired old men." And to emphasize this contention, the GOP nominated a young, vigorous political figure, Thomas E. Dewey, governor of New York, who had won an enviable reputation as a "racket-buster" in corruption-ridden New York City.

On the surface, it seemed like a contest between youth and age, but the Democrats transformed it into one between experience and immaturity. More important, however, than the question of age, was the unshakable grip which Roosevelt and the New Deal had on a broad spectrum of the populace as the champions of the common man. Dewey, for all his "youth," represented the party of Herbert Hoover and the Republican old guard, whose favorite son, Governor John W. Bricker of Ohio, received the vice-presidential nomination. The Dewey forces urged, "Win the war quicker with Dewey and Bricker," but the Democrats countered with the slogan which had stood both Lincoln and Wilson in such good stead, "Never swap horses while crossing a stream." It was an argument which, try as they might, the Republicans could not overcome:

REPUBLICAN BATTLE HYMN
Tune: "John Brown's Body"

They say to change your horse while in the middle of the stream,
Is not the smartest thing to do, but this can plain be seen,
A horse that's run twelve years should be retired to pastures green,
So vote Republican.

Vote for Dewey and for Bricker,
Win the war and do it quicker,
Vote for Dewey and for Bricker,
And keep our Country free.

They both are honest, capable, and men of proven worth,
Their heads are clear, their minds are strong, their feet
  are on the earth,
They're trained to guide our destiny, they'll put our Country first,
So vote Republican.

Our Country needs a leader who will work for unity,
And build our Nation up again—we'll have prosperity,
For Labor, Farmer, Business Man—with that you should agree,
So vote Republican.

From *Dewey-Bricker Songsheet.*

But it wasn't all standard rah-rah for our candidates stuff. At least one little jingle came a lot closer to the real Republican sentiments than the hand-on-the-heart songs which were both predictable and colorless.

Tune: "Good Night, Ladies"

Good night, Perkins,
Good night, Ickes,
Good night, Browder
You're leaving us at last.

Pack your grip and roll along,
Roll along, roll along,
Pack your grip and roll along,
[*Slow*] And clearing with Sidney is past!

From *Dewey-Bricker Songsheet.*

The personalities mentioned in the song above were all favorite targets of the Republicans. As might be expected, the song attacked two members of FDR's cabinet, Miss Frances Perkins and Harold Ickes. Republicans had always found Roosevelt's cabinet good targets, because it included a great variety of unorthodox figures who devised many of the New Deal's most interesting programs. Miss Perkins, the first woman to serve in a presidential cabinet, was secretary of labor. Ickes, secretary of the interior, was a political maverick with strong liberal ideas.

Other favorite Republican whipping boys who figured in the lyrics were Earl Browder and Sidney Hillman. Browder, then General Secretary of the Communist Party, had received a presidential pardon after being convicted of passport fraud. Sidney Hillman was the director of the CIO Political Action Committee and one of the most important labor leaders in the country. Roosevelt presumably used the phrase "Clear it with Sidney" in some discussion of preconvention strategy. The Republicans made much of the phrase. In the dying days of the campaign, Dewey had talked about the Roosevelt supporters as "Hillman, Browder & Co."

The Roosevelt campaign was pegged to the theme of national unity, winning the war, and extending the New Deal into peacetime America. The CIO Political Action Committee, which had played a key role in the 1940 campaign, became the National Citizen's Political Action Committee in an attempt to remove the stigma of "party politics" from the Democratic campaign. A songbook issued by the Committee included ditties by such theatrical pros as Harold Rome, Irma Jurist, Earl Robinson, Mary Lou Williams, Jay Gorney, Edward Eliscu, Lewis Allan and others.

HE'S THE PEOPLE'S CHOICE

Words: Bernice Fields
Music: Irma Jurist

(From *Songs for Political Action*)

In No-vem-ber for-ty-four, On the sev-enth day, Mis-ter and Mis-sus A-mer-i-ca, Will step up to have their say. They said it once in nine-teen thir-ty-two; They've said it twice since then—

{Now the mold-er and the min-er, ev-'ry last as-sem-bly lin-er,}
{Now the typ-ist and the tai-lor, and the sol-dier and the sail-or,} Will say it once a-gain.— He's the peo-ple's choice!— He's the Na-tion's voice!— For the peo-ple all a-gree, what we need is u-ni-ty, And we'll march to Vic-to-ry with Mis-ter Frank-lin Dee! He's the peo-ple's choice!— He's the Na-tion's voice!— And our votes will re-af-firm we want him for an-oth-er term! They term!

MY FRIEND FRANKLIN
Words and music: Harold Rome

(From *Songs for Political Action.* Copyright 1944. Used by permission of the author.)

My friend, Frank-lin, steered us thru some storm-y skies,— Might-y few can meas-ure to— his size! My friend, Frank-lin, He's the one who knows the score.— 'Round our way we like what he— stands for. He's as high a-bove his ri-val as the top of a stee-ple. They say ev-'ry-one's a-gainst him, Ev-'ry-one ex-cept the peo-ple! My friend, Frank-lin, He's the chief to guar-an-tee— That we win the peace as well— as vic - to - ry! My friend, Frank - lin D._____

The Postwar Years

*The Decline of
Campaign Singing*

The decline in campaign singing which first set in after World War I was further accelerated after the second great war. By 1948, in the advanced electronic age, election campaigning had become a mammoth enterprise. Radio and television were rapidly replacing the old-fashioned campaign rally, and by the sixties, the new "cool" media completely dominated the vote-getting process. The old-fashioned campaign song simply had no function any longer. If an appropriate popular song could be found or adapted for the candidate, that would be pretty much the extent of musical propaganda.

Rarely has an incumbent president been faced with such certain defeat in his bid for re-election as seemed to be the prospect for Harry Truman in 1948. Possibly Andrew Johnson, also the successor to a president who died in office, would have been overwhelmed at the polls, but no one thought of nominating him. Herbert Hoover's chances weren't bright, but at least he had a unified party behind him.

Truman, in the shadow of Roosevelt for almost four years, was confronted with inner-party revolts from both the left and the right. Henry Wallace, denied renomination by the

Democrats in the 1944 convention battle over the vice-presidency, broke with Truman over the latter's "cold war" foreign policy, and eventually organized the Progressive Party for the 1948 race. At the same time, a revolt by southern Democrats over the civil rights issue produced a fourth candidacy, that of Senator Strom Thurmond of South Carolina, who promised to make sizable inroads in the usually solid Democratic South.

In retrospect, one can see that both defections probably did Truman more good than harm. He conducted an aggressive stump-speaking campaign in which he hammered away at civil rights; the Wallace candidacy enabled him to move somewhat to the left while avoiding the charge of being pro-Communist.

I'm Just Wild About Harry

In many ways, it was a one-man effort by Truman, and the fact that his main campaign song was a reworking of that ragtime hit of the early twenties, "I'm Just Wild About Harry," was an appropriate touch to a battle which very few thought could be won.

I'M JUST WILD ABOUT HARRY
(Campaign Version)

Adapted from the original song by Noble Sissle and Eubie Blake

("I'm Just Wild About Harry" [Sissle-Blake] © 1921 by M. Witmark & Sons. Copyright renewed. All rights reserved. Used by permission of Warner Bros. Music.)

For the Republicans, victory was in the air. Once again they went with Thomas Dewey and this time it seemed as though the New Yorker could not be de-nied. At the Republican Convention, the Meyer Davis band played the party's theme song for the coming campaign:

DATE IN '48
Words: Charles Lee
Music: Meyer Davis

(Copyright 1948 by Campaign Music Publishing Co., New York. Used by permission.)

So confident was the GOP of victory that it conducted a cautious campaign designed to offend no one. As it finally turned out, Dewey had the polls, Truman had the votes, and Wallace had the songs. Henry Wallace failed to attract the masses of voters he thought would follow him, largely because of rising cold war sentiment, but if a vote had been taken among the folksingers, Wallace would have won hands down. Paul Robeson, Pete Seeger, Woody Guthrie, E. Y. Harburg, and scores of others—famous and unknown—flocked to the Wallace cause. The guitar and the banjo became the symbols of this left-wing crusade. In fact, Wallace's running mate was Glen Taylor, Democratic senator from Idaho, and himself a guitar-playing singer.

The Wallace songs, some of which focused on the man, were concerned with such issues as peace, equal rights, political liberty, and the rights of labor. Here is a small sampling of the best of those songs—about all that remains of that ill-fated cause:

THE SAME MERRY-GO-ROUND

Words and music: Ray Glaser and Bill Wolff

The don-key is tired and thin, The el-e-phant thinks he'll move in, They yell and they fuss, But they ain't fool-in' us, 'cause they're broth-ers right un-der the skin. It's the same, same, mer-ry-go-round, Which one will you ride this year? The don-key and el-e-phant bob up and down on the same mer-ry-go-round.

The elephant comes from the North,
The donkey may come from the South,
If you'll look you'll find,
The donkey's behind,
But they got the same bit in their mouth!

If you want to end up safe and sound,
Get offa the Merry-go-Round;
To be a real smarty,
Just join the New Party,
And get your two feet on the ground!

From *Songs for Wallace*. Copyright 1948 by
Ray Glaser and Bill Wolff. Used by
permission.

STAND AND BE COUNTED

Words: Pete Seeger and Alan Lomax   Music: Traditional

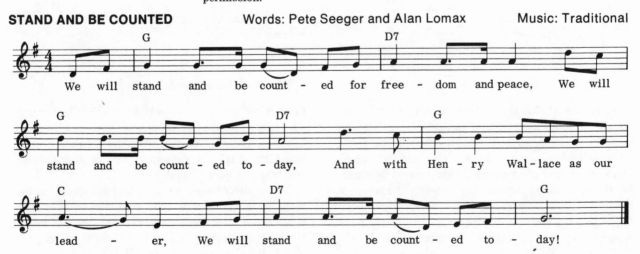

We will stand and be count-ed for free-dom and peace, We will stand and be count-ed to-day, And with Hen-ry Wal-lace as our lead-er, We will stand and be count-ed to-day!

We will stand and be counted against Jim Crow,
We will stand and be counted today,
And with Henry Wallace as our leader,
We will stand and be counted today.

We will stand and be counted for the right to have our say, etc.

We will stand and be counted, don't say it can't be done, etc.

From *Songs for Wallace,* ©1948 by Stormking Music Inc. Used by permission.

THE WALLACE-TAYLOR TRAIN

Words: Woody Guthrie

Music: Adapted from "The Wabash Cannonball"

From the high Ca-na-dian Rock-ies to that land of Mex-i-co, The
Lis-ten to the jin-gle, The rum-ble and the roar, She's a-

cit-y and the coun-try, wher-ev-er you may go, Thru the
roll-ing thru New Eng-land, The West Pa-cif-ic shore. It's a

wild and wind-y weath-er, The sun, the sleet and rain, Comes a-
long time we been wait-ing, Now she's whis-tling round the bend, Now we'll

whis-tling thru the coun-try, This Wal-lace-Tay-lor Train, Oh
ride in-to the White House on the Wal-lace-Tay-lor

Train!

There's lumberjacks and teamsters and sailors from the sea,
And there's farming boys from Texas and the hills of Tennessee;
There's miners from Kentucky and there's fishermen from Maine,
Every worker in the country rides that Wallace-Taylor Train.

There are folks of every color, and they're sitting side by side,
From the swamps of Louisiana and across the Great Divide;
From the wheat fields and the orchards and the lowing cattle range,
And they're rolling on to victory on the Wallace-Taylor Train.

This train pulled into Washington one bright and happy day,
When she steamed into the station, you could hear the people say:
"There's that Wallace-Taylor Special, she's full of union men,
And they're headed for the White House on that Wallace-Taylor Train."

Yes, the crooked politicians, they knew their time had come,
'Cause the Union men and women put the gamblers on the run,
They sealed 'em in a box-car, and switched them off the main,
And they cleared the people's railroad track for the Wallace-Taylor Train.

From *Songs for Wallace*. Copyright 1947 by Woody Guthrie. Used by permission.

GREAT DAY   Words: People's Songs members, New York   Music: Traditional (Negro spiritual)

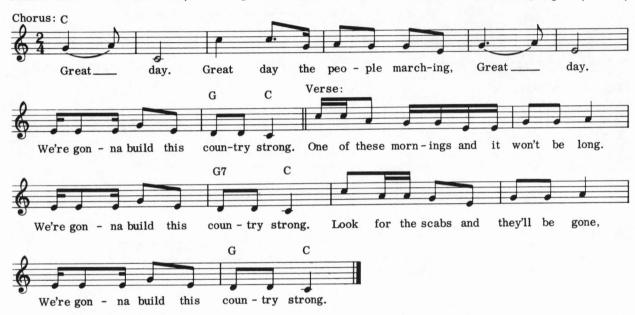

Great____ day. Great day the peo - ple march-ing, Great____ day.

We're gon - na build this coun-try strong. One of these morn-ings and it won't be long.

We're gon - na build this coun - try strong. Look for the scabs and they'll be gone,

We're gon - na build this coun - try strong.

We want no cowards in our band,
We're gonna build this country strong,
We call for valiant-hearted men,
We're gonna build this country strong.

One of these mornings bright and fair, etc.
Truman and Dewey won't be there, etc.

One of these days and it won't be long, etc.
Jim Crow laws will all be gone, etc.

One of these mornings in our land, etc.
We'll all be marching hand in hand, etc.

Sing this song in every state, etc.
Wallace and Taylor in '48, etc.

From *Songs for Wallace*. Copyright 1948 by Stormking Music Inc. Used by permission.

They Like Ike

Sooner or later, the Republican drought had to end, and in 1952, after twenty uninterrupted years of Democratic rule, the Grand Old Party returned to power. To do so, it adopted an old Republican habit from the nineteenth century—nominating a wartime hero, a military figure only vaguely identified in the public mind as a party man.

The Republicans turned to Dwight David Eisenhower, whom some Democrats had courted for the presidential nomination in 1948. Radiating a warm smile and a reassuring tone, Eisenhower seemed the perfect answer to the years of hard-nosed politics which had dominated the country during Truman's two terms. He pledged an end to the war in Korea, a continuation of the social welfare programs of the New and Fair deals, an end to corruption and a crackdown on "Communists in government." Again, but this time convincingly, the slogan was "It's time for a change!"

When the ballots were finally counted, it turned out that Eisenhower had scored a sweeping personal victory, but that the Republican Party, while mustering a majority in the Congress, lagged far behind their popular candidate. The voters liked Ike, even if they weren't too sure about his party.

I LIKE IKE

Words and music: Irving Berlin

The "Uncle Joe" who was worried by Ike's popularity in Irving Berlin's song was, of course, Joseph Stalin.

Another popular Eisenhower song was this one, inspired by a campaign speech of Ike's in Philadelphia which concluded with the phrase, "Look ahead, neighbors!"

LOOK AHEAD, NEIGHBOR
Words and music: Mann Holiner and Alberta
Nichols

The Democrats, recognizing that Eisenhower was a formidable opponent, decided once again to run against Herbert Hoover and Thomas Dewey. Invoking memories of the depression while avoiding the unpopular war in Korea, they nominated Gover-nor Adlai Stevenson of Illinois, grandson of Grover Cleveland's vice-president, and proclaimed, "You never had it so good" and "Don't let 'em take it away!"

DON'T LET 'EM TAKE IT AWAY!   Words: Robert Sour   Music: Bernie Wayne

289

2nd Chorus:
The bus'ness man knows what's in sight;
He's a fellow can sleep at night. [*Clap, clap*]
DON'T LET 'EM TAKE IT AWAY!
It's worth your while to stay alive,
Even after you're sixty-five! [*Clap, clap*]
DON'T LET 'EM TAKE IT AWAY!
[*Repeat last half of first chorus (B).*]

3rd Chorus:
Just take a look at your home town—
Homes goin' up as slums come down! [*Clap, clap*]
DON'T LET 'EM TAKE IT AWAY!
Behind a desk, behind a plow,
Ev'rybody's got a future now! [*Clap, clap*]
DON'T LET 'EM TAKE IT AWAY!
[*Repeat last half of first chorus (B).*]

The scenario for 1956 was virtually unchanged. Once again it was Eisenhower versus Stevenson, and although the Democrat had managed to inspire a small cult of admirers among the liberal intellectuals of the country, the outcome was foreordained.

Eisenhower had ended the war in Korea and, almost inadvertently it seemed, also ended the meteoric career of the famous "junior senator from Wisconsin," Joseph R. McCarthy. The Democrats were "Madly for Adlai," but the country still liked Ike.

WE'RE MADLY FOR ADLAI

Words and music: Gilbert S. Watson

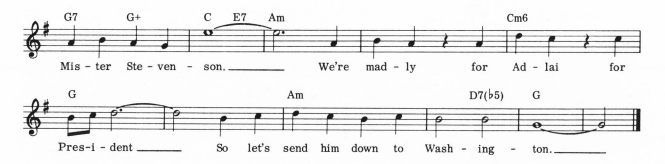

Mis - ter Ste - ven - son._____ We're mad - ly for Ad - lai for
Pres - i - dent ____ So let's send him down to Wash - ing - ton.____

Some of the qualities which Stevenson projected
were captured by this song, which enjoyed a small
vogue during the '56 campaign:

BELIEVE IN STEVENSON   Words: Anne Croswell   Music: Ed Scott

(Copyright 1956, Robert Lissauer Publishing Corporation. Used by permission.)

If you want a man who speaks his mind right out,__ A man whose
choose to have a bet - ter gov - ern - ment,__ Then choose this

hon - est - y you'll nev - er doubt,__ A Wil - son and Roo - se - velt in
Gov - er - nor for Pres - i - dent.__ To get pri - vate in - t'rest on the

one ____ Be - lieve in Stev - en - son. ____ If you
run ____ Be - lieve in Stev - en -

son.____ He won't take us in with a hand - shake or grin And he'll

keep ev - 'ry prom - ise to the let - ter.____ He'll tell us the

score and he'll tell us, what's more, that it's time for a change for the bet - ter!

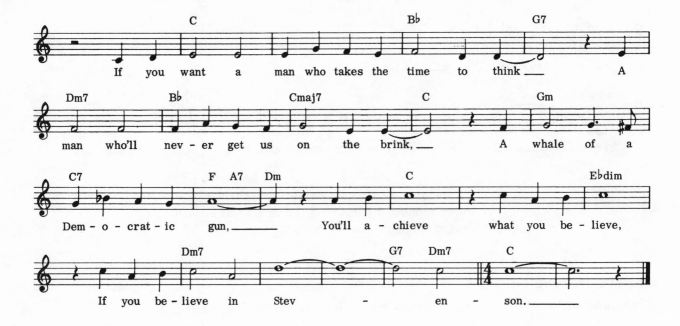

Stevenson songs, suitable for sound-truck broadcasting, were composed by Frederick Loewe and Alan Jay Lerner, co-authors of *My Fair Lady* and *Paint Your Wagon,* Dick Adler, co-author of *Damn Yankees* and *The Pajama Game,* Mitch Miller and Johnny Green. It was a measure of the esteem in which the traditionally liberal Broadway and Tin Pan Alley professionals held the Democratic candidate.

ADLAI'S GONNA WIN THIS TIME

Music and words: Frederick Loewe and Alan Jay Lerner
(to the tune of "Get Me To The Church On Time" from their show, *My Fair Lady*)

We'll start campaigning in the morning,
Ding, dong, the bells are gonna chime,
Pull out the stopper,
Let's have a whopper,
For Adlai's gonna win this time.

He's getting started in the morning,
Spruced up and feeling in the prime,
Stand up and shout it,
No doubt about it,
That Adlai's gonna win this time.

He's gonna lead us to victory,
He's gonna move to Washington, D.C.

For we're getting started in the morning,
Up, up the votes are gonna climb,
No one could doubt him,
There's no way to stop him,
Adlai's gonna win this time.

This parody is based upon the original work "Get Me to the Church on Time." Copyright ©1956 Alan Jay Lerner and Frederick Loewe. The parody was made and reproduced by permission of Chappell & Co., Inc.

292

STEVENSON, STEVENSON

Words: Mary Rodgers Beaty
Tune: "My Pony Boy"

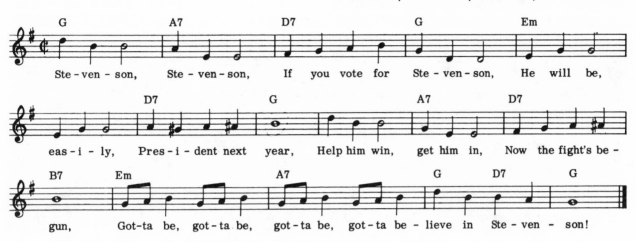

Ste-ven-son, Ste-ven-son, If you vote for Ste-ven-son, He will be, eas-i-ly, Pres-i-dent next year, Help him win, get him in, Now the fight's be-gun, Got-ta be, got-ta be, got-ta be, got-ta be-lieve in Ste-ven-son!

LET'S GO WITH AD-A-LAI
Words: Dick Adler

Tune: "Ta-ra-ra Boom-de-ay"

(Used by permission of Richard Adler.)

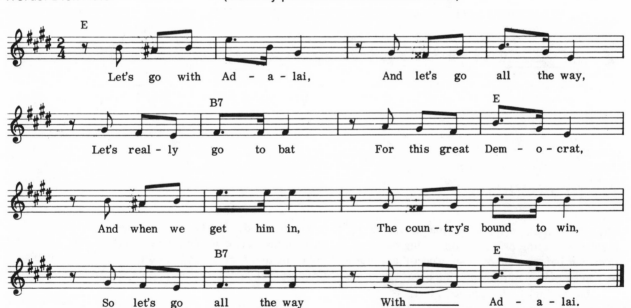

Let's go with Ad-a-lai, And let's go all the way, Let's real-ly go to bat For this great Dem-o-crat, And when we get him in, The coun-try's bound to win, So let's go all the way With ____ Ad-a-lai.

But despite the Democratic hoopla, the Republicans still had their campaign favorite, "I Like Ike," and that was how the voters felt.

Once again Meyer Davis struck the Republican theme, but this time he was a more fortunate prognosticator than in 1948.

VICTORY IN '56
Words and music: Meyer Davis

(Copyright 1956 by Meyer Davis. Used by permission.)

High Hopes

The accelerating decline in campaign singing of the past two decades has not meant an absence of music from the electioneering process. Nominating conventions, streamlined for television, have probably had more music than ever before. And one can expect that radio and TV campaign commercials in future years will rely heavily on contemporary music—much the way advertising of other products has.

Increasingly, the music which is sung and played on behalf of presidential candidates has devoted itself not so much to a presentation of issues or even a delineation of personality, but seems to have been directed more at a certain emotional essence of the campaign. Thus, the one song which came to be identified with John F. Kennedy in the 1960 campaign was the Academy Award-winning song of 1959 from the film *A Hole in the Head,* "High Hopes." To the Democrats, it projected the image of a new era and young blood, a time in which it might be possible to elect the first Catholic to the American presidency.

HIGH HOPES (Special Campaign Version)

Words: Sammy Cahn
Tune: "High Hopes" by James Van Heusen

Everyone is voting for Jack,
'Cause he's got what all the rest lack,
Everyone wants to back Jack,
Jack is on the right track.

'Cause he's got high hopes,
He's got high hopes,
1960's the year for his high hopes,
Come on and vote for Kennedy,
Vote for Kennedy,
And we'll come out on top.

Oops! There goes the opposition ker-
Oops! There goes the opposition ker-
Oops! There goes the opposition. Kerplop!

K-E-Double N-E-D-Y
Jack's the nation's favorite guy.
Everyone wants to back Jack,
Jack is on the right track.

'Cause he's got high hopes,
He's got high hopes,
1960's the year for his high hopes,
Come on and vote for Kennedy,
Vote for Kennedy,
He'll keep America strong,

Kennedy, he just keeps rolling a-
Kennedy, he just keeps rolling a-
Kennedy, he just keeps rolling along.

© Copyright Maraville Music Corp. Used
by permission.

Richard Nixon, on the other hand, projected a much more conservative image. One songwriter summed it up this way:

Nixon is the man for me,
He knows his way around,
His thoughts are safe and sound.

From "Nixon is the Man for Me,"
by J. Maloy Roach, copyright 1960.
Used by permission.

Another said:

The White House needs a man who's tried and true....
If you like Ike, you've got to like this great American.

From "Vote for Nixon," words and music by Leonard Keller. Copyright 1960 Len-Art Music Publications, Miami, Fla. Used by permission.

And if anyone in the Republican National Committee was embarrassed by this one, nothing was said to disturb party harmony:

CLICK WITH DICK

Words and music: Olivia Hoffman, George Stork, and Clarence Fuhrman

(Permission for reprint granted by Elkan-Vogel, Inc., copyright owners.)

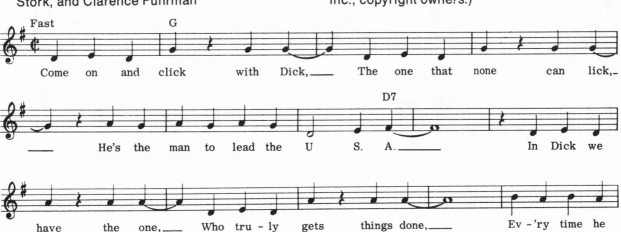

Come on and click with Dick,___ The one that none can lick,___ He's the man to lead the U. S. A.____ In Dick we have the one,___ Who tru-ly gets things done,___ Ev-'ry time he

has his say. _____ He's a man of peace and rea - son ___ ___ For the job in ev - 'ry sea - son. And he knows how to fight, _ ___ When he is in the right, ___ So let's all click with Dick. _____

Campaign sound-trucks urging Nixon's election
played records of songs like the following:

HERE COMES NIXON

Tune: "Merrily We Roll Along" ("Goodnight, Ladies")

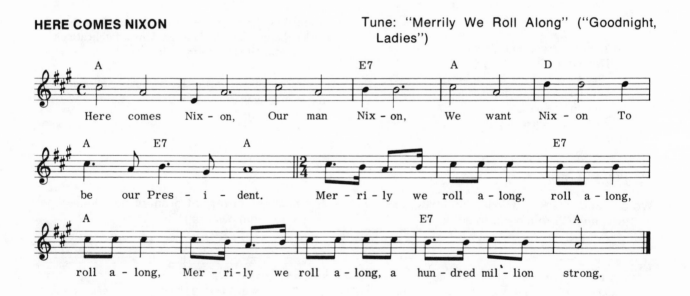

Here comes Nix - on, Our man Nix - on, We want Nix - on To be our Pres - i - dent. Mer - ri - ly we roll a - long, roll a - long, roll a - long, Mer - ri - ly we roll a - long, a hun - dred mil - lion strong.

BUCKLE DOWN WITH NIXON
Tune: "Buckle Down Winsocki"

Buckle down with Nixon, buckle down,
We can win with Nixon, if we buckle down;
We can always fight, when we know we're right,
And we know we're right, so buckle down.

Make 'em yell for Nixon, make 'em yell,
We can win with Nixon when we make 'em yell;
If we don't give in, take it on the chin,
We can always win if we'll only buckle down.

He has been in 50 lands across the sea,
And they know he stands for peace and liberty.
He has friends everywhere—over here, over there,
What a President he'd make for you and me!

Buckle down with Nixon, buckle down,
We can win with Nixon, if we buckle down;
He has set the pace, we will win the race,
Yes we'll win the race with a Nixon victory!

This parody is based upon the original work "Buckle Down Winsocki." Copyright © 1941 by Chappell & Co.,
Inc. Copyright renewed. The parody was made and reproduced by permission of Chappell & Co., Inc.

The Rise and Fall of Lyndon Johnson

The dominant figure in the elections of both 1964 and 1968 was Lyndon Johnson. Assuming the presidency late in 1963 after Kennedy's assassination, Johnson did not begin to rule in his own right until his smashing electoral triumph over Barry Goldwater in 1964. It was a victory, much like Wilson's in 1916, which was based on the idea that Johnson would not involve us in a foreign war. Many who voted the Democratic ticket did so out of fear that Goldwater would escalate the war in Vietnam, bomb the North and commit massive numbers of American ground troops to the conflict in Southeast Asia. The country went all the way with LBJ and in keeping with the campaign songs of recent elections, Tin Pan Alley adapted the theme song from the Broadway hit show *Hello, Dolly* and sang:

HELLO, LYNDON
Words and music: Jerry Herman

Hello, Lyndon,
Well, hello, Lyndon,
We'd be proud to have you back where you belong.
You're lookin' swell, Lyndon,
We can tell, Lyndon,
You're still glowin', you're still crowin',
You're still goin' strong.

We hear the band playin',
And the folks sayin'
That the people know that you've got so much more,
So . . . flash that smile, Lyndon,
Show us that winning style, Lyndon,
Promise you'll stay with us in '64!

We hear the band playin',
And the folks sayin'
"Let's all rally 'round the one who knows the score,"
So . . . be our guide, Lyndon,
Ladybird at your side, Lyndon,
Promise you'll stay with us in '64!

© Copyright 1963 and 1964 by Jerry Herman. All rights
controlled by Edwin H. Morris & Company, Inc. Used
by permission.

The Republicans proclaimed Barry Goldwater "A choice—not an echo," thus recalling the years of anguish in which old-fashioned conservative Republicans had to settle for the likes of Wendell Willkie, Thomas Dewey and Dwight Eisenhower when they really wanted Robert Taft and Herbert Hoover. And so in 1964 the Republican Convention booed down Nelson Rockefeller and made short shrift of the Eastern Establishment, going with the man about whom they would say, "In your heart, you know he's right." Goldwater was their man. This was their song:

GO WITH GOLDWATER

Words: Tom McDonnell
Music: Otis Clements

But in 1968, Goldwater had gone and no one was singing "Hello, Lyndon." College students were chanting "Hell, no! We won't go!" while a country which had voted for peace found itself enmeshed in a war for which it had neither the heart nor the commitment. In the face of a deteriorating military and political situation in Southeast Asia and massive discontent with the war at home, Johnson decided against running for re-election. But nomination of Johnson's vice-president, Hubert Humphrey, meant that the Democrats were forced to run on the Johnson record. Nominated in the midst of a riot in Chicago and with pandemonium raging on the convention floor, Humphrey unsuccessfully tried to campaign on the politics of joy.

The Democrats stepped to the rear, the reinvgorated Dixiecrats, under the banner of George Wallace's American Party, whistled Dixie; and for Republicans, promising that their man had a solution to the unpopular war in Southeast Asia, Nixon was the one.

NIXON'S THE ONE

Words and music: Moose Charlap and Alvin
 Cooperman

As the above examples demonstrate, much of the originality, dedication, partisan zeal, sassiness and colorful vitriol have departed from presidential campaign songwriting. There seems no reason to suppose that the decline of campaign songs will be reversed in the future. The only exception might be the emergence of a significant third party movement which, differing sharply from its two opponents, could once again arouse some of the crusading fervor which has marked the best singing campaigns of the past. Henry Wallace in 1948 was able to stimulate such a movement and many believe that Eugene McCarthy might have in 1968. A big factor here, of course, is that third parties generally do not have the same access to mass media and must, therefore, rely more on direct techniques of campaigning.

Whatever the future holds, however, campaign songs will continue to be written; and they will continue to reveal something of the way in which the American people regard their politicians and the issues on which their campaigns are fought.

The Outsiders
Are In

*After Vietnam and Watergate, ballads
favor the "outsiders."*

Although Kennedy, Johnson, and Nixon had moved into the White House out of the maelstrom of Washington politics, Watergate and the collapse of the Nixon presidency made such associations an insurmountable handicap in the election campaigns that immediately followed.

The first to pay the price for too close an association with the Washington political establishment was Nixon's successor, Gerald Ford. An amiable individual, Ford went into the 1976 campaign saddled not only with a Republican Party tarnished by the disgraced Nixon but also with his own action in granting the ex-president a full pardon for his Watergate activities.

Aware of this burden, the Ford campaign committee tried to depict their candidate as one who stood in stark contrast to the gloom and doom—represented principally by the Vietnam War and Watergate—that had preceded him. A song written by a member of the campaign staff, "I'm Feeling Good About America," tried to associate with Ford the idea of a change for the better. In what may have been a campaign first, the song was recorded in various styles—country-western, hard and soft rock, California sound, marching band, and full chorus. A Spanish version in Latin music style was aimed at the growing number of Hispanic voters. All this probably helped enliven the Ford campaign—but not enough.

I'M FEELING GOOD ABOUT AMERICA

Words and Music: Robert K. Gardner

There's a change that's come o-ver A-mer-i-ca,— A change that's great to see,— We're liv-ing here in peace a-gain, We're go-ing back to work a-gain, It's bet-ter than it used to be.— I'm feel-ing good a-bout A-mer-i-ca,— And I feel it ev-ery-where I go.— I'm feel-ing good a-bout A-mer-i-ca,— and I feel you ought to know— That I'm feel-ing good a-bout A-mer-i-ca;— It's some-thing great to see.— I'm feel-ing good a-bout A-mer-i-ca,— I'm feel-ing good a-bout me.

If, in 1976, the country was looking for an outsider to the Washington establishment—preferably a Democrat—no one seemed to fill the bill better than the one-time governor of Georgia: folksy, born-again Jimmy Carter. Never mind that this astute southern politician was a keenly knowledgeable and sophisticated individual who came to the presidency better prepared than many who had occupied the Oval Office. For election purposes, the image of good-old-boy Jimmy as a Georgia peanut farmer who could bring plain horsesense to the presidency was by far the better part of campaign wisdom.

Among a spate of songs on the same theme, this one by K. E. and Julia Marsh could well serve as a prototype. Its tune borrows liberally from a southern Civil War song, "Eatin' Goober Peas."

ODE TO THE GEORGIA FARMER
(Eatin' Goober Peas)

By K. E. and Julia Marsh

(Copyright 1976 by Brim Music.)

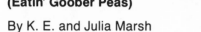

General Sherman rode through Georgia and marched on to the sea,
The burning of Atlanta went down in history.
The South is gonna rise again and have a little fun—
That Farmer's gonna plant him a peanut patch on the White House lawn. (Cho.)

We've had our New Frontier and Great Society;
It's time we all came down to earth, not be so high and mighty.
Them high-falutin' candidates just seem to lose their backers,
And the farmer boy who got the votes is just a Georgia cracker. (Cho.)

Now Roosevelt he promised us a chicken in every pot;
He gave us all a New Deal, and chicken's what we got.
Now we've got a better deal, and people, let's don't knock it—
That Georgia farmer's promised us a goober in every pocket. (Cho.)

Ronald Reagan's campaign songs in 1980 weren't nearly so colorful as Carter's goober ballad, which only proves that songs have been replaced by mind-molding devices more suitable to the high-tech age of electronic media. One can hear the strains of the one-time California governor's conservative political base in the following song. It manages to suggest the populist, antigovernment theme that Reagan so successfully exploited in his campaign for the presidency. In 1984 he played the role of the outsider again, soundly defeating an old Washington insider, Walter Mondale.

STAND UP AND CHEER FOR RONALD REAGAN

Words and Music by E. F. Moss

(Copyright 1970 by E. F. Moss, and 1980 by Apex Music Studios.)

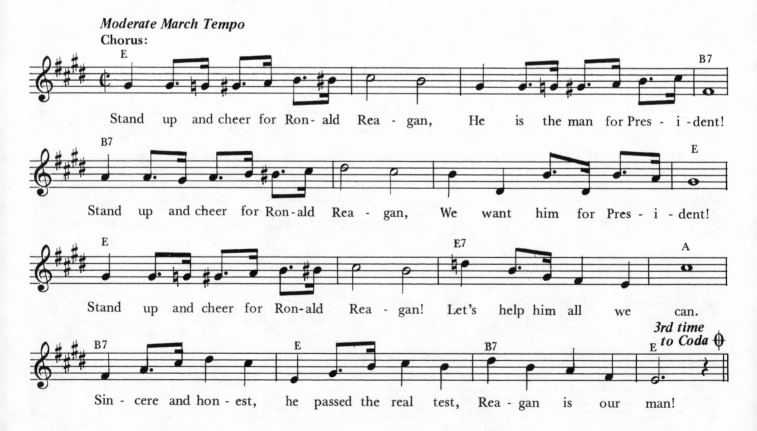

Moderate March Tempo
Chorus:

Stand up and cheer for Ron-ald Rea-gan, He is the man for Pres-i-dent!

Stand up and cheer for Ron-ald Rea-gan, We want him for Pres-i-dent!

Stand up and cheer for Ron-ald Rea-gan! Let's help him all we can.

3rd time to Coda

Sin-cere and hon-est, he passed the real test, Rea-gan is our man!

Instrumental Interlude

1. Now is the
2. We've been a-

time___ Yes, it's the time___ For all good men___ and wom-en too, To
sleep___ like lit-tle sheep___ We must a-wake,___ it's time to shake The

stand up! face up! Raise all our voic-es loud and clear.___ We've been too
shack-les, cack-les, Bad el-e-ments that we have seen.___ Why should we

still,___ oh, far too long.___ We've got to show___ them just how strong The
bow___ to tyr-an-ny___ of such as these___ and all their spleen. Oh,

good folks in this great coun-try real-ly are!___ } Let's all just
A-mer-i-ca, God's peo-ple real-ly care!___

Coda

Grandioso

Rea-gan is our man! Rea-gan is our man! REA-GAN IS OUR MAN!!

Bibliography of Election Campaign Songsters, Pamphlets and Songbooks

1788
 THE AMERICAN SONGSTER. Samuel Campbell, New York.

1796
 THE DEMOCRATIC SONGSTER, being a collection of the newest and most admired Republican songs, interspersed with many originals, to which is added some of the most admired French airs. Printed for Keating's Book Store, Baltimore, 1794.

1800
 THE AMERICAN PATRIOTIC SONGBOOK, a collection of political, descriptive and humorous songs of national character and the production of American poets only. John Bioren, Philadelphia, 1816.

 THE FEDERAL SONGSTER, being a collection of the most celebrated Patriotic Songs hitherto published, with a variety of others, etc. Printed by James Springer, New London, Conn.

1836
 SONGS FOR THE WHIG CELEBRATION, JULY 4, 1834. J. H. Eastburn, printer, Boston.

1840
 THE BROOKLYN TIPPECANOE SONG BOOK. Compiled by the Brooklyn Tippecanoe Glee Club, Brooklyn, N.Y.

THE HARRISON AND LOG CABIN SONGBOOK. Columbus, Ohio.

THE HARRISON MEDAL MINSTREL; comprising a collection of the most popular and patriotic songs illustrative of the enthusiastic feelings of a grateful but power-ridden people towards the gallant defender of their country. Grigg & Elliott, Philadelphia.

HARRISON MELODIES, published under the direction of the Boston Harrison Club. Weeks, Jordan & Co., Boston.

THE LOG CABIN AND HARD CIDER MELODIES, a collection of popular and patriotic songs respectfully dedicated to the friends of Harrison and Tyler. Charles Adams, Boston.

A MINIATURE OF MARTIN VAN BUREN, with a selection of the best and most popular Tippecanoe songs. Published and printed anonymously.

THE TIPPECANOE SONG BOOK, a collection of popular and patriotic songs respectfully dedicated to the friends of Harrison and Tyler. Harrisburg, Pa.

1844

THE AMERICAN REPUBLICAN SONGSTER. Composed and arranged by P. De Lee Ree for the American Republican Party, New York.

THE DEMOCRATIC SONGSTER. Turner & Fisher, New York.

THE HARRY CLAY MELODIST. Benjamin Adams, Boston.

THE LIBERTY AND ANTI-SLAVERY SONG BOOK. S. D. King, Boston, 1842.

THE LIBERTY MINSTREL. Compiled by George W. Clark, S. W. Benedict and Co., New York, 1845.

THE NATIONAL CLAY MELODIST. Boston.

THE NATIONAL CLAY MINSTREL. George Hood, New York.

THE WESTERN DEMOCRATIC MELODIST, Simon Pure Edition. D. M. Dewey, Rochester, N.Y.

THE WHIG BANNER MELODIST. Published for the Whigs of the Union, Philadelphia.

WHIG SONGS FOR 1844. Greeley & McElrath, *New York Tribune,* New York.

1848

THE FREE SOIL MINSTREL. Martin & Ely, New York.

FREE SOIL SONGS FOR THE PEOPLE. Boston.

THE ROUGH AND READY MINSTREL. The National Rough and Ready Club, Philadelphia.

1852

THE PRIZE REPUBLICAN SONGSTER, composed of original songs by writers in all parts of the Union presented to the Philadelphia Republican Club in answer to its offer of prizes for the most meritorious.

SCOTT AND GRAHAM MELODIES, being a collection of campaign songs for 1852 as sung by the Whig Clubs throughout the U.S. New York.

THE SCOTT SONGSTER, compiled expressly for the Presidential Campaign of 1852.

1856

FILLMORE AND DONELSON SONGS FOR THE CAMPAIGN. New York.

THE FREEMEN'S GLEE BOOK, a collection of songs, odes, glees and ballads published under the auspices of the Central Fremont & Dayton Glee Club of the City of New York and dedicated to all, who, cherishing Republican liberty, consider FREEDOM WORTH A SONG. Miller, Orton & Mulligan, New York and Auburn.

FREMONT & DAYTON CAMPAIGN SONGSTER. San Francisco, 1855.

FREMONT SONGS FOR THE PEOPLE. Compiled by Thomas Drew, Boston.

THE REPUBLICAN CAMPAIGN SONGSTER: a collection of lyrics, original and selected, specially prepared for the friends of freedom in the Campaign of 'fifty-six. Miller, Orton & Mulligan, New York and Auburn.

THE ROCKY MOUNTAIN SONG BOOK, published for the use of the Fremont Flying Artillery of Providence.

1860

THE BELL & EVERETT SONGSTER FOR THE CAMPAIGN . . . as sung by the Constitutional Glee Clubs. Philadelphia.

THE BOBOLINK MINSTREL; or Republican Songster for 1860. Edited by George W. Bungay.

CONNECTICUT WIDE-AWAKE SONGSTER. Edited by John W. Hutchinson, New York.

THE DEMOCRATIC CAMPAIGN SONGSTER, Douglas and Johnson Melodies. New York.

HUTCHINSON'S REPUBLICAN SONGSTER for the Campaign of 1860. Edited by John W. Hutchinson for the Hutchinson Family of Singers. New York.

UNION SONGSTER FOR THE CAMPAIGN OF 1860 (Bell and Everett). Baltimore.

THE WIDE-AWAKE VOCALIST or Rail-Splitter's Songbook. E. A. Daggett, New York.

1864

CAMPAIGN DOCUMENT NO. 19 (McClellan). New York.

CAMPAIGN SONGS FOR CHRISTIAN PATRIOTS AND TRUE DEMOCRATS, by Rev. William D. Potts, M.D., of Newark, N.J. Published in New York.

COPPERHEAD MINSTREL, a choice collection of Democratic songs and poems for the use of political clubs and the Social Circle. Bromley & Co., New York.

LINCOLN CAMPAIGN SONGSTER. Mason & Co., Philadelphia.

McCLELLAN CAMPAIGN MELODIST, a collection of patriotic campaign songs in favor of the Constitution and the Union, the election of General McClellan, the restoration of the Federal Authority, and the speedy extermination of treason, by Sidney Herbert. B. W. Hitchcock, New York.

THE PRESIDENT LINCOLN CAMPAIGN SONGSTER. New York.

THE REPUBLICAN CAMPAIGN SONGSTER FOR 1864. Cincinnati.

SONGS FOR THE UNION. Printed for the Union Congressional Committee by John A. Gray & Green, New York.

1868

THE GRANT CAMPAIGN SONGSTER. New York.

THE GRANT SONGSTER for the campaign of 1868. Root & Cady, Chicago.

HOLMES' PATRIOTIC SONGS FOR COMING CAMPAIGNS, by S. N. Holmes. Syracuse.

REPUBLICAN CAMPAIGN MELODIST AND REGISTER, by Sidney Herbert. Dick & Fitzgerald, New York.

SEYMOUR & BLAIR SONG BOOK AND DEMOCRATIC REGISTER. New York.

1872

THE FARMER OF CHAPPAQUA SONGSTER, containing a great number of the best campaign songs that the unanimous and enthusiastic nomination of the Hon. Horace Greeley for President has produced. New York.

GRANT & WILSON CAMPAIGN SONGSTER. New York.

GREELEY & BROWN CAMPAIGN SONGSTER. New York.

THE HORACE GREELEY CAMPAIGN SONGSTER. George Munro, publisher, New York.

NATIONAL REPUBLICAN GRANT & WILSON CAMPAIGN SONG BOOK. Published by the Union Congressional Committee, Washington, D.C.

THE SUN'S GREELEY CAMPAIGN SONGSTER, by Amos J. Cummings. New York.

1876

HAYES AND WHEELER SONG BOOK. Published by the Union Republican Congressional Committee, Washington, D.C.

THE HAYES ILLUSTRATED CAMPAIGN SONG AND JOKE BOOK. The American News Co., New York.

HELMICK'S REPUBLICAN CAMPAIGN SONGBOOK as sung by the Springfield, Ohio Glee Club. F. W. Helmick, Cincinnati.

THE ILLUSTRATED CAMPAIGN TILDEN SONG AND JOKE BOOK. The American News Co., New York.

1880

GARFIELD AND ARTHUR CAMPAIGN SONG BOOK. Published by the Republican Congressional Committee, Washington, D.C.

GARFIELD AND ARTHUR CAMPAIGN SONGS, as sung by the Central Quartette. Published by Donnelley, Gassette & Lloyd, Chicago.

GARFIELD & ARTHUR CAMPAIGN SONGSTER. Popular Publishing Co., New York.

GARFIELD AND ARTHUR REPUBLICAN CAMPAIGN SONG BOOK, 1880. Compiled by L. Fayette Sykes. Published by the Republican Central Campaign Club of New York.

HANCOCK & ENGLISH DEMOCRATIC CAMPAIGN SONG BOOK. W. R. Swan & Co., Cincinnati.

1884

BLAINE AND LOGAN BUGLE CALL. P. T. Schultz & Co., Cincinnati.

BLAINE AND LOGAN SONGSTER. Thomas Hunter, Philadelphia.

CLEVELAND AND HENDRICKS SONGSTER. E. Y. Landis, Philadelphia.

FACTS AND SONGS FOR THE PEOPLE, prepared especially for use in the Blaine and Logan Campaign. Cleveland, Ohio.

HAMILTON DEMOCRATIC GLEE CLUB SONGSTER. Hamilton, Ohio.

1888

ACME SONGS, Republican Glee Book and Cartridge Box of Truth for the Campaign of 1888. Acme Publishing Bureau, Syracuse, N.Y.

HARRISON AND MORTON CAMPAIGN SONGSTER. Cincinnati.

THE HARRISON LOG CABIN SONG BOOK OF 1840 revised for the Campaign of 1888 with numerous new songs to patriotic airs. Edited by O. C. Hooper. Columbus, Ohio.

PROTECTION CAMPAIGN SONGS AND RECITATIONS by Edward Fitzwilliam. Boston.

REPUBLICAN CAMPAIGN SONGS FOR 1888. Words ,and music by M. H. Rosenfeld. Pub. by R. M. Collins, New York.

RED HOT DEMOCRATIC CAMPAIGN SONGS FOR 1888. S. Brainard's Sons, Chicago.

SONGS FOR THE PRESIDENTIAL CAMPAIGN OF 1888, respectfully dedicated to the Hon. Benj. Harrison of Indiana, Hon. Levi P. Morton, New York. New York.

THE TIPPECANOE CAMPAIGN SONGSTER. W. F. Shaw Co.

TRUE BLUE REPUBLICAN CAMPAIGN SONGS FOR 1888. S. Brainard's Sons, Chicago.

YOUNG REPUBLICAN CAMPAIGN SONG BOOK. Compiled by Henry Camp. Pub. by John W. Lovell Co., New York.

1892

CLEVELAND & STEVENSON CAMPAIGN SONGSTER for 1892. W. F. Shaw.

THE HARRISON CAMPAIGN SONGSTER, by D. E. Bryer. Logansport, Ind.

NATIONAL REPUBLICAN RALLY RHYMES. El Dorado, Kans.

1896

THE GOLDEN-GLORY REPUBLICAN CAMPAIGN SONGSTER for 1896. Compiled and published by the Echo Music Co., Lafayette, Ind.

THE LIBERTY BELL RINGING. Songs and poems by James G. Clark and others. Pub. by Salyer & Robinson, Los Angeles.

NATIONAL CAMPAIGNER; Marching Songs of the Republican Clubs. Philadelphia.

RED HOT: Democratic Campaign Songs for 1896. S. Brainard's Sons, Chicago.

REPUBLICAN CAMPAIGN PARODIES AND SONGS. Betts & Burnett, South Butler, N.Y.

REPUBLICAN CAMPAIGN SONG BOOK. Denver, Colo., 1894.

REPUBLICAN LEAGUE CAMPAIGN SONG BOOK. Compiled and published by K. L. Chambers. Denver Music Co., Denver, Colo., 1894.

SIX REPUBLICAN SONGS FOR THE 1896 CAMPAIGN. Pub. by W. H. Pettibone, Chicago.

THREE GRAND CAMPAIGN SONGS. Pub. by Chas. H. Scott, Cincinnati.

THREE OF THE GREATEST REPUBLICAN CAMPAIGN SONGS OF THE SEASON. Pub. by L. S. Lyman, New York.

1900

CAMPAIGN PRIZE SONGS as published by the New York Journal on behalf of the National Association of Democratic Clubs.

CAMPAIGN SONGS by Edwin A. Hartshorn. New York.

CAMPAIGN SONGS WRITTEN FOR THE COSMOPOLITAN MALE QUARTET by Edwin A. Hartshorn. New York.

COLONEL JOSEPH H. SPRAGUE'S POPULAR REPUBLICAN CAMPAIGN SONGS. Norwalk, Ohio.

*THE DEMOCRATIC NATIONAL CAMPAIGN SONG BOOK FOR 1900, as sung with great success by the Hoi
Polloi Glee Club of Tacoma.* Words by Harry H. Johnson. Tacoma, Wash.

THE NATIONAL DEMOCRATIC SONG BOOK FOR 1900. Words by J. J. Kavanaugh, music by W. A. Sullen-
barger. Chicago.

THE NATIONAL REPUBLICAN SONG BOOK, by W. W. McCallip. Columbus, Ohio.

SIX RED HOT SONGS written and composed especially for the Campaign of 1900. Pub. by O. G. Hursen Co.,
Chicago.

1904

PARKER CAMPAIGN SONG BOOK. Logan S. Porter, Logansport, Ind.

PARKS' REPUBLICAN CAMPAIGN SONGS. J. A. Parks Co., York, Nebr.

ROOSEVELT CAMPAIGN SONGSTER. Logan S. Porter, Home Music Co., Logansport, Ind.

1912

FAIRBANKS' REPUBLICAN CAMPAIGN SONGS, by George E. Fairbanks. South Cornish, N.H.

PARKS' REPUBLICAN CAMPAIGN SONGS for 1912.

UP-TO-DATE PROGRESSIVE PARTY CAMPAIGN SONGS. Compiled by J. Burgess Brown. Indianapolis.

1920

SONGS FOR THE HARDING & COOLIDGE CAMPAIGN OF 1920. The Glee Club of the Republican League of
Massachusetts.

1932

ROOSEVELT SONGS by Wallace Le Grande Henderson.

1936

CAMPAIGN SONGS FOR LANDON & KNOX.

1936 FRANKLIN ROOSEVELT SONGBOOK. Thomas O'Dowd, New York.

1940

WILLKIE-McNARY RALLY SONGS. Whole World Inc., New York.

1944

DEWEY-BRICKER SONGSHEET, songs from the Republican Madison Square Garden Rally, Nov. 4, 1944, New
York.

SONGS FOR POLITICAL ACTION. National Citizens Political Action Committee, New York.

1948

SONGS FOR WALLACE. Edited by Waldemar Hille, Pete Seeger and Irwin Silber. Pub. by People's Songs, New
York.

1964

REPUBLICAN SONG BOOK, Fritz Purnell, Hank Wells. Pub. by the Bobbs-Merrill Co.

GREENBACK PARTY

NATIONAL GREENBACK CAMPAIGN SONGS as sung by the Des Moines Greenback Glee Club. Des Moines,
Iowa, 1878.

THE POLITICAL CATECHISM AND GREENBACK SONG BOOK. Compiled by Dr. J. H. Randall. Pub. by Rufus H. Darby, Washington, D.C., 1880.

PEOPLE'S PARTY (Populist)

THE ALLIANCE AND LABOR SONGSTER; a collection of labor and comic songs for the use of grange, alliance and debating clubs. Compiled by H. Leopold Vincent. Winfield, Kans., 1891.

FARMERS' ALLIANCE SONGS, a collection of songs for Alliance meetings, farmers' institutes, etc., by E. O. Excell and Dr. D. Reid Parker. Chicago, 1890.

NEBRASKA FOLKLORE PAMPHLETS prepared by the Federal Writers Project, 1938 and 1939:

#16—Ballads
#18—Farmers' Alliance Songs of the 1890s
#20—More Farmers' Alliance Songs of the 1890s.

THE PEOPLE'S SONGSTER, for campaign purposes and a jolly time generally. C. S. White. Vincent Bros., Indianapolis, 1892.

POPULIST AND SILVER SONGS. Words by Henry W. Taylor, music by J. B. Herbert. S. Brainard's Sons, Chicago. 1896.

PROHIBITION PARTY

FILLMORE'S PROHIBITION SONGS, a collection of songs for the Prohibition Campaign, patriotic services and all meetings in the interest of reform. Edited by Charles M. and J. H. Fillmore. Fillmore Bros., Cincinnati, 1900.

THE NATIONAL TEMPERANCE SONGSTER, by W. O. Moffitt. Pub. by O. C. Williams, Providence, R.I., 1879.

PROHIBITION PARTY CAMPAIGN SONGS, by Horace B. Durant. Claysville, Pa., 1884.

THE PROHIBITION SONGSTER. Compiled by J. N. Stearns. National Temperance Society and Prohibition House, New York, 1885.

SOCIALIST PARTY

SOCIALISM IN SONG. Edited by Rev. M. A. Smith and Rev. S. J. Oslin. Pub. at Campbell, Tex. and Stigler, Okla., 1916.

SOCIALIST SONGS WITH MUSIC. Compiled by Charles H. Kerr. Pub. by Charles H. Kerr & Co., Chicago, 1901.

SONGS OF SOCIALISM, by Harry P. Moyer. Brotherhood Publishing Co., Battle Creek, Mich., 1905.

TOWNSEND PLAN

TOWNSEND CONVENTION SONGBOOK. Cleveland, Ohio, 1936.

UNION LABOR PARTY

LABOR SONGS dedicated to the Knights of Labor. J. D. Talmadge, Chicago, 1888.

WOMAN SUFFRAGE MOVEMENT

MANUAL FOR POLITICAL EQUALITY CLUBS, by Harriet May Mills and Isabel Howland. The National-American Woman Suffrage Assn., 1896.

SONGS SUNG AT THE NATIONAL-AMERICAN WOMAN'S SUFFRAGE CONVENTION, Feb. 26 to March 1, 1891.

SUFFRAGE AND TEMPERANCE MELODIES, by L. May Wheeler. Minneapolis, 1884.

Index of Composers, Lyricists and Songwriters

Index of Song Titles

The letter (M) immediately after a page number means that the melody of the song is included with the lyrics. The letters (Exc.) immediately after a page number means that only an excerpt (or excerpts) from the lyrics is printed. The title of a tune which accompanies a song with words different from those which originally accompanied the tune and which is used for only one song in this book is printed in italics. For titles of tunes which accompany the words of more than one song in this book, consult Where to Find Often Used Melodies on p. 13.

Addenda